P9-CFT-012

PARAPSYCHOLOGY
THE CONTROVERSIAL SCIENCE

PARAPSYCHOLOGY

THE
CONTROVERSIAL SCIENCE

Richard S. Broughton

Institute for Parapsychology
Durham, North Carolina

BALLANTINE BOOKS
New York

133
Bro
cop. 1

Copyright © 1991 by Richard Broughton

All rights reserved under International and Pan-American Copyright
Conventions. Published in the United States by
Ballantine Books, a division of Random House, Inc.,
New York, and simultaneously in Canada by Random House
of Canada Limited, Toronto.

Library of Congress Cataloging-in-Publication Data

Broughton, Richard (Richard S.)
Parapsychology : the controversial science
Richard Broughton.—1st ed.
p.   cm.
Includes index.
ISBN 0-345-35638-1
1. Parapsychology.   2. Parapsychology—Controversial literature.
✓ I. Title.
BF1031.B7457   1991
133—dc20   90-24320
CIP
Manufactured in the United States of America

First Edition: July 1991

10 9 8 7 6 5 4 3 2

CONTENTS

ACKNOWLEDGMENTS

As I am not naturally inclined toward the writer's craft, I must acknowledge a great deal of assistance from the many people who have helped to make my work easier, even possible.

My first debt of gratitude is owed my many colleagues in the field, only some of whose names appear in this book. Their work has stimulated and excited my scientific curiosity; their conversations have broadened my horizons; and their friendships have fortified me. I am most grateful to those colleagues who have permitted me to quote from their publications and, in some cases, from their raw data. Several have also kindly supplied some of the illustrations in this book. There are too many of these generous persons to list here, but you will find them acknowledged in the notes.

My colleagues and good friends at the Institute for Parapsychology have been unstinting in their advice and encouragement. Moreover, they have been tolerant of my frequent extended absences from our busy laboratory engendered by my need to write in solitude. These stalwarts are Anne Carroll, Linda Vann, Iris Oliver, and Michelle Davis, who bore the brunt of the consequences of my absences. Among my professional colleagues, Carlos Alvarado, Jim Carpenter, H. Kanthamani, Anjum Khilji, John Palmer, Dorothy Pope, and Nancy Zingrone have all helped in various ways. Of course none of this would have been possible without the encouragement of our director, K. Ramakrishna Rao, and his generosity in permitting me to do so much of the writing on "company time."

The person who most directly aided me in this endeavor is my friend and colleague, Debbi Weiner. Her editorial skills have made your job, dear reader, very much easier, and her broad knowledge of parapsychology provided a much-needed touchstone for my own thoughts. Whatever errors and confusions remain, however, are entirely my own.

Since I already indicated that I am not inclined toward writing, you may rest assured that someone else was responsible for starting this project. Sydelle Engel is that person. Her gentle efforts to turn a researcher into a writer, her words of encouragement, her tolerance of missed deadlines, and her determination to get a book on parapsychology out of me have resulted in what you are reading.

Finally my deepest thanks must be reserved for the three women in my life: my wife, Kathleen; and daughters, Sally and Stephanie. Their love, support, and forbearance through this project, and always, sustain me more than words can express.

PART I

Parapsychology: A Study of Experiences

INTRODUCTION

A Controversial Science

The newspaper reporter sat in front of my desk, flipping through her notepad, looking for any questions she had missed. We had talked for quite a while, and I had shown her several of the experiments under way at the lab. She looked up from the pad, hesitated slightly, and began, "Dr. Broughton, there is just one final question I would like to ask . . . ."

I knew what was coming, and it was not through ESP, only experience. The Institute for Parapsychology is perhaps the most famous parapsychology laboratory in the world. Parapsychology first achieved worldwide recognition through the work of Dr. J. B. Rhine and the Duke University Parapsychology Laboratory, which he created in 1930. Over the decades J. B. Rhine, with his wife Dr. Louisa E. Rhine and the many researchers who trained and worked at the Duke lab, created the foundations for the science as we know it today. As J. B. Rhine approached the age of mandatory retirement for Duke, he created the Foundation for Research on the Nature of Man (FRNM). Upon his retirement in 1965 an agreement with the university made the Institute for Parapsychology, the FRNM's research arm, legal heir to the Duke University Parapsychology Laboratory, in terms of both its reputation and records and its modest financial support. With a heritage like that, our lab has become a mecca for journalists working on stories about parapsychology.

". . . Dr. Broughton, do you believe in this ESP and psychokinesis stuff?"

"No, I don't believe in it," I replied, and then I watched the reporter's face take on a familiar perplexed look. Of course I then had to explain to the startled reporter that I regard "belief" as something appropriate in matters of faith, such as in religious questions, but not in matters of science. One's religious beliefs might require what theologians would call a "leap of faith" precisely because there is no evidence to support them. As a scientist I do not take leaps of faith with my subject matter. I study the evidence.

I have been studying the evidence for over two decades. My initial readings in the subject convinced me of two things: (a) There is an enormous amount of evidence for what we call psychic ability that remains to be explained and understood; and (b) hardly anyone is doing anything about it. Having spent most of my undergraduate days championing politically unpopular causes, it was but a small step into the arena of the intellectually unpopular, so I ignored all the best advice of my friends and colleagues and embarked upon a career in parapsychology. Four years in the psychology department of the University of Edinburgh, Scotland, led to a Ph.D. (one of the few in Britain for work that included parapsychology), and that was followed by a couple of years working at Europe's only state-supported parapsychology laboratory at the University of Utrecht, Holland. A stint in "ordinary" psychology with the State University of New York convinced me that the challenges that fired my scientific curiosity were those of parapsychology, so in 1981 I was happy to accept FRNM director K. Ramakrishna Rao's invitation to join the world's most famous parapsychology laboratory. Now, as director of research, I spend a lot of time with reporters, telling them I am still studying the evidence.

Let me assure you, however, that I am not lacking in commitment or passion for my chosen field. It is just that my commitment is not to a set of beliefs or abstract concepts. My commitment is to the scientific process, and my belief, if we may call it that, is that science will ultimately help us understand a wide variety of baffling phenomena and experiences that have been puzzling human beings since time immemorial.

Occasionally you will hear some scientific pundit proclaim there is no evidence for parapsychological phenomena, therefore parapsychology is a pseudoscience with no subject matter to study. That is patent nonsense. For over two thousand years people have been reporting a class of human experiences—the kind commonly called psychic—and for almost as long, scholars and scientists have been trying to understand them. Two millennia of human experiences *is* a subject matter. Surveys have repeatedly shown that anywhere from one-half to three-quarters of the population have had experiences that they believe were psychic. That constitutes a subject matter with a rather large initial data base. There is no doubt that people have experiences that are apparently psychic in nature, and therefore parapsychology *does* have something to study. The question put to parapsychology as a science is, How are we to explain these experiences?

Obviously the very first step in dealing with experiences of this kind is to examine how far "normal" or conventional mechanisms and knowledge can go in explaining them. Investigators must consider such factors as malobservation, faulty memory, and deceit (and the list can be quite lengthy). If it proves that all normal explanations fail to explain the experience adequately, then what do we have? Actually all we have at that point is an anomaly, something that science at its present stage is unable to explain.

Anomalies are what fuel scientific advances. Facts that do not fit existing theories, observations that cannot be accounted for by current knowledge—these are what continually push forward the boundaries of human knowledge. Anomalies, if they persist, eventually force science to revise its theories and bring about a new and more complete understanding of nature.

At any particular time science is confronted by a variety of anomalies. Meteors—stones falling from the sky—were long dismissed as the ravings of lunatics. X rays were thought by many scientists to be a hoax. N rays, also greeted with skepticism, proved to deserve it. The anomalies encompassed by parapsychology are only a small portion of the anomalies that face science today. Persistent reports of unidentified flying objects or unusual creatures also present anomalies, and there are many other less notorious anomalies stretching the imaginations of scientists.

Undoubtedly the best way to approach these reports of inexplicable experiences is with a healthy skepticism. I use the word *healthy* deliberately, for it is all too easy for skepticism to become corrosive.

For a parapsychologist, the most important intellectual tool is an appropriate amount of "critical doubt."

Skepticism can go too far, and many scientists choose to deal with anomalies simply by denying their existence. Even when they cannot deny the experiences or observations that underlie the anomalies, they may force the observations into a more acceptable explanation, no matter how implausible it may be.

Parapsychologists, and their predecessors who were called psychical researchers, have chosen to confront some of nature's anomalies that seem most intimately connected with the human mind. To do this, they have posited certain constructs, such as extrasensory perception (ESP) and psychokinesis (PK), to serve as crude hypotheses for what they think might be happening. In so doing they have embarked upon a research program that undoubtedly must be the longest-running controversy in all of science.

Reading the newspapers over the last couple of decades, I have often had the feeling that there is a curious parallel between parapsychology and political scandals. In a political scandal it almost seems a rule of thumb that the more vehemently the allegations are denounced, the more likely they are to have struck home. I have often wondered if that same rule could apply to the controversy that surrounds the claims made by parapsychology.

CHAPTER 1

What Is a Psychic Experience?

On a sunny winter afternoon some years ago I was sitting in my office working on a paper when the receptionist called up on the intercom to announce a phone call. It was a woman who wanted to discuss an experience she had had, and it was my afternoon to be on duty for that sort of call. (The Institute gets a couple dozen phone inquiries each day. The majority are for information about parapsychology in general or for our research in particular, but a few are from people wishing to discuss personal experiences, often troubling ones. The five-member research staff deals with these latter calls.*) After years of taking such calls, my colleagues at the Institute for Parapsychology and I have found that there is little that can shock or surprise us in what folks want to discuss,

---

*As you might suspect, a certain percentage of the personal-experience calls are from emotionally disturbed individuals. The best we can do in such cases is sympathetically to suggest that the person seek professional care in his or her own locale. Many calls, however, are from persons who seem perfectly sane but have simply had a puzzling experience that they believe to have been psychic. For these we can offer information, suggest reading material, or otherwise help the person better understand the experience. We log all such calls, but we do not record them in detail or attempt further investigation.

but occasionally there is a call that makes us think hard about the enterprise in which we find ourselves. This was to be one of those.

From the quaver in her voice it was clear that this was a young woman who was fighting hard to keep her composure. She explained that she had buried her husband less than two weeks ago and was just now able to talk about a disturbing experience surrounding the event. Several weeks prior to his death she had had a vivid dream in which her husband was out hunting and had been accidentally shot and killed by his hunting partner. It had been an unusually vivid dream—unlike her normal dreams—and she had awakened from it in a cold sweat. Her husband did go hunting occasionally and she debated whether or not she should tell him about the dream. Since he had no immediate plans to go hunting and he had already announced that his schedule would not permit him to do so that season, the woman decided not to mention the dream. About two weeks later her husband was unexpectedly invited to go hunting, and equally unexpectedly he found the time to do so. Again the woman debated whether or not to tell him about the dream, but this time she feared that perhaps the act of telling him might somehow bring the event to pass, and she knew in any case that her husband would ridicule her concern over "just a dream." On the evening before the scheduled day she implored her husband not to go, but she did not tell him why. He assured her that both he and his partner were careful hunters and that there was nothing to worry about.

The next morning her husband did go hunting, and in a freak accident almost exactly like the one the woman had seen in her dream, his partner accidentally shot and killed him. Her question to me, as "someone who knows about these things," was, had she done the right thing?

Would that parapsychologists knew enough about these experiences to be able to say what one should do in such instances. Unfortunately we do not. All we can do is help people try to understand them, even as we try to understand them ourselves. Was it just coincidence? The woman herself had thought long and hard about that possibility—hoping to alleviate her own guilty feelings—but it just did not fit. She could not escape the feeling that she had somehow received information from the future and had perhaps failed to heed its warning. "Is it really possible to see the future like I did, or am I going crazy?" she asked.[1]

Exploring Human Experiences

People often think that it is the more flamboyant phenomena of parapsychology—the ghost stories and poltergeists, people who work miracles, and the like—that keep researchers hammering away at a subject matter that at times seems very reluctant to give up any secrets. Not so. For me—and I suspect for many, if not most, of my fellow researchers in parapsychology—the driving force behind our efforts can be found in the unusual experiences of thousands upon thousands of quite ordinary men and women. It is those "observations of nature" that simply do not fit into our conventional understanding of the way the world works and that cry out for better explanations than the dismissive ones that are usually offered. These are the experiences that we commonly call *psychic*. In some cases people acquire information in ways that, on the surface, seem to go beyond any of the conventional communication pathways that biology and psychology have identified. In other experiences people appear to cause events to happen at a distance, also by means other than the mechanisms normally associated with human action.

Were parapsychologists confined to studying only the occasional gifted individual, or limited to certain rare events, it is unlikely that this field would make any progress at all. But the fact is that *many* people report experiences that seem to involve extrasensory perception or, less commonly, psychokinesis. This suggests that psychic phenomena, as they are called, are the result of some sort of ability that may be widely distributed in the population, perhaps even universal, and thus can be studied just as other human abilities are.

Whether psychic ability is a universal human ability or is relatively uncommon remains a completely open question. It is not unusual to hear opinions such as, "Everybody has psychic ability; they just have to learn to use it." Perhaps that is true, but for the present there are no data to provide unqualified support for that claim. Having an experience or two does not translate into having an ability that a person can use at will, despite the publication of books that claim to teach people how to enhance their psychic powers. We simply do not know if psychic ability is something everyone has, but we do know that psychic experiences are widespread.

I mentioned previously that surveys have repeatedly demonstrated that anywhere from one-half to three-quarters of the population claim to have had one or more psychic experiences.[2] However, when parapsychologists are able to follow up these surveys with more detailed questioning, it usually turns out that only a much smaller number of these experiences can be considered *possibly* psychic by the parapsychologist's stricter standards, which aim to weed out the more obvious "normal" explanations. An estimate accepted by many parapsychologists is that between 10 and 15 percent of the population have had an experience (ESP or PK) that cannot reasonably be explained by normal means. That still amounts to quite a few people.

What Is a Psychic Experience?

Psychic experiences can be as different as the people who report them, but we can look at some representative cases. For these examples we shall rely on the work of Dr. Louisa E. Rhine, who has examined more reports of spontaneous psi experiences than any other parapsychologist.

As the work of the Duke University Parapsychology Laboratory became widely known, people would write the lab and describe their unusual experiences. Often the writers asked the Duke researchers to explain these occurrences, but usually these correspondents were just volunteering to share their experiences in the hope that this might further the research. By 1948 quite a few such letters had accumulated, and Louisa Rhine decided that a systematic study was in order. For the next thirty years, until her retirement in the mid-seventies, she collected and studied these reports, amassing nearly fourteen thousand cases, which remain in the files of the Institute for Parapsychology.

The first thing Rhine did was to eliminate those reports that were either too vague or were easily explained by normal factors. The accounts had to describe explicitly what the experience was like as well as the actual event and surrounding circumstances to which the experience seemed to relate. If the report was sufficiently detailed, Rhine made a "face validity" judgment as to whether or not the experience was likely to have been psychic. More than half of the reports that came in to the laboratory were eliminated, and the rest became part of the collection.

Louisa Rhine never claimed that her criteria for acceptance were rigorous or that any particular case was "proof" of the existence of psychic phenomena. The cases she amassed simply reflected the correspondents' "good faith" efforts to relate strange and sometimes troubling experiences. Rhine's purpose was to collect a large number of reports of unusual human experiences and let the numbers speak for themselves. She hoped that through examining these cases, patterns would emerge that would guide future experimental research. Naturally her approach drew criticism from other parapsychologists, who felt that unless each case was thoroughly investigated by an experienced parapsychologist, there was no way of telling if the experience was genuinely psychic or even if the story was authentic. But Rhine felt that even a thorough investigation of such reports could never *prove* the existence of psychic phenomena. Only the experimental approach as embodied in her husband's work could do that. Louisa Rhine was searching for patterns of psychic experiences in real life, and she wanted to cast her net widely. She believed that problems with individual cases—faulty memory, embellishment, and even fabrication—would "come out in the wash" when she studied large groups of cases.[3]

One of the first patterns to emerge was not particularly surprising. The largest number of psychic experiences—nearly 60 percent of the collection—occurred during dreams. The next largest group—almost 30 percent—was what were called waking impressions: intuitions or hunches that arrive without any imagery or forethought. Least common were actual sensory hallucinations, which comprised less than 10 percent of the collection.[4]

Psychic Dreams

Psychic dreams come in two forms. The most common form is the *realistic dream.* Typical of this experience is the following (summarized by Louisa Rhine):

> One night a California grandmother awoke from a frighteningly vivid and very realistic dream. In it she thought she saw her baby

grandson struggling and smothering in his blankets. His movements were getting weaker and weaker. It was almost the end. She awoke. It was 3:45 A.M. Her daughter and her husband lived across town. Should she call them?

As she said, "After all, it was only a dream. I thought, If I call and wake them they'll think I'm crazy. But if I don't and anything happens . . ." So she phoned and got a surprised son-in-law on the line.

"What on earth are you calling for at this hour?" he cried.

"Go to the baby at once," she said. "He's smothering."

"Yes, he was. We're up. We heard him."[5]

In this case the grandmother's dream was a reasonably realistic representation of what was actually happening at the time. Not only did she sense that her grandson was in danger but she identified what the danger was.

Often these realistic psychic dreams are extremely detailed. Sometimes parts of the "scene" may be obscured, almost as if the dreamer were watching events unfold from a particular vantage point. One such example came from the district manager of a Canadian sheet-and-tin-plate company. One summer he and several fellow industrialists spent about two weeks in the Canadian deep woods on a fishing trip. On the night before they were to return home, the district manager had a dream so clear and vivid that he could not sleep afterward. He described his experience as follows:

One of our locomotive cranes that was unloading a car of scrap iron, together with the car, was on the track near the bank of a river alongside the water tower that served the locomotives. For some unaccountable reason, as the huge magnet swung around with a heavy load of scrap, it suddenly toppled over the riverbank. The operator, whom I called by name, jumped clear of the crane and landed below it as it came bounding, tumbling and bouncing down the riverbank, and he finally disappeared from view as the crane came to rest twenty feet below at the water's edge. I particularly noted the number of the crane and the number and positions of the railroad cars, and was able to tell how the crane operator was dressed. Furthermore, I noticed the approximate damage done to the crane. I did not know, however, what had finally happened to the operator. He had disappeared under or behind the crane after it had come to rest. In other words, I was observing the accident from somewhere in or across the river.

Upon my return to the mill the following day, the first man I met was the master mechanic. He told me to come with him to the machine shop to inspect the crane of my dream, to talk with the operator, who had emerged without a scratch. The operator explained his lack of injury by the fact that the crane had fallen over in front of him as he made his last jump and it made its last bounce. The record showed the smallest detail to be as I had dreamed it, with one exception. The exception was that the accident had happened two hours after the dream.[6]

Another type of psychic experience is the *symbolic dream*. Almost one-third of psychic dreams are quite unrealistic; the relevant information is conveyed in more or less symbolic terms or through outright fantasy. Since ordinary dreams often consist of symbolic or fantastical reinterpretations of waking experiences, it is not surprising that information somehow acquired extrasensorily will similarly be transformed. For this reason symbolic dreams that might be psychic resemble the strange dreams that we all have, but psychic dreams often appear to carry a certain conviction of importance to the dreamer that sets them apart. A good example of a symbolic dream that appeared to convey information psychically was one of the many cases that came in to the Duke lab following World War II. In this case a woman from San Francisco wrote:

In January 1945 I dreamed that my young son, an only child, who was overseas in combat duty in the South and Southwest Pacific theater, came to me while I was busy in the kitchen and handed me his uniform, which was sodden, soaking, and dripping wet. He had a most distressed expression on his young face, and feeling disturbed and confused, but saying nothing, I mechanically began to wring the water from the uniform, the navy-blue dye clouding the water in the process and increasing the disturbed and confused bewildered feeling.

Billie, standing next to me, took the uniform from my hands and, dropping it into the laundry tub, turned me around and took me in his arms saying, "Isn't this terrible! Oh, Mom—it's all so terrible!"

Although he had never given me any cause for concern when it came to getting into any mischief of any major degree in the "growing-up" process of his nineteen years, I thought—in the dream—that he might have gotten into some sort of difficulty that he thought would therefore be distressing to me, for he said, "This is the one thing, Mother, that I had so hoped you would never have to hear!" So I said to him, as I had at times when he was growing up, "Billie dear, remember?

There is nothing so terrible that we can't sit down together and talk it out."

We went into the living room, and when I sat down in the chair he sat down in my lap, put his arms around my neck and his head on my shoulder—sobbing—but quietly. I held him in my arms and suddenly he was a little infant again and I was rocking him as I had in his babyhood! As his sobbing ceased, I awakened abruptly, but the dream remained with me most vividly.

That was on a Monday night. The following Sunday afternoon a chaplain from the Thirteenth Naval Base in Long Beach, California (I was living in southern California at that time) came to me with the message that something had happened to Bill's ship, the USS S——, a long list of those missing—and his name was among them. It was later established that all those listed as missing—two hundred fifty lads—were killed . . . at the time the ship . . . was torpedoed by the enemy . . . on that very night of January twentieth when I had dreamed so vividly of Billie in the dream here recorded.[7]

Even though the occurrences in this dream bore little relationship to the actual event, the sad news was conveyed nonetheless in the mixture of fantasy, dramatization, and the mother's memories.

In the many cases she examined, Louisa Rhine observed that it was rare to find a psychic dream report in which realistic and un-realistic elements were mixed. Why this should be is not known, nor is there any firm answer to the question of why some people develop apparently psychic information into a shockingly accurate picture of actual events while others transform similar information into dramatized fantasies or symbolic scenarios. Undoubtedly a good part of the answers to both questions will be found in the experient's own psychological makeup and predisposition to certain types of dreaming.

Waking Impressions

Like dreams, intuitions, or waking impressions, are familiar to all of us. They are the sudden hunches, ideas, and insights that seem to arrive without any deliberate effort, sudden "bolts from the blue" that suggest courses of action or help solve problems but often seem to have no apparent logic behind them. Just like dreams, the vast bulk of waking impressions are probably the result of ongoing ordinary psychological processes at the unconscious level—the unconscious fitting together of little bits of information from many sources resulting in a sudden "click" and a leap into consciousness of the insight or intuition. However, there is also a type of apparent psychic experience that resembles intuition but would be very hard to explain on the basis of unconscious processes. Probably all of us have at one time or another had the feeling that so-and-so will telephone today and then received the expected call. Often there are ordinary components in such a hunch—for example the person is overdue to make such a call, or perhaps some shared news events caused two people to think of each other. In the following case from a man living in Seattle, however, normal explanations seem inadequate. While he was a college student in 1907 and on a vacation at his home in Iowa, he witnessed an experience of his mother's that he described as so unforgettable that in all the intervening years it still stood out.

> My parents had been divorced in 1905. To my mother it was a matter of shame and sorrow—divorce being deemed a defeat. While both parents had frequently written to me off in school, they had not corresponded with each other. When with one of them, I never mentioned the other—I had early learned not to do so.
>
> Seated chatting with my mother that day, I saw her face take on a sudden expression of astonishment—possibly agony. I exclaimed, "Mother, what's wrong?"
>
> She replied, "Your father is getting married."
>
> I laughed. "Impossible. He would have told me. I had a letter from him only a few days before I came here."
>
> But no assurance from me could change her complete conviction that at the moment my father was remarrying. In contrast I continued to be convinced that he would have advised me in advance, my relation to him being very close and our letters very intimate.
>
> However, in due course I received a letter from my father telling me of his marriage. The marriage had taken place in New York on the evening of the day my mother and I were visiting in Iowa.[8]

By their nature, intuitions involve little or no imagery, so there is no point in classifying them as realistic or unrealistic. The experient just "knows" something, and often that knowledge comes with an unexpected degree of conviction.

Hallucinations

The least common type of apparent psychic experience, the hallucination, can be realistic or unrealistic. Hallucinations seem to fall partway between the "direct" knowledge of intuitions and the pictorial or dramatized information that appears in dreams. Like intuitions, hallucinations occur when the person is awake, but like dreams the information is inferred from simulated sensory information. In a hallucination, the person thinks he is receiving this sensory information (usually sight or hearing, but also touch and pain) when in fact there is no stimulus. Although hallucinations seem to present new information, they are typically based on memories and other unconscious material, and they come into consciousness in a way that causes the person to feel that the experience is being freshly presented to the senses. Like the other forms of psychic experience, hallucinations are a familiar, though somewhat uncommon, psychological experience. They can even be induced in a variety of ways, ranging from sensory deprivation to hallucinogenic drugs.

Hallucinations that are apparently of a psychic nature can occur in circumstances that might trigger ordinary hallucinations—extreme stress, fatigue, and the like—but they can also occur when there seems to be no particular cause. The distinguishing feature of a psychic hallucination is that the information conveyed by it could not have come from past memories or present inferences. The following experience is fairly typical of a visual hallucination:

> In December 1951 my husband was drafted into the Marine Corps. We had only been married three months and of course were very close.
>
> He had been down in Parris Island about a month; it was a very cold spell and according to the weather broadcasts even the South was having bad weather.
>
> I stayed at my mother's house several nights a week, as I was lonely. On this Friday night I fell asleep and about 1:30 A.M. I woke up and Richard (my husband) was standing in the room next to me. It was as clear as this paper. He didn't speak but just stood there as if sort of pleading.
>
> When I got up the next morning, I told my mother I was very

worried something might be wrong. I didn't hear from him that day—but the next day, Sunday, I received a long-distance phone call from Charleston, S.C., Navy Hospital. He had pneumonia.

At the time he appeared to me on the Friday night he was standing twelve-to-four fire watch. As you know, Marine Corps boot training is pretty rigid, and when he complained of being sick, they thought he was trying to plead out of fire watch and he was forced to stand it anyway.

He had a fever of over 104 and was very sick, and at those moments when he appeared to me, he told me that he was walking the watch, just praying so hard that he could be home with me.[9]

Hallucinations of this type, in which people are at that moment in some particular crisis, are often referred to as "crisis apparitions." In this case the husband was in a relatively mild "crisis." Most commonly, however, crisis apparitions involve seeing a person near death or at the moment of death. As long as the apparition is "private," that is, experienced by only one person, we may be justified in considering it a hallucination, induced perhaps by psychic means. In the rarer cases where more than one person "sees" the apparition (as we shall see in chapter 7), to call it a hallucination may not be the best explanation.

Although the popular notions would suggest that visual hallucinations should be most common, the fact is that in Louisa Rhine's collection the most common type is actually auditory—people hearing their name being called, and so on. Another large category is that of hallucinated pain, as in the next example from an Indiana woman who was very close to both her mother and a childless aunt who lived with her mother. As they became elderly, the two relied upon the younger woman for assistance.

On November 8, 1961, shortly after I had arrived at the school where I teach, I went into the office. Suddenly an extremely severe pain struck my shoulder and chest, so intense that it made me cry out. The principal and other teachers who were in the office were alarmed. However, the intensity of the pain did not last, and I went on with my work.

About an hour after this, my principal came to my room to tell me that I had a long-distance call. My aunt had suffered a heart attack as she and my mother were going downstairs. She had died instantly, with only my mother there. As well as we could estimate, it had happened about the time the severe pain had struck me.[10]

These examples typify the principal ways in which people seem to experience paranormal phenomena in their lives. The examples are slightly misleading, though, to the extent that they all portray the experience as conveying important information. It is true that the great majority of apparently psychic experiences do convey important, sometimes lifesaving, information, but in a surprisingly large number of cases the information conveyed is trivial. For instance sometimes a person will have a vivid dream of being in a certain situation or meeting some particular people and later—perhaps days or weeks later—the event is played out in minute detail. The correspondence between the event and the dream may be uncanny, yet the event itself may be of little significance to anyone involved. Nevertheless experiences like this, whether important or not, do raise one of the most difficult questions parapsychologists encounter: Can we use information acquired through psychic experiences to change the future?

Seeing the Future

More than half of all psychic experiences are *precognitive*—they convey information about an event that has not yet taken place. Behind this academic observation, however, can lie a great deal of human anguish, as in the case that opened this chapter. Many psychic experiences do appear to be glimpses or previews of the future; what we do not know is whether or not someone can *intervene* to prevent a foreseen tragedy. If the experience is genuinely paranormal, is it revealing what *will* inevitably happen, or is it warning about what *might* happen if steps are not taken to avoid it? Unfortunately the answer that comes from the many reports of such experiences is equivocal.

In one of her many papers Louisa Rhine looked at this question in detail.[11] From a batch of more than 1,300 apparently precognitive experiences, she culled 433 cases in which the event was recognized as precognitive at the time of the experience and the foreseen event was such that anyone would have wanted to prevent it. In about two-thirds of the cases no attempt was made to prevent the event, either because the experient simply forgot or because she or he feared the ridicule that might ensue should the premonition prove false, or for some other reason. Rhine set aside these cases, too, leaving her with 162 cases in which people attempted to prevent a foreseen event from taking place. For her study she added 29 similar cases taken from earlier collections, giving a total of 191.

In sixty (31 percent) of the cases, the attempted intervention was unsuccessful, most often because the psychic experience had failed to convey enough information to permit the experient to take adequate steps. Strangely enough for a matter so seemingly important, the bulk of precognitive experiences come in the form of unrealistic dreams—the most difficult to recognize as potentially important and the least likely to convey useful details—or as intuitions, which, by their nature, convey few details. Parapsychologists can only speculate why this should be. It seems clear that most apparently psychic experiences—contemporaneous or precognitive—are somehow "constructed" by the mind from existing memories of past experiences, so it is possible that events that have not happened yet are simply more difficult to represent. However, there is no hard evidence on this issue, and such speculations are little more than educated guesses.

An example of an unsuccessful attempt to prevent a foreseen event was reported by a woman in New York. Her experience seemed convincingly like a premonition to her, but it involved too many elements for her to be able to take effective action, though she tried. She reported:

> I had clearly seen [in a dream] a plane crash at the shore of a lake and the roof of the third cottage on that dirt track in flames as a result. There was only one man and he burned up. I tried to write two overdue letters that morning, but I found myself telling my correspondents about it [the dreamed accident] and also the fact that the fire engine would go in by the canal and be unable to get to the plane until it was too late. It was so clear that I was conscious of every plane that went over that day. Late in the afternoon the lights were on and I was at the electric range stirring something for dinner when I said, "That's the plane—the one that's going to crash! Robert, stop the firemen before they try the canal; they have to take the basin road and they don't know it."
>
> My husband went outdoors to listen, [and] put his head in to say, "That plane's all right," only to have me shriek, "It is *not!*" Within seconds the plane crashed, the firemen took the canal instead of the basin road, and the pilot was burned to a crisp. The cottage was only

slightly damaged . . . and I was a wreck for weeks wondering how I could have prevented it.[12]

The remaining 131 cases (69 percent) were more successful, in that people were able to take steps to avoid the undesirable consequences of whatever appeared to have been "foretold" in their experiences. In one case a man who operated a streetcar in Los Angeles had a strikingly vivid dream concerning an intersection where cars leaving a certain street exit often made illegal turns across the streetcar tracks. Of course it would be normal to find such worrisome situations incorporated into the dreams of a streetcar operator, but in this case the man's dream had a different character.

I dreamed that I was operating a "one-man" car on the "W" line going south on Figueroa Street. I pulled up at an intersection, Avenue 26, loaded with passengers, and waited for the signal to change. All the things in the dream were as they *actually* were; I mean the streets, stores, traffic conditions. Everything was in the dream just as they were in real life.

When the signal said, "Go," I proceeded and crossed the intersection. As I crossed the intersection I saw a northbound "5" car approaching. I waved to the motorman and went on. As the cars passed, my car was at the point of this exit. Suddenly, without warning a big truck, painted a solid bright red, cut in front of me coming from the exit, and the truck making the illegal turn could not see my car because of the other streetcar. There was a terrific crash. People were thrown from their seats on the streetcar and the truck overturned. There had been three people in the truck, two men and a woman. The two men were sprawled on the street, dead, and the woman was screaming in pain. I walked over to the woman and she looked at me with the largest, bluest eyes I had ever seen. She repeatedly shouted at me, "You could have avoided this. You could have avoided this."

I awoke with a start, my pajamas soaked with perspiration. It was nearly time for me to get up anyway, so I stayed up, quite shaken by the dream.

I reported for work and for one reason or another I do not remember, I was given a run on the "W" line. I had recovered my composure by then and had put the dream out of my mind. I made one trip south. On my second trip I pulled up to Avenue 26 just as in my dream and loaded passengers. I was waiting for the signal to change, still not thinking of the dream, when suddenly I became sick to my stomach. I was actually nauseated. I felt provoked at myself and hoped it would go away. As I left the intersection on the signal change, I saw, just as in my dream, a Number 5 car, northbound. Now I was definitely sick. Everything seemed to have happened before, and my mind seemed to be shouting at me about something. When I waved to the motorman on the "5" car, the dream came to me. I immediately shut off the power and applied the brakes, stopping the car. A truck, not a big truck completely red as in my dream but a panel delivery truck, with the space for advertising on the side painted over with bright red, shot directly in my path. Had I been moving at all, I would have hit it as surely as I did in the dream.

There were three people in the truck, two men and a woman. As the truck passed in front of me, the woman leaned out of the window and looked up at me with the same startled, large blue eyes I had seen in my dream, and without realizing what it meant to me, I'm sure, she waved her arm and hand, thumb and forefinger circled in the familiar "okay" gesture.

I was so upset I had to be relieved [from duty].[13]

Examples like this seem to indicate that sometimes it is indeed possible to "change the future," *if* the psychic experience was showing the future. But it is worth noting that in more than a few cases people who tried to intervene felt that their attempts to prevent something from happening actually could have contributed to its occurrence.

What, then, is one to do if faced with an experience that seems to be a glimpse into the future? Louisa Rhine counseled a pragmatic approach: If the experience leaves the person with a conviction that it is a warning of some sort, then it should be treated as such, and reasonable steps should be taken to avoid the problem. On the other hand, since we know so little about these apparently precognitive experiences and since the world is often misled by cranks and fanatics, Rhine advised against issuing public warnings. Also, it is apparent that efforts to prevent tragedies will often fail for reasons that are completely beyond the control of the person who had the experience, so, at this stage of our knowledge (or perhaps our ignorance) about such experiences, there is no reason whatsoever to feel guilty over such failures.[14]

As you might suspect, precognitive experiences are among the most difficult to accept at face value. People are willing to allow that there might be unknown means of communicating information between people contemporaneously, but to foresee a future event—that is just too much to swallow. Among the various types of psychic experiences, precognition, were it to be true, is seen as the most threatening to the conventional worldview.

What Separates the Normal From the Paranormal?

While we can go on listing these unusual human experiences, we must not lose sight of the fundamental issue: Do these experiences require the attention of the special science of parapsychology, or can they be explained by perfectly ordinary means? Should we not choose the "normal" explanation over the paranormal one whenever possible? Of course, but deciding whether or not a normal explanation adequately accounts for a seemingly psychic experience is not a clear-cut process. A great deal depends on one's initial attitude. Those who feel that parapsychological phenomena are impossible are likely to prefer any explanation that does not invoke constructs such as ESP, no matter how improbable the normal explanation, while those who are firmly convinced that psychic phenomena are real are likely to find a parapsychological interpretation more satisfying, perhaps even to the point of overlooking a likely normal explanation. This holds true in evaluating any paranormal claims. Human nature makes it difficult to be as objective about these claims as textbook notions of science would like us to be.

Of course none of the cases in Rhine's collection would be there if she had had any reason to believe that there were any *obvious* normal explanations for them. As we have seen, she rejected about half of all the reports that came in. Not everybody needs to accept her criteria, however.

What are some of the alternative explanations that must be considered? Perhaps the most commonly offered alternative is simple coincidence: The seemingly psychic experience and the related event just happened by chance, and the natural tendency to link similar events gave the apparently psychic experience greater importance than it deserved. This explanation applies best to situations in which the psychic element is part of a normally occurring experience, such as a dream. A person may have lots of strange dreams, and every once in a while something similar to a dream may happen in real life. The person then recalls the dream and makes a connection. Pure coincidence. This approach is less successful, however, at explaining those experiences that of themselves may be extremely rare—such as a full-blown hallucination or sudden psychosomatic pains—and are later connected to a confirming event.

While we all know people who seem inclined to impart mystical significance to any two events that seem remotely connected, the fact is that most adults can keep coincidence in reasonable perspective in their daily lives. The cases that were volunteered to the Duke lab were given precisely because they seemed to exceed the threshold of chance. In general what makes the cases stand apart from simple coincidences is the *preciseness of the fit* between the experience and the event. It is one thing to dream about a plane crash, but it is quite another to dream about a plane crashing into a particular house on a particular lake shore with the fire engine taking the wrong road, and then watch the event unfold as in a film.

Might there still be a satisfactory normal alternative explanation for apparently psychic experiences? To find out, it is necessary to consider some additional factors. We must keep in mind that the Rhine collection is composed only of reports. Might the reports be entirely fabricated? Actually this is not a likely explanation. In the several other major case collections in which the reports were rigorously investigated, it turned out that incidents of fabricated reports were very rare. Might the report be accidentally inaccurate? This is a much more likely possibility. Often an individual's recollection of the psychic experience becomes more and more like the confirming event as time goes on. Just as a tale grows in the telling, the recollection of the experience—which itself may have been vague in the first place, especially if it was a dream or an impression— may come to "fit" reality far more closely than it did originally. A dream of an auto accident that is coincidentally followed by a real auto accident may grow to seem more precognitive as details of the real event become intermingled with recollections of the dream.

Yet there are many cases in the Rhine collection in which the psychic experience was so dramatic or troubling that the individual either recorded or communicated the details to another person before the confirming event took place. There is less chance here that the memory of the experience is molded to fit the event. Even so, might not this individual's perception of the confirming event be colored by his or her memory of the seemingly psychic experience? The dramatic or frightening nature of the psychic experience might cause a person to misperceive the details of a complicated event in such a way that they appear to "confirm" the psychic experience. But then there are cases in which the event is witnessed by others who corroborate these details, and so on and so on. . . .

Where does all this leave us? It is perfectly possible for a rational individual to take the position that all experiences that appear to be psychic can be explained by one or more completely normal psychological mechanisms. If paranormal phenomena are impossible, then those are the *only* explanations. On the other hand, it is possible for an equally rational individual to look at all these reports and decide that the proposed normal explanations are inadequate and that we should continue to look for explanations. I do not think one of those positions more scientific than the other. It is simply a matter of where one draws the line in accepting explanations. My colleagues and I fall into the camp that feels that all of the answers are not in yet, and that is why we do what we do.

What Separates Psychic Experience From Mental Disorder?

According to all the surveys that have been done, more than half of the people reading this book believe they have had one or more psychic experiences. *You* may feel that you have had a psychic experience. Even after playing devil's advocate and trying to account for your experience by normal means, you may still be convinced that you have had a genuine psychic experience. How do people cope with these experiences? Are they something to fear?

People sometimes ask me, "Is there something wrong with me?" or, "Am I going crazy?" It is hard to read the letters in Louisa Rhine's collection without coming away with the feeling that the vast majority of these persons are normal, sane, healthy individuals who have simply had a strange experience. They are not crazy. They are not delusional, and it is precisely their firm grip on reality that makes an apparently psychic experience so puzzling and unique for them. Nonetheless the *official* answer from the psychological professions to the question "Is there something wrong with me?" is, "Yes, I am afraid there *is* something wrong with you." According to the third edition of the *Diagnostic and Statistical Manual of Mental Disorders* (often referred to as the DSM-III) published by the American Psychiatric Association and considered the bible of mental-health evaluation, a person who claims to have seen the future, reports hearing voices or seeing visions that tell him what is happening at distant locations, experiences pains that he thinks might be connected with some distant person's pain, and so forth, is displaying symptoms of mental disorder. Such "presenting symptoms" could typically result in a diagnosis of one of the schizophrenic disorders or any of several other mental illnesses.

Time and time again, when clinical psychologists and psychiatrists who are familiar with the parapsychological literature evaluate a person who has had an apparent psychic experience, they find that standard tests reveal a perfectly normal, well-adjusted individual—who happened to have had a strange experience. There is in fact a world of difference between the cases that we have been considering and those experiences that *are* symptomatic of mental illness. The apparent psychic experience is usually a solitary event. It happens infrequently in an individual's life, usually only once or twice. It is not an ongoing condition. The person who has had the experience usually recognizes that it *is* unusual, that it is something outside his or her normal mental experiences. Most importantly these occasional psychic experiences do not interfere with a person's ability to carry on a normal life.

The sort of report that one is likely to get from a schizophrenic is easily recognized as such. Any laboratory that studies parapsychological phenomena gets it share of these contacts either by phone or letter. Typical of the sort of schizophrenic "report" that our laboratory staff might receive is:

> I know what you people are doing. You're beaming thoughts into my head—trying to make me go crazy. Don't tell me you're not. I've read about your lab. My ex-wife's paying you to do this, isn't she? Well, it's going to stop. When I get through to the CIA, they'll close you down in a minute. You just wait.

Or perhaps one that would sound less belligerent:

> Actually I am quite psychic. I can tell when people are thinking about me right away because I can pick up their thoughts. Like when I am in a bar, I can tell when a good-looking chick really wants to meet me because I can hear her thoughts in my head—like she is hoping I'll come over to her. Of course, when I talk to her she'll deny that she was thinking of me because she's afraid to admit that I have such powers.

The spectrum of mental experiences and of mental illnesses is far broader than we can discuss in this chapter, and sometimes it is necessary to seek professional help in sorting out troubling experiences. Although there is abundant evidence from parapsychology that normal, well-adjusted individuals can have psychic experiences, and that such experiences typically produce no long-term problems, there will be some instances where appropriate professional assistance might be needed. In such cases it might be wise to "shop around" for a mental-health professional in the same way that one might look for a family physician. Parapsychologists often find themselves at odds with colleagues in the mental-health professions, who accuse them of supporting and even encouraging delusional thinking. Parapsychologists, on the other hand, object to the knee-jerk reaction of many psychologists and psychiatrists who regard any report of a psychic experience as an automatic diagnosis of mental illness. For the present the onus remains on parapsychologists to gain a greater understanding of psychic experiences, but clinicians could put themselves in a better position to help their patients if they were more familiar with the abundant professional material that examines apparent psychic experiences in greater depth than is found in the regular training programs.

There are many approaches to clinical psychology, and some are more sympathetic to apparent psychic experiences than others. Jungian psychoanalysts tend to be willing to explore such experiences in some depth before making a diagnosis. Clinical psychologists with an orientation toward transpersonal psychology or humanistic psychology are usually more willing to accept psychic experiences at face value and work toward helping the person integrate the experience into his or her life.

Shamanism: Psi Experiences in Other Cultures

Our particular view of parapsychological experiences comes to us filtered through the eyes of a technologically advanced culture imbued with centuries of scientific and rational thought. Paranormal phenomena do not, at present, fit in comfortably with conventional scientific thinking, so psychic experiences are not readily assimilated into our culture. Although poll after poll has shown that more than half of the population accepts the existence of psychic phenomena, the culture as a whole is not ready to grant fully "normal" status to psychic experiences. They remain something extraordinary—something we should be skeptical about. We must recognize, however, that our modern perspective is relatively recent in the history of mankind, and though we may like to think of it as advanced and as the goal to which all mankind should be striving, it remains in many respects still a minority view.

Outside of our Western, scientific culture we find that many cultures we consider less developed or "primitive" have a very different attitude toward what we would call psychic phenomena. For these people psychic phenomena are not unusual, rare, or "unbelievable" events. They are incorporated into the most basic religious and cultural beliefs of the society. In such societies it is normal for certain persons to have the ability to communicate with spirits to get information about future events. It is perfectly acceptable for a healer to diagnose a disease by going into a trance or by casting diviner's "bones" and then consulting the spirits for a remedy. Sometimes we consider the people in these cultures to be naive, but in fact it would be very naive of us to think that they believe in the efficacy of their healers or their "clever men" simply because of ingrained religious superstitions. Anthropologists have confirmed that they maintain these beliefs in large part because they get tangible results. The anthropologist E. F. Torrey has shown that tribal healers using what we might be tempted to label magic tricks are at least as effective in treating mental disorders among their fellow tribesmen as Western psychiatrists are in dealing with their patients.[15]

Just because the magical practices of a primitive culture seem to work is no reason to assume that anything paranormal is involved, however. Traditional primitive methods of diagnosis and healing no doubt involve a great deal of folk wisdom that is passed from generation to generation and that has been effectively surrounded by certain rituals and ceremonies to convince the patient that the healer has the power to produce a remedy. (In some ways it is not so different from our own system of medicine.) Tribal clever men and diviners may have learned the same skills that Western "psychics" use to convince clients that they can read minds or see the future. In addition, people who accept paranormal phenomena as just a fact of life might be much less critical of what they see and more likely to accept simulations of these phenomena as genuine.

For much of this century most anthropologists' attitudes toward psi phenomena in primitive cultures ranged from thinly disguised scorn for such gullible superstition to paternalistic condescension that advised fellow researchers not to laugh or make fun of such beliefs. The work of professional anthropologists is full of reports that could possibly have a paranormal basis, but only in recent years have a few anthropologists been willing to entertain the possibility that some of those "miracles" may be the same phenomena that parapsychologists have been studying. Today some anthropologists are attempting to investigate apparent instances of paranormal phenomena in other cultures, not only by viewing them but also by participating in certain practices. The result is that the people of these very different cultures are not looking quite so naive and foolish as they once seemed.

More and more investigations are focusing on the power of the shaman in primitive societies. Today the shaman is rather loosely defined as a tribal miracle worker who intercedes with the spirits for the benefit of the tribe and the individuals of whom it is comprised. Most "primitive" and developing cultures have people who fill the role of the shaman, whether it be the medicine man of the Native Americans, the sangoma of southern Africa, or the clever man of the Australian aborigines. In general the shaman serves as a healer, diviner, intermediary between ancestral spirits and the living, and general-purpose psychic. Almost by definition the shaman possesses abilities that, if they are genuine, are paranormal.

Across Africa the shaman is regarded as an important member of society. Even in the developed areas of South Africa and other countries, shamans can be found in the cities as well as in the bush.

Their abilities are sought even when the best Western medicine and technology is available. The most common type of African witch doctor or shaman is the *sangoma*. This can be a man or woman who has been called to the profession in the traditional manner—through a particular type of sickness diagnosed by another sangoma—and who has undergone a training period that ranges from six months to several years. The sangoma serves as a diagnostician, healer, finder of lost objects, prognosticator, conveyer of information from distant relatives—whatever the spirits will permit. Excellent examples of how a sangoma is chosen and how he or she operates have been provided by Adrian Boshier, an Englishman who worked for the Museum of Man and Science in Johannesburg and who spent many years living in the bush in remote areas of South Africa. In his years of working with different sangomas both in the field and at the museum, Boshier was convinced that he had witnessed genuine psychic abilities on many occasions. Eventually Boshier suffered a "calling" illness, and in the early seventies he himself was trained and initiated as a sangoma.

The actual training involves various physical regimens and instruction by the *Baba*, or teacher. Certain exercises seem explicitly designed to develop psychic abilities. The Baba will often hide objects and require the novice, or *twasa*, to go out at any time, day or night, to find them. Eventually the Baba gives her commands telepathically, or so it seemed to Boshier. When the Baba decides the training is complete, there is an elaborate coming-out ceremony, and the newly qualified sangoma can begin her practice. If at some time in the future the new sangoma feels that her powers are getting out of hand, or that the spirits that visit her have become too difficult to work with, she must find a more highly qualified teacher and begin a second training, called the "second pot." There are twelve "pots" altogether, and the very few sangomas who reach the highest level are considered extremely powerful individuals.

Boshier provided a description of how a sangoma operates that was related by another sangoma with whom he had worked extensively at the museum in Johannesburg:

A patient comes into my house and says *Sia cou lega*—I want to know. I leave him and go into my room, put on my clothes, pick up my switch and begin to sing. I ask my ancestors to tell me what is wrong with this person. I sing and sing, walking around until I feel the spirit coming. When it comes it feels like a heavy weight on the back of my head and my shoulders. Very heavy on me. Then I must go to that patient and start to talk. I must talk until the spirit goes. I cannot stop until it is finished. Sometimes I don't even know what I was saying and the patient must tell me. Sometimes I can hear my words, but don't understand them. When I come back afterwards I feel like I have been dreaming.[16]

Psychic Surgery

When called for, the sangomas of Africa usually employ traditional herbal medicine, sometimes combined with chanting, incantations, and advice for the patient. This is all very tame compared with the sometimes shocking displays of the so-called psychic surgeons who appear to cut open the body of a patient and perform an "operation" with their bare hands. In the late sixties and early seventies psychic surgery was a flourishing business in the Philippines, sought out by planeloads of ill patients from Europe and North America.

Psychic surgery has a long history, having been noted as one of the feats of the Koryak shamans of northern Asia as early as the turn of the century. In its contemporary guise a healer, usually ill educated and ignorant of Western medicine, will select a site on the patient's body, according to the healer's diagnosis of the complaint. With minimal concern for antiseptic conditions, the psychic surgeon will appear to draw open an incision with his finger, insert his fingers (or whole hand), feel around a bit, and eventually withdraw the offending item, which he will typically identify as a tumor, kidney stone, or whatever seems appropriate. Blood is seen, sometimes in quantity, but when the "incision" is wiped clean, there is little or no mark on the skin. Generally when the "operation" is over the patient claims to be cured and simply walks away on his own.

When psychic surgery became a fad, there were of course a number of investigations. Most of these turned up rampant fraud. Many psychic surgeons palmed small balloons filled with animal blood, which they released as they pressed their folded hands into soft areas of the body. "Tumors" turned out to be animal flesh, and "kidney stones" were ordinary pebbles. What healing effects there were— and many were reported—could be attributed to placebo effects.

Healers who were caught defended their practices by saying that the show was necessary to make the patients believe in the healing and thus heal themselves (or let the spirits do it).

Away from the glare of publicity and scattered across southeast Asia and South America, however, reports continue to come in of "psychic surgeries" that are not so easily explained as simple tricks. But the difficulties in disentangling fraud from genuine effects, and in understanding the body's own remarkable abilities to heal itself when the mind is suitably disposed, have effectively removed psychic surgery from the list of claims that parapsychologists can profitably investigate at present.[17]

Psychic healing itself, whether by prayer and meditation, incantations, laying on of hands, spirit intervention, or sacred herbs, is a major component of most shamanic traditions around the world. It also figures prominently in many evangelical Western religions and can be seen any week on television. How much of this is truly a paranormal phenomenon—something that is completely beyond modern medicine—remains unclear and will probably stay that way for some time.

Psychic Injury

The flip side of psychic healing is psychic injury—"hexing" or voodoo death. Though less common than healing, these functions are part of the repertoire of shamans in several parts of the world. In 1971 Joseph Long, a medical anthropologist, accompanied a local physician to observe the trance ceremonies of the Kumina people in southeastern Jamaica. During the ceremony Bongo, an eighty-year-old sorcerer or "obeah-man," made repeated sexual overtures to a dancing priestess, all of which were rejected. Suddenly the priestess went into a deep trance, and all the usual methods used by the participants to awaken her failed. The physician examined her and, after observing no change for over two hours, demanded that he be allowed to take her to a hospital. He did that and returned to the ceremonies. Both Long and the physician visited the hospital around 2:00 A.M., and the priestess was still in the trance. Her breathing was normal, and her pupils appeared normal and reacted properly. She died at 6:00 A.M. with no further symptoms, according to the hospital records.[18]

There are a variety of explanations for reports of hex death. Most common is the suggestion that the victim, who shares the same beliefs in the effectiveness of hexing as the hexer, literally dies of fear and overwhelming anxiety—death due to extreme stress. In some societies in which hexing is accompanied by social isolation, the victim, ostracized in an already isolated society, may commit a kind of suicide. There are, however, numerous reports of hex deaths occurring in societies in which it is considered of the utmost importance that the victim *not know* that he has been hexed, lest he take steps to ward off the hex.[19] These cases would appear to negate the roles of stress and isolation, and as such they are part of a large group of reports that have no satisfactory medical or psychosocial explanation. As with psychic healing, though, the absence of a normal explanation does not mean that something paranormal is happening, though the suggestions are intriguing. It only means that there is yet one more class of unusual phenomena that deserves further investigation.

I could go on indefinitely citing examples of apparently paranormal experiences from virtually every culture and every corner of the globe. It is undeniable that experiences that appear to be paranormal (and are considered as such by those involved) are a fundamental part of human existence. Perhaps, in time, these widespread experiences may be lumped together with the many other delusions and misconceptions that have fallen before the march of science. Many think they belong there already. Yet science itself has a history of prematurely foreclosing on nature's anomalies. To scientists who see foreclosure as a danger, these experiences may be seen as manifestations of abilities possessed by humans that science is now only dimly beginning to comprehend. For the present, keeping this debate alive and keeping the research going are tasks that fall largely to those few scientists who take a genuine interest in this fascinating facet of human nature.

CHAPTER 2

Mapping the Territory

As we have already seen, the subject matter of parapsychology grows out of a variety of human experiences, commonly called psychic, which, when closely examined, seem to defy explanation by conventional means. Over the decades parapsychologists have evolved a certain classification system of the phenomena and a terminology to go with it. Broadly speaking, there are two principal abilities with which parapsychology is concerned: extrasensory perception and psychokinesis.

Extrasensory Perception

Extrasensory perception, or *ESP*, refers to the apparent ability of a human being to acquire information without using the ordinary senses of the body and without depending on logical inference. The *extra* simply means "outside" of the sensory channels (at least as we understand them today); *perception* can refer to anything from vividly "seeing" or dreaming an event to having a vague hunch or even obtaining information that never reaches one's consciousness but in some way affects his or her behavior.

There are several older terms that reflect subdivisions of the broader category of ESP.

Telepathy refers to "mind to mind" contact, wherein a person seems to acquire information directly from another's mind without the mediation of the senses. A typical telepathic experience would be the case of a wife who is at home and suddenly "hears" her husband call or cry out or suddenly "just knows" that he has been hurt. Later she learns that at that very moment he had been involved in a serious auto accident. In this type of case the inference is that the "distress message" was somehow communicated to the wife telepathically from her husband's mind.

Clairvoyance is the acquisition of information about a place, event, or object without sensory mediation. Unlike telepathy, clairvoyance does not depend upon direct contact with another person. One of the most famous examples of clairvoyance came from the eighteenth-century Swedish scientist and later spiritual leader Emmanuel Swedenborg. At a dinner in Göteborg he reported to his host that he saw a great fire raging in Stockholm, some three hundred miles distant. He described the scene as it developed over the next two hours, and the governor was notified. Eventually a courier arrived from Stockholm with news that confirmed Swedenborg's visions precisely. Somewhat less famous, but no less puzzling, are the many cases in which someone has found a lost object (frequently lost by someone else) by "seeing" it in a dream or vision, or the many instances in which someone appeared to "witness" a distant event.

Both telepathy and clairvoyance are assumed to happen in real time, that is, the impression by the percipient happens more or less at the same time as the event. However ESP often involves some future event, in which case it is called *precognition*. Although precognition usually manifests itself as clairvoyance (where a person seems to "see" a future event or scene), some precognitions appear to be telepathic (as when a person experiences the future emotions or distress of another person). Precognition is surprisingly common among the reported experiences of ESP.

Now that the distinction between telepathy and clairvoyance has been made clear, we can pretty much forget about those two terms. Today parapsychologists generally prefer to use the term *GESP*, or *general ESP*, to encompass both phenomena, because they cannot be distinguished in laboratory experiments. No matter how one designs the experiment, it is impossible to rule out clairvoyance as a possible explanation. In any experiment, at some point the "target," even a telepathic one, must be communicated to the person who will check if it is correct. For that moment the target exists either as a written record or as an event that could be picked up by clairvoyance (perhaps precognitively). Over the years some pretty ingenious experiments have tried to get around this problem, but none has done so conclusively. So parapsychologists have shelved attempts to distinguish the two classes rigorously and simply talk about ESP or GESP.

Psychokinesis

The second ability parapsychologists study is *psychokinesis*, or *PK*. This is the apparent ability of a human being to affect objects, events, or even people around him or her without using the usual intervention by the muscular system. Derived from two Greek words, *psychokinesis* literally means "soul (or mind) motion" and is often described today as the direct influence of consciousness on physical systems. PK is popularly referred to as "mind over matter," but this expression is a bit too loose to be of much use, since it can often refer to such things as self-healing and placebo effects in medicine that are not part of parapsychology.

Psychokinesis is a much less frequently reported phenomenon than ESP and hardly ever occurs spontaneously, apart from poltergeist activity or the occasional stopping of a clock at the moment of someone's death. Examples of apparent deliberate psychokinesis would be the reports of the physical mediums of the Victorian era (about whom we shall read more in the next chapter), who were said to move objects around the room, levitate tables, and so on, or the demonstrations of individuals such as the Russian Nina Kulagina (whom we shall meet in chapter 6). Psychokinesis, like ESP, has been studied in the laboratory for some time now. Most contemporary research into PK involves examining the direct influence of consciousness or the mind on finely balanced electronic devices—PK on atomic particles—and this has become known as *micro-PK*. Not surprisingly, the traditional PK, object movement or object deformations such as bending metal, is now frequently called *macro-PK*. The distinction is largely based upon whether one can simply see the effect (macro-PK) or whether one needs a statistical evaluation to determine if something unusual happened (micro-PK). Nevertheless there remain a few experiments, such as dice-throwing tests, that tend to fall somewhere in between.

Collectively, the phenomena covered by the terms *ESP* and *PK* are called *psi phenomena* (from the letter that begins the Greek word for "soul," the root word of all our *psych-* terms), or sometimes just plain *psi*. Although it is common to see phrases such as "I think psi was operating here . . . ," we must always keep in mind that psi, and all other terms that we have discussed, are just constructions to describe certain classes of reported phenomena. It is sometimes necessary even for parapsychologists to remind themselves that psi or ESP or PK are not independent existing forces, abilities, or "things" that can be measured and quantified in some way. These terms are merely labels, a type of shorthand used to describe those interactions that constitute anomalies in our present scientific understanding of the world.

Other Psychic Phenomena

The term *parapsychology* was adopted from German usage by J. B. Rhine in the thirties to describe the strictly experimental approaches to the study of psychic phenomena. If you had ghost stories to tell, you had to take them elsewhere. Over the decades common usage has overcome the boundaries that Rhine and his colleagues tried to erect, and once again parapsychology includes the puzzling reports of ghosts or apparitions and the often-bizarre happenings found in reports of poltergeists. Although these happenings are not part of the mainstream of parapsychological research, they do constitute a significant body of data in the discipline.

Early psychical researchers proposed that the investigation of apparitions and poltergeists could provide evidence to demonstrate that human beings have a soul, or an independently existing consciousness that is separate from the body and indeed even survives the death of the body. As we shall see in chapter 7, poltergeists no longer provide support for this notion, and apparition research is virtually nonexistent today. Yet among some parapsychologists the search for such evidence remains important, and they have brought to parapsychology investigations into reincarnation and a variety of quasi-experimental attempts to answer the ultimate question of what, if anything, survives bodily death.

Finally there are several phenomena that straddle the border between parapsychology and orthodox medical and psychological fields. This area includes near-death experiences (NDEs) and out-of-body experiences (OBEs). The NDEs, reported by people who are brought back from near death, are of interest to some parapsychologists for what these reports have to offer regarding the life-after-death issue; the medical profession regards them as unusual hallucinatory experiences. OBEs, sometimes called *astral projection* or *traveling clairvoyance*, interest some parapsychologists again because of what these reports may indicate about the possibility of the mind "detaching" itself from the body. Psychologists regard them as unusual misperceptions or hallucinations possibly brought about by distortions in body image.

What Parapsychology Is Not

Having outlined the topics that parapsychology includes, it is probably a good idea to mention a few topics that parapsychology does not embrace. Astrology, the belief that the sun, planets, and stars influence events on earth, with its associated methods of predicting future events or explaining present and past ones, is not part of parapsychology. Neither are unidentified flying objects (UFOs). A few scientists have suggested that at least some UFO sightings might represent a modern-day apparition phenomenon, but for the present and the foreseeable future, parapsychology leaves the UFOs to UFOlogists.

The last topic that is often mistakenly included in the field of parapsychology is the matter of strange, unidentified creatures—Bigfoot, the Loch Ness Monster, and so forth. Like sightings of UFOs, the reports of such creatures, if accurate, represent anomalies that science must address, but in this case it is a job for the cryptozoologists.

Parapsychology Today

By the mid-fifties parapsychology had become quite popular, and researchers began to spread out from the original center of activity, the Duke University Parapsychology Laboratory. The leading scientists in the field began to see the need for a professional organization that would both set the standards for parapsychology and facilitate communication between the increasingly far-flung researchers. In 1956 the Parapsychological Association (PA) was formed to serve as the international organization of professional researchers investigating psi phenomena.

Most people have misconceptions not only about the phenomena being studied but also about just who parapsychologists are. The two most common misconceptions are: (a) that there are a large number of parapsychologists working both in universities and in relative secrecy at discreetly located government-sponsored labs; and (b) that there are only a few oddball cranks who work in garages and at ill-funded private institutes. (Since the popular film *Ghost-busters* came out in 1984, there has been a third image of the parapsychologist, but that need not detain us here.) As usual, the truth is somewhere in between. You may be surprised to learn that there are not very many parapsychologists. I would estimate that there are probably fewer than fifty scientists in the English-speaking world and in Europe who conduct parapsychological research on a more or less full-time basis. When you realize that there are probably more people now involved in this research than ever before, you can see why progress in this field is slow.

Researcher is the operative word in describing the members of the PA. Parapsychologists are not psychic practitioners, nor do they all necessarily even accept the reality of psi phenomena. They are, for the most part, scientists and academics with a sincere commitment to trying to understand psi phenomena using the tools of science. In fact the membership of the PA is quite diverse, with psychologists, psychiatrists, M.D.'s, physicists, biologists, sociologists, philosophers, and professionals from many other fields represented. The PA is one of those organizations whose membership criteria are designed more to keep people out than to invite them in.

The current membership has remained static at roughly three hundred.

Of course not all scientists who are working in parapsychology are members of the PA. Many have quite legitimate reasons for not wanting to be labeled parapsychologists, since it does little for one's career and can often serve as an excuse for exposing to question one's work in other areas. But for the past two decades the annual conventions of the PA have been the main forum for presenting and discussing new research in parapsychology, and the affiliated professional journals of the PA are the chief outlets for published research. These journals—the *Journal of Parapsychology*, *Journal of the American Society for Psychical Research*, *Journal of the Society for Psychical Research*, and *European Journal of Parapsychology*—are, like most other scientific journals, *refereed* journals. That is, any paper that is published is first read and approved for publication by other scientists with experience in the relevant area. Additionally some of the journals, such as the *Journal of Parapsychology*, have a statistical editor who reads every paper that employs statistical analyses. Needless to say, it is not easy even for a parapsychologist to get published in the *Journal of Parapsychology*, which rejects two or three papers for every one it publishes.

In 1969 the Parapsychological Association was granted affiliation with the august American Association for the Advancement of Science (AAAS). This was an important milestone in parapsychology's struggle for scientific acceptance.[1]

Twenty-five years ago our own research center, the Institute for Parapsychology, was the world's leading producer of research in parapsychology and the only major research center in this country. Fortunately for the growth of the field, this is no longer the case. Since 1979 a small but energetic group of researchers has been investigating psi phenomena at Princeton University. The group was started by Robert Jahn when he was dean of the College of Engineering and Applied Science, and it is located in the Engineering Department. Researchers there regard the direct interaction of mind and matter as something of an engineering problem, and the lab goes by the name of the Princeton Engineering Anomalies Research (PEAR) Laboratory. On the West Coast, in the large contract research firm SRI International (formerly known as the Stanford Research Institute), one of parapsychology's most ambitious research programs proceeds under the direction of physicist Dr. Edwin May. SRI has discreetly conducted parapsychological research for a variety of contractors (including the U.S. government) for well over a decade. In San Antonio, Texas, a small research team at the Mind Science Foundation has kept up a steady stream of innovative and well-conducted research since the mid-seventies. Regrettably one of our most productive laboratories—the Psychophysical Research Laboratories (also in Princeton, New Jersey)—recently had to suspend operations because of funding difficulties. Prior to these recent difficulties Charles Honorton and his colleagues at PRL made major contributions to parapsychology research with the development of a robust and repeatable ESP experimental technique that we shall examine in chapter 5.

In Europe parapsychology research goes on much as it does in the United States. In Great Britain, home of the venerable Society for Psychical Research (SPR), there is a long tradition of small institutes conducting psychical research. Presently the flagship of British parapsychological research is the Parapsychology Laboratory of the University of Edinburgh in Scotland, endowed in 1983 by the writer and philosopher Arthur Koestler. In 1985 the university appointed one of America's leading parapsychologists, Dr. Robert Morris, as the first Koestler Professor of Parapsychology, and the lab is attracting researchers and graduate students from around the globe.

On the Continent modest parapsychological laboratories exist at the University of Freiburg in Germany and at the Sorbonne in Paris. The most active continental country for parapsychological research is the Netherlands, with small but active parapsychology labs in Amsterdam and Eindhoven. At the University of Utrecht, there has been a chair of parapsychology held by a Swedish parapsychologist, Martin Johnson, and, up to fairly recently, a prospering parapsychology laboratory. Unfortunately the Dutch government has been forced to make sweeping cutbacks in the entire university system, and Utrecht's parapsychology lab fell victim to these cuts. Even in the face of this setback the Dutch researchers are hoping to reorganize as a privately funded institute.

A good deal of important research also comes from individual scientists at different universities pursuing their own modest research programs in departments of psychology, physics, medicine, or whatever. There are dozens of such committed individuals throughout the United States and Europe and in many other countries.

How Parapsychologists Work

The research methods used in parapsychology are the same as those widely employed in all the social sciences. Increasingly the high-technology methods of the physical sciences are being applied to parapsychology in such labs as the PEAR lab at Princeton and at SRI in California. Often students are dismayed to learn that there are virtually no opportunities for undergraduate study in parapsychology, but this is not such a bad thing. The specialized training for parapsychological research is best acquired on top of a solid foundation in the basic principles of scientific method, since these underlie virtually all parapsychological research. The standard advice we give would-be parapsychologists is to get a solid degree in science first—any science—and then take up parapsychology.

In parapsychology today there are three principal methods of investigating psi phenomena: case studies, field investigations, and experimentation.

Case Studies

The case-study approach to psi phenomena, frequently called the *spontaneous-case approach*, is a natural way for researchers to begin studying psychic experiences. A case study typically comprises a testimonial about an unusual experience that a person might label "psychic" plus, in some instances, corroborating testimony and the results of additional investigations by a researcher. One of the first tasks the British Society for Psychical Research undertook was to collect spontaneous cases of ESP. After rigorous examination of thousands of cases, in 1886 the SPR investigators eventually published more than seven hundred of the best-documented cases in a two-volume work entitled *Phantasms of the Living*. To this day *Phantasms* remains one of the richest sources of human experiences involving psi phenomena. Years later, in 1951, the SPR's sister society in the United States, the American Society for Psychical Research (ASPR), published a collection of four hundred cases (out of some 1,200 reports received in response to a published appeal). In a similar manner, in 1963 investigators at the University of Freiburg in Germany amassed a collection of one thousand cases.[2]

Investigators for the SPR collection, the ASPR collection, and the German collection (known as the Sannwald collection after its chief investigator) took great care to validate the cases, since questionable cases could jeopardize their hard work. However, case-study investigators have always been aware of the problems inherent in basing investigations on human testimony. Faulty memory or the natural tendency to mold perceptions to fit expectations or to embellish or reinterpret memories are ever-present hazards, not to mention the possibility of outright fabrication. Even so, in many cases the evidence is very compelling, and some testimonials are particularly strong. Often there are written records (for example, a letter describing an apparition that was written and mailed before an event occurred—say, the death of a distant person).

A rather different approach to case studies was adopted by Louisa E. Rhine for her monumental collection discussed in chapter 1. Unlike the other case collectors, Rhine did not attempt to verify each case. Apart from a "first cut" inspection (which actually eliminated about half of the reports), if the case were intelligently written and in apparent good faith and fulfilled the basic criteria for a psi experience, then it was made part of the collection.

The difference in the two approaches can be traced to the difference in the philosophy behind the studies. The SPR investigators and those who followed their approach were primarily concerned with verifying the existence of these phenomena. Rhine, on the other hand, believed that the reality of psi phenomena was already well established, and thus she could be more adventurous in her collecting, hoping that her collection might naturally reflect the wide diversity of psi experiences in life. Sheer weight of numbers would smooth over the less trustworthy cases.

Despite the best efforts of verifiers, case collections alone can never be sufficient to establish the reality of psi phenomena. Their greatest usefulness has always been to shape and guide the experimental efforts, to provide possible hypotheses for experimental verification. The rich detail of the collections indicates not only how psi phenomena transpire in ordinary life but also how people interpret and assimilate information that appears to be paranormally acquired.

Today the case-study method remains an important part of parapsychology. Not only do the existing case collections contain a wealth of untapped information, but new collections, often of a more specialized nature, continue to be developed. In chapter 8 we shall be examining Professor Ian Stevenson's large and growing collection of cases suggesting that reincarnation is a possibility. We shall also look at Dr. Karlis Osis and Dr. Erlendur Haraldsson's collection of cases, in which physicians and nurses report visionlike experiences of dying patients.

By their nature, most spontaneous cases are one-time events. Even when one person reports several experiences, they are usually unrelated and unpredictable. Parapsychologists obviously can't be on the scene to investigate the experience while it is happening; we hear about it later. There are, however, certain types of psi experiences that do occur for long enough periods of time that parapsychologists can make direct observations. In such cases parapsychologists are able to conduct field investigations.

Field Investigations

Field investigations can present unusual opportunities for parapsychologists to investigate apparent psi effects of a magnitude far beyond what is typically seen in the laboratory. Unfortunately field investigations usually also bring with them a large number of potential pitfalls. Typically a field investigation is hurried and somewhat improvised, and all too frequently the circumstances are such that conscious or unconscious fraud on the part of some of the affected parties is a distinct possibility.

Field investigations are not particularly common in contemporary parapsychology. The best known field investigations usually involve hauntings or poltergeists, which we shall examine more closely in chapter 7. The stereotypical image of a psychical researcher sitting out lonely nights in an old mansion hoping to catch a glimpse of an ancient specter, or better yet record it on film, is not too wide of the mark, but that is only a small part of the investigation of a haunting. Extensive interviewing of all persons involved and much archival research also forms an important part of the investigation of hauntings or recurrent apparitions.

Poltergeist "outbreaks" are perhaps the most flamboyant of all the opportunities for parapsychological field investigations. Poltergeist phenomena are unique in that they typically provide from several weeks to several months of "activities" that can be examined by experienced investigators. It is not uncommon for parapsychologists to be called in while alleged poltergeist activities are still under way. Not only do the field investigators have an opportunity to make detailed observations, but occasionally they can suggest remedies to bring about the cessation of the phenomena.

Poltergeist field investigations are extremely difficult to conduct. This is not because poltergeists are dangerous—there is very little recent evidence of that. The main reason is that often the person or family involved was already experiencing severe psychological tensions before any poltergeist phenomena began. Indeed there is evidence that such circumstances can trigger the phenomena. Thus the investigator must be prepared to deal with possibly severe emotional problems in addition to whatever paranormal phenomena may be occurring. Such cases typically involve adolescents or young adults in whom the temptation to keep (or even generate) the interest of the investigators provides a strong incentive to "help" the phenomena along. In fact most initial poltergeist reports turn out to be kids playing tricks (adults can be guilty too) and they are quickly found out by field investigators. Nonetheless each decade about two or three examples of apparently genuine poltergeist activity are reported (and often hotly debated) in the professional parapsychological literature.

Fascinating as the case studies and the field investigations are, they are destined to play only a small role in the establishment of parapsychology as a science. Despite the extremely thorough work by investigators, we are ultimately left with a collection of anecdotes—stories that tell us once upon a time this or that happened. The systematic collection and examination of these testimonies do provide invaluable information about how these apparently psychic phenomena affect ordinary people in everyday life, or how apparent psi abilities might actually be controlled and used in other cultures. Testimony alone, however, can only take us so far. Even in the presence of lots of evidence we lack the explanations, or even the certitude that there is something behind all these stories that needs explanation. For that we need an experimental approach.

The Experimental Method

The essence of the experimental method in all branches of science is control and measurement. The experimenter seeks to control certain variables and measure what effect this has on some other particular variable in which he is interested. Let's suppose, for example, that a psychologist is interested in learning how reading comprehension might be affected by different styles of type on the printed page. To find out, he will start by controlling some variables, keeping them fixed and unchanging—for example, the content of the text to be read, room lighting, comfort of the chair and desk, quality of eyesight of the subjects, and perhaps the sex of the subjects or even the room temperature. Of course there will be an infinite number of other variables that the experimenter expects to be unrelated to what he is interested in—for example the phase of the moon, time of the school year, and so forth—and these are allowed to vary by chance. The experimenter will control the variable of interest, the typeface, by varying it systematically. Thus some subjects will see the text in a sans-serif typeface, others in Roman, and so on. Finally the experimenter will have a standard instrument (in this case some form of reading-comprehension test) by which to measure what effect varying the typeface had. In the terminology of science, the typeface is known as the *independent variable*, and the reading comprehension demonstrated by the subjects is known as the *dependent variable*, because it is assumed to depend on the variation of the independent variable.

Experimental method has been part of parapsychology from the very beginning. In 1874 the physicist Sir William Crookes conducted experiments to measure the forces involved in some of the extraordinary effects produced by the famous medium D. D. Home. Later other Victorian investigators tried to test for telepathy using ordinary playing cards. It was the work of J. B. Rhine at Duke University in the early thirties, however, that established the experimental method as the primary means of investigating psi phenomena. This emergence of parapsychology as an *experimental science* finally made the rest of the scientific world take notice.

Early psychical researchers used decks of ordinary playing cards to test for telepathy (we would call it GESP today) by having one person concentrate on the cards, one at a time, and try to "send" the identity of that card to another, suitably isolated person. The person acting as "receiver" would guess which card was being viewed by the sender. Various methods—signaling, timing, and so on—were used to synchronize the sending and receiving. It is easy to see that the odds of making a correct guess by chance alone are 51-to-one, so if it turned out that the receiver was able to guess correctly substantially more than one out of fifty-two cards, then the experimenter could conclude that something other than chance was involved. That "something" could have been ESP.

Using playing cards had some shortcomings, however. For one thing, even if a person was able to guess cards correctly quite a bit more than once per deck, he or she would still be getting most of the guesses wrong. That is hardly an ideal way to keep up the morale of one's subjects. If, as was sometimes done, the receiver tried only to guess the suit of the cards, then the experimenters were left to deal with a lot of extraneous information on the cards that could lead to recording errors. J. B. Rhine's simple and elegant solution to the problem was to design a better card deck.

Working with a colleague in the Duke University Psychology Department, Karl Zener, Rhine tried various designs, eventually settling on the five symbols illustrated in figure 1. These are the now-famous ESP cards, which have been used in thousands of experiments since the early thirties. There is absolutely nothing mystical about the five symbols, although they are often used on book jackets and in magazine articles rather the way stars and moons are used to decorate a wizard's cap. The five symbols were selected because they are easy to tell apart, easy to remember, and of roughly equal visual weight. Five were chosen because a one-in-five chance-hit ratio seemed about right for holding a subject's interest; five of each symbol were included to create a conveniently sized deck.

The core procedure of Rhine's early experimental method was to have a subject guess the sequence of the symbols in a deck of ESP cards. The deck was very well shuffled to ensure that the order of the symbols was *random*, that is, completely unpredictable. Of course for a typical experiment many such decks would be prepared and the subject would go through deck after deck.

Figure 1. ESP Card Symbols.

In this type of experimental session the subject would make a number of "hits," or correct guesses. For a deck of twenty-five ESP cards we would expect *on average* that five would be guessed correctly by pure chance. This is called the *mean chance expectation* or MCE. The point of the experiment, however, is to see whether the subjects can guess correctly *more often* than chance would predict. So how does one determine when a subject exceeds chance's boundary?

To answer this question, Rhine turned to the field of statistics, which in those days was still in its infancy. The basic aim of most statistical tests is to determine whether a particular experimental result could be explained by *chance* variation in the scores. Take for example the following situation: A subject guesses through ten decks of ESP cards. By chance one would expect him to get about 50 hits from these 250 cards. Fairly frequently, by chance alone, the subject might get 55 hits, or 45. Scores of, say, 60 or 40 might show up every once in a while. But what should we make of a score of 75? Is that just chance variation?

By using a simple statistical formula the experimenter can determine what the *odds against chance* are, that is, the odds against chance alone accounting for the event. In the social sciences the convention is that when the odds against chance for a given result are better than one-in-twenty, then chance is "ruled out" and the result is said to be *significant*. In situations where the experimenter feels a need to be more conservative (and this applies to most parapsychology experiments), he may hold out for odds against chance of one-in-100 or even one-in-1,000 before he is willing to say that chance is ruled out as an explanation. Usually these figures will be expressed as the *probability value* (*p*) being less than .05 or .01 or .001, respectively. In our example above, a score of 75 would give us $p < .001$. In other words the odds of a score of 75 happening solely by chance are less than one-in-1,000, so we would say that we have ruled out chance as an explanation for that result. (Although this example is given for ESP, various types of PK tests are evaluated in the same manner.)

It is important to note that a statistical test does not automatically tell us that ESP was demonstrated. It merely gives us a certain confidence that the results were not simply chance variation. Whether or not we are willing to say that the high score was due to ESP depends on how well we exercised the controls that are part and parcel of the experimental method. Since what we are calling ESP is the acquisition of information without using the normal senses, then the most fundamental control that the parapsychologist needs to employ is to ensure that there is no way by which the subject could obtain information about the cards through normal means. Conversely, for PK research the fundamental control is to ensure that the subject has no way of affecting the object or test equipment by normal means.

Controlling card-guessing experiments is a pretty straightforward matter. The Duke lab developed routine procedures involving several experimenters performing duties in isolation. Some experiments were conducted with the cards and one experimenter in one building and the subject and other experimenters in another, with yet a third experimenter receiving record sheets from each team independently. With different types of experiments, different precautions will be necessary, and sometimes these are not obvious at first. Parapsychologists do slip up from time to time by overlooking a possible area of *sensory leakage*—that is, some means by which the subject might obtain sensory clues about the target—but such goofs are usually caught by colleagues when the results are presented at a convention or submitted for publication. Ultimately the bottom line for all parapsychological experiments is whether or not all possible *normal* means of accomplishing the task are denied the subject. Only then can we posit ESP or PK to account for the anomalous results.

Obviously control is a matter of degree, and different levels of control will be necessary for different circumstances. An experiment that uses many different subjects, each of whom contributes only a little bit to the final result, will need a different level of control from an experiment with one subject who produces the entire result. If, for example, the subject is someone who makes a living by demonstrating psychic feats on stage, then the experiment will need a very high level of control, and the experimenter would be wise to enlist the assistance of specialists such as professional conjurers or mentalists.

If all the controls are adequate and the results of the experiment show that the subjects were able to make use of information that was not available to them through normal channels, then the experimenter can claim to have demonstrated a communication anomaly, which we call ESP. However, simply demonstrating anomalies isn't enough; parapsychologists must also focus on trying to understand what is *behind* these anomalous phenomena, what patterns and regularities can be uncovered. To do this, most parapsychologists today manipulate all sorts of variables in their experiments. Are certain personality types more successful in ESP experiments than others? Can conditions be created in the lab to facilitate ESP? Can it be learned? In later chapters we shall see what sort of picture is emerging.

It is at this point that parapsychology begins to resemble any other experimental social science, particularly psychology. Different classes of subjects, say extraverts and introverts or artists and accountants, are compared on their performance in one or another type of ESP test. Experimenters introduce different conditions, say whether the subjects are relaxed or are actively striving to guess the identity of the target. In fact, apart from that fundamental control against "normal explanations," most parapsychological experiments are virtually indistinguishable from psychological ones. But it is precisely that issue—whether or not the experimenter has ruled out all normal explanations—that is at the heart of the controversy that rages about parapsychology.

CHAPTER 3

Origins of the Science

Can I not number all the grains of sand,
And measure all the water in the sea?
Tho' a man speak not I can understand;
Nor are the thoughts of dumb men hid from me.
A tortoise boiling with a lamb I smell:
Bronze underlies and covers them as well.[1]

That poetic reply by the Pythia, priestess of Apollo at Delphi, represents the successful conclusion of the very first parapsychological experiment on record. According to the Greek historian Herodotus, it was conducted around 550 B.C. by the ambitious King Croesus of Lydia. Croesus had grown concerned about a buildup of forces by Cyrus of the rival kingdom of Persia and he wished to consult the oracles for advice about what the future might hold. But whom to consult? Which oracles were reliable?

The king decided to do his own consumer testing. He sent delegations to the seven best oracles of the day with instructions to approach the oracle on the hundredth day after departure and ask, "What is the king of Lydia doing today?" This was not an experiment in seeing the future. It was a telepathic (or clairvoyant) experiment, and even the messengers would not know the correct answer—to preclude leakage of information. On the appointed day the king chose to do something very unkinglike—to make a lamb-

50

and-tortoise stew in a bronze kettle—in order to reduce the possibility of chance coincidence.*

Five of the oracles were completely wrong. The oracle of Amphiaraos had a near miss. Only the Delphic oracle was exactly correct. Convinced of the Pythia's powers by this test, Croesus asked whether he should go to Persia and attack Cyrus. The oracle replied, "When Croesus has the Halys crossed, a mighty empire will be lost." Believing fate to be with him, Croesus attacked, but he had failed to reckon on the notoriously ambiguous nature of Delphic advice: Croesus was defeated, and it was *his* empire that fell.** What Herodotus made of this story is not known, but the great historian once commented, "My duty is to report what I hear—but I am not obliged to believe everything equally."

There are other references to successful tests of oracles in the classics, and it is clear that among the ancient philosophers the reality of paranormal phenomena was as hotly debated as it is today. Religious scriptures, especially the Old Testament, are replete with examples of prophetic dreams and other parapsychological phenomena. Some scholars have viewed the Old Testament as a record of the shamanistic practices of divination (foretelling the future) and magic as they evolved from a fairly primitive form to an organized religion. Moses, for example, can be viewed as a typical shaman, having had his calling made known to him by mysterious signs and wonders and having established his credentials by besting Pharaoh's priests in a contest of magic.

Around the world the historical record up to the nineteenth century shows paranormal phenomena to be inextricably bound up with religious beliefs. In most cultures paranormal events such as miracles or foretelling the future typically seemed to serve at least two purposes. First, such an event helped the group to avoid some calamity—destruction by an enemy, a plague, and so on—or to gain

---

*Many historians have assumed this story to be apocryphal, though others, citing the very Lydian characteristics of the story, claim there may be an element of truth among the Delphic propaganda. In any event it is not a bad experimental design for its day.

**Given the Greeks' propensity to kill messengers bearing bad news, it is not surprising that the oracle would disguise unwanted news. Actually Croesus asked four questions in all, and he misinterpreted all of the answers in a way that missed the warnings contained in them.

some advantage and; second, it reinforced faith in the power of the gods or their representatives on earth. Fairly early on, as religion became more institutionalized, the leaders of the Roman Catholic church, in particular, began to realize that uncritical belief in miracles and other phenomena that we would consider paranormal could be a threat to orthodox beliefs.

Lives of the Saints

Some of the best-documented early reports of paranormal phenomena come from the investigations of individuals declared saints by the Roman Catholic church. Over the centuries the Catholic church developed strict standards for evaluating reports of miracles. As the monastic movement grew through the Middle Ages, more and more reports emerged of miracles happening in the presence of particularly devout men and women, supplementing the already long tradition of miracles related to shrines and relics. Far from embracing every claimed miracle as another example of God working in the world, the Catholic church actually took a very skeptical and hard-nosed stance toward these reports. Before any individual could be declared a saint, the Church would conduct a long and rigorous investigation of his or her past, including reports of miracles associated with the person.

The Church created the post of *promotor fidei*, more popularly known as the devil's advocate, to conduct these investigations. In due course the case for canonization would be argued much as a court case would, with the *promotor fidei* doing all that he could to discredit the testimony and evidence of the would-be saint's advocates.

Despite this relatively hostile approach to miracles, the records of the lives of many of the saints contain amazing accounts of paranormal phenomena. Among the most dramatic, and often the best attested, was the phenomenon of levitation. Levitation stories are associated with many of the better known Catholic saints, and one might be tempted to dismiss it all as mere hagiography or pious embellishment of the record. Some of the cases, however, are backed by impressive amounts of eyewitness testimony.

In the sixteenth century Saint Teresa of Avila was observed on

many occasions, typically when she was deep in prayer, to rise anywhere from a few feet to as high as the ceiling of the room. A fellow
sister, Anne of the Incarnation at Segovia, testified that one afternoon she observed Sister Teresa enter the choir and kneel in prayer
for about ten minutes.

> As I was looking on, she was raised about half a yard from the
> ground without her feet touching it. At this I was terrified, and she,
> for her part, was trembling all over. So I moved over to where she
> was and I put my hands under her feet, over which I remained
> weeping for something like half an hour while the ecstasy lasted.
> Then suddenly she sank down and rested on her feet and turning
> her head round to me, she asked me who I was, and whether I had
> been there all the while.[2]

A bishop further testified that Teresa levitated just after she had
received communion from him, and he watched as she grasped at
the choir grillwork to stop her upward floating. Saint Teresa provided an account of her own feelings and experiences—of how it
seemed impossible to resist being "carried away" and how she was
most distressed by the embarrassment her flights caused—which
was submitted to the censors of the notorious Inquisition while she
was still alive. The Inquisition accepted her testimony.

The case of Saint Joseph of Copertino is stranger yet. As a Fran-
ciscan monk in the mid-seventeenth century, Joseph began levitating
during services and was often observed by whole congregations. His
superiors did not welcome his activities, and at times he was disciplined and made to do penance for his displays. Among the many
persons who witnessed Joseph's levitations was a pope (Urban VIII)
as well as many laypersons, including non-Catholics. The Spanish
ambassador to the papal court watched Joseph fly over a crowd
to a statue of the Immaculate Conception and back again (the ambassador's wife fainted). Johann Friedrich, duke of Brunswick, hid
himself in a stairwell to observe one of Joseph's levitations. On later
observing a second levitation, the duke renounced his Lutheran faith
and became a Catholic.[3]

Centuries of investigating the claims of miracles as part of the
canonization process have provided the Catholic church with a
wealth of information regarding paranormal phenomena. Indeed the
Catholic scholars who investigated these cases could properly claim

to be the first psychical researchers. Chief among these investigators was Prospero Lambertini,* whose treatise *De Servorum Dei Beatificatione et Beatorum Canonizatione* was a thorough guide to what was known about paranormal phenomena by the eighteenth century. Interestingly many of Lambertini's observations remain valid to this day. For one thing, Lambertini noted that "knowledge of things to come, things past, present events distant in space, and the secret places of the heart" did not come to saints alone but also to ordinary persons. The same was true for apparitions of the dead and the living. He also noted that seeing the future was more likely to occur during sleep than during waking, and that often predictions of the future came in symbolic form rather than as a literal representation of what would take place. Often, Lambertini notes, the "prophet" is unable to distinguish between his own thoughts and "divine messages."[4]

The Emergence of Secular Psychical Research

In addition to the Church's circumspect interest in paranormal phenomena, there has always been a lively, if not well organized, interest in such matters among lay scholars and scientists. The alchemists of the Middle Ages included among their studies many experiments that we would consider parapsychological. In the mid-1500s John Dee, mathematician, astronomer, and astrologer to Queen Elizabeth, began experimenting with the divining rod and pendulum to locate lost objects. Later he attempted to gain information from spirits employing a somewhat disreputable colleague as a medium, but Dee devised a complex code for the spirits to use to prevent his colleague from cheating. For many years Dee labored to understand the process of divination. Dee's activities could have landed him in trouble had he not already won the confidence of the queen, who relied on the intelligence he provided regarding what was being plotted on the Continent. In Her Majesty's service as an

*Lambertini was regarded by his peers as a man of common sense and a sharp, critical intellect. He was elected pope (Benedict XIV) in 1740.

intelligence agent Dee's code name was 007, which was derived from the colophon he used to sign his reports.[5]

Interest in parapsychological phenomena continued throughout the sixteenth and seventeenth centuries. Many noted scholars and scientists of the time conducted investigations into cases of poltergeist or haunting activity, or of individuals with unusual abilities. The late eighteenth century, however, saw two developments that led directly to the organized study of psychic phenomena and eventually to parapsychology as we see it today: mesmerism and spiritualism.

Mesmerism

During his medical studies at the University of Vienna in the 1760s, Franz Anton Mesmer developed a theory that the sun, moon, and stars influenced all organized bodies "through the medium of a subtle fluid, which pervades the universe, and associates all things together in mutual intercourse and harmony." This theory owed much to earlier alchemical and astrological notions and had a practical counterpart in the form of healing forces that could be guided and strengthened by ordinary magnets. Mesmer's experiments led him to develop "treatments" using first mineral magnets and later the "animal magnetism" of the healer (himself), which was imparted through sweeping movements of his hands and other gestures. Patients often lost control of their limbs, suffered convulsions, or went into trances, all of which was regarded as part of the healing process. His treatments found little favor in Vienna, but when Mesmer moved to Paris in 1778, the reception was rather different. Although the medical authorities in Paris were no more sympathetic to his new theory of animal magnetism than were their Viennese counterparts, the public interest in his magnetic treatments—which now included baths in "magnetized" water—was enormous. This prompted a number of scientists to investigate Mesmer's claims; however, there was little agreement as to their validity. Eventually King Louis XVI set up the Royal Commission of Inquiry to decide one way or the other. The commission included some of the most eminent scientists of the day and was headed by Benjamin Franklin, then U.S. ambassador to France.

The commission's conclusion that the claimed effects were probably caused by suggestion did not dampen public enthusiasm, and many investigators continued mesmeric research. Among the latter was Chastenet de Puységur, a former president of the Lyons Medical Society and a disciple of Mesmer. Puységur is best known for his discovery of the hypnotic trance (which was not part of Mesmer's original treatments). From the start of the mesmeric craze there were reports that mesmerism facilitated clairvoyance, "thought transference," and other psychic phenomena. Puységur was initially skeptical of such reports, but he was surprised to discover that one of his patients, Victor Race, not only obeyed his spoken commands while under hypnotic trance but also responded to unspoken ones. Eventually Puységur found that Victor could provide clairvoyant diagnoses of his other patients. One of Puységur's skeptical colleagues, J. H. Pététin—also a past president of the Lyons Medical Society—undertook some experiments of his own with Victor and was very impressed with the results.

The French Revolution of 1789 scattered the supporters of mesmerism, but by 1826 scientific curiosity about the topic had revived to such a degree that the Academies of the Sciences and of Medicine appointed a second commission of inquiry. Although the authorities expected that this second report would be as dismissive as the first, a number of striking demonstrations of the trance state as well as several very careful studies of clairvoyance caused the commission to come to rather different conclusions. The commission acknowledged that they could not precisely identify what the trance state was but that they were convinced that it was genuine. Moreover, they felt it could give rise to "new faculties which have been designated by the terms clairvoyance, intuition, interior prevision." Finally they urged the academies to encourage further research into "magnetism," which they regarded as a "very curious branch of psychological and natural history." The leaders of the academies were not pleased with the report and did nothing to follow the commission's recommendation.

The battle for acceptance of mesmerism and the "higher faculties" that it appeared to engender was not limited to France. Noted scientists all over Europe and Britain began to investigate these mysterious powers. For decades the controversy raged in scientific and medical circles before mesmerism was finally refined into what we know today as hypnotism. In the meantime other developments were underway that were to contribute to the establishment of psychical research.[6]

Spiritualism

The teachings of Swedish savant Emmanuel Swedenborg are generally credited with providing a focal point around which coalesced the quasi-religious belief that living persons could converse with the spirits of dead persons. Swedenborg himself believed that many of his insights came from spirits, and after his death in 1772 something of a religious sect developed around his teachings. Over the next half century the Swedenborgians spread across northern Europe, Britain, and the United States.

Swedenborg's followers quickly discovered that the mesmeric trance seemed to facilitate the spirit communication they were seeking, even though the mesmerists themselves generally believed that the "higher phenomena" (clairvoyance, thought transference, and so on) were *natural* phenomena, with no particular connection to spiritual or religious entities. By the second quarter of the nineteenth century things began to change, and even some of the mesmerists' trance subjects began to claim that they were receiving communications from spirits.

Around the time all this was happening, the United States had become a fertile ground for the growth of new and unconventional religious movements. (Two religious movements still strong today— Mormonism and Adventism—sprang up during this period, in 1830 and 1831, respectively.) There was also tremendous popular interest in mesmerism, particularly in the increasing tendency for mesmerized clairvoyants to "teach" revelations attributed to various spirits. One of the better-known instances is the case of Andrew Jackson Davis of Poughkeepsie, New York. This poorly educated son of a leather worker was mesmerized when he was eighteen, at which time he discovered that he had clairvoyant powers. Soon he was regularly going into trances without the aid of hypnotism and allegedly receiving teachings from none other than Swedenborg himself, along with several other notables. He produced lectures on philosophical and scientific subjects that were published in several books and were very well received by the public. One of these, *Principles of Nature*, was published in 1847 and went through thirty-four editions in less than thirty years.* The stage was thus set for a sequence of events that launched one of the most remarkable religious movements in the modern Western world.[7]

On December 11, 1847, the Fox family—John; his wife, Margaret; and two of their daughters, Margaretta, fourteen, and Catherine, twelve—moved into a small wooden house in Hydesville, New York. The following March the Fox family began to have their nights disturbed by mysterious rapping and banging sounds with no apparent origin. On March 31, 1848, the family, fed up with the disturbances, resolved to retire early that evening and take no notice of the noises. But it was not to be an undisturbed night. In the words of Mrs. Fox's statement of April 11, 1848:

> My husband had not gone to bed when we first heard the noise on this evening. I had just laid down. It commenced as usual. I knew it from all other noises I had ever heard in the house. The girls, who slept in the other bed in the room, heard the noise, and tried to make a similar noise by snapping their fingers. The youngest girl is about 12 years old; she is the one who made her hand go. As fast as she made the noise with her hands or fingers, the sound was followed up in the room. It did not sound any different at the time, only it made the same number of noises that the girl did. When she stopped, the sound itself stopped for a short time.
>
> The other girl, who is in her 15th year, then spoke in sport and said, "Now do this just as I do. Count 1, 2, 3, 4," &, striking one hand in the other at the same time. The blows which she made were repeated as before. It appeared to answer her by repeating every blow that she made. She only did so once. She then began to be startled; and then I spoke and said to the noise, "Count ten," and it made ten strokes or noises. Then I asked the ages of my different children successively, and it gave a number of raps, corresponding to the ages of my children.[8]

Mrs. Fox went on to ask if it was a human or a spirit making the

---

*The parallels with modern phenomena of "channeling" are obvious, not only in general form but also in the reaction to the messages. Modern "channeled" texts tend to enjoy enormous popular appeal and publishing success, even though more critical observers dismiss the material as bland platitudes derivative of well-known religious teachings.

noises. The raps answered that it was a spirit. Eventually the raps revealed the "spirit" was that of a thirty-one-year-old man who was buried beneath the house and who had left a family of five children, all still living, and a wife who had died two years earlier.

This all took place by 7:30 in the evening. The Foxes called in various neighbors and by 9:00 P.M. more than a dozen people were present. Several proceeded to question the spirit further and learned more details that seemed to describe a murder. The spirit rapper also seemed to know much about the neighbors as well, and one commented, "I think that no human being could have answered all the questions that were answered by this rapping."

As word of the occurrences spread, the Fox household began to draw crowds of onlookers. Impromptu committees were formed, and guards were posted in different parts of the house to try to catch any trickery. At first observers thought the Fox family had nothing to do with the noises, but later it became clear that the sounds were associated with the two younger girls. A publisher from nearby Canandaigua arrived in mid-April and collected testimonies from the principal witnesses, which he later published.[9] More and more visitors besieged the sisters for communications with the spirit world. Eventually the Fox daughters (now including the eldest sister, Leah) went public, and in time they were giving demonstrations all over the country. Commissions were set up to investigate them, and the press jumped in as well. Most of the investigators were satisfied that the effects were genuine. Some, however, were not convinced. Three professors from the Buffalo School of Medicine claimed that the sounds were produced by the dislocating and "popping" of the girls' knee joints.[10] The professors, as well as those who repeated this criticism, never explained how joint poppings could produce the range of sounds that echoed around large meeting halls in the girls' presence.

As the years went by, the Fox sisters' careers declined, partly due to increased competition from the growing ranks of professional mediums. By 1888 the two younger sisters had lost their husbands, were both alcoholics, and were nearly penniless. In October of that year Margaretta confessed that the rappings had been fraudulent all along. Although at the time Kate seemed to agree with this statement, she denied Margaretta's claims soon after. Later Margaretta herself retracted her confession, admitting to having taken a $1,500 bribe to make it. This temporary confession provided their detractors with ample reason to dismiss the Fox sisters as charlatans. Other commentators have also produced evidence to show that the younger sisters had staged the confession at least in part to discredit their older sister, Leah, still a successful medium, with whom they had had a severe falling out over family matters.[11]

Apart from the joint-popping theory, no one found any way of explaining the phenomena that the Fox sisters produced. Joint popping could easily be demonstrated, and those who had witnessed the rapping of the early years maintained that this was nothing like what they had heard. In addition, no one was able satisfactorily to explain how the raps were able to provide the answers so many questioners (often skeptical ones at that) had sought, including information the sisters could not have known or deduced.

Whatever one believes about the Fox sisters, there can be no doubt that they launched Spiritualism as a religious movement. Although Spiritualism never developed the formal belief system or hierarchical organization characteristic of conventional religions, its central tenet was simply that the human personality (in the form of a soul or spirit) survives bodily death and that dead persons can communicate with the living through specially gifted individuals known as mediums. Perhaps the most amazing thing about that religion was its phenomenal growth. Within a few years there were hundreds of practicing mediums. Only five years after the Hydesville affair an English observer claimed that there were not less than thirty thousand "recognized media" in the United States, with more than three hundred "magnetic circles" in Philadelphia alone. At the movement's height most large cities in Britain and the United States had Spiritualistic "congregations," only a few of which survive today.

Mediums

The enthusiasm for Spiritualism brought forward small armies of practicing mediums, persons who claimed they could facilitate communication between the natural and the spirit worlds. The more spectacular of these were the *physical mediums*, whose repertoire included physical effects in addition to the usual communications from the dead to the living. Tables and objects would move, untouched musical instruments would produce sounds and melodies, and strange lights might be seen, among other things. Not surprisingly the ranks of the mediums included all manner of persons, ranging from well-meaning amateurs to calculating charlatans who exploited the gullibility of bereaved clients. In general the physical mediums of Spiritualism's heyday enjoyed a most unsavory reputation—except for a few. Over the years there emerged several men and women whose abilities impressed the more critical investigators of the time. However, investigators usually found that even some of the best would resort to cheating when given an opportunity. There was only one exception to this pattern: D. D. Home.

Daniel Dunglas Home (pronounced "Hume") was born in Scotland in 1833 but was brought up by an aunt in Connecticut. As a child he had precognitive visions, and at the age of seventeen raps began to be heard in his presence and furniture was observed to move. His aunt thought it was the work of the devil and put him out of her home, but with the Hydesville happenings in recent memory he was quick to find people who were willing to avail themselves of his paranormal gifts. He began to give séances, and his reputation quickly spread.

Early in his career Home was examined by two experienced investigators of Spiritualism: William Cullen Bryant, the noted journalist and critic, and Prof. David Wells of Harvard. Along with two other Harvard colleagues they paid a visit upon Home with the specific intent of exposing any trickery they might find at one of his séances. As became Home's custom, the investigations were permitted to take place in a well-lit room and the investigators were given every opportunity to inspect the room and the table about which they would sit. During the sitting the table began to move around in all directions, violently at times, even with Wells sitting on it. At one point the table reared up on two legs when no one was in contact with it. The investigators reported:

Three gentlemen, Wells, Bryant and Edwards, seated themselves simultaneously on top of the table, and while these men were so seated, the table started to move in various directions. After some time the table was seen to rise completely from the floor and floated about in the air during several seconds, as if something more solid than air was upholding it.

The investigators concluded their testimony with "this one emphatic declaration—*we have the certainty that we were not imposed upon and neither were we the victims of optical illusions*."[12] Thus began what is undoubtedly the most amazing career in the annals of psychical research.

The record of Home's activities over the next decade or so is voluminous and includes testimonies from numerous literary, scholarly, and scientific figures. Two extended reports of Home's phenomena—based primarily on notes taken during or immediately after events—were published, including one by William Crookes, a noted British physicist, chemist, inventor, and Fellow of the Royal Society, who was a respected pillar of the scientific establishment and highly critical of Spiritualist claims when he began his investigations.

The range of phenomena observed during Home's séances was truly amazing, all the more so since his séances were usually given in good light. In addition to the raps, which were common, musical instruments of various kinds played melodies, and strange moving lights were observed. Levitations were frequent. Among the most spectacular effects was that of fire handling, or incombustibility, which Crookes and many others witnessed. Crookes observed as Home walked over to the coal fire and picked up "a red-hot piece nearly as big as an orange." Home then cupped his hands around it and blew until it became white-hot and Crookes was able to observe flames licking around his fingers. When Crookes examined Home's hands afterward, he found them "soft and delicate." On another occasion Home stirred embers of a fire into flame and then, "kneeling down, he placed his face right among the burning coals, moving it about as though bathing it in water."[13]

Perhaps most important for the development of psychical research were the series of experiments Crookes conducted with Home. Assisting Crookes were Dr. William Huggins, an astronomer and Fellow of the Royal Society, and Sergent Cox, a barrister who served as observer. One of these experiments tested Home's ability to play an accordian without touching the keys. (Instruments playing themselves were a frequent feature of Home's séances.) Under Crookes's careful observation the accordian played "a well-known sweet and plaintive melody." A second experiment tested Home's ability to deflect a specially designed balance beam.[14]

In 1871 Crookes published his experiments (in considerable detail, with drawings and diagrams), but inevitably his report attracted the derision of many of his colleagues. Undaunted, Crookes patiently published rebuttals to all their criticisms and went on to conduct additional experiments using even more sophisticated apparatuses designed to prevent or detect ordinary physical forces. These experiments employed automatic recording devices to guard against the charge that Home hypnotized all the observers, causing them to misread their instruments. Furthermore this time Crookes confirmed the effects with another medium who was not a professional.

Not long after his work with Crookes, Home's health—which had never been very good—deteriorated, and on the advice of his doctors he moved south to the Mediterranean. He never returned to England. Crookes, for his part, continued his psychical research for several years, but he eventually gave it up as his orthodox research began to consume more time. As if to belie those who had snidely insinuated that he was getting senile or losing his scientific acumen, Crookes went on to develop his radiometer, and some years later he produced the Crookes tube, a high-vacuum tube that facilitated the discovery of X rays.

Despite all his detractors—and there were many—never did any creditable report emerge that Home had used trickery. To this day the best that Home's critics can do is simply conjecture how some of his phenomena *might* have been produced fraudulently. But when these conjectures are compared with the voluminous, detailed eyewitness testimony, they are shown to be feeble indeed.

The Society for Psychical Research

In January 1882 a group of scientists and scholars gathered in London to discuss the scientific investigation of Spiritualism and the formation of a learned society to facilitate these investigations. On February 20, with Prof. Henry Sidgwick, a highly respected (and politically well-connected) Cambridge University philosopher, at its head, the Society for Psychical Research (SPR) was formed. Its aim was "to investigate that large body of debatable phenomena designated by such terms as mesmeric, psychical and spiritualistic." It was pledged to do this "without prejudice or prepossession of any kind, and in the same spirit of exact and unimpassioned inquiry which has enabled Science to solve so many problems, once not less obscure nor less hotly debated."[15]

The founding of the SPR fundamentally changed the nature of psychical research. Prior to 1882 psychical research was largely pursued as an avocation or part-time interest, with the resulting unevenness in quality and haphazard dissemination of results. The leaders of the SPR moved quickly to establish standards of evidence for case studies and methods for experimental research. Almost immediately the SPR began publishing a scholarly journal and the proceedings of its scientific meetings in order to provide an outlet for its work and that of other scientists around the world. In short, psychical research was becoming a *science*, with disciplined experimental methods and standardized methods of description, established by some of the finest minds of the day.

The leaders of the SPR plunged into research with vigor. Within a few years of the society's inception, the research output was filling about 550 pages each year.

The SPR was notoriously tough in its investigations. The poet William Butler Yeats, a one-time member, complained, "It's my belief that if you psychical researchers had been about when God Almighty was creating the world, He couldn't have done the job."[16] This critical approach was evident in one of the first investigations undertaken by the SPR, that of Madame Blavatsky. As a recent immigrant living on New York City's Lower East Side, Blavatsky took up Spiritualism and became the founder of the Theosophical Society, a mystical religion that numbered nearly one hundred thousand adherents at its peak in the late 1880s. Since much of her support came from Britain and her admirers included many British notables, when she visited London in 1884, the SPR organized a committee to examine the psychical manifestations that she had become known for. The SPR's verdict was harsh: Madame Blavatsky was described as "one of the most accomplished, ingenious, and interesting imposters in history." With the publication of an official report the Theosophical Society went into a decline.[17]

It would be incorrect to think that all the early SPR researchers did was to chase after mediums, exposing the vast majority of them as frauds. They did enough of that, of course, but it was by no means all that occupied their time. Charles Richet, professor of physiology at the medical school of the University of Paris and a future Nobel Prize winner, conducted a number of experiments for clairvoyance using ordinary playing cards. In 1884 he published a paper on the application of probability statistics in experiments of "mental suggestion." In an 1889 paper he reported on experiments with a hypnotized subject whose task was to identify playing cards enclosed in opaque envelopes.[18] Not only did Richet pioneer the methodology that Rhine was to use to great advantage about forty years later, but he also observed the curiously unstable nature of the subject's clairvoyant ability, something that plagues psi research even today.

A variety of other experimental studies were conducted over the years, but the most enduring contribution of this era was the collection of apparition cases that was eventually published as *Phantasms of the Living*. One of the several SPR investigative committees—the Literary Committee—was charged with collecting reports of psychic experiences, which they did through private inquiries as well as announcements in the press. The committee was particularly impressed with the number of "crisis apparitions" that they received. These were cases in which a percipient sees (or hears) an apparition of a distant person who at that time is experiencing a trauma or crisis (injury or, often, death).

The committee made a monumental effort to verify and corroborate each case. Letters were written (some ten thousand in one year alone), witnesses interviewed, official records examined, and libraries combed. The amount of research is staggering, and the documentation (still in the SPR archives) comprises forty-two boxes of material. In 1886 the SPR published the results of the massive study and in so doing established a methodology for casework and evaluation of eyewitness testimony still valid today. The committee's conclusions challenged the spirit hypothesis by arguing that these crisis apparitions are really hallucinations by the percipient that are generated by some sort of telepathic message from the person in the crisis. To this day the 1,300-page *Phantasms* remains the starting point for all case studies in parapsychology.

The enormous enthusiasm and energy of the SPR's founders could not last, and as these early giants died, the quantity of research declined. By the early part of the twentieth century psychical research had quieted down considerably. Certainly work continued, with important experiments being conducted in Holland, in France,

and at several universities in the United States. But what parapsychologist John Beloff has called the Heroic Age of psychical research
had passed, and the young science had to await the emergence of a
new figure to rejuvenate it.[19]

J. B. and L. E. Rhine

Undoubtedly the best-known name in parapsychology is that of
Joseph Banks Rhine, but in fact his career is not easily separated
from that of his wife, Louisa E. Rhine. While J. B. (as he was
always known to his colleagues) became the charismatic leader of a
revolutionary new science, this probably would not have happened
were it not for the intellectual and emotional support of "Louie," a
very capable and innovative researcher in her own right.

J. B. Rhine and Louisa Weckesser were friends from their teenage
years, when they found they shared a common interest in deep religious questions and a dissatisfaction with the traditional answers
of organized religions. Following undergraduate work at different
colleges (and a World War I stint in the Marines by J. B.), they were
married in 1920. Both then went on to complete Ph.D. degrees in
botany at the University of Chicago.

J. B. obtained a good position at the University of West Virginia,
and both he and Louisa were at the start of promising careers in
botany, but it was a lecture they had heard in 1922 while still in
Chicago that made them start wondering if their careers should take
a different direction. Sir Arthur Conan Doyle, creator of Sherlock
Holmes, had been on a speaking tour promoting psychical research
and Spiritualism. Doyle's sincerity and the list of distinguished scientists about whom he spoke deeply impressed the Rhines. After
much thought, in 1926 J. B. gave up his West Virginia post and a
career in botany to begin training in philosophy and psychology for
a career in psychical research.

In the summer of 1926 the Rhines arrived in Boston, a city that
had two attractions for them. One was the medium Margery Crandon, who had been the subject of controversial investigations for
some years. The other was the presence of William McDougall at
Harvard University. McDougall was a distinguished British psychologist who strongly supported psychical research. As luck would

have it, the Rhines caught up with McDougall just as he was leaving on a year-long trip. While the taxi waited, McDougall hurriedly gave Rhine advice about who to see and how he might get some money to support a year of research.

On July 1, the Rhines had a sitting with Margery Crandon that proved to be a bitter disappointment. To J. B. and Louisa, complete newcomers to psychical research, it seemed that this famous medium's physical phenomena were phony, and they were quick to say so. Writing to the American SPR (who had championed Margery), Rhine said he was disgusted with the case and with the ASPR's attitude and declared, "The whole case is sure to crash some of these days and where will our reputation be then? We will be the laughing stock of the world for years to come!"[20] The Rhines eventually published an exposé, which brought them to the attention of the more conservative wings of both the American and the British SPRs, though it did little to dampen the loyalty of Margery's supporters. Ironically one of those most put out by the Rhines' "colossal impertinence" was Sir Arthur Conan Doyle himself.

Perhaps the most important effect of this experience with Margery was to crystallize for J. B. Rhine the belief that progress could be made in psychical research only if it became primarily an *experimental* science. For J. B. and Louisa Rhine there was no future in the séance room and the old-style psychical research.

In spring of 1927 the Rhines learned that McDougall would not be returning to Harvard. He had accepted an offer from the newly endowed Duke University in Durham, North Carolina, to become head of the psychology department there. Initially this seemed another setback for the Rhines, but eventually McDougall secured funding for Rhine to do a semester of research at Duke University.

While scholars regard the founding of the SPR in 1882 as the start of psychical research as a *science*, they consider the arrival of the Rhines at Duke University in September 1927 as the start of its *professionalization*. Although Rhine began working without any long-term expectation of employment at Duke, McDougall offered J. B. a position in the psychology department for the 1928–29 academic year. Part of the time he assisted McDougall with some controversial experiments dealing with Lamarckian inheritance (the notion that acquired abilities or traits can be passed on to succeeding generations). This particular research experience impressed upon

Rhine the need for statistical reasoning in controversial areas of science. The next year Rhine was given a joint appointment in the departments of philosophy and psychology.

In the summer of 1930 Rhine finally had an opportunity to start his own research. He started with card guessing using local children and cards stamped with numerals. In the fall a colleague, Karl Zener, suggested that they try guessing tests with their classes using numerals or letters sealed in envelopes. Because this work was not particularly successful, Rhine asked Zener, a specialist in perception, to design a new set of cards that could be easily distinguished and easily remembered. The result is the well-known ESP cards discussed in the previous chapter.

One of the many students tested with the new cards, a sophomore by the name of A. J. Linzmayer, displayed a consistent ability to guess the cards better than chance—404 correct out of 1,500, where 300 would be expected by chance. The following year Linzmayer provided another 2,000 trials and continued to guess above chance, although Rhine noticed a decline in his ability. In the fall of 1931 Rhine was joined by two graduate students, Charles E. Stuart and J. Gaither Pratt. Through careful self-testing, Stuart found that he himself had a modest clairvoyant ability, and Rhine and Pratt uncovered another high scorer in divinity student Hubert Pearce. After adjusting to the testing procedures, Pearce quickly reached scoring levels higher than Linzmayer, with no sign of a decline. Within six months the program of experimentation with these subjects had become the main focus of Rhine and his colleagues.

In 1932 Rhine justifiably felt that he was on the verge of a breakthrough. Not only had he and his associates *demonstrated* the existence of psychic phenomena, which Rhine named "extrasensory perception," with solid experimental evidence, but, more importantly, they were able to show that ESP seemed to *reveal natural relationships* in the same manner as ordinary psychological phenomena. For instance both Linzmayer and Pearce lost their ability under the influence of the drug sodium amytal. Their performance seemed to follow predictable patterns such as fatigue curves—the falling off of scores during intensive testing. Showing that psychic ability obeyed certain natural laws, Rhine felt, would do more to make its study acceptable to other scientists than any number of "miracle" demonstrations.[21]

Rhine's team discovered five more students with abilities similar to those of Pearce and Linzmayer. New experiments examined the differences between telepathy and clairvoyance—if any could be found—as well as the effects of distance between agent and subject. Most importantly, testing conditions became increasingly stringent as the researchers sought to exclude every possible opportunity for sensory leakage.

The classic example of these later experiments is the Pearce-Pratt series, which took place between different buildings on Duke's West Campus. Pratt, the agent, was located in what was then the Physics Building. Once a minute he picked up a card from a precut and preshuffled pack. *Without turning it up or looking at it*, Pratt moved the card facedown onto a book. (Since this experiment was meant to test clairvoyance, it was not necessary for Pratt to see the card.) At that very minute Pearce, located with a synchronized watch in the library one hundred yards away, tried to perceive the card on the book. Without meeting, both men deposited sealed records with Rhine—Pratt of the targets (which he recorded after the run) and Pearce of his calls—and then met to check results. Although Pearce started off with only chance scores, as was typical for him when confronted with a new situation, he quickly resumed his high scoring level and averaged 9.9 hits per run of 25 (where chance predicts 5 hits) over the 300 trials. Pearce was then moved to the medical school, over 250 yards away, and, after the customary adjustment period, continued his high scoring. Ultimately four separate experiments were done with a total of 558 hits out of 1,850 trials (where 370 would be expected by chance). The odds against chance for the series were literally astronomical, 22 billion-to-one.[22]

While this was going on, Rhine was preparing a report of the research to date. Its publication as the monograph *Extra-Sensory Perception* in April 1934 was a landmark in the history of psychical research. The initial response from fellow psychical researchers was generally extremely favorable, though Rhine's professional colleagues, particularly the British, were quick to voice criticisms, primarily of the book rather than of the research itself. They complained that Rhine's description of the experimental conditions was inadequate; they could not determine whether or not sensory leakage had been adequately excluded, and it was not clear whether or not some methods of testing might have permitted a certain amount of logical inference. Although some of Rhine's more skeptical colleagues had reservations about certain experiments, they found more than enough in the other experiments to convince them that this was important work. Perhaps the most difficult pill for these researchers to swallow, though, was the ease with which Rhine seemed to find exceptional subjects. For many psychical researchers who had labored long with little or nothing to show for it, this was the most incredible aspect of Rhine's research. To be sure, no one before had approached ESP testing with the drive and vigor that Rhine had, and however incredible Rhine's results may have seemed, other researchers in America and abroad began duplicating his methods almost immediately.

While work continued at Duke—the team began precognition experiments in 1934 as well as psychokinesis studies, the latter being kept very quiet—other researchers began to report some success using Rhine's methods. Word came of successful replications at Tarkio (Missouri) College, Bard College in New York State, and from England. Word also arrived that a young German researcher, Hans Bender, had conducted a successful series of clairvoyance experiments, which Rhine regarded as an independent corroboration of his own work. As momentum built, Rhine was able to secure additional funding, and more researchers joined the team.

News of Rhine's research was picked up by the popular press. Articles on parapsychology (as it was now being called by the Duke researchers) appeared in *Time*, *Reader's Digest*, *Scientific American*, and *Harper's*, among other publications. As more scientists learned of the research and got hold of copies of Rhine's monograph, the criticism began to mount. A psychologist at Clark University, R. R. Willoughby, launched a series of articles essentially declaring Rhine's statistical procedures to be faulty. After extended correspondence with Rhine and Charles Stuart he conceded, in September 1936, that his statistical objections did not hold up. Almost immediately another attack on Rhine's statistics came from the McGill University psychologist C. E. Kellogg, who questioned the fundamental underpinnings of Rhine's statistical approach. Rhine and other researchers responded to these criticisms and eventually the Institute for Mathematical Statistics gave its blessing to the statistical methods used by the Duke researchers.

Criticism also focused on the question of whether all sensory cues had really been excluded. Critics quickly noticed that the cards in some of the early commercially produced ESP decks could be read from the back because of the printing impression. But these were not the same cards that had been used in the early Duke testing, and of course the problem did not exist in the many experiments in which the subject was not permitted to see even the back of the cards. This did not stop some critics from trying to portray the entire body of results as worthless, however.

The year 1937 was something of a watershed. The *Journal of Parapsychology* was inaugurated, officially demarcating the area of psychical research that comprised parapsychology: Parapsychology was to be the strictly experimental approach to psychic phenomena. In September 1937 the Zenith Radio Corporation began a series of nationwide broadcasts about psychic phenomena and ESP in particular. Along with this went a special version of the ESP cards (with the Zenith logo on the back) that were sold in bookshops for people to test themselves in conjunction with the weekly radio program. The following month Rhine's popular account of the Duke research program, *New Frontiers of the Mind*, hit the bookshops and was selected by the Book-of-the-Month Club.[23] By the end of that year few people in the United States had not heard of ESP or the research at Duke University.

Of course the massive publicity brought renewed attacks on the research. Some of the reviews of *New Frontiers* rehashed old statistical and methodological criticisms, as did articles now appearing in the semipopular science press. Criticism became increasingly vicious. It began to appear that the objective of many leading psychologists of the day was not to criticize but to discredit the research entirely, lest the enterprise reflect badly on orthodox psychology.

The controversy came to a head in the professional community at the annual convention of the American Psychological Association in September 1938. The APA arranged for a session to debate "Experimental Methods of ESP Research." On the panel were three supporters of ESP research—J. B. Rhine; T.N.E. Greville, one of Rhine's statisticians; and Gardner Murphy, a well-respected psychologist who supported the Duke work—as well as three critics of the research, L. D. Goodfellow, H. O. Gulliksen, and J. L. Kennedy. Rhine had not been looking forward to this meeting— referring to it as his "heresy trial"—but in the end it went rather well. Rhine and Murphy were able to rebut much of the criticism. Several well-known critics harshly denounced the work, but Rhine's patient and well-reasoned responses, as well as his ability to point to examples of his team's continued methodological improvements, were warmly applauded.

It would be wrong to leave the impression that organized psychology was ready to embrace parapsychology. Far from it. But the grudging tolerance from professional psychology that Rhine had earned was better than nothing. At least Rhine understood how he was going to have to present his findings to his professional colleagues in the future. Almost immediately his thoughts turned to a project that would present all the accumulated research on ESP to a professional audience.

What Rhine had in mind was another book, but this one would be a collaborative effort of nearly all the researchers in the laboratory. Throughout the spring and summer of 1939, the entire team worked on what would be the definitive report on ESP research. Not only were all of the experiments of the last decade reported thoroughly in this volume, but the mathematical and statistical treatments were explained in detail. Furthermore the book took on all of the principal criticisms that psychologists had leveled over the years—thirty-two, by Rhine's count—and then demonstrated how the six "best" parapsychological experiments could not be explained away by any combination of these criticisms. Before publication the authors showed these arguments to their principal critics and invited their replies, which were included in the volume. The resulting book, *Extra-Sensory Perception After Sixty Years* (the word *sixty* referring to the founding of the SPR in 1882), appeared in 1940.[24]

The professional response to *ESP-60*, as it came to be called, was far more positive than it had been to Rhine's earlier monograph. Most of the principal professional psychological journals reviewed it. This time many of the reviewers, even if they were unwilling to accept the reality of ESP, at least gave a sober and careful hearing to the arguments. By now psychologists seemed willing to accept that parapsychology was a legitimate scientific activity, whether or not they were personally convinced by the evidence. No one was more surprised than Rhine when *ESP-60* became assigned reading for the introductory psychology classes at Harvard for the 1940–41 academic year.

Now that parapsychology had gained a measure of acceptance, researchers at other universities were able to take up ESP research without ridicule, and many did. Already a massive replication and extension of the Duke work had been completed at the University of Colorado. As World War II clouded the horizon, Rhine and his co-workers hoped that their academic battles were behind them.[25]

When the war ended, a fresh influx of new students attached themselves to the Duke University Parapsychology Laboratory. These students later started research programs at other universities. The data base upon which parapsychology rested became increasingly broad. The network of researchers grew, too, and soon there were regular international meetings to discuss research. Parapsychology continued to grow and change over the decades, and J. B. Rhine's influence was powerfully felt right up until his death in 1980.

Still, the academic battles were not over in 1940 as Rhine had hoped. They are not over today. Rhine could give other researchers ESP cards and teach them the methods of the Duke lab, but he could not give them ESP. Many researchers were able to confirm Rhine's findings, but many others simply found no evidence of ESP, and they remained skeptical. The evidence for ESP and psychokinesis is incomparably stronger now than it was half a century ago when *ESP-60* was published, yet, as the next chapter reveals, parapsychology has yet to find universal acceptance within the scientific community.

CHAPTER 4

Why Does the Controversy Continue?

For the last ten years, we have been arguing about what constitutes science and scientific method and what societies use it. We even changed the By-Laws about it. The PA uses statistics and blinds, placebos, double blinds and other standard devices. The whole history of scientific advance is full of scientists investigating phenomena that the establishment did not believe were there. I submit we vote in favor of this Association's work.[1]

There is nothing that one can't research the hell out of. Research guided by bad judgment is a black hole for good money . . . Now is the time for everyone who believes in the Rule of Reason to speak up against pathological science and its purveyors.[2]

Both of those quotations refer to the same organization—the Parapsychological Association. Both of them were delivered to our nation's premier scientific organization, the American Association for the Advancement of Science (AAAS). The first statement was made in December 1969 by the renowned anthropologist Margaret Mead, who spoke from the floor in support of the PA's application for affiliation with the AAAS. Following her statement, the membership voted five-to-one in favor of granting that affiliation.

The second statement was made by the noted physicist John A. Wheeler in an address to the AAAS in January 1979. It was the opening salvo in a campaign to "drive the pseudos out of the workshop of science" that he launched in the hope of getting the PA disaffiliated from the AAAS. The campaign failed.*

In or out of the halls of the scientific establishment, parapsychology has a way of stirring passions and provoking amazing reactions. Robert Jahn was dean of the School of Engineering and Applied Science at Princeton University and a noted authority on aerospace engineering with a long record of work for NASA and the Department of Defense when he decided that certain parapsychological problems were worth investigating. Did his colleagues applaud his pioneering spirit? Not exactly. They as much as said he was crazy and a disgrace to science and the university. The university even convened an ad hoc committee to oversee his research—something unheard of for a scientist of his stature. Yet not all established scientists reacted that way, as Jahn noted in a 1983 address to the PA. Speaking about the Princeton Engineering Anomalies Research program, he said, "We have had commentary on our program from no less than six Nobel laureates, two of whom categorically rejected the topic, two of whom encouraged us to push on, and two of whom were evasively equivocal. So much for unanimity of high scientific opinion."

Roots of the Controversy

Robert Jahn's experience is not an isolated one. In fact it is fairly typical of what distinguished scientists who dare to stray from orthodoxy have had to endure ever since the noted physicist William Crookes began examining the phenomena of Spiritualism more than

*Wheeler's address, "Drive the Pseudos Out of the Workshop of Science," can be found in the *New York Review of Books*, April 13, 1979. When he originally delivered the address to the AAAS, Wheeler injudiciously replied to a question with statements accusing Rhine of fraud in his pre-parapsychological research. The accusation was groundless, and Wheeler subsequently retracted it in a "correction" published in the AAAS magazine *Science* (13 July 1979, p. 144). Nonetheless AAAS legal counsel disallowed distribution of the cassette tapes of that part of the conference.

one hundred years ago. There is a long history of scientific journals discriminating against parapsychological reports, and an almost equally long history of principal government funding agencies that deny funding for parapsychological research. Although there is great public interest in the topic, the popular scientific press often prints vehement attacks on parapsychological research (and on the researchers themselves). Parapsychology is controversial, no doubt about it, but *why* this is so turns out to be a fairly complicated issue.

Fundamental to the controversy are the *claims* of parapsychology. Parapsychological hypotheses at the very least claim that humans can acquire information or affect external physical systems in ways that science, in its present state, cannot explain. If these claims are correct, then the existing worldview that science gives us will have to be modified—the so-called laws of physics will have to be rewritten. Of itself this should not be controversial, since the scientific worldview is always undergoing modification and the laws of physics have been rewritten several times in just the last century. This is called scientific progress. Yet some scientists are profoundly uncomfortable with this possibility and feel that the domain of human communication and action is already completely understood, so any apparent need for modification is spurious.

Just how controversial parapsychology is depends on whom you ask. The public does not think of parapsychology as a particularly controversial science, since surveys frequently show that most people either accept the reality of ESP or have had psychic experiences themselves. Oddly enough, even a very large percentage of scientists and academics see nothing wrong with parapsychology, or at least parapsychology's main topic of study. Over the decades several surveys have been made of scientists' opinions on ESP. The percentage of scientists who think that ESP is "an established fact" or that ESP is a "likely possibility" has climbed from a low of 8 percent (in a survey of 352 members of the American Psychological Association in 1938, just as the Duke University work was becoming known) to highs of 67 percent and 75 percent in two large (well over 1,000 respondents each) surveys conducted in the early seventies.[4]

With such evidence indicating that so many scientists are willing to consider ESP a likely possibility, you may wonder why parapsychology courses are not routinely found in colleges and universities and why there are so few labs doing research in this area. A more recent survey conducted by University of Maryland sociologist Dr. James McClenon in 1981 may suggest some reasons.[5] McClenon surveyed the "administrative elite"—the council and selected section committees of the AAAS. These scientists were more skeptical of ESP, with just under 30 percent believing that ESP was an "established fact" or a "likely possibility." Those in the social sciences (where parapsychology courses would normally be categorized) were even more skeptical (20 percent were believers) than those in the natural sciences (30 percent believers). Clearly the percentage of scientists willing to entertain the possibility of ESP (and presumably the study of it) is much lower among those who run the scientific establishment than among average working scientists.

Science is not just the steady accumulation of little facts, one building upon the other. It is a steady accumulation of little facts punctuated periodically by major upheavals in the whole scientific view. Minor revolutions in science, such as the acceptance of continental drift, happen all the time. Major revolutions, such as Einstein's theory of relativity, happen less frequently. Change, from minor revisions to major revolution, is the very essence of scientific progress, and change never comes easily. From the discovery of anomalies—pieces that do not fit into the prevailing scientific picture—to the general acceptance of a revised picture that makes sense of the anomalies, is often a long and difficult road. The prevailing scientific view will not give in easily to a challenger, and the battle is waged not only with data and reasoned debate but also with ridicule and scorn, censorship and denial, and just about every other rhetorical and political tactic.

Parapsychology may or may not contain the seeds for a major upheaval in science. Only time will tell. Many a scientific anomaly has come and gone without provoking a scientific revolution. What is clear is that the controversy surrounding parapsychology bears the hallmarks of at least a potential revolution. Sociologists of science see this both in the activities and strategies of those who believe the claims of parapsychology should be rejected and in parapsychologists' efforts to win the approval of orthodox science. Frustrating as this struggle may be to those who champion the unpopular cause, we must accept that this is part of the give-and-take of normal science, the winnowing of the wheat from the chaff of human knowledge.

The pivotal point about which the entire parapsychological controversy turns is whether or not "normal explanations," which are compatible with the existing worldview, have really been excluded for any given parapsychological claim or experimental result. Could the subjects in researcher X's experiment in fact have obtained the information through some normal means? Did subject Y have an opportunity to cheat in such-and-such an experiment? This is where scientific control becomes so important. But there is another, equally important but often unacknowledged, factor: a person's *a priori* concept of just how *improbable* the phenomena are. If a person's *a priori* conviction is that psi phenomena cannot possibly exist, then any "normal" explanation, no matter how bizarre and convoluted it might have to be, will be preferable to an explanation that invokes psi phenomena.

Are psi phenomena really "impossible" according to contemporary science? As Robert Jahn's experience with the Nobel laureates revealed, the answer will depend upon whom you ask. Certainly there has been a tradition both in philosophy and in science that would make psi phenomena "impossible." This is the tradition (or philosophy) of *materialism*, which holds that *all* phenomena, whether they are chemical reactions or mental events such as memories, can ultimately be reduced to discrete, analyzable bits of matter and observable interactions between such particles. From this perspective the idea that information can be transferred from one person to another, or from some object to a person without a material transmission medium, or that action can take place at a distance without material connecting the cause and the effect, is purely and simply *impossible*.

Fortunately the march of scientific progress is usually only temporarily slowed down by people saying "impossible." For a long time meteorites were declared "impossible." The idea that continents could drift around on the surface of the earth was ridiculed for decades. The history of science is full of other "impossibilities" that have become ordinary parts of everyday life. A number of leading physicists, acknowledged giants of the field, such as Henry Margenau, David Bohm, and O. Costa de Beauregard, have repeatedly claimed that there is nothing in quantum physics that forbids psi phenomena. De Beauregard maintains that certain axioms of quantum physics virtually *demand* that psi phenomena exist.[6]

Nobel laureate Brian Josephson, a strong supporter of parapsychology, has stated that some of the most convincing evidence he has seen for the existence of psi phenomena comes not from the diligent work of the parapsychologists but from experiments in quantum physics.[7]

So, science does not speak with one voice on the matter of parapsychology. Such is life on the frontiers of knowledge. All we can say now is that the jury is still out.

From a scientific point of view, what we are calling psi phenomena can be explained in one of two ways. Either they can be attributed to such constructs as ESP, PK, and so forth, explanations that are paranormal *for the present* but will become normal if they are brought within the general scientific worldview, or they can be attributed to ordinary, normal factors, unrecognized by the investigators but perfectly explicable by today's science.

Parapsychologists, obviously, are betting on the first explanation, skeptics on the second. Actually *skeptic* is not the best word to describe those who reject the possibility of psi phenomena. A true skeptic is inclined to question easy answers from whatever point of view. I prefer to use an expression advocated by my colleague John Palmer, who recommends that people preferring the second type of explanation be called *conventional theorists*, that is, those who try to explain apparent psi phenomena in terms of conventional scientific knowledge.[8]

Conventional explanations of psi phenomena are as varied as the imagination can devise, but they basically fall into two classes: incompetence and fraud. The conventional theorist will maintain that if one carefully examines any given parapsychological experiment, one will find methodological flaws and lapses in controls that could permit the subject or subjects to accomplish the task through perfectly normal means. The subject may be as unaware as the experimenter that he is using ordinary sensory information. Furthermore this claim can apply as easily to spontaneous-case investigations as it does to laboratory experimentation, and even if there is no obvious evidence of incompetence in the investigation, there is always the possibility of fraud.

The objections of conventional theorists are not without merit. Certainly there have been parapsychological experiments that, after being reported and generally accepted, are later found to have weaknesses. For example, in one type of experiment subjects were asked to judge which art print out of a set of five was being viewed by an agent elsewhere. The agent would have spent some time trying to communicate one of those pictures, usually by holding it and looking at it. In a few early experiments the experimenters had only one set of pictures, so the same set that the agent used was later used by the subject. Might not the subject have noticed that one picture had been handled recently? Whether or not the subjects actually did make use of "handling cues" is not known, but the fact that they *could* have undermines our confidence that all sensory information had been excluded.

Errors in statistical analyses of experimental results may lead an experimenter to conclude that chance had been eliminated as an explanation when in fact it had not. Not surprisingly most slipups in experimental methodology or statistics are caught by fellow parapsychologists. They, more than anyone else, feel the obligation to keep their experiments as near to perfect as possible.

Fraud, too, is a problem from time to time. In the days of psychical research quite a few mediums were found to be faking psychic effects, and even in the laboratory a few subjects have been caught cheating. Even worse, on one occasion a parapsychologist was caught cheating by his colleagues, and in at least two other cases there is strong circumstantial evidence that the experimenter faked parapsychological data. Worth noting is that in all of these cases it was other parapsychologists who brought the evidence forward. While fraud by experimenters is utterly reprehensible, it is reassuring to me that parapsychologists are doing a pretty good job at least of policing themselves. Recent media coverage of fraud in science suggests that parapsychologists are well ahead of their colleagues in other branches of science in rooting out fraud.

Hundreds and hundreds of experiments in parapsychology have provided good evidence of psi phenomena. Are they all fatally flawed or the result of fraud? That is quite a sweeping indictment, but some critics would answer, "Probably so." Their reasoning is that even in experiments where they cannot point to specific flaws, they are quite sure they are there—it just might take a sharper eye to find them.

Accusations of fraud are even more sinister than accusations of flawed methodology. Critics frequently see no problem in alleging fraud without even a shred of evidence. One famous example of this took place in 1955, when Dr. G. R. Price, then a research associate in the Department of Medicine at the University of Minnesota, published an article in the prestigious journal *Science*. Price argued that ESP was scientifically impossible and that therefore J. B. Rhine and British investigator S. G. Soal must be fraudulent experimenters. Appearing as it did in such an authoritative journal, this article was taken by many otherwise uncommitted scientists as the final dismissal of ESP research. It was not until 1972 that Price admitted he was mistaken and withdrew some of his accusations. Later, he further admitted that he had written the original article in *Science* without even a slight attempt to find evidence of fraud and in fact had been under the mistaken assumption that Rhine was trying to promote some sort of religious belief.[9]

The Rise of Fundamentalism

Parapsychologists have nothing to fear from responsible criticism. Unfortunately the past decade has seen the growth of a form of scientific fundamentalism that threatens to undermine the productive, if not always amicable, relationship parapsychology has had with its critics. This movement, characterized by its unquestioning acceptance of the authority of the existing scientific worldview and its vehement condemnation of any deviations from orthodoxy, can trace its origins back to a magazine called *The Humanist*, a philosophical journal known primarily for its attacks on religion. The editor, Dr. Paul Kurtz, a philosopher at the State University of New York at Buffalo, had mounted several editorial campaigns against "pseudo-sciences," most notably astrology. In 1976 Kurtz, along with Dr. Marcello Truzzi, a sociologist with a long-standing academic research interest in occult beliefs and practices, and several other scientists and academics formed the Committee for the Scientific Investigation of Claims of the Paranormal (CSICOP). The goals for CSICOP were indeed laudable, "the critical investigation of paranormal and fringe-science claims from a responsible, scientific point of view and [the dissemination of] factual information about the results of such inquiries to the scientific community and the public."[10] No reasonable scientist could possibly take issue with goals such as these, and CSICOP was quickly able to attract distinguished members from a broad spectrum of scientific and academic disciplines.

It quickly became clear that the plans Kurtz had for CSICOP were rather different from the professed goals of the organization. After only one year Truzzi, who was serving as cochairman with Kurtz, resigned. Truzzi felt uncomfortable with CSICOP's excessive negative zeal and its crusading, inquisitional approach to anomalies, which was rapidly replacing the scholarly, scientific approach that Truzzi had envisioned. Several other noted academics also resigned for similar reasons. Truzzi had been editor of *The Zetetic*, a journal that was to be CSICOP's organ for scholarly debate, but on his resignation Kurtz replaced him with Kendrick Frazier, who headed CSICOP's new journal, *Skeptical Inquirer*. Under Frazier's editorship the *SI* abandoned all pretensions to scholarship and has become a propagandistic organ that trades chiefly on ridicule, titillating innuendo, and a "fellow traveler" camaraderie among like-minded individuals who are already convinced that the study of a wide range of anomalies has nothing to offer science.* Backed by an aggressive marketing campaign, *SI* has achieved wide circulation in recent years.

Two examples will illustrate how CSICOP members "investigate" parapsychological claims. One of parapsychology's better-known academic critics is the British psychologist Prof. C.E.M. Hansel. Although his critical attacks on parapsychology predate the formation of CSICOP, he has been one of CSICOP's fellows from the beginning, and CSICOP's publishing house, Prometheus Press, issued an update of Hansel's 1966 examination of parapsychology under the title *ESP and Parapsychology: A Critical Reevaluation*. Hansel makes no bones about his basic assumptions: ESP is impossible; therefore investigating an experiment simply means finding out how the trick was done or where the loophole occurred. His strategy is to devise "rational reconstructions" of how a given experiment took place and then suggest how the fraud was perpetrated.

Typical of Hansel's approach was his examination of the famous Pearce-Pratt series of ESP experiments conducted at Duke Univer-

---

*In a 1989 issue of the *Journal of Scientific Exploration* (vol. 3, no. 1) Prof. Henry H. Bauer, of the Virginia Polytechnic Institute and State University, reported an exchange of letters with Frazier in which *SI*'s editor argued that "the magazine's purpose is not to consider what the best evidence for anomalous claims might be but to argue against them" (Bauer's words).

sity in the late thirties, discussed in the preceding chapter. Before Hansel's visit to Duke University some twenty years *after* the Pearce-Pratt experiments there had never been even the slightest suggestion of fraud in this classically designed card-guessing experiment. Hansel looked over the layout of the two locations that had been used and subsequently claimed that he had found the manner in which Pearce, the subject, had probably cheated. Pearce had obviously left his assigned post in another building, returned to the building where Pratt, the experimenter, was recording the ESP cards by a timed schedule at a desk, and either peeked over *two* transoms or gained access to the attic and peeked through a trapdoor in the ceiling. Near the end of the session Pearce would have hustled back to his assigned station and turned in his record sheets in the expected manner. (Of course Pearce would have had to repeat this performance over thirty times without having been detected, and done this even though Rhine himself was present for many sessions.) It did not concern Hansel that there was never a shred of evidence that any part of this activity ever took place, nor did it bother him that the layout of the rooms upon which he based his scenario had been substantially altered since the days of the experiment. Even the discovery of blueprints of the original layout that demonstrated that much of his scenario was simply impossible did not deter Hansel from standing by his accusations in the reissued version of his book.[11] From Hansel's point of view, evidence is not needed. It is sufficient to demonstrate the merest possibility of fraud to allow one to dismiss an experiment altogether. However, other staunch critics of parapsychology, such as University of Oregon psychologist Dr. Ray Hyman, have said that Hansel's hypothetical fraud approach is neither scientific nor helpful.[12]

Probably one of CSICOP's best-known advocates is the magician James Randi. Born in Canada as Randall James Zwinge, Randi achieved national exposure through his efforts to debunk the self-proclaimed Israeli psychic Uri Geller. Randi has always been harshly critical of parapsychologists who investigate alleged psychokinetic effects such as object movements or metal bending because he claims they consistently overlook the tricks of his trade—conjuring. Actually parapsychologists have a long history of collaborating with conjurors and mentalists, but Randi's criticisms did serve as a salutary reminder to the latest generation of researchers. In 1979 and 1980,

under the code name Project Alpha, Randi arranged for two young
magicians to pose as psychics and hoax the researchers at the recently established McDonnell Laboratory for Psychical Research at
Washington University in St. Louis, Missouri. Several times over
the next eighteen months the two young men were flown in for
research sessions at the laboratory. All of this work was classed as
exploratory and done under relatively relaxed conditions. At the
1981 convention of the Parapsychological Association, the Mc-
Donnell Lab researchers presented a videotape of some of these exploratory sessions that they felt captured some possibly genuine
phenomena. The researchers made it clear that they were making
no claims and that they were really seeking the advice of colleagues
on how to proceed. Nevertheless the videotape was practically
hooted down by their parapsychological colleagues, who saw numerous weak spots in the setup. Chastened by that experience, the
researchers returned to St. Louis and restructured their experiments
according to advice from Randi (who had been offering it all along)
and of other parapsychologists. Under the more rigorous conditions, the two young men were able to produce no seemingly psychic
effects, and the researchers reported this lack of results at the following year's convention. Subsequently they discontinued work with
the two men.

That might have been the end of the affair, not unlike others that
have wasted the time of parapsychologists. When it became obvious
to Randi that no further work was going to be done with his
"plants," he called a press conference (with the sponsorship of *Discover* magazine) where he announced to the world that he had conducted a "sociological experiment" to test whether parapsychologists
were capable of detecting fraud. Although privately Randi had told
the McDonnell researchers that they had "passed the test" and that
his two magicians were unable to cheat after the more rigorous
conditions were imposed, at the press conference and in all the
following publicity Randi lambasted and ridiculed the earlier exploratory work. It went largely unnoticed that the McDonnell
researchers had *never* made any formal claims that the two alleged
psychics were producing psi phenomena.[13]

Afterward some science commentators, notably William Broad of
The New York Times, observed that had Randi been a psychologist
conducting that experiment, his hoax would probably have landed

him in trouble with the ethics committee of the American Psychological Association.[14] At the 1983 Parapsychological Association convention, Project Alpha was roundly condemned by some of Randi's own colleagues in the magic profession, who had gathered there to discuss how magicians can collaborate with parapsychologists. Despite the ethical backlash, Project Alpha has been warmly embraced by CSICOP members as one of their most audacious exposés.*

Of course the real function of CSICOP is as an advocacy group to lobby for a particular point of view. Certainly the organization is effective in this way, and few would deny that there is often a need to counter the public's credulity. But somewhere along the line CSICOP abandoned the *objectively* critical spirit of science and adopted a "stop at any cost" approach toward any topic that it deems off-limits to science. Fortunately the scientific controversy over parapsychology will not be resolved at press conferences and in the media. Only in the appropriate professional forums can the give-and-take of science go on. Science is a marvelously self-correcting system. If there are errors or bad science, this will be

---

*One might wonder if CSICOP is capable of conducting any "scientific investigations," as its name implies. The answer appears to be a resounding *no*. CSICOP has conducted only one organized investigation of what could be called a paranormal claim—observations by the French chronobiologists Michel and Françoise Gauquelin that the birth times of sports champions bear an unusual, but quite regular, relationship to the position of the planet Mars in the heavens. In 1977 CSICOP inherited a controversy about this quasi-astrological claim from Kurtz's *The Humanist*, and Kurtz organized a committee of himself and two other members with astronomical and statistical expertise to conduct certain control tests and a replication of the Gauquelins' work. This resulted in several articles in the *Skeptical Inquirer* claiming there was no such effect. Shortly afterward the project's statistician, Dennis Rawlins (who was a member of CSICOP's executive committee), published a scathing denunciation of CSICOP's handling of the investigation. Rawlins claimed that Kurtz and his associates had manipulated the data and had demonstrated gross incompetence. Then they engineered a massive cover-up of the whole thing when he had tried to bring this to the attention of other CSICOP fellows. The furor that ensued resulted in additional defections by other prominent members of CSICOP as well as several subsequent exposés of the investigation by additional former CSICOP fellows. Since that fiasco CSICOP has undertaken no further scientific investigations. (For a recent history of CSICOP, including the Gauquelin affair, see "Skeptics and the New Age" in J. Gordon Melton, Jerome Clark, and Aidan A. Kelly, *New Age Encyclopedia*. Detroit: Gail Reasearch, 1990, pp. 417–427.)

weeded out in due course. Science does not need vigilantes to guard the gates.

Parapsychologists ask for nothing more than to have their experiments, their methods, and their data examined without distortions or misrepresentations, without prejudice or predisposition. The work that we shall examine in part II represents the broadest representation of recent parapsychological research that space will permit. For each area we shall look at the evidence and examine whatever reasonable criticisms should be taken into account. In some of the areas we will find that the evidence is inconclusive, but that does not mean it should be altogether dismissed or rejected. In other areas the evidence for psi phenomena is very strong, and scientists are beginning to feel that some real progress is being made. As you make your own evaluations of the data, resist the temptation to decide whether something is "real" or "not real"; the real question is whether the scientific quest is worthwhile.

PART II

Surveying the Field

CHAPTER 5

Contemporary Extrasensory Perception Research

Parapsychologists frequently speak of the phenomena they study as not being constrained by space and time. Taking my cue accordingly, I shall adopt a fairly elastic interpretation of the word *contemporary*. My approach in this and succeeding chapters in this section shall be to focus on particular research themes or programs that have been instrumental in shaping parapsychology as I know it today. In practice this means that I shall concentrate on, but not limit myself to, developments of the past twenty or twenty-five years. While this may seem an overly generous interpretation of *contemporary*, the fact remains that parapsychology is not a rapidly evolving field, not yet at least. Perhaps what follows may help to accelerate progress.

A Parapsychologist's Dream

In the basement of the Maimonides Medical Center in Brooklyn, New York, Dr. William Erwin, a Manhattan psychoanalyst, lay asleep in the special soundproof chamber of the Maimonides Dream Laboratory. Thin wires led from electrodes taped to his skull to a small box on the wall. In the adjacent room experimenter Joyce Plosky sat, idly flipping through a magazine and trying not to fall asleep.

Suddenly the pens on the polygraph monitoring Erwin began chattering with the sounds characteristic of rapid-eye-movement (REM) signals. Examining the polygraph chart as it passed under the pens, Plosky determined that Erwin was just entering a dreaming period. Immediately she hit a button; a buzzer sounded in a distant room where a young City College student sat, waiting for his cue.

Minutes ticked away as Plosky watched the chart. Eventually the REM signals became sporadic and then stopped. Erwin's dream had ended, but instead of letting Erwin slip peacefully into deeper sleep, the experimenter turned on the intercom.

"Bill, Bill. Wake up. Can you tell me what you've been dreaming about?"

Erwin groaned, but, after all, he had volunteered for this. "A storm. Rainstorm. It reminds me of traveling—a trip—traveling one time in Oklahoma, approaching a rainstorm, thundercloud . . ."[1] A few moments later he mused, "For some reason I got a feeling of memory, now, of New Mexico when I lived there. There are a lot of mountains around New Mexico, Indians, Pueblos. . . . You're surrounded by mountains . . . the name of one of the mountain ranges in New Mexico, Sundre Christo [Sangre de Cristo] . . ." A few minutes later Erwin was back asleep.

This routine was repeated as Erwin had a second and third dream, each different from the first. In his fourth dream Erwin returned to the traveling theme; in his fifth and last dream he recalled the old World War II advertising slogan "Lucky Strike green has gone to war . . ."

As you may have suspected, Bill Erwin had sacrificed an undisturbed night's sleep for the sake of ESP research. He was to do this many more times throughout the summer and fall of 1964—and over the next couple of years—but at the moment he was one of the first subjects in a new type of ESP experiment. Neither he nor the rest of the experimental team realized that decades later, parapsychologists would consider these dream studies to be the start of a new era in ESP research.

Erwin and Plosky were not the only ones giving up their nights for ESP research. Alone in a small room elsewhere in the hospital was the "other half" of this ESP experiment—the agent, a City College doctoral student named Sol Feldstein. His job was to try to communicate to Erwin by ESP the contents (visual, emotional, and so on) of an art print. Earlier that evening Feldstein had chatted with Erwin and the rest of the team to establish a rapport with the dreamer. Once Erwin entered the sleep room, however, Feldstein had to remove himself to the small room for the rest of the evening. After Erwin went to sleep, Feldstein used a special procedure to select randomly one envelope from many in a file drawer. Only when the buzzer from the sleep lab signaled the start of Erwin's dream period did Feldstein open the envelope. Until he heard the signal marking the end of the dream period, Feldstein concentrated on the picture, trying to get it across to Erwin. When Erwin was not dreaming, Feldstein could rest, but once he heard the buzzer, it was back to the same picture. In the morning Feldstein slipped out of the hospital without any contact with Erwin or the experimenters.

On awakening, Erwin was asked to recall any aspects of his dreams that stood out. He immediately went to his first dream: ". . . my first dream impressed me very much . . . I spent a few summers in Santa Fe . . . and during the Fiesta a great many of the Indians came in with their wares . . . it seems there were heavy clouds behind this . . . Perhaps the coloring of New Mexico fits it, the mesa as it runs up to the mountains." A bit later he commented, "Here it gets into this epic type of thing . . . a DeMille super-type colossal production. I would carry along with it such ideas as the Pueblo going down to the Mayan-Aztec type of civilization."

When Erwin had finished reviewing his dreams, he was free to go. His part in that trial was now complete. It remained only for Plosky to seal up the recording of all Erwin's comments and send it off to be transcribed. After several more trials the transcripts would be given to several "outside judges," who would rank the nightly dream transcripts against the possible targets. Standard statistical procedures would tell the researchers whether the dreams actually matched the targets better than chance would predict.

And the target for Erwin's session? It was *Zapatistas* by Carlos Orozco Romero, a painting that depicts Mexican-Indian followers of the Mexican revolutionary Emiliano Zapata. The painting is dominated by a row of marching, armed men, followed by shawled women and accompanied by carrillera-bedecked horsemen. Dark mountains and ominous clouds fill the background. Among other characteristics, the Zapatistas traced their ancestry to the ancient Mayans and Aztecs. Considering Erwin's repeated references to the American Southwest, along with the storm imagery, the war and traveling references, the judges classified that session as a "striking hit."

Despite Erwin's impressive performance that evening, this pioneering series got off to a shaky start. The overall results did not provide significant evidence of ESP, but they certainly were promising, and the researchers had learned a lot that would improve later sessions. Some subjects (like Erwin) seemed particularly good at incorporating the target material into their dreams, whereas others did not. Also, the two senders achieved very different results. Feldstein, who had actually helped design the series, did very well: His subjects got five hits and one miss. Plosky, who alternated with Feldstein, was not so successful. The investigators even began to suspect that Feldstein might be "contaminating" the dreams. One subject reported a very confusing dream in which the words *left* and *right* kept coming up. It had nothing to do with the target, but later the researchers learned that moments before he attempted to "send" the target picture, Feldstein had been studying a psychology problem in which animals had to learn a sequence of left and right turns. And then there was the time when Feldstein became engrossed in a *Life* magazine article about topless bathing suits . . . .

Dreams and ESP

Dreams, of course, have always been a common vehicle for extrasensory information. History records many famous psychic dreams, and a large proportion of the apparently psychic experiences of ordinary folks happens in dreams. Why dreams should be such good vehicles for extrasensory information is not known, but there has been much speculation. The man who did more than anyone else to bring dreams to the attention of science, Sigmund Freud, once stated that it is an "incontestable fact that sleep creates favorable conditions for telepathy."[2] Freud thought telepathy might be an archaic method by which individuals could understand one another, a method that was replaced through evolution by more efficient language. Dreams, with their origins in the depth of the psyche, may reveal vestiges of this ancient means of communication.

More recently investigators have speculated that since dreams unfold without the conscious mind's constraints on what is or is not possible in perception, perhaps our dreaming minds simply do not filter out extrasensory information that our waking consciousness might. Whatever the reason, dreams and extrasensory perception have been closely linked for the entire history of our field. The literature of psychical research and parapsychology contains numerous investigations that collect and examine spontaneous psychic dreams. Likewise there have been many reports of attempts to influence dreams telepathically. Yet it was only with certain technological developments and advances in understanding the physiology of dreaming that it became possible for the study of psychic dreams to be brought into the laboratory.

The immediate impetus for the development of this new research technique came from certain winds of change that were blowing in the parapsychological community. In the late fifties and early sixties the consensus among many parapsychologists was that card guessing had run its course. This highly artificial and basically rather boring technique had provided the necessary evidence to establish the scientific credentials of ESP, but it seemed incapable of telling us much about how ESP works in real life. In a sense the social spirit of the so-called rebellious sixties also swept the parapsychological community as many researchers sought to break away from the card-guessing methods and the conservative approach they felt Rhine and the Duke lab represented. Radically new approaches were needed, new trails had to be blazed.

This conviction was strongest among those parapsychologists who were psychiatrists or clinical psychologists—persons who often found startling evidence of ESP in their day-to-day practices. Two such individuals were Montague Ullman, then director of the Maimonides Community Mental Health Center in Brooklyn, New York, and Stanley Krippner, director of the Dream Laboratory at Maimonides. Along with Sol Feldstein they developed the method of investigating ESP in dreams that we just encountered, thus starting down a trail that would lead to the first real alternative to forced-choice ESP methods like card guessing.

The technical development that facilitated ESP dream research was the discovery by psychologist Nathaniel Kleitman that when people dream, they exhibit distinct physiological responses such as rapid eye movement (REM). By placing electrodes alongside the eyes to detect these characteristic bursts of movement and by monitoring brain-wave activity, an experimenter can detect when a sleeper starts and ends a dream. If the sleeper is awakened during or just after a REM period, he is far more likely to report a dream than if awakened at other times.

Determining when the subject is dreaming was only part of the ESP dream research. The other main component was the ESP test itself. Since one could hardly expect someone to dream his way through a deck of ESP cards, a more suitable test had to be devised. The targets had to be complex, with visual, emotional, or thematic content that could conceivably manifest itself in the dreams of the subject. The Maimonides team started with small reproductions of art prints, as in Erwin's session above, but they expanded this concept into creative alternatives, as we will see later. To make best use of the richness of the dreams and the art-print targets, the Maimonides team abandoned the guessing-game style of forced-choice testing. Instead they revived and updated an old method—the "free response" approach. As the name implies, with this method the subject responds freely, reporting whatever comes to mind in the form of images, thoughts, memories, and so on. In the dream research the subject merely recalled what he was dreaming about, no matter how strange or bizarre it might seem at the time.

Naturally the other essential elements for an ESP test were also incorporated into the procedure. The researchers randomly selected the target for each night and took steps to ensure that once the target had been selected, there was absolutely no leakage of information back to either the sleeper or the personnel in the sleep lab. To assess whether the content of the dreams matched the target, the researchers had outside judges rank each dream transcript according to its similarity to each of the pictures that had been used in the series. The judges—usually psychologists familiar with dream interpretation—did not know which picture had actually been used for any given session. If the dream transcript contained elements found in the picture, then the judges would accord it a best rank (1 being the top rank). As an example of this procedure in practice, the three judges gave Erwin's *Zapatistas* session an average rank of 1.7 (out of 12).

With this basic method the Maimonides "dream team" went on to complete dozens of screening sessions* as well as several extremely successful series with selected individuals.[3] Erwin went on to do an additional fifteen sessions, thirteen of which were scored as hits.

Dreaming About the Future

One of the most striking and dramatic features of the psychic dream is that it often appears to be about future events. Could this type of psychic dream be created in the laboratory? Flushed with their initial success with "real time" dream ESP, the Maimonides researchers attempted exactly that.

Malcolm Bessent was a young English psychic who had studied for many years under Douglas Johnson, a well-known British psychic, at the London College of Psychic Studies. Bessent's personal experiences suggested that he had a gift for precognition. Whether or not his studies had anything to do with his ability is not clear;** in either case he came to the attention of the Maimonides researchers in 1969. After a couple of sessions with the standard dream-telepathy arrangement, the team decided to test Bessent's

---

*Among the many people who participated in these screening sessions was Chester A. Carlson, the inventor of the xerography process. Carlson was a strong supporter of parapsychology research and was a financial benefactor of several laboratories, including ours.

**The question of whether or not one can learn to be psychic is hotly debated among parapsychologists. Evidence from experimental attempts to train psychic ability has been largely negative, and evaluations of several commercial methods that claim to train psychic ability have been equally unimpressive. Yet it is worth noting that another of Johnson's pupils, Alan Vaughan, also proved to be a good subject in the dream experiments, and he has continued to be a good subject in ongoing research at several labs on the West Coast. What this might show, however, is that an instructor may help individuals who already have some psychic ability to recognize and use it, but they may not be able to help those who lack psychic ability. An analogy with artistic training may be apt: Training will measurably improve those with innate artistic talent but have little effect on those without.

forte—dreaming about the future. To do this effectively, it was necessary to modify the procedure somewhat. For the precognition sessions Bessent would sleep and report his dreams as usual, but there
would be no agent and no target selected for the night. Instead the
following morning a member of the team who had had no contact
with the night's activities would use a random procedure to select a
picture target. This time, however, the picture would also indicate
the theme for a multisensory experience Bessent would undergo. To
guarantee the integrity of the data, the tape of Bessent's dream review was packed and mailed to the transcriber before the target
selection started.

Could Bessent dream about this future event? His results speak
for themselves. On one of the first nights Bessent reported, "a large
concrete building . . . a patient upstairs escaping . . . had a white
coat on, like a doctor's coat." In the third dream he noted a feeling
"of hostility toward me by people in a group I was in daily contact
with. . . . My impression was that they were doctors and medical
people."[4]

Krippner was assigned to select the target on the following morning. Using a complex randomization process, he selected Van Gogh's
Hospital Corridor at Saint-Rémy. As Bessent left the sleep room, he
was escorted down a dark corridor resounding with cackles of hysterical laughter. Staff in white coats greeted him as "Mr. Van Gogh."
Bessent was given a pill and "disinfected" with acetone on cotton
swabs while viewing slides of paintings done by mental patients.
When the judges came to rate Bessent's dream for that night, they
had no trouble assigning *Hospital Corridor* a "direct hit."*

In that series of eight sessions Bessent scored seven hits and one
miss. Clearly he was able to incorporate elements of an event that
he *was yet to experience* into his dreams. One of the most perplex-
ing of all psychic experiences now had a laboratory analogue.

The following year Bessent returned to Brooklyn for a more involved series, which achieved equally impressive results. The second

---

*Lest you think that the medical theme of this example target made it an easy one
to dream about (given that the experiment was conducted in a hospital), it should
be noted that none of Bessent's other dreams in the series mentioned hospitals or
mental patients and that the other targets included such possibilities as "parka
hood," "desk," "teaspoon," "leaves," and "elbow."

series with Bessent was designed to compare his ability to dream *precognitively* about a target with his ability to dream *normally* about a target that he had just seen. This time the targets were short slide shows, each on a specific theme, with an accompanying sound track. The target was not selected until the evening following the dream, at which time Bessent would see the slide show. That night Bessent would attempt to dream about the slide show he had just seen; this was the control condition. Thus each slide was compared against the dreams of two nights, those from the previous night (precognition) and those following the slide show (normal). In order to ensure that no bias entered into the process of monitoring Bessent's dreaming and recording his descriptions, fresh EEG technicians (who neither knew nor cared what the experiment was about) were brought in from New York University.

Although the Maimonides researchers anticipated good results, the night of September 13, 1970, surprised even them. "We looked into the sky. There was a dark blue color in the sky," was one of the comments that Bessent made after his first dream. After his second dream he again remarked about the color blue being very strong. The third dream provoked more specific comments: "It involved Bob Morris. His experiments with birds. The general reaction to him would be of his interest, I felt . . . that once the target was seen, it would explain everything. The target is of emotional interest to Bob Morris.* The color of deep blue is important. The sea or the sky."

Bessent recalled nothing of his fourth dream, but the following morning he recalled further details about all the dreams. From the first dream he recalled the dark blue colors; about the second dream he recollected, "I had an enormous sack on my back which was stuffed with letters like a mailman, and yet the sack was completely weightless . . . something important happened around water . . . Everything was blue . . . It was as if there was a blue light, almost, so that everything, although you knew it really wasn't blue, appeared to be blue."

Commenting on his third dream, Bessent said, "Bob Morris does

*This is Robert L. Morris who, at the time, was a graduate student studying animal behavior (mostly birds). In 1985 Morris was appointed Koestler Professor of Parapsychology at the University of Edinburgh, Scotland.

research on animal behavior and, more specifically, birds. . . . He's been doing various research and studies with birds and he's taken me out to see his sanctuary place where all the birds are kept. . . . I remember seeing various different kinds of doves. Ring-tailed doves, ordinary doves, Canadian geese. There were many, many different kinds of varieties. . . . I just said, 'Oh, well, you'll understand everything when you see the target. I don't have to explain it now. It's self-explanatory, so you'll have to wait a while.' "

Although during the night he remembered nothing of the fourth dream, in the morning a little more came back. "The only thing I think of is just water. Just a lake of water. Kind of greeny-blue. . . . A few ducks and things. It's fairly misty, but there are quite a lot of mandrake geese and various birds of some kind swimming around in rushes of reeds. . . . Birds . . . I just have a feeling the next target material will be about birds."[5]

On the evening of September 14 a team member who had had no contact with Bessent or the technicians randomly selected the target. That evening Bessent was treated to a bird show—slides of all sorts of birds, birds in water, birds on land, birds against the blue sky, and so forth. Along with this was a sound track of aviary noises and bird calls. As the saying goes, "He could not have done better if he had tried." And try he did that evening. The experimental protocol required that for the control condition he try to dream about birds, but nary a bird appeared in those dreams.

The Maimonides Dream Lab closed in 1978. As funding declined, the core members of the team had all moved on to other jobs, and the lab died a quiet death. By the time the researchers had finished, they had amassed an impressive record—over one dozen formal studies and several compilations of pilot and screening data, all of which was reported. In 1988 Alan Vaughan, one of the participants in the dream project, and Jessica Utts, a University of California statistician, did a statistical appraisal of the entire project. Using the Maimonides definition of a hit as a mean ranking by the judges that fell in the upper half of the possible range, Vaughan and Utts found there were a total of 233 hits in 379 trials, or an accuracy rate of 83.5 percent (where chance would be 50 percent). The odds against chance for this are better than a quarter of a million-to-one.[6] Psychic dreams—about the present and the future—had been brought into the laboratory.

The success of the Maimonides lab did not spark many imitators or successors. There were a few isolated replication attempts, but little beyond that. It may seem surprising, perhaps even suspicious, that such exciting results were not followed by many similar studies. The reason for this is depressingly prosaic: Dream laboratories are expensive to equip and run. Most parapsychologists—myself included—feel that the Maimonides team has established evidence for ESP in dreams in a dramatic way, but given the limited budgets we work with, there are more cost-effective ways of pursuing ESP, at least one of which is the successor to the dream studies.*

In addition to their impressive record of experimental successes, the Maimonides researchers had opened a door to a whole new style of ESP research, not just to a new test technique but to a new arena, ESP in states of consciousness other than the normal waking state. This newfound freedom among parapsychologists led to many innovative research programs that examined ESP in various altered states of consciousness. The most fruitful of these has been a technique developed by one member of the Maimonides lab, Charles Honorton.

ESP in the Twilight Zone: The Ganzfeld

"I hope my performance is worth all this trouble," said Anne** to experimenter Nancy Zingrone. Anne, a volunteer subject at the Institute for Parapsychology in Durham, North Carolina, made her comment as Zingrone fussed with the halved Ping-Pong balls that she was positioning over Anne's eyes. "Don't worry, you'll do fine. I'll be through in a second," replied Zingrone as she deftly secured the Ping-Pong ball halves with surgical tape.

A few minutes later Anne was stretched out in a reclining chair, listening through earphones to the sound of waves breaking upon the shore and a soothing voice leading her in relaxation exercises.

---

*Of course if funding for psi research were not a problem, I can think of several parapsychologists or laboratories, including ours, who would be eager to continue ESP dream research.
**Subjects will not be identified here unless they have already been identified in published research reports.

Her eyes were open, but she could see only a warm, pink glow caused by the red lights shining on the Ping-Pong ball halves that covered her eyes. After about fifteen minutes the relaxation exercises ended, and the voice began some new instructions. For the next thirty minutes, she was told, she should describe whatever thoughts and images came to mind. "Do not hold back anything. Just say whatever comes." Then the waves faded into a steady, not-unpleasant hiss that she had been told was "white noise."

In the control room Zingrone waited for Anne to start describing her imagery. Unfortunately Anne didn't seem to be having much imagery, or at least she was not sharing it. "Perhaps she misunderstood the instructions," Zingrone wondered to herself. Ordinarily Zingrone would be recording her subject's comments and taking detailed notes for later review with her, but not much was coming. This session was starting to look like a washout. At the end of the thirty minutes the white noise faded, and Zingrone returned to remove the headphones and the Ping-Pong balls. She sat down and asked Anne if she had had any imagery during the session.

"I didn't get a lot of images, except something going round. . . . I kept picking up something about horses," Anne remarked. "There was a road, but . . . it wasn't a gravel road, it was a pebble road, a hard-packed pebble road. . . . And, there was a very fleeting image of being inside of a car and I could see just the rearview mirror. . . . A feeling of going very rapidly, everything was like if you are in a car or train and you are going very fast." Later she commented, "Also, at one point, the feeling of being out in the country and wide open spaces. . . . I had the feeling of driving out in the country, wide open areas, countryside landscapes."

Zingrone then excused herself for a moment and retrieved an envelope from just outside the control-room door. Checking that the seals were intact, she brought it into the room with Anne and began to open it. "Now I am going to show you four pictures. One of these was the target for this session," explained Zingrone. "Let's look at them carefully and then I want you to rank them according to how much they resemble what had been going through your mind during the session."

The envelope contained a set of four pictures, and that set was one of thirty-six such sets that comprised the pool of possible targets for this series of experiments. The pictures came from various sources. Some were art prints, as in the Maimonides dream studies; others were culled from magazines of various kinds. All were selected on the basis of visual or emotional impact, and each set was constructed so that the pictures in the set were different from one another. While Anne was doing her relaxation exercises, Zingrone's co-experimenter, George Hansen, had gone to the computer and used a special program to select randomly first the set (out of thirty-six) and then the particular picture (out of four). After fetching the envelope containing the pictures, Hansen left the "judging set" by the door to the control room and then took the four individually sealed envelopes to another room in the building.* Fifteen minutes into the experiment, as Anne ceased her relaxation exercises, Hansen opened the designated envelope. For the next thirty minutes he concentrated on that picture.

As Zingrone opened the judging set, she had no idea what the target picture might be. The first picture was a painting of a Chinese nobleman in ornate dress. Next was a floral still life with an Oriental aspect. Then came a photo of rows of cars snowbound in a parking lot. The last picture was a *National Geographic* photo of countryside, possibly Kentucky or Tennessee. The photo was taken from an elevated position, and dominating the center of the scene was a curving country road with a solitary pickup truck traveling down it. "That's it," Anne said when she saw the picture, "that's what I've been seeing." And so she had. It was a direct hit.[7]

The experiment that Anne had just been in is known as an ESP-ganzfeld experiment, or simply, the *ganzfeld*. The ganzfeld is a technique whereby the subject is placed in a mild state of sensory deprivation; it had been sporadically used in perceptual psychology since the mid-thirties. The term comes from the German for "whole field," which describes what the experimenter is trying to do—create

---

*Notice that there are two sets of pictures, one for the agent and another for the subject to use in judging. Researchers quickly realized that if only one set was used for both agent and subject, it might be possible for the subject to recognize which picture had been the target by external cues such as fingerprints, temperature differences, or other traces of having been handled for the past thirty minutes. Research has shown that subjects are not likely to actually use such cues—unless they are specifically instructed to look for them—but for well over a decade all good free-response experiments have avoided this problem by using duplicate picture sets.

whole, homogeneous sensory fields with no pattern or detail to distract the subject. The halved Ping-Pong balls (which are carefully
cut to fit comfortably) reduce the subject's visual input to a uniform
pink (when red lights are shone on the subject). The hiss to which
the subject listens is unpatterned white noise that masks any other
auditory input. Having the subject relax comfortably in a reclining
chair helps minimize tactile input. The ganzfeld serves to cut the
subject off gently from outside distractions and disturbances.

Why all the trouble? you may ask. Does one really need to go to
all that fuss to observe ESP in the lab? In fact there are some very
good theoretical reasons why the ganzfeld might produce a state
especially conducive to ESP. To see what these reasons are, let us
trace this technique back to its roots in the Maimonides Dream
Laboratory.

As the dream research picked up steam, a young parapsychologist
by the name of Charles Honorton joined the group in 1973. As a
high school student he had developed a passion for parapsychological research that led him to spend several summers at Rhine's
lab in Durham, North Carolina. Eventually, however, Rhine's approach proved too restrictive for Honorton (and for many of the
parapsychologists of his generation), and he found himself more at
home with the fresh, pioneering spirit of the Maimonides lab. While
working as a research associate in the dream lab, Honorton became
keenly interested in exploring not only dreaming but also similar
states of consciousness that appeared congenial to ESP. As the
dream-lab activities began to wind down, Honorton began to search
for a technique that did not require the considerable overhead (all-
night sessions for staff and subjects, expensive EEG equipment, and
so on) that dream research entailed.

Honorton was not simply seeking economy, though. Drawing
upon his years with the dream subjects, as well as from three other
traditions about ESP, Honorton had developed very specific ideas
about what was needed to observe successful ESP in the laboratory.
Starting with the logical assumption that ESP is similar to a weak
form of our ordinary senses, Honorton reasoned that ESP might
normally occur more frequently than we recognize, but that it is
usually overwhelmed by all the stronger signals constantly besieging
us through our conventional sense organs. It seemed to Honorton
that the dream state facilitated ESP simply because it is during this

period that stimuli from the external world are markedly reduced and that the focus of attention during dreams is inward. Would it be possible to capture the elements of dreaming that are important for ESP without the actual dreams? Studies of spontaneous cases indicate that a close runner-up to dreams for ESP frequency is a state that can best be described as "almost asleep"—very relaxed, just on the verge of sleep, daydreaming, or lost in a reverie. This was the state that Honorton wanted to reproduce.

Another tradition involving apparent ESP also influenced Honorton's thinking. Eastern religions that employ meditational techniques have often included paranormal powers in the repertoire of phenomena arising from meditation. Perhaps the strongest association can be found in the Vedas—the ancient Hindu scriptures of India—in which paranormal powers, known as *siddhis*, were considered to be undesirable side effects of meditation—undesirable because of their tendency to distract the meditator from the true purpose of his or her exercises. Writing about 3,500 years ago, Patanjali, in his *Yoga Sutras*, described yoga meditation as a succession of stages in which outside distractions are reduced and attention becomes "absorbed" in a single object, which, in turn, effects a "oneness" between meditator and object. First, distractions due to emotion and desire are reduced, then bodily sensations, as the meditator seeks to isolate consciousness from the sensory signals impinging from the external world. In the stages of the meditational process—termed *Samyana*—paranormal phenomena may be produced, most commonly a feeling of clairvoyant omniscience but sometimes including physical effects such as levitation, object movements, and healing.

The final observation that struck Honorton came from writings and comments by the field's best psychics. A common theme ran through the descriptions of how they employed their gifts: the need to "still the mind," "eliminate distractions," and so forth. Often psychics engage in a sort of meditational technique to "wipe the slate of the mind clean." Mary Sinclair, wife of the novelist Upton Sinclair and apparently a very gifted subject, recommended that "you first give yourself a 'suggestion' to the effect that you will relax your mind and your body, making the body insensitive and the mind a blank." Many contemporary psychics—Malcolm Bessent, for example—routinely meditate before psi tests.

From these converging themes Honorton created a new strategy for

ESP research—the noise-reduction approach. By "noise" he meant the everyday concerns and sensory input that might drown out the weak "signal" that ESP may represent. If the subject could somehow reduce all the sensory clutter vying for attention, quiet his mind, and in a sense clear the way for weak or faint signals to reach consciousness, then we might just see a good deal more ESP in the laboratory.

It is easy to see why the ganzfeld technique seemed like such an ideal tool to enable Honorton to put his ideas into practice. It reduces outside distractions and helps the subjects to focus on inner mental processes, not unlike meditation. The relaxation exercises and use of a reclining chair*—which are not part of the ganzfeld itself—serve to reduce bodily sensations and distractions and help to clear the subject's mind of the day's cares and worries. Just how successful the ganzfeld technique is in achieving the state that Honorton is looking for depends very much on the individual subject. In most instances it at least produces a very different state of consciousness from the subject's ordinary waking state.[8]

From the example with Anne it is easy to see how the ESP-test component of the ganzfeld experiment was adapted directly from the dream experiments. Sets of possible targets had been prepared. At the appropriate time an experimenter employed a procedure to select randomly the actual target for the session. Often the targets were pictures, as in Anne's case, but Honorton was quick to explore more exciting target material in the hope of obtaining more dramatic results. Stereoscopic View-Master slide sets were used for many experiments, and lately videotape excerpts from movies and cartoons have been giving excellent results. The subject's task is to receive, by ESP, impressions of the selected target, but ganzfeld experimenters generally caution the subject not to try to "get" the picture or strain to figure out what the agent is looking at. Instead the subject is advised just to relax and effortlessly let the images flow.

As with most free-response ESP experiments, the statistical treatment that ultimately determines whether the subjects did produce imagery that was closer to the actual target than chance would allow is based on similarity ratings of the imagery to each of the possible tar-

---

*Subjects are also encouraged to remove shoes and loosen collars or other tight clothing.

gets.** Most ganzfeld experiments differ from the dream studies in that the subject does his or her own matching. This design is based on the assumption that the subject is the best person to judge just what had been going through his or her mind.*

In the more than fifteen years since Charles Honorton conducted the first ganzfeld-ESP experiment, more than fifty similar experiments have been completed in laboratories around the world. Have they all demonstrated ESP? Certainly not. Hardly any experiments that involve human psychology work every time. Nevertheless the ganzfeld-ESP experiments have had enough successes that many parapsychologists believe that this technique may be the key to the repeatable ESP experiment that has so long been sought after. In part III we shall examine some of the statistics behind the ganzfeld's claim to repeatability, but for now we shall see how that experiment is helping parapsychologists to understand the type of person who will succeed in ESP tests.

Making Sense of the Extrasensory

A lovely spring afternoon in May 1989 found Charles Honorton in his office at the Psychophysical Research Laboratories (PRL), the private research institute that he had headed since leaving Maimonides some ten years earlier. During those years his laboratory spearheaded the ganzfeld-ESP research that was now really beginning to produce results. Yet he was deeply worried, for his lab, lavishly set up (by parapsychologists' standards) by aircraft pioneer James S. McDonnell and the McDonnell Foundation, was now facing a financial crisis. After its

---

**This is usually either a ranking or a rating method (or sometimes both). In the first the subject ranks the pictures in order of similarity with rank number 1 given to the picture most similar to the subject's mentation. With ratings the subject gives each picture a numerical value (typically on a scale of 0 to 99) that represents the amount of similarity. Larger numbers indicate higher degrees of similarity.

*This assumption need not necessarily be true, however. As in dreams, ESP target material might be distorted or incorporated in some symbolic way that is not obvious to the subject. It remains an open question as to whether, say, psychoanalytically trained judges are better than the subjects themselves in seeing connections between the mentation and the targets.

founder's death some years earlier, the McDonnell Foundation had turned its attention and largesse in a different direction, and now Honorton was finding it nearly impossible to interest other funding sources in supporting a parapsychology laboratory with such high overhead. Space in Princeton's prestigious Forrestal Center research campus did not come cheaply.*

Yet none of those concerns showed when Honorton went to greet the newly arrived subject for the latest ganzfeld series. This was PRL Subject Number 332, a young actor from the renowned Juilliard School in New York City. In fact, all the subjects in the current series were from the Juilliard School. For the past few weeks a steady stream of young artists had been arriving at PRL for a special project designed by Marilyn Schlitz, a visiting researcher from the Mind Science Foundation in San Antonio, Texas. Schlitz, an anthropologist by training and a gifted subject herself, was interested in how outstandingly creative individuals would do in ganzfeld experiments.

After some coffee and a little chatting, Schlitz escorted the subject into the suite of rooms used for the ganzfeld experiments. As often happens, Subject 332 expressed some misgivings as Schlitz led the young man through the massive, vaultlike door into the soundproof room, but his experimenter assured him that there was nothing to worry about; the friendly attitude of all the people whom he had met there had already convinced the student of that. Schlitz pointed out the items that would be used later in the experiment—the TV and the computer hand controller for judging the targets—and then she set about preparing Subject 332 for the ganzfeld.

Back in his office Honorton glanced over the subject's file. "Hmmm, this one is an ENFP," he thought to himself. "And some personal psi experiences too. This guy ought to give us a pretty good session." But Honorton kept this to himself and lingered in his office working on other matters.

After Schlitz completed preparing the subject she shut the door to the soundproof chamber and joined Honorton in the experimenter's room for a final check-out. Today Honorton would be the experimenter, operating the computers and video equipment. Some years

---

*The Psychophysical Research Laboratories shut its doors at the end of September 1989.

earlier, PRL had completely automated their ganzfeld experiments, and there was not too much for the control-room experimenter to do except to start the programs and ensure that the right videocassette was in the machine. An Apple II computer would select the target, find it on the videotape, and present it to the agent.

All of the PRL targets were stored as sets of four video clips on videocassettes. Some were still pictures, others were excerpts from films, cartoons, and even advertisements. None of the clips was longer than sixty seconds. During the half-hour period in which the subject would report his imagery, the computer would show the selected target of the four clips to the agent six times. When the session was over, the computer would turn on the TV in the subject's chamber and present all four of the pictures in the selected set to the subject. Just as in the manual ganzfeld, the subject would rate each of the possible targets for similarity with his imagery, indicating his rating by using the computer hand controller to move a pointer along a scale on the screen.

Schlitz had drawn agent duty for this session, so she settled down into the comfortable chair in the agent's room. Right on schedule the TV came to life and the target flashed on the screen. Schlitz was slightly disappointed when she saw the target. It was a still—she preferred the film clips—but the picture was a venerable old veteran of the Dream Lab days, so she would give it her best. The screen showed a magazine ad for Coca-Cola that appeared some Christmas season in the 1950s. A classic Santa Claus is holding a Coke bottle in his left hand. Enough of the Santa figure shows so that three buttons of his suit are visible. Behind Santa and to the left a large bottle cap displaying the Coca-Cola logo rests against an ornamented Christmas tree. For about sixty seconds Schlitz tried her best to put herself in a thirsty, Christmassy mood, then the screen faded. There was a pause and then the picture appeared again, for a total of six showings.

In the soundproof chamber, Subject 332 was thoroughly relaxed. He began to describe the images that came to him. "There's a man with a dark beard and he's got a sharp face . . . There's another man with a beard. Now there's green and white and he's in bushes and he's sort of colonial. He looks like Robin Hood and he's wearing a hat . . . I can see him from behind. I can see his hat and he has a sack over his shoulder . . . Window ledge is looking down and there's a billboard that says 'Coca-Cola' on it . . . There's a snowman again and it's got a carrot for a nose and three black buttons coming down the front . . . There's a white beard again. There's a man with a white beard . . . there's an old man with a beard . . ."[9]

In the PRL setup, the agent listens to the subject's running commentary as a way of increasing motivation and helping the agent concentrate on the task. As Schlitz listened to the actor describe his images, she thought to herself, "This one is good, very good. Easily a direct hit."

What was it that tipped off Honorton that this was likely to be a good session, and what is an ENFP? Parapsychologists are on the verge of fulfilling one of their earliest research goals: to be able to identify those people who are likely to do well in a particular experiment. Now, that does not mean that we are able to say who has ESP and who does not. That is a different issue. But we are reaching a point where we can say with some confidence that a person with certain traits and interests stands a good chance of doing well in a specific type of ESP experiment.

This knowledge has been a long time coming. Trying to find reliable ESP performers has been a preoccupation of parapsychologists from the very start of the science, but until very recently it has been a hit-or-miss affair. Good subjects—those who could consistently score well in psi tests—always turned up from time to time, but there was little rhyme or reason to their appearance. Try as they might, parapsychologists remained unable to find sufficient common ground among these individuals to enable them to say what it was that made a good subject.

Part of the problem was that parapsychologists were not at all sure what they were supposed to be looking for in the search for good subjects. Throughout the history of the field there have been two principal interpretations of psi ability. One interpretation holds that psi ability is a relatively rare gift possessed by only a few persons—analogous perhaps to artistic ability. The other interpretation is more egalitarian, maintaining that everyone has some degree of psi ability. This latter view grew with the rise of psychology as an academic discipline and the corresponding influence it had on the design of parapsychological experiments. It also received implicit support from the fact that such a high percentage of the general population reports apparent psychic experiences.

The two interpretations lead to rather different research strategies. If a researcher feels that psi ability is rare, he simply has to
keep testing and testing, as Rhine did in the early Duke work, until
he finds a few good subjects. Conversely if the researcher feels that
most everyone has psi ability, he can either try to coax psi out of
subjects by designing clever experiments or he can try to see if psi
ability varies systematically with other, more easily identified traits
and abilities. Unfortunately just finding a few unusual subjects reveals very little about who makes a good subject and why. Experiments with "psychic stars" remain isolated events which have little
generalizability to other persons or situations, though these individuals can be important in certain kinds of research.

The bulk of ESP research in the decades following Rhine's initial
experiments was designed on the second interpretation—that pretty
much everyone has some degree of psi ability. In a typical experiment an investigator might be looking to see if, for example, believers in ESP do better than nonbelievers, and he might find that, on
the whole, believers do indeed get higher scores than nonbelievers.
Yet none of the believers may have produced individual evidence of
ESP ability, and even as a group their combined performance may
have differed from chance by only a barely significant degree. Admittedly a single such finding will not inspire much confidence in
the reality of a "believer effect." However if many studies also point,
even if only weakly, in the same direction, then our confidence may
grow. This is precisely what has been happening.

Many dozens of experiments over the decades have now made it
possible for parapsychologists to venture some cautious generaliza-
tions about the type of person who will succeed in an ESP test. Not
surprisingly parapsychologists have found that persons who believe
in the reality of ESP (called "sheep") actually do better in ESP tests.
Curiously those who do not believe in ESP (called "goats") often do
more poorly than chance would predict. If the subjects had no psi
ability, they should score around chance, not below. In about 80
percent of all "sheep-goat" experiments, the sheep score higher than
the goats—not exactly a massive effect, but a consistent one.[10]

Extraversion—the tendency to be gregarious and outgoing—has
shown an even stronger relationship with ESP performance. Considered by psychologists to be one of the most reliable and easily measured
human traits, the extraversion-introversion dimension of personality

has also been the one most studied by parapsychologists. Over sixty studies by seventeen different investigators have been published, examining whether extraverts or introverts do better in ESP tests. The verdict is that extraverts have a clear edge over introverts.[11]

However Honorton's hunch about Subject 332's performance was not based so much on the research of prior decades as it was on PRL's own work. For the past six years his staff had been systematically collecting personality information on their subjects and testing them in a uniform ESP-test environment—the autoganzfeld described above.

The personal information that the PRL researchers gathered came from two sources. One was a lengthy, PRL-designed inventory—called the Personal Information Form, or PIF—of one's history and interests as they might relate to parapsychological matters. The second source was a well-known personality-assessment test, the Myers-Briggs Type Indicator (MBTI). Based on the personality theory of Carl Gustav Jung, the MBTI constructs its dimensions of personality without any negative aspects. There are no personality types that can be construed as less desirable than others, since Jung firmly believed that mankind needs all its diverse types for a healthy society.

There are four aspects to the MBTI classification scheme. The first describes a person's general orientation to the world. Although this dimension is labeled extraversion/introversion (E/I) and embodies characteristics of the popular notion of extraversion and introversion, its definition is more specific. Extraverts are "oriented primarily toward the outer world of objects, people, and action, having a tendency to get caught up in whatever is happening around them," whereas introverts have a "more inward orientation and tend to detach themselves from the world around them."[12] The second aspect describes one's perceptual style, which can be either sensing or intuitive (S/N). Sensing types tend to feel most at home with concrete and practical matters, whereas intuitive types prefer to deal with abstractions, inferred meanings, and hidden possibilities. Decision-making style is the third aspect of the MBTI, and this can be either thinking or feeling (T/F). Thinking types excel at organizing material, weighing facts, and making true-false judgments impersonally, whereas feeling types are better at understanding the feelings of others and analyzing subjective impressions. Feeling types are usually very interested in human values and interpersonal relationships. The final aspect of the MBTI concerns the way a person deals with the outer world, which, in the MBTI scheme, can be either judging or perceiving (J/P). Judging types tend to be "organized and systematic; they live in a planned, orderly way, aiming to regulate life and control it." Perceiving types are "more curious and open-minded; they tend to go through life in a flexible, spontaneous way, aiming to understand life and adapt to it." Where each of us falls along the four dimensions, our MBTI "personality type," is usually indicated by the four-letter combination of our types (for example an ENFP is an extraverted, intuitive, feeling, perceptive type).

After only a few years of systematic data collection with the PIF and MBTI, the PRL team began to see a pattern emerging. By 1986 Honorton and his colleague Ephraim Schechter were able to publish some very interesting findings and to issue a bold challenge to other researchers.

Honorton and Schechter had identified four factors that predicted successful initial* performance in their ganzfeld experiments. The first factor was whether or not the subject had personally experienced what he or she felt were psychic events. Those who did report personal psi experiences were more likely to do well in the ganzfeld than those who did not. This first factor is a fairly obvious one, and many other researchers have reported similar findings related to other types of ESP experiments.[13]

The second factor was whether or not the subject practiced (or had ever practiced) a mental discipline, such as meditation, regular relaxation, or biofeedback exercises. Those with experience in a mental discipline did quite a bit better in the ganzfeld than those who had none. This factor certainly made sense in light of Honorton's noise-reduction theory: Persons who practice mental disciplines may have developed the ability to quiet the mind in a way that helps them be aware of ESP information, or they may be more in touch with their inner mental processes. Alternatively those who seek out such practices may simply be more interested in their own mental activity and thus are more motivated to succeed in the ganz-

*Honorton and Schechter were examining the ganzfeld performance of those participating in the ganzfeld for the first time, since they felt this is when the personality factors might have their biggest impact.

feld. This could explain why even subjects who were not currently practicing a mental discipline, but had done so at one time, also did well. Like the first factor, this second factor did not surprise parapsychology researchers.

The really new findings came from the MBTI. As expected, the extraverts (E on the E/I scale) did better than the introverts. Likewise the intuitives (N on the S/N) did better than the sensing types. The really dynamite subjects, however, were those who were both feeling (F on the T/F scale) and perceiving (P on the J/P) scale. The thirty-three subjects who were both F and P achieved an impressive 55 percent success rate (where 25 percent is expected by chance). Recall that PRL Subject 332 was an ENFP. Honorton's hunch was a pretty safe bet.

The fourth factor was not likely to be of too much practical use because it rarely occurred. That was whether or not the subject had participated in psi experiments other than in the ganzfeld: Those who had been in other experiments were more likely to succeed in the ganzfeld than those who had not. Generally this applied only to very dedicated subjects or to visiting parapsychologists. Odds are that this factor probably reflects a higher level of motivation.

Honorton and Schechter proposed a formula that would predict successful performance in the ganzfeld for first-time subjects: prior psi experiences + mental disciplines + FP on the MBTI + prior psi testing. There were only four subjects who fit this model—too few for a proper statistical assessment—but these four had a 100 percent success rate. A more practical model for other researchers was a three-factor model of prior psi experiences + mental disciplines + FP. The twenty-eight subjects who fit that picture achieved an astounding success rate of 64 percent.

Of course Honorton and Schechter recognized that these findings had to be confirmed on a new data base, so they effectively issued a challenge to other parapsychologists. Based on their data, Honorton and Schechter estimated that the true ganzfeld scoring rate for any population of three-factor subjects should lie between 43 and 87 percent. From this they calculated that it would take about thirty-six such subjects to achieve significant above-chance scoring.

Meeting the Challenge

Only one other laboratory in the world has a comparable data base of ganzfeld subjects: our lab at the Institute for Parapsychology. Some years earlier we had deliberately chosen to collect the same personal information that the PRL researchers were obtaining so that we would be in a position to confirm whatever effects the PRL team uncovered.

As you may have gleaned from the description of Anne's session, our ganzfeld experiments are not the high-tech operations that they are at PRL. Our targets are ordinary pictures—not videotapes—and we do not have a computer run the sessions. Our subjects are different too. Most of them are students from nearby Duke University, whereas PRL's subjects come from all over and have to make a greater effort to get to that lab. Thus PRL's subjects tend to be more interested in psi research. Finally our results, in terms of ganzfeld successes, are generally not as good as PRL's. So it was not without some trepidation that, in May 1989, we decided to take on PRL's challenge.

Up to that point we had not examined our ganzfeld data with the personality information, so we had no clue as to how well PRL's findings would hold up in our data. For our analysis we had personal data on 102 first-time ganzfeld subjects. The pattern that emerged from these subjects was very similar to PRL's: Mental-discipline practitioners did better than nonpractitioners; FP types did better than non-FP types; people with prior psi experiences did better than those without. We had 28 subjects who fit the three-factor model of successful ganzfeld performers. They achieved a statistically significant scoring rate of 43 percent. *The PRL model had been confirmed.*[14]

In other fields of science this would not be such a big deal. So what if one lab confirms another's findings? Isn't that the way it is supposed to happen? Yes, but in parapsychology that is not so common, and therein lies most of parapsychology's problems with the rest of the scientific community. Parapsychology has many experiments demonstrating consistent effects but relatively few in which an entirely independent experiment closely replicates specific findings of another researcher. Virtually no experiment before this ever replicated a prediction as tightly formulated as that of Honorton and Schechter. This prediction and confirmation of a relationship between ESP and specific personality factors is only a single case, but it marks the growing maturity of our science. Not long ago some parapsychologists would have despaired of ever obtaining such a result. Now we are likely to see additional relationships emerge before too long. Improved statistical tools, coupled with an awareness of the importance of large-scale data collection using a stable, subject-centered test environment, may force ESP to give up more of its secrets.

Before I leave this topic, let me clarify a source of potential misunderstanding. None of the results we have been examining addresses the issue of whether or not a given individual has psi ability or how much of it he or she might have. The PRL three-factor model does not identify certain people as *more psychic* than others. It only means that they exhibit psychic ability in the ganzfeld more readily than the rest. Quite possibly in a different test setting a different "type" of subject might excel. Similarly the consistent findings showing that extraverts do better than introverts in ESP tests does not mean that extraverts have ESP and introverts do not. It only means that extraverts are more likely to show their ability to the experimenter. That, of course, is precisely what one would expect, since introverts are far less likely to reveal anything about themselves to strangers.

Parapsychologists simply do not have any means of measuring "raw" psychic ability. It is unlikely that they will in the foreseeable future either. Everything we have learned so far indicates that psychic ability is not under conscious control. Thus how psychic ability is used by the subject probably depends very heavily on the situation in which he or she is asked to use it. An inexact analogy can be drawn with the way a novice might try to study verbal-communication ability. Were he to study verbal ability only in large social gatherings, he might erroneously conclude that only extraverts had any appreciable amount of this ability. If that novice later studied verbal ability in small groups of friends, he might be surprised to learn that introverts, too, had verbal ability. Parapsychologists have only recently graduated from the position of the novice in many of their studies. Now that they have, the pace of progress should accelerate.

Remote Viewing

Hal Puthoff—physicist, laser specialist, and senior staff scientist at SRI International—was not thinking of ESP cards or even the ganzfeld that morning in early 1974 as he got out of a car in the parking lot of the Redwood City Marina near San Francisco. Puthoff was nonetheless participating in an ESP experiment. He and colleague SRI physicist Russell Targ were in the midst of their second formal series of experiments in what they termed "remote viewing." Puthoff's job was to spend about fifteen minutes "taking in" the scenery and then return to the SRI laboratory. Back at the lab a subject was trying to describe what Puthoff was seeing.

This day the procedure had been changed slightly. Ordinarily Puthoff would leave the lab in which Targ and the subject were getting ready and go to the office of their division director. There he would receive from the director an envelope containing the target location. Once off the SRI premises, Puthoff would open the envelope and proceed to the location. The division director had been following the results of the series, however, and found them hard to believe. This time he would drive Puthoff to the location himself.

Deliberately driving in an aimless manner, following whatever traffic flow he felt like, the division director found his way to the Redwood City Marina, a small harbor for local boating enthusiasts. For fifteen minutes Puthoff gazed over the neat rows of small sailboats with their bare masts and furled sails. He stared at the marina's restaurant, a curious building with a stepped roof that gave it an Oriental appearance.

Back at SRI Targ was in an electrically shielded room with one of their special subjects, Pat Price, a former police commissioner and vice-mayor of Burbank, California. Price, who thought that his psychic gift had often helped in his police work, had heard of the SRI research and had offered to help. Usually the SRI researchers, like parapsychologists at other labs, politely turn down such offers, but Price was different. Some informal work convinced the SRI team that Price was indeed gifted.

This was trial 4. After a half hour of polite chat—to allow Puthoff to reach his destination—Targ and Price got down to business. Apart from knowing that it was within a half-hour drive, neither Price nor

Targ had any inkling of the target location. Price relaxed and closed his eyes; Targ switched on the tape recorder.

"What I'm looking at is a little boat jetty or dock along the bay. . . . Yeah, I see little boats, some motor launches, some little sailing ships, sails all furled, some with the masts stepped and others are up. Little jetty or little dock there." Price continued. "Funny thing—this flashed in—kinda looks like a Chinese or Japanese pagoda effect. It's a definite feeling of Oriental architecture that seems to be fairly adjacent to where they are." Price went on to describe other details of the marina with such uncanny accuracy that later, as they were listening to the tape, Puthoff actually wondered if Price and the division director were somehow in collusion to test his ability to detect trickery.[15]

Remote viewing is not a direct descendant of the ganzfeld experiment, but it has benefited from the refinement of basic free-response procedures that had taken place in both the ganzfeld and the dream experiments that preceded it. SRI remote viewing employed no special consciousness-modifying techniques, such as the ganzfeld or dreams, largely because the SRI researchers did not feel they were needed. From the beginning SRI researchers used selected (and generally quite gifted) subjects, so the ganzfeld, which is designed to elicit evidence of ESP from subjects who do not necessarily have a history of unusual ability, probably would not be necessary. Later researchers have tried combining remote viewing with deliberate subject-relaxation techniques—though not the full ganzfeld—but SRI's results certainly demonstrated that their subjects, at least, did not require such procedures.

The idea of remote viewing as an experiment is credited to one of parapsychology's better-known subjects, Ingo Swann, a New York artist who had been participating in psi experiments at New York labs for some time. Puthoff invited Swann to SRI for some psychokinesis experiments, but although he reportedly provided some astounding demonstrations, he soon told his SRI hosts that he found them boring. Swann had enjoyed some experiments that he had done at the American Society for Psychical Research in New York, in which he had been asked to move his viewpoint (but not his body) to a remote location and describe what he saw. The ASPR experiments, investigating out-of-body experiences, had Swann shifting his viewpoint to the next room; what Swann wanted to do now was to move his viewpoint *anywhere in the world.*

This was more than the SRI scientists had in mind, but on Swann's insistence, they tried a few pilot tests—just for fun. In the pilot studies Swann was given map coordinates for locations on the globe and then asked for a virtually instantaneous description of the locale. The results were interesting. For example, once the coordinates were latitude 64 degrees north, longitude 19 degrees west (about 20 degrees east-northeast of Mount Hekla, a famous volcano in Iceland); Swann's immediate response was "Volcano to southwest. I think I am over ocean." Not bad, but it was clear to the SRI researchers that this sort of performance could be explained by an exceptionally good knowledge of world geography.

From the pilot study the SRI scientists moved on to a more exacting test. This time scientists outside SRI would choose the coordinates, and Swann's descriptions would have to be far more specific. On Swann's first attempt he described, in considerable detail, the features of the small French-administered island of Kerguelen in the southern Indian Ocean, including the layout of buildings and what appeared to be equipment of a joint French-Soviet meteorological research installation. He even drew a passable map of the island. A little later, using coordinates supplied by a "skeptical colleague on the East Coast," Swann described (and drew) a site that he felt might be some sort of military installation. "Is this a former Nike [missile] base or something?" he asked during the session. Swann never got an answer to that specific question, but several weeks later the East Coast colleague reported that his description was correct in every detail.

We shall learn more about SRI's friends on the East Coast in a later chapter, but for now the important fact is that Swann's performance in this more rigorous experiment convinced Puthoff and his colleagues, as well as their funding sources, that a full-scale investigation into remote viewing was warranted.

A typical remote-viewing session had the essential elements of its free-response predecessors. The subject was closeted with an experimenter at the start of the experiment, and neither person had any communication with the outside world until the end of the session. (During the program the SRI researchers tried cloistering subject and experimenter in a special electrically shielded room, but this made no difference in the results.) There was no deliberate attempt to have the subject relax or enter a special state of mind, but the test room was designed to be comfortable and relaxing. After the subject and experimenter were set, the "target demarcation team"—one or more researchers and sometimes other SRI staffers—went to the director of the Information Science and Engineering Division to receive from the office safe an envelope containing the location of the target site. The target envelope was selected randomly from a pool of one hundred sites that had earlier been chosen by the director and were known only to him. Upon receiving the envelope, the demarcation team left the SRI campus by car. After they left the campus, the team opened the envelope and proceeded according to the directions to the selected site. Once there, the demarcation team spent fifteen minutes looking, wandering around, and generally taking in the sights and sounds of the spot.

Back at the lab, once the allotted thirty minutes for travel time had passed, the experimenter asked the subject to begin attempting to "view" where the team was. Often the subject would supplement his or her verbal description with sketches. Since the experimenter had no idea where the target site was, he was free to question the subject to elicit further detail. Often the experimenter had to remind the subject not to be too analytical about his or her impressions: "Just describe it—don't try to figure out what it is."

A good example of this process came from a session in which the subject was a visitor to the SRI lab, the author of *Jonathan Livingston Seagull*, Richard Bach. Early in the session Bach described seeing an airline ticket office with the counter on the right. The experimenter, Targ, prodded Bach to explain why he had this impression. Bach described a "white block about three-by-three-by-eight," which he thought was covered with white Formica. On the wall behind that "counter" was "the logo of the company. . . . It looks like a big gold fleur-de-lis." The target team was not in an airline office. They were in a very modern Methodist church. The altar was a large block of marble, with roughly the dimensions Bach gave, and behind it was a large gold cross, the "company logo," one might say.

Each impression session lasted fifteen minutes and was recorded or videotaped. At the completion of a trial the target team returned to the lab for an informal comparison of the results, and usually the subject was then taken to the site for feedback. In due course a typed transcript of the session was prepared for later judging.

For the statistical analysis of each series, the response packets containing the transcript and any drawings were given to another SRI staff member not connected with the remote-viewing research who served as an independent judge. (In some cases several judges, acting independently, were employed.) The response packets were unlabeled, of course, and presented randomly. The judge visited each site in the series and ranked all packets from best to worst match against each site. The site-packet rankings were then summed, and the resulting "sum of ranks" score could be compared with what chance would predict. For example in the first of the Bay Area experiments, with Pat Price as the subject, there were nine sessions. The sum-of-ranks scores could therefore range from 9 (all best matches) to 81 (all worst matches). The sum-of-ranks score for this session was 16 (seven direct hits) and the statistics show that the odds against chance for this result are better than 30,000-to-one.

Eventually the SRI researchers published the results of fifty-one trials with nine subjects. Most sessions used targets that were local sites, but twelve—the "technology series"—involved various pieces of lab, office, and shop equipment. A few trials were done precognitively, that is, the remote-viewing session took place some twenty minutes *before* the target was selected and about thirty-five minutes before the target team was in place. These sessions provided some of the best direct hits recorded. The combined results for the fifty-one sessions were highly significant, with astronomical odds against chance as the explanation.

As we well know, however, astronomical odds simply mean that chance is not likely to be the reason for the results. They only indicate that ESP is involved when all normal causes are eliminated. After Targ and Puthoff published the results of their first two series in the prestigious British science journal *Nature*,[16] quite a dispute broke out about whether or not the judging procedure was adequate. The transcripts that had gone to the judges were not edited at all, since the SRI scientists did not want to risk being accused of "fitting" the transcripts to the targets. What they had not anticipated (since they had not done this before) was that the subjects sometimes referred to earlier trials in their descriptions. Two psychologists,

David Marks and Richard Kammann, published a criticism of these experiments (also in *Nature*) that pointed out that if the transcripts had not been randomized before the judges saw them (that is, if the judges knew the order in which they had been done), then they could have used these cross-referencing clues to infer the correct matches.[17]

Well, it did turn out that the transcripts for the very first series (nine trials) had not been randomized, so at least for a small portion of the data there could have been a non-ESP explanation for the results. Hoping to resolve the dispute, Charles Tart, a well-known psychologist and parapsychologist at the University of California, Davis, edited out the problematic comments and gave the transcripts (randomized of course) to a new judge. The results proved to be about the same as those of the original judge.[18]

Some critics, Marks in particular, are not entirely convinced that Tart's rejudging has exonerated that first series. The fact remains, however, that the problem existed in only a small part of the SRI data. Two years after the original *Nature* paper, Targ and Puthoff published additional successful remote-viewing studies that did not have the randomization problem in the *Proceedings of the IEEE* (Institute of Electrical and Electronic Engineers).[19] Nor is it the case that successful remote viewing is confined to SRI anymore. Several laboratories, including the Princeton Engineering Anomalies Research lab at Princeton University and our own lab, have reported significant evidence of ESP using the remote-viewing approach.

Remote Vacationing

On a November morning in Detroit, parapsychologist Marilyn Schlitz was wishing she could exchange roles with her coexperimenter in this remote-viewing experiment. He was in Rome, preparing to visit some probably wonderful tourist site; she was in cold Michigan, trying to imagine what he would shortly be seeing. "I'd sure like to be vacationing there, not just remote-viewing it," she thought to herself.

As 11:00 A.M. approached, Schlitz had just arrived home from running some errands. She went directly into the sitting room and drew the curtains to darken the room. She picked up a writing pad and sat down in her favorite chair. Sinking deep into the chair, Schlitz closed her eyes and tried first to catch her breath and then to clear her mind of all distractions. In Rome it was 5:00 P.M., and her coexperimenter, German parapsychologist Elmar Gruber, was to be on location, a randomly selected place out of forty possible target sites in and around the city.

For a while not much came, just idle thoughts on the morning's irritations. Then Schlitz felt her perspective change. On her pad she noted, "Flight path? Red lights. Strong depth of field." A rather distinctive image, but not very Roman. She noted that her coexperimenter seemed detached from the scene. Later she noted, "A hole in the ground, a candle-shaped thing. Flower—maybe not real." As the fifteen-minute session drew to a close, Schlitz noted, "Outdoors. See sky dark. Windy and cold. Something shooting upward."

When the session had ended, Schlitz flipped to a fresh page and proceeded to summarize and elaborate upon her impressions:

> The impressions that I had were of outdoors and Elmar was at some type of—I don't know if institution is the right word—but some place. Not a private home or anything like that—something—a public facility. He was standing away from the main structure, although he could see it. He might have been in a parking lot or a field connected to the structure that identifies the place. I want to say an airport but that just seems too specific. There was activity and people but no one real close to Elmar.[20]

Only a few months earlier Schlitz had read Targ and Puthoff's book *Mind Reach*, and the story about how author Richard Bach had misinterpreted his impressions stuck in her mind. That is why she was reluctant to be too specific—just relate the impressions, don't interpret them. She also had a clear recollection of a drawing of an airport that was in the same book, but declined to mention that.

Schlitz made sure the date and time were on all the sheets and then placed them in the folder marked "Trial 6." She was halfway through the planned twelve consecutive daily sessions.* When the series was complete, Schlitz would make two copies of her daily reports and forward one copy to her coexperimenter and another to Hans Bender, a noted German parapsychologist, who would hold

---

*External difficulties caused Schlitz to be unable to do two of the sessions, so only ten trials were completed and evaluated.

security copies of both Schlitz's reports and the notes and target information from Gruber.

Perhaps the most frustrating part of this experiment for Schlitz was that it would be months before she would find out where Gruber had been for the session, and still longer before the complicated evaluation process was completed. Gruber had to have her transcripts translated and independently checked for accuracy, and finally edited to remove any possible clues to the order of the trials (following the Marks and Kammann criticism). This latter step was just a precaution, since Schlitz had no feedback and had no idea whether any particular trial was correct during the experiment. Finally, the experiment required five persons to serve as judges and to independently rank Schlitz's impressions against each target site.

In the end it was worth the wait. The experiment was very successful, with odds of over 200,000-to-one against chance. Six of the ten trials were direct hits (where chance predicts 2.5), including trial 6. On that day Gruber was standing on a little hill beside Rome International Airport. He was a short distance from the main structure, where he could see both the activity at the terminals and the planes taking off. The hill upon which he stood was pockmarked with holes where clandestine antiquity hunters had searched for Roman coins.

Not all the sessions provided such strikingly close matches, but several others were equally impressive. All but one of the five judges had little difficulty matching Schlitz's transcripts with the target sites.*

Schlitz and Gruber's experiment (published in the December 1980 issue of the *Journal of Parapsychology*) is one of a growing number of independent replications that confirm beyond a doubt that the dramatic initial remote-viewing experiments of the SRI researchers were not just a flash in the pan. Whatever problems may have existed in SRI's early data, the effectiveness of remote viewing as a technique for eliciting ESP evidence no longer rests on their work alone. Besides the Schlitz and Gruber study, there are several other individual replications. The Princeton Engineering Anomalies Research

---

*As an extra precaution against potential criticism, Schlitz and Gruber later conducted a complete re-judging of the transcripts with Gruber's on-site comments and observations edited out. The results remained very significant.

Laboratory at Princeton University has been amassing a substantial data base of remote-viewing trials.

Although many of the remote-viewing experiments have achieved impressive statistical results, the real promise of these experiments for many parapsychologists lies in the fact that so many subjects seem to be able to produce truly self-evident hits. Such strikingly accurate correspondences suggest there might be practical applications lurking behind this simple technique. You can be quite sure that it is not just parapsychologists who are eager to find out where this research might lead, as we shall see in chapter 10.

Random Number Generators and Precognitive Research

"How am I doing with this thing?" Otto asked after he had been sitting punching buttons for about half an hour. "We'll take a look anytime you are ready. Do you want to take a rest now?" replied the scientist sitting in the room with him. "Five more minutes, then that's enough for tonight," was Otto's answer.

"Tonight" was a spring evening in 1969. Otto's attention was focused on the shoe-box-sized aluminum device on the table in front of him. There were four colored lights in a row and four largish buttons, one below each light. On the back of the box were four counters that the experimenter had explained recorded each trial and hit in duplicate. From the rear of the button box was a thick cable running to a larger device in the corner of the room. This machine punched coded holes in a paper tape to record each button press and each light that came on.

This was not Otto's first encounter with the box or the scientist. He had been introduced to both at a meeting of the spiritualist group that he occasionally dropped in on. The scientist had explained that this was an ESP test—precognition, to be exact—and that everyone was invited to try it. Otto, who fancied himself an amateur psychic, was one of the few who gave it a try. He was quite surprised when some days later the scientist phoned to ask if he could bring the ESP tester around to his house for some more work.

"Blue this time," thought Otto, and with a little flourish he pressed the button under the blue light. *Click, click,* went the counters. *Kerchunk, kerchunk,* went the punch-tape machine. And on came the blue light. "Bingo! Got another one," exclaimed Otto. Then he pressed the red button. *Click, click, kerchunk, kerchunk,* and on came the green light. A miss.

Over the course of several months in the spring of 1969, Otto and two other volunteers *click*ed and *kerchunk*ed their way through 63,066 trials. Their task was to guess—predict, if you will—which of four lamps would light on the next button press. By chance they should get about 25 percent of the guesses correct. Their actual total was 16,458 correct, nearly 700 more than would be expected by chance. Their hit rate of just over 26 percent may not seem too spectacular until you realize that the statistical odds against this happening by chance are more than 100 million-to-one.

The scientist who conceived this experiment is Helmut Schmidt, a German-born physicist who, at the time, was senior research scientist at the Boeing Scientific Research Laboratories in Seattle, Washington. This modest experiment, which he undertook without much fanfare, though with Boeing's official support, marked the beginning of a second revolution in ESP research and the beginning of the contemporary period for forced-choice guessing, the method pioneered by J. B. Rhine at Duke nearly forty years earlier.

Schmidt's revolution was not as profound as the rise of free-response testing that followed the Maimonides experiments. The Maimonides work broke away from the traditional ESP testing framework that had dominated the field for decades, whereas Schmidt stayed firmly within it. What he brought to the traditional approach, however, was a level of automated experimental control and sophistication that rapidly became the standard by which forced-choice research would be measured. As we shall see in the next chapter, Schmidt had a truly revolutionary impact on psychokinesis research—comparable to the free-response revolution in ESP research—but in his early ESP experiments he elegantly set the standard for the automated (and eventually computerized) experiments to come.

Because of the amount of drudgery associated with forced-choice research—recording, scoring, double-checking, and so forth—parapsychologists had begun attempting to automate research very early. In the attic above my office are the remains of several ingenious gadgets from the early days, and archive photos testify to other noble efforts. Despite these efforts, effective automation of ESP research had to wait until the technology was easily accessible.

In the early sixties researchers in the U.S. Air Force were the first truly to automate ESP research. They constructed an electromechanical device called VERITAC that automatically generated the targets (digits 0 through 9), recorded the subjects' responses, and calculated the results. The only reported work with VERITAC involved a modest number of subjects, and the Air Force researchers did not obtain any evidence of ESP. Apart from its automation, it would have been a pretty unremarkable piece of research were it not for the fact that one of parapsychology's severest critics, C.E.M. Hansel, had singled it out for high praise in his 1966 book *ESP: A Scientific Evaluation.* Hansel called VERITAC "an acceptable model for future research."[21] This judgment may have had more to do with the fact that it did not produce evidence of ESP than with the general quality of the research. Hansel's praise notwithstanding, the Air Force experiments were hardly a model of careful ESP experimentation, but parapsychologists realized that a methodological gauntlet had been cast down. In the future the best research would have to be automated.

What Hansel did not want to see—a carefully automated ESP experiment that *did* produce impressive results—came only three years later, when Schmidt published the results of his first experiments in 1969.[22]

At one level Schmidt's research was simply a progressive step in the automation of ESP research. His test device automatically chose the target, registered the subject's guess, recorded the trials and hits on counters, and stored the entire sequence of targets and guesses on punched paper tapes. No chance of human recording errors here!

At the next level Schmidt's machine broke new ground for experimental security, that is, it reduced the opportunities for the subject to cheat. The machine had dual sets of counters: one pair could be reset to zero at the start of a run, and the other pair was nonresettable, counting every trial and hit. The tape-punch recorder was connected to the tester by a heavy, shielded cable, and recorded every target and guess. Finally the electronics in the device absolutely precluded more than one guess being registered at any time.

Schmidt's most important innovation, however, was in the way that the targets were generated. To "shuffle" the targets in his ESP tester, Schmidt made use of one of nature's most elementary chance processes, the decay of radioactive atoms. Specifically, Schmidt used a small sample of the isotope strontium 90, fixed so that a Geiger tube would register the irregular arrivals of electrons from the decaying atoms. It is easy to measure the average number of electrons arriving at the Geiger tube over a given period of time, but according to the laws of physics, *it is impossible to predict the exact moment that an atom will decay and throw out an electron.* It was these unpredictable electrons that Schmidt's subjects were, in essence, predicting.

How this all worked is best seen in Schmidt's precognition test device known as the four-button machine—the one Otto was contending with at the start of this section. (Over the years Schmidt has created ESP testing devices in various designs; most are based on similar principles.) This machine has four colored lamps in a row and a corresponding response button for each. The subject's task is to "guess" or predict which lamp will come on by pressing the button below the lamp of his choice. Inside the machine is a high-speed counter that steps through the numbers 1, 2, 3, 4, 1, 2, 3, 4, . . . at the rate of one million steps per second. When the subject presses a button, a circuit is enabled so that the *next electron* that hits the Geiger tube will stop the high-speed counter. That, in turn, causes the corresponding lamp to light. Since the electrons in this machine arrive approximately ten per second, there might be a barely perceptible delay between the button press and the lamp lighting, but even in that fraction of a second the counter will have cycled through all the lamp positions several thousand times.

It is important to understand that the act of pressing the button simply registers the subject's prediction and starts the sequence that permits the next electron to stop the counter. It is the *random timing of the electron's arrival* that selects which lamp will light. This use of a process that is, by the best understanding of quantum physics, completely random, became the hallmark of Schmidt's research. In later designs the radioactive source was replaced by an electronic component, usually one or more Zener* diodes. These diodes pro-

---

*This is not the same Zener who helped Rhine design the ESP cards. The reappearance of this name in parapsychology is pure coincidence.

duce random electronic noise in the form of sharp voltage spikes that rise above some preset threshold in a random way, analogous to the arrival of an electron on the Geiger tube. Schmidt has published the designs of his devices, and many other researchers have duplicated or developed similar devices for their research. Collectively these are generally called random-number generators (RNGs), though some researchers prefer the term random-event generators (REGs).*

Today parapsychologists use RNGs in dozens of different types of experiments. RNGs have been constructed in forms ranging from a two-choice "electronic coin-flipper" to an eight-bit (0 to 255) RNG-on-a-board that plugs into a microcomputer. All of this began because Boeing Industries was in a bit of a slump and one of their physicists had a deep interest in psychic phenomena!

In Schmidt's next experiment he tried to see if his subjects could control their ESP. In this study the subjects selected in advance whether they were going to aim for a high score (by guessing the lamps correctly) or a low score (by avoiding the lamp that would come on). For the second experiment Schmidt decided upon a total run of 20,000 trials and, as before, subjects could break this up into manageable sessions. One subject did 5,000 trials in the "low-aim" condition, another did 5,000 in the "high-aim" condition, and a third did 10,000 split roughly equally between the two conditions. Once again, Schmidt's subjects were able to hit (or miss) the lights just a little better than chance. The combined high-score trials yielded a scoring rate of nearly 27 percent, while the low-score trials came in at under 23 percent. Again, not large percentages, but the odds against this result happening by chance are *better than one-billion-to-one.*[23]

---

*It is important to note that these random-number generators are *not* the same as those commonly found on computers. Computer random numbers are derived from a mathematical calculation, whereas Schmidt's random numbers are based upon true quantum mechanical processes (electron tunneling effects in the case of Zener diodes). In psychokinesis research parapsychologists always use true RNGs, but in ESP research, good-quality computer algorithms are sometimes used. Normally parapsychologists are quite explicit in describing the type of RNG used in an experiment, but for the layperson this distinction may get blurred, especially since today it is very common for a researcher to connect a true RNG device directly to a computer.

This evidence for precognition—knowing which lamp will come on a fraction of a second in the future with an accuracy of about 2 percentage points greater than chance—seems light-years away from the real-life cases that we looked at in chapter 3. It is hard to believe that getting a few "extra" correct guesses is the same process as dreaming of an airplane crashing into a particular house across the river. Schmidt's experiments, however, demonstrate precognition in the way that scientists like to see phenomena demonstrated—in quantifiable terms with impeccable, repeatable methodology.

It is precisely those quantifiable terms that leave little room for doubt that *something* is happening. Combining the two experiments gives truly astronomical odds against chance as the explanation. If one does not want to accept the parapsychological explanation, then the only alternative is to look for some defect in the methodology. But even there, Schmidt covered his bases extremely well. With parallel sets of counters (one set of the nonresettable type), electrical interlocks against multiple guesses, and a separate punch-tape recorder, the system was virtually fraudproof. Schmidt was present for all but a couple of sessions. The equipment ruled out recording errors and it produced perfectly random numbers that could be checked in various ways. Years later University of Oregon psychologist Ray Hyman, a staunch critic of parapsychological research, remarked, "By almost any standard, Schmidt's work is the most challenging ever to confront critics such as myself. His approach makes many of the earlier criticisms of parapsychological research obsolete."

There remained yet another question nagging at Schmidt: Is it possible that the subjects are somehow using psychokinesis to *cause* the lights to match the button presses? In other words, perhaps what they are demonstrating is not ESP at all but PK. To answer that question definitively, Schmidt conducted a third experiment. This time the targets would not come from the Geiger-counter RNG but from a punched paper tape containing a large supply of random numbers compiled from a commercially available table. When the subject pressed the button to select one light, a tape reader in another room advanced and read the next punched hole. There was no possibility that a subject could use PK to influence the results in this experiment; only clairvoyance of the punched-tape targets was being tested.

Following the procedure of the second experiment, six subjects contributed a total of 15,000 high- and low-aim trials. The result was 260 more hits than chance expectation—yet another highly significant (250,000-to-one) finding. Since the scoring rates were nearly the same across all three experiments, it seems safe to say there was no appreciable difference between the precognition (and possibly PK) experiments and the clairvoyance experiment.

Having satisfied himself that ESP was indeed possible with his atomic-RNG machine, Schmidt went on to revolutionize PK research, as we shall see in the next chapter. In ESP research other parapsychologists were quick to follow his lead, especially since Schmidt had published the designs of his test machines and even constructed several for other laboratories. One of the first labs to have an automated precognition tester was the Maimonides Dream Lab. They did not use it in the dream research, but their precognitive dreamer, Malcolm Bessent, scored a significant number of hits in a separate experiment comprising over 15,000 binary (two-choice) trials.[24]

In the ensuing years the trend toward automated ESP research blended nicely with the rise of the microcomputer. Parapsychologists eagerly combined Schmidt-type RNGs with these tiny computers to produce experiments that were not only exceptionally well controlled—better than anything Hansel could have imagined in the mid-sixties—but also fun to do. Among the leading labs in this respect we find—once again—Honorton's Psychophysical Research Laboratories in Princeton, New Jersey. In the early eighties this lab developed a hardware and software package called Psilab—a parapsychology laboratory in a box. The box was the then-popular Apple II computer with a specially designed RNG built right in. Along with this came several programs that permit an experimenter to conduct and analyze both PK and ESP experiments that are methodologically unassailable.

Return of the Dreamer

"ESPerciser is an ESP feedback trainer. Your goal is to identify which of four images has been selected as the target for each trial." So ran the instructions on the computer screen. Things had certainly changed a lot since the last time he'd been in an ESP experiment, the subject thought, but that was nearly two decades ago. "Today's date?" asked the computer. "July 14, 1987," typed the experimenter. "Subject's name?" The experimenter's practiced fingers replied, "Malcolm Bessent."

The experimenter left the room, and in a few moments the computer screen displayed what looked like four empty windows in a bright blue panel. The word *ESPerciser* was displayed prominently at the top; the instruction "Press button when ready" was at the bottom. This display marked the beginning of the "impression period," during which Bessent was free to see if any psychic impressions came to mind. However, he was eager to see what his choices would be for this trial, so he pressed the button. With that a different picture filled each window—a cartoon pig, a knee, a queen, and a bee. "I love your pictures, Chuck," Bessent shouted (with more than a hint of playful sarcasm) to the experimenter who was outside the room. On the previous trial the pictures had been the familiar ESP symbols against a purple background. For some reason the bee felt like it was the right choice. Bessent adjusted the knob on the hand controller until the arrow pointed to the bee; he pressed the button. "HIT!" flashed the screen as the computer beeped enthusiastically.

After an absence of eighteen years, Malcolm Bessent was back at ESP testing. After his work with the Maimonides lab Bessent returned to England, where he established himself as a successful businessman. Often he found that his psychic abilities helped him in his business, but he never participated in any further ESP research. When a business trip in July 1987 brought him to New York City, he took the opportunity to phone his old friend and experimenter, Charles Honorton. When Honorton casually inquired why he had not done any more ESP experiments, Bessent's reply was simple: "No one ever asked me."

Honorton remedied that oversight on the spot with an invitation to spend a few days at PRL. The years of development work on the Psilab system came in handy at a time like this, since Honorton knew that he could do a top-quality experiment practically at a moment's notice. ESPerciser, one of the Psilab modules, is a classic forced-choice ESP test with a new twist; it incorporates some of the advantages of free-response testing by using a wide range of different "card decks" throughout the experiment. On one turn the targets might be the traditional ESP symbols, on the next it might be a selection of freehand drawings, abstract symbols, or even words in different typefaces. Subjects can either rely on visual imagery, as in a free-response experiment, or just take a guess, as in a forced-choice test. ESPerciser was a perfect experiment for Bessent because it can run either in a clairvoyance mode, where the target is already selected by the computer before the subject guesses, or in a precognition mode, in which the target is not selected until after the subject registers his guess. The program switches between the two conditions without the subject being able to tell the difference. In this way not only could Honorton see if Bessent still had the knack, but he could compare Bessent's precognitive ability with his clairvoyant ability.

Bessent was in Princeton only four days, but true to his record of generous service to parapsychological research, he spent a good deal of that time in front of the ESPerciser screen. Honorton had arranged for two test series of five hundred trials each, and Bessent completed both, even though the second was completed in a single marathon session on his last day. Bessent's 280 hits (where 250 was expected by chance) were statistically significant with odds against chance of about 100-to-one. With a scoring rate of 28 percent, Bessent's performance was very similar to that of Schmidt's subjects working on the four-button machine.

Was his precognition better than his clairvoyance? Before the experiment Bessent felt that he would do equally well in both conditions, but the data proved otherwise. In a total of 490 precognitive trials Bessent averaged over 30 percent (significant at odds better than 250-to-one), whereas in the 510 clairvoyance trials he averaged only 26 percent.[25]

As experiments go, Bessent's four-day fling was not an earthshaking affair, but it does have an importance beyond its modest statistics. It confirmed that one individual's psychic abilities could stretch over nearly twenty years and across several very different types of experiments. Is that a big deal? Actually it is, because many critics of parapsychology would like to believe that the so-called psychic stars that appear in the research literature are at best merely statistical flukes who quickly regress to the mean, or at worst simple cheats who master a narrow range of skills that enable them to fool the experimenters over and over again. Bessent's latest performance shows that, at least for some persons, psychic ability demonstrable in the laboratory is stable over time and generalizable to different situations.

Emotional ESP

On an early summer morning in 1988 a group of about a half dozen individuals were gathering in the office of our institute's director, Dr. K. R. Rao. He was overseas at the time, and the group had commandeered his office because its sunny aspect and soft furnishings suited the little experiment that was underway. The group was equally balanced between men and women and ranged in age from mid-twenties to late forties. All of them had training in parapsychology and psychotherapy or clinical psychology.

Light banter and greetings filled the air as the group assembled. They arranged themselves in a circle and, as the last person arrived, almost automatically quieted down. Soon they were talking about deeper topics. Long silences were punctuated by earnest bursts of conversation, often clearly laden with strong emotions.

To the casual observer this meeting would look like a group-therapy session, but with no obvious leader. Indeed in a sense it is a therapy group, but therapy is not the primary goal—it is actually an ESP experiment, and it is not supposed to have a leader.

On this particular morning the discussion has centered on two men, who begin to recall fragments of their once-very-close friendship that had cooled over the years. They discuss at length some of the close times they shared. Eventually they reveal some of the issues that had come to divide them over the years. Others in the group share their thoughts and feelings and support the two men as they tentatively reach out to each other. As the session draws to a close, it becomes clear that the two are about to start a new chapter in their lives. A sense of relief and a feeling of having accomplished something very important pervades the group.

All in all, this would have been a successful group-therapy session, but this group wasn't finished. Shortly after the group had assembled for this session, John Palmer, a member of our senior staff, went to the computer and used the random-number-generating program to select two numbers, one to identify an envelope and the other to indicate one of four pictures in that envelope. Then he pulled the appropriate envelope from a pile in his office and set it on a desk next to the director's office. One of those pictures was the ESP target for the group session. If all went well, their discussions would incorporate sufficient elements of the picture to enable them to identify it.

Now, as the session winds down, one person leaves the room briefly and returns with the envelope. He opens it and lays out the pictures. Immediately one of the two older men exclaims, "Damn! That one looks like Mayola's Chili House!" Unknown to all but one other member of the group, Mayola's was a beer hall and café—long gone from the local scene—in which the two older men had shared many of the significant experiences they had been recalling. The picture was a black-and-white photograph of a highway diner with rather grim-faced patrons sitting on stools at a counter. The other pictures in the set are of a gentleman's midsection cloaked in a shiny vest and displaying a rabbit's foot; a colorful, vividly patterned wingback chair; and a row of American Indian adobe houses. The group discusses the pictures, paricularly how they might relate to elements of the morning's discussions. Then they each rank the pictures from their first to last choice as the target picture. Today there is universal agreement as to which is the most significant picture. Then the group each rates (on a scale of 1-to-5) the level of emotional depth and intensity and group involvement for the day's session. With an average rating of 3.9, this is clearly one of the more intense sessions.

Nearly ninety minutes after they had first gathered, the group troops down to the library, late (as usual) for the regular Thursday research meeting. Jim Carpenter, one of the group, is toting up the group's target rankings. "What was the number, John?" he asks. "Three! It has to be three," interjects another member. "Three it is," says John matter-of-factly. The diner photo was the target.

Over the past couple of years something like this little scene has been reenacted well over forty times. Of course not all sessions are quite so therapeutic, and not all result in ESP hits, but they are uncovering some interesting hints about the relationship between ESP and our deeper, emotional selves. The project is the brainchild of James Carpenter, a clinical psychologist and longtime associate of our institute.

Carpenter's years of work as a psychotherapist had reinforced for him observations that psychiatrists and psychotherapists have been making for decades: The process of uncovering and resolving deep emotional tensions is a rich source of striking anecdotal evidence of ESP. Numerous psychotherapists who are willing to entertain the possibility of ESP (the majority are not) have reported instances where they had sudden, therapeutically valuable insights that they felt sure could only have come through ESP. In other cases they report that the patient somehow described personal (and sometimes very private) details about *the therapist*, often without even realizing what they were talking about. Although many respected analysts and therapists have noted these instances and have urged parapsychologists to pay more attention to them, there have always been great difficulties in bridging the gap between the therapist's couch and the researcher's laboratory. The closest parapsychologists had come to bridging this gap is to use dreams as a vehicle for ESP, as we saw in the Maimonides dream studies. This was, in part, due to psychiatrist Montague Ullman's experiences in seeing ESP arising in the dreams of his clients.

Since those pioneering days the dream work evolved into the ganzfeld technique, and the use of the free-response method of eliciting ESP from subjects has grown to be a major part of psi research. Without realizing it, parapsychologists have to a certain degree recreated the psychoanalyst's couch in the lab. Not only are subjects practically reclining (in ganzfeld experiments at least), but they are expected to more or less "free-associate" their images in the hope of picking up impressions of the target. Yet the parapsychologist's laboratory is not the psychotherapist's office, and the researcher's goals are very different from the therapist's.

Among those parapsychologists using the ganzfeld technique it is no secret that better ESP results seem to come from the labs and the researchers who are able to provide a warm, supportive, and caring atmosphere for their subjects. There are no statistics to back up this observation, yet it is a pervasive bit of lab lore that probably has more than a grain of truth behind it. It was also an important clue for Carpenter, one that eventually led to a fresh perspective on the nature of the free-response type of ESP experiment.

For Carpenter the patient's attempt to gain personal insight and understanding in psychotherapy and the subject's attempt to uncover the hidden ESP target were strikingly similar. Information about the ESP target may well be in the subject's unconscious, but how can one dredge it up and recognize it for what it is? Those are the same tasks facing the therapy patient with regard to deep emotional wounds or other problems. What is more, it may be naive of the researcher to expect the subject's impression of the ESP target to be a straightforward graphic reproduction of the original. More likely it will be transformed and given new, personal meaning by the subject. A picture of a diner may become an old chili house, laden with poignant memories and the sadness of a cooled friendship. Perhaps, speculated Carpenter, free-response ESP sessions are really mini therapy sessions, and the best ESP results come from sessions that are most like very good therapy sessions.

The obvious way to explore these issues was to merge the therapy session with the free-response experiment, and that is what Carpenter is trying to do. With such a novel approach, however, a certain amount of "feeling one's way" is needed. Carpenter started with several members of our staff and a few of the participants in our 1987 Summer Study Program. Not all members of the group were clinically experienced, and the first few sessions were awkward. Under Carpenter's guidance a "method" gradually evolved among the group that facilitated the in-depth discussion of feelings and emotions while retaining an awareness that any part of the group meeting might bear on the ESP target.

The pilot experiment ran for twelve sessions. As it progressed, technical details were ironed out, and a number of very striking hits left the group with a feeling that there was real promise in the technique. For example in one of the later sessions, two of the group dominated the conversation. One talked about her vivid images of brightly painted red fingernails, and she did some role-playing on that theme. The second person saw himself as a tree, with roots planted in the center of the group and his arms and fingers stretching toward people all over the world. When the time came to decide which of the four pictures was the ESP target, all agreed on a picture of a bright red telephone with advertising copy touting the connections among people around the world. It was the target. In the pilot series about half of the trials produced direct hits (where one-quarter is expected by chance), but the group did not need statistics to encourage them to continue.

Carpenter and his group then embarked on their first formal study. Twenty sessions were planned using the same group technique. This time, however, both the therapeutic quality of the sessions and the ESP results seemed more variable. By session 8 the group had the feeling that the better sessions therapeutically were also producing better ESP results. To assess this impression scientifically, they began to rate the "quality" of the session before leaving the room to discover the target. In their rating scheme higher numbers reflected sessions of greater intensity, spontaneity, risk, and depth. The overall results for the twenty sessions were disappointing—the results were exactly at chance. However, when they grouped the results by the session-quality ratings, something interesting emerged. The sessions that earned high ratings (reflecting greater intensity and depth) produced six binary hits (rank 1 or 2) and one miss (rank 3 or 4). Sessions earning low ratings produced one hit and six misses. This relationship between session quality and ESP success was statistically significant.

A second formal series was started in mid-1988. Again, twenty sessions were planned, but Carpenter was no longer expecting overall evidence of ESP. He predicted that the better-quality sessions would show ESP while the poorer sessions would not. Among the early hits of this series was the session that I described at the beginning of this section. Altogether this series produced twelve hits and eight misses, but more importantly, the results confirmed the relationship between session quality and ESP scores. Excluding four sessions in which the ratings fell exactly in the middle of the range, the higher-quality sessions produced seven hits and one miss, whereas the poorer-quality sessions produced two hits and six misses. Again the results were statistically significant.[26]

As I write this, a third formal series is under way. Sessions are still on Thursdays (but after the research meeting now) and they have moved to Carpenter's nearby clinical offices (though the targets are still selected at our lab). Today's session produced a striking hit, as did last week's, but it is too early to say how the series is going. It is clear, however, that Carpenter (and his colleagues, for it is truly a group effort) are blazing an important new trail in the search for understanding how ESP may function in our emotional lives.

Precognition by Any Other Name . . .

Ed May stared silently at the line and the graphs on the computer screen. Every few seconds he would strike one of the keys, and a fresh line would zigzag its way across the screen and the graphs would change. These days May was spending a lot of time staring at computer screens, but most of the time he was staring at reports and spreadsheets in his capacity as director of the parapsychology research program at Stanford Research Institute. (Yes, the same organization that did the remote viewing.) It is no small job running parapsychology's only multimillion-dollar research contract.

At the moment, however, he was wearing a different hat. May, a senior staff scientist at SRI, was acting as his own subject in an experiment that he had designed with Dean Radin, a human-factors psychologist on loan to SRI from AT&T Bell Laboratories. The screen that he stared at was not flashy and colorful like the ESP tests used by labs that rely on subjects from the general public. The screen on his ESP test conveyed just the essential information to tell him how he was performing. In recent years SRI has been drawing its subjects from among its own scientists and other staff so that they keep their displays utilitarian, the way scientists like it. Besides, this was not really an ESP test either; it was a test of "intuitive data sorting."

May and Radin were working on a problem that traces its roots back to Schmidt's first three experiments. As we saw, Schmidt recognized that the precognition experiments with his atomic RNG could also be testing psychokinesis—the subject may have been causing a particular light to come on rather than predicting which one would come on. There are now hundreds of PK experiments in which subjects *try* to make the lights come on in a certain way. These comprise a massive data base showing unequivocally that something other than chance is operating. Is it PK? That is what many parapsychologists would say, but May and Radin are trying to turn the tables on them. Instead of arguing that precognition experiments with RNGs might really be PK, May and Radin are gathering evidence to show that PK experiments with RNGs are really precognition. The mathematics behind their argument derive from information theory and are too complicated to go into here, but their essential point is that the subjects in PK experiments are not *affecting* the RNG by PK. They are using precognition to know when to start the series of trials to take advantage of momentary short-term biases that are normal in RNGs.

The experiment May was engaged in is a prototype of what he and Radin think might be happening in RNG-PK experiments. Each time May hit the key, he initiated a "run" of a certain number of individual binary (two-choice) trials. May's task was to accumulate as many 1s as possible out of a random string of 0s and 1s. The moving line and the graphs on the screen told him how successful he was on each run. Superficially this experiment looks like many PK experiments in which the experimenter asks the subject to *make* the RNG produce more 1s than 0s, but in this case PK is impossible. Why?

PK was impossible in this experiment for the same reason it was not possible in Schmidt's third experiment. The random numbers are not *truly random* but instead came from a source of *pseudorandom* numbers. The SRI experiments used a pseudorandom-number generator (PRNG) of the type commonly used by computer scientists for modeling situations that require a certain amount of unpredictable behavior. A PRNG works by using a *seed number* in a mathematical formula and calculating from that an indefinitely long sequence of random numbers. While these sequences will appear to be random for most practical purposes, they differ from Schmidt's atomic RNG in an important way: They do not come from a true random (for example, subatomic decay) process. The PRNG sequences are completely determined by the seed number and the mathematical formula. If you give the PRNG the same seed number a second time, you will get precisely the same sequence of random numbers.

Since the PRNG sequences depend on the starting seed numbers, the crucial part of the experiment lies in the way these seed numbers are selected. The experiment was programmed to take a number derived from the computer's internal clock at the moment the key was pressed and use this to generate the fixed length of binary random numbers that comprised one trial. The computer clock ticked at the rate of fifty times a second, and the program was set up to have ten thousand different seed numbers. In the same way that sometimes one will get eight heads in ten coin-flips, just by chance, some of those seed numbers would produce strings with more hits than others. To succeed in the test, the subject had to press the key at the right moment to "grab" a good seed number as they flew by with the ticks of the clock.

The Radin-May experiment involved prediction within a very tight window—20 milliseconds, to be precise. In fact for the average person reaction time is typically several times greater than the "window of opportunity" in the Radin-May experiment. Thus, even if the subject were told that a "good" seed number was coming, he would not be able to press the button fast enough to catch it. The idea that a person could predict when to initiate the muscular movements that will result in a key press at precisely the right 20-millisecond moment seems absolutely mind-boggling. Yet that is exactly what the SRI experiment demonstrated. Both May and the other SRI subject were able to predict the right moment to hit the key so that they could get the "better" sequences. In the terminology coined by the SRI researchers, the subjects used intuitive data sorting to sort the good sequences (those with more 1s) from the rest. To the rest of us that looks like precognition.

The control tests that Radin and May conducted were just as important as the subjects' performance. These tests verified that the available seed numbers produced a properly random distribution of scores, and that seed numbers and the PRNG sequences had not been affected by PK. The most interesting control test, however, was one that asked, What if the subject had pressed the key one clock tick (20 milliseconds) before or after he or she actually did? In fact they examined that "what if?" possibility for five clock ticks before and after the key press. *Only key presses at the precise moment chosen by the subject yielded significant scores.* Radin and May not only demonstrated precognition but also that it could be effective within a 20-millisecond window.[27]

Slow But Steady Progress

In most sciences, for every flashy, headline-grabbing experiment there are many, many studies that more prosaically lay the groundwork and later replicate and confirm the findings. In this respect parapsychology is no different from its fellow sciences. Throughout the period that I have been considering as contemporary ESP research, there have been far more experiments than the few that we have looked at in this chapter. For every one on which we have focused there have been dozens of similar experiments that have not been as ground-breaking nor have used such interesting personalities as these. Not every one has obtained significant positive results, but many have. Quite frankly not all have been as well-conducted as these, but most of them meet the exacting standards that publication in the professional journals of parapsychology requires.

We have seen free-response research move from a creative reemergence in parapsychology through the dream-ESP research to arrive at its present place as the cornerstone of one of parapsychology's most robust experimental techniques, the ganzfeld. We have seen the ganzfeld experiment win grudging acceptance from some of parapsychology's toughest critics—even if only to the point that they agree that *something* is happening. We have also seen the free-response approach adopted by researchers who are pushing to develop practical applications of psi ability in the form of remote viewing.

The preferred method of the pioneers of parapsychology—forced choice—continues to be a mainstay for parapsychologists, particularly for investigators of precognition. Technological advances and the experimental ingenuity of scientists such as Helmut Schmidt have virtually removed this line of research from debates about the "methodological quality" of the research, and increasingly critics are left with nothing to criticize.

Is the breakthrough in understanding ESP just around the corner? Probably not. A century of research has taught us that those elusive human abilities that we now label psychic will not favor us with breakthroughs. At best we can hope for a gradual increase in our understanding of the mind's mysteries, born of patient and meticulous experimentation. The past two decades have certainly fulfilled that hope, and I have no doubt that the next decades will continue to do so.

CHAPTER 6

Contemporary
Psychokinesis Research

On a Friday evening in October 1970 Gaither Pratt and his associate, Champe Ransom, waited nervously in their Leningrad hotel room. Pratt and Ransom were experiencing the anxious anticipation that comes with the possibility of seeing a miracle but not quite knowing if it will take place. Pratt, a longtime associate of J. B. Rhine at Duke University and then a member of the Division of Parapsychology at the University of Virginia, Charlottesville, had seen his share of miracles—and had his share of disappointments—in his long career in parapsychology. He and Ransom had just completed some strikingly successful card-guessing experiments with a gifted subject, Pavel Stepanek, in Prague, Czechoslovakia, but what they eagerly awaited in their hotel room could be psychic effects of a different order entirely.

At the appointed hour there was a knock at the door; Pratt welcomed the visitors: Dr. Genady Sergeyev, a physiologist and mathematician with the A. A. Uktomskii Physiological Institute and his colleague, Mr. Konstantin Ivanenko, a mathematician and computer expert. With them was an attractive, middle-aged woman by the name of Nina Kulagina and her husband, a marine engineer. Sergeyev, who had been studying Kulagina for several years, had arranged this meeting at short notice on Pratt's be-half.

Kulagina was already known to Western parapsychologists for her claimed ability to move small objects by psychokinesis, but few parapsychologists outside Russia had had the opportunity to ob-serve her. After exchanging the usual social pleasantries, Kulagina got down to the business at hand. Pratt and Ransom had brought a small box of wooden matches and a compass in a plastic case, which Sergeyev placed on a table in front of the seated Kulagina. "She will need a few minutes to get in the right mood," Sergeyev explained and he suggested that the group step outside. As the group chatted outside the room, Pratt watched through the open door. Kulagina stretched her hands out toward the objects on the table and appeared to concentrate very hard. As Pratt watched, the matchbox suddenly moved several inches toward Kulagina while she remained still. Rather matter-of-factly, Kulagina replaced the matchbox in the center of the table and resumed concentration. Again the matchbox moved toward her. In Russian Kulagina an-nounced to Sergeyev that she was ready.

Sergeyev and Ivanenko were interested in seeing if Kulagina could affect a roll of Polaroid film that Pratt had brought. In their lab the Soviet scientists had observed that while making objects move, Kulagina caused exposurelike effects on sealed photographic film. Moved objects actually left distinct traces across the sealed film. For the Soviets the luxury of instant developing that Pratt's Polaroid film afforded led them to focus on this feature for the demonstration. Ransom set up the roll of film as a bridge between a small block of wood and the target object, a small cylinder of nonmagnetic mate-rial. With the intention of affecting only the film, Kulagina began concentrating, but as Pratt and Ransom watched, the cylinder moved slowly under the film.

When they put the film in the camera and developed the prints, there were no unusual exposures, but that seemed of little consequence com-pared with what they were observing. Pratt asked Kulagina for one further demonstration that he could film with his home movie camera. As Pratt set up the camera, Ransom spread a patch of aquarium gravel in the center of the table, placed the nonmagnetic cylinder upright in the midst of the gravel, and inverted a tall glass over it. Kulagina con-centrated, Pratt filmed, and within moments the cylinder began tracing a path through the gravel. When the perimeter of the glass seemed to restrict the cylinder's movement, Ransom lifted it and Kulagina again concentrated. Again the upright cylinder plowed a path through the gravel as the camera rolled.

That evening Pratt and Ransom had witnessed a remarkable demonstration by a remarkable woman.[1] As demonstrations go, however, it probably would not have been terribly convincing even to other parapsychologists were it not for the fact that it was only the latest in a long series of demonstrations and scientific experiments that had established Kulagina* as one of the most studied PK subjects in recent years. All of this research has taken place in the Soviet Union—most of it by Soviet scientists, although several Western scientists have observed her, and one has even conducted experiments. This has simultaneously engendered skepticism among Western scientists distrustful of Soviet methods and fear among others that the Soviet Union is leaping ahead of the West in their understanding of psychic phenomena. The fear of Soviet advances has proven unfounded—so far—and the distrust of the research has been laid to rest by increased contact between Soviet and Western scientists in recent years.

Apart from these unusual abilities, there was little in the life or manner of Kulagina to suggest that she was anything but an ordinary Russian woman. Western scientists always found her to be friendly and hospitable, with a calm manner and a willingness to submit to any task they devised for her. Born in the mid-twenties, she served with distinction in the defense of Leningrad during World War II as a senior sergeant in a tank regiment. Until her death in April 1990, she resided in that city with her engineer husband in a small apartment, which they shared with a married daughter.

Kulagina came to the attention of the renowned Soviet parapsychologist Leonid L. Vasiliev in 1963. He immediately set about investigating her unusual abilities, the likes of which had not been seen—East or West—since the decline of physical mediumship in the thirties. Following Vasiliev's death in 1966, investigations continued under the supervision of an associate, Zdenek Rejdak, a Czech parapsychologist and scientist at the Prague Military Insti-

---

*In some reports, particularly earlier ones, she is referred to by her maiden name, Nelya Mikhailova.

tute, and other Soviet scientists such as Sergeyev. Western scientists first learned of Kulagina when films made by Rejdak and other researchers were shown at an international parapsychology conference in Moscow in June 1968.

The films of Kulagina were indeed impressive, not to mention longer and somewhat better produced than Pratt's. One film excerpt shows her moving a cigar tube standing upright on a playing card inside a closed, clear plastic case. With her hands in her lap or at her sides, Kulagina stares intently at the cigar tube, occasionally bending over and around the case as if to coax the tube along. The cigar tube, still upright, slowly moves to the right and slightly toward her. The card moves along with the tube and rotates slightly in a counterclockwise direction. Other film excerpts show Kulagina selectively moving one or two matchsticks among several scattered on a table as well as moving several objects simultaneously in different directions.[2]

Soviet investigations of Kulagina were extensive. Besides studies by Soviet scientists openly interested in psychic phenomena, Kulagina was also investigated by committees and individuals from impartial scientific and medical institutes. The investigations appear to be quite competent regarding the elimination of fraud. Typically Kulagina was searched for magnets, strings, and other paraphernalia that might be used to simulate PK. For one series of filmed investigations she was examined by a physician and X-rayed for hidden magnets or traces of shrapnel from a war wound that could possibly act as a magnet. Often she was required to move nonmagnetic objects in sealed containers to eliminate magnetism or concealed threads as explanations.

The Soviets were interested in more than just eliminating fraud. Given the strictly materialist orientation of Soviet science, their scientists worked exceptionally hard to see if some form of normal energy, perhaps present in abnormal quantities, might explain what they were seeing. Some reports noted unusually high electrostatic or magnetic fields near Kulagina, but could not directly connect these with the movements of objects near her. Other investigations concentrated on Kulagina's physiology, and here researchers noted effects not unlike those that had been observed decades earlier with physical mediums. Despite her outwardly calm composure, Kulagina seemed to expend prodigious amounts of physical energy. Her heartbeat sometimes reached 240 beats per minute. After a session her blood sugar would be elevated and her weight reduced by as much as three pounds. In any sustained investigation it was necessary to allow rest periods for Kulagina to recover. Sergeyev, only one of Kulagina's many investigators, claimed to have performed over two hundred experiments with Kulagina, and he and his colleagues were completely convinced of the genuineness of her phenomena.

The visit by Pratt and Ransom in 1970 was primarily observational, as were most visits by Western parapsychologists. Only one scientist from outside the Eastern-bloc countries—British physicist Benson Herbert—has done any amount of experimentation with Kulagina, and even that was limited. In April 1973 Herbert, along with colleague Manfred Cassirer, was able to set up a temporary laboratory in a Leningrad hotel. His equipment included cameras, objects of varying composition and weight, and a device for measuring electrostatic charges. The centerpiece of this impromptu lab was a hydrometer, a glass-bulb-and-tube device used for measuring specific gravity, that floated upright in a saline solution. The entire system was surrounded by an electrically grounded screen. Herbert had hoped Kulagina might be able to depress the hydrometer, thus giving him a means of measuring the amount of psychic "force" being used.

When Kulagina arrived for the experiments, Herbert was dismayed to learn that she was ill and did not feel up to doing any experiments. Shortly into the visit, however, Kulagina became fascinated with the hydrometer apparatus and tried to move it in the water, but with only slight success. After a few moments she quit and plopped into a chair, tired by even this small effort. The chair was three or four feet from the apparatus, and Herbert, his colleague, and Sergeyev (who had brought Kulagina) several times walked between Kulagina and the table. Then they noticed that Kulagina was staring intently at the hydrometer from the chair. Slowly she raised her arms in the direction of the apparatus. Within moments the previously motionless hydrometer floated in a straight line to the far side of the vessel. After resting there for about two minutes, it then retraced its path and continued to the near side. All of this took place under the close watch of the two British investigators, who were able to confirm there were no strings or hidden wires between Kulagina and the device several feet away.

Later in that session Herbert asked Kulagina to try rotating a compass needle. After trying for a while with only marginal success, she fell back in the chair, exhausted. As she sat motionless, Herbert bent over closely to examine the compass. Suddenly the entire compass, case and all, turned about 45 degrees counterclockwise, as he put it, "right under my nose." Over the next minute, as Herbert ran his fingers over and under the table looking for threads and Kulagina sat motionless, the compass case did a zigzag dance about the table.

This was Herbert's only experimental session with Kulagina, but he spent the rest of his time conferring with Sergeyev and other scientists who had worked with her. Both he and Cassirer, an experienced British parapsychologist, came away convinced of Kulagina's integrity and very favorably impressed by the capabilities of Kulagina's Soviet investigators.[3]

The Soviet authorities eventually discouraged further visits by Western scientists, but Soviet scientists were permitted to continue their work. During the period 1978 to 1984 Kulagina was studied, primarily by physicists, at the Institute of Precise Mechanics and Optics in Leningrad, the Research Institute of Radio-Engineering and Electronics in Moscow, and the Baumann Higher School of Technology, also in Moscow. Much of this research was aimed at exploring possible physical mechanisms for her abilities, and scientists reported detecting unusually strong magnetic and acoustic fields around Kulagina's hands. In other experiments, Kulagina reportedly decreased the intensity of a laser beam by affecting the physical properties of the gas through which it passed.[4]

Kulagina, of course, drew her share of critical fire. The usual counterexplanation for her abilities is that she employed typical magician's methods, such as hidden magnets or extremely fine threads. However, repeated searches by many investigators consistently failed to turn up the slightest evidence of any such aids. To my knowledge not a single parapsychologist who had an opportunity to observe her closely ever expressed any doubts as to her authenticity. Kulagina never made any attempt to exploit her abilities, and, if anything, her notoriety was something of a burden in her own country. Although she was never caught using tricks, this has not deterred Western critics from dismissing her as a fraud, but when the Soviet journal *Man and Law* accused her of trickery, she brought legal action against it. Two members of the Soviet Academy of Sciences testified on her behalf, and early in 1988 the court ordered the journal to publish a retraction.[5]

Judging from the reports, Soviet scientists have measured just about everything that can be measured in and around the objects Kulagina moved. They have also investigated Kulagina's physiology fairly thoroughly during her feats. Although some of the investigators have ventured what could best be described as "creative" hypotheses as to what is happening, we really do not have any better idea of how Kulagina accomplished these movements than our Victorian predecessors had about D. D. Home. "It is not normal movement, therefore it must be PK," the parapsychologist is likely to conclude, but that only invites the next question. How does this so-called PK work?

Obviously we do not have the answer to that question yet. I must confess that I do not think we are even close to getting an answer, but at least we are seeing signs that PK may not remain an impenetrable mystery forever. Certainly this hope motivates our Soviet colleagues. Sustained work with Kulagina stopped in the mid-1980s when her health declined, though similar research reportedly continues quietly with other subjects.*

Kulagina's abilities may not have been as rare as they seemed. At least one Soviet scientist, physicist Victor Adamenko, claims to have trained several other persons to produce effects similar to Kulagina's. During a recent stay at our laboratory he demonstrated his method by starting a couple of members of our staff on moving small, rollable objects around on a Plexiglas table. Adamenko begins by teaching subjects to move objects using common electrostatic effects, the way anyone can move Styrofoam cups or packing chips simply by first rubbing one's hands on a woolen sweater. Gradually, over many sessions, Adamenko replaces these objects with ones that cannot be moved by electrostatic forces. If all goes well, Adamenko eventually eliminates every possibility of electrostatic effects by electrically grounding the person's hands. The ra-

*In the mid-seventies there was a crackdown on Soviet parapsychologists who were too open in their dealings with Western parapsychologists. One can only hope that the age of glasnost will facilitate renewed cooperation among scientists of the East and West. Recent reports indicate a strong resurgence of interest in paranormal issues among Soviets, which, in turn, may lead Soviet scientists to talk more openly about research once considered taboo.

tionale behind Adamenko's method is one that can be found in several techniques designed to foster PK. First build up confidence in the subject by *simulating* PK through normal means, but then gradually wean the subject off the normal to the paranormal.

Oddly enough, the best-known American version of Nina Kulagina did not follow Adamenko's method at all. In 1971, not long after Kulagina had become known in the West, Felicia Parise, a young hematologist, was in the small audience of staff and volunteers of the Maimonides Dream Laboratory gathered to watch a recently arrived film of the Russian marvel. Parise worked in the medical center and had served as a subject—and a very successful one at that—in the Maimonides ESP-dream experiments. Watching the film, Parise felt that if that Russian woman could do PK, she could too. For the next several months, each day when Parise got home from work, she would take out a small plastic container (which was meant to hold her cosmetic eyelashes in alcohol) and try to move it by sheer concentration.

For weeks Parise continued this ritual with no success. Then, one evening, in a moment of personal stress (she had just received word that her ill grandmother had taken a turn for the worse), she had the distinct impression that the little vial suddenly slid away from her hand as she reached for it. After this incident Parise discovered that if she worked herself up to a level of concentration that involved a truly intense physical effort, she could actually "will" the container (alcohol and all) to move. Before telling anyone of this newfound ability, Parise went on to learn how to move a compass needle as Kulagina did and to move pieces of aluminum foil.

Eventually Parise felt sufficiently confident about her abilities to let the Dream Laboratory parapsychologists in on her little project. Charles Honorton, with whom she had worked closely as an ESP subject, was the first person to investigate her PK abilities. On his initial visit to Parise's apartment Honorton watched as she placed the vial on the kitchen counter about a foot from the edge. She placed her hands at the edge of the counter and stared—silent and unmoving—at the vial. Several minutes passed as Honorton watched closely. At one point Parise said it had moved, but Honorton had not noticed anything. All of a sudden, as Honorton watched, the vial moved nearly two inches to the right and away from Parise. Honorton grabbed the vial and checked it closely to see if anything was attached or if there was any moisture on the base that might enable it to slide. It was clean. Honorton replaced it on the counter and tried to see if it would slide by itself normally. It remained where he placed it. Parise resumed her staring stance. After a few moments the vial began moving again, this time in a curved trajectory to Honorton's right. It moved slowly, stopping several times, and eventually traced a path of about four and a half inches. Then it reversed direction and returned several inches closer to Honorton before stopping.

On this visit, and on the several others that followed, Honorton and his colleagues watched closely for possible tricks. On one occasion Honorton employed a cameraman who was also a magician to film Parise. On that visit she moved the vial, a compass needle, and pieces of aluminum foil. The latter two items were both covered by a bell jar.[6]

In 1973 Parise visited our laboratory in Durham for an experiment devised by parapsychologists Graham and Anita Watkins. Parise's target was a compass located inside the coil of a commercial metal detector. Sealed packets of photographic film were placed under the detector and at intervals up to three meters from it. Seated in front of the apparatus, Parise—after some effort— was able to move the needle 15 degrees to one side. As the needle moved, the continuous tone from the metal detector changed in pitch, but as the needle stopped moving, in the Watkinses' words, "a total shatter of the tone occurred." (According to the researchers, the only way they could duplicate the shatter effect was to drop a two-pound coil of solder into the center of the detector coil.) Parise moved to the far corner of the room, but the needle remained at its 15-degree deflection. Even more strangely, the compass needle did not deflect when a magnet was placed nearby. After about twenty-five minutes the needle gradually returned to normal behavior. When the sealed film was developed, the packs near the target were strongly exposed, with the exposure decreasing with the distance from the target. This effect on sealed film is similar, though not identical, to that which the Soviet scientists had observed with Kulagina. Also, as with Kulagina, Parise expended an enormous amount of physical energy in these demonstrations (as well as in practice sessions that she felt were needed to maintain her ability). After the studies at the Institute for Parapsychology, Parise stopped this work, feeling that it was taking too much time and effort.[7]

At this point readers may be wondering just how big a part of what we are calling "contemporary psychokinesis research" the dramatic demonstrations of Kulagina and Parise are. The fact is that they form only a small part of contemporary PK investigations. Researchers have learned little about PK from these demonstrations. Even the extensive Soviet investigations of Kulagina (and several similar performers) have yielded little except a long list of possible normal forces that are unlikely to account for the observed phenomena. To that extent this work has simply paralleled the work that Crookes did with D. D. Home a century earlier. An important difference, however, is that now the subjects of the investigations are ordinary persons—not psychic superstars—who more or less "learned" how to create the phenomena.

The principal contribution of the Kulagina and Parise investigations has been to relegitimize a category of psychic phenomena that had been considered off-limits by mainstream parapsychology for over thirty years: directly observable PK effects.

In the thirties J. B. Rhine revived PK research with his dice-tossing experiments. The PK Rhine studied, however, was very different in character from its predecessors. It was *statistical* PK. You could not observe it directly but only infer it from the numbers. Thus if a subject were able to get dice in a tumbling machine to come up with the desired target face more often than chance would predict, a statistical evaluation might rule out chance and suggest the operation of PK, but you could not tell by watching the dice roll. Rhine's PK research was very different from watching a table lift off the ground, but for several decades it was virtually the only PK research that was done. Kulagina, and to a lesser extent Parise, managed to return directly observable PK to the parapsychological arena, but now it was stripped of the quasi-religious trappings of mediumship. Parapsychologists once again felt comfortable turning their attention to what is perhaps the most mind-boggling of all psychic phenomena.

Imaginary Ghosts and PK

On a cold January evening in 1974 a small group had gathered in a room of the New Horizons Research Foundation in Toronto, Canada. The eight persons came from varied backgrounds—some engineers, others housewives, nurses, accountants—but all were members of the Toronto Society for Psychical Research and shared a serious interest in psychic phenomena. They had assembled this evening, as they had nearly weekly for the past couple of years, for a rather special experiment. This experiment was under the supervision of Dr. A.R.G. Owen, a British mathematician, now resident in Canada, who was a longtime parapsychologist with a special interest in poltergeist activity and directly observable psychokinesis. He was not part of the assembled group, however, and the weekly sessions were generally organized by his wife and colleague, Iris.

The participants filed into a small room set aside for their experiment and sat on the folding metal chairs that surrounded a well-worn card table. On the table were a pair of fencing foils and a dish of candies, items that represented two of the fondnesses of the soon-to-be-invoked guest of honor. The room was lit normally. Each member of the group assumed the position that had become part of the regular ritual: hands lightly placed, palms down, flat on the table. Sue began the evening's activities: "Hello, Philip." Immediately there was a loud rap that seemed to come from the table directly below her hands. "Wow, I really felt that one," she commented. Then Sidney spoke, "Hello, Philip." Another rap came from the table below his hands. This continued around the table until all sitters had offered their greetings.

With the social amenities over, the group began to "chat" with Philip, asking questions that could be answered by "yes" or "no"— one or two raps, respectively. Suddenly the table shifted slightly. At once Andy apologized, "Sorry, my knee hit the table." One of the strict codes of the group was that any accidental movements of the table must be immediately acknowledged, and anyone who thought another member was unconsciously causing movement had to say so. Soon, however, the table began to tilt, and then slide across the floor. The sitters had to leave their seats to keep their hands on the table. This time no one claimed responsibility. "Philip, is that you?" asked someone. A solitary rap "yes" was the answer. One of the sitters playfully told the table to get back to its position, which it did, and the sitters—hands still lightly on the table—resumed their seats. Then they began urging Philip to levitate the table—something they had been urging almost every visit, since they ultimately wanted to capture such an event on film. For a moment the table was still, then *one* leg only (the other three were squarely on the floor) began to rise. The top of the table began to twist out of shape; sounds of straining wood and metal could be heard. Someone whispered, "He's going to break the table," but the one-legged lift continued. Eventually someone tried to push the corner down, but the table resisted. It finally took four of the sitters to push the table down. Even though all could see that there was nothing under the table or the errant leg, those who pushed it down said that it distinctly felt as if someone were resisting their efforts. Interesting, but not the levitation they were hoping for. Later the candies were passed around, and as customary, one was set out for Philip. Someone jokingly reached to take Philip's candy, whereupon the table tipped up at an angle of 45 degrees to take the candy out of reach, *but the candy stayed put.* With the table tipped, the sitters placed several other types of candy—all examined to be sure they were not sticky—beside Philip's; they stayed in place too. After the session was over, the sitters performed some tests, finding that when the table was tilted by hand, the candies slid off well before the tilt even reached 45 degrees.

Several months later they got the complete levitation they were working for.[8]

All of this must sound like it might have taken place in 1874 instead of 1974, but there is at least one big difference. All the sitters knew that their visiting spirit, Philip, was entirely fictitious—the product of their own imaginations. In fact it was one member of the group, Sue, who had invented their imaginary ghost and given him a history as an aristocratic Cavalier in the time of Cromwell. Unlike their Victorian counterparts, the Toronto group was not interested in communicating with someone on "the other side"; they wanted to re-create the *physical* phenomena so often a part of the Victorian séance. Philip was simply a means to this end.

How one gets from a phony ghost to large-scale PK effects is not exactly obvious, but a pathway can be traced with the help of a new perspective on nineteenth-century séances. In the fifties Kenneth Batcheldor, a British clinical psychologist, pondered the often-noted fact that the physical phenomena associated with séances declined seemingly in proportion to the increased scientific (and often suspicious) approach of the investigators. The later investigators seemed to embark upon their investigations with the intent of discovering fraud. While circumstances may have made this necessary to maintain appropriate scientific rigor, it certainly did not create the psychological conditions that might be said to nurture the phenomena. Batcheldor came to two conclusions. First, in common with some of the earlier researchers, Batcheldor thought that PK ability was simply an unusual human behavior—not a rare gift—so séance-room phenomena could be produced by most anyone, given the right conditions. Secondly Batcheldor concluded that the psychological conditions prevailing at the time the phenomena are being sought are of the utmost importance for the elicitation of PK.

Batcheldor's basic idea was that doubt and suspicion hinder the production of psychic phenomena, whereas belief and expectation facilitate it. This is a common notion, of course, but Batcheldor's version was more specific. Not only was a general belief and expectation helpful, but conditions had to be such that the persons involved felt an almost tangible expectation that a miracle was about to take place. Clearly this was more than just sitting around wishing—it was a specific state of mind that had to be induced.

Two factors militated against successful PK production, according to Batcheldor. One, what he called "witness inhibition," was the initial reaction of shock or fear that arises when one actually sees a paranormal event. Witness inhibition, he felt, served to block any further demonstrations. The other factor, ownership resistance, was a tendency to fear that one might be responsible for or causing the phenomena oneself. Whatever techniques could reduce these inhibiting psychological factors were likely to produce the right conditions for PK demonstrations, Batcheldor concluded.

In many ways the traditional séance was just the ticket, and Batcheldor, along with a few friends, began a series of experimental séances. Devoid of the traditional spiritualist trappings, these séances were held in an ordinary room, with an ordinary table. All participants maintained an objective, experimental approach, but during the sittings there was much lighthearted banter and playfulness. The sitters were careful to address their requests for movements to the table, rather than to themselves, thus trying to avoid responsibility for any movements that might ensue.

Over the course of ten sittings the sitters became used to a variety of minor effects: the table tilting or rocking, sliding, or even hopping. All of these could be attributed to the normal but unconscious muscle action of the sitters, but the small effects helped build confidence. At the eleventh sitting, though, the table—all forty pounds of it—actually rose off the floor. All participants' hands were on top of the table. Batcheldor noted in his report that even though this was exactly what they had been striving for, it was still very shocking when it occurred. The next sitting produced numerous levitations and other activity, but the one after that produced nothing. Batcheldor surmised that the rather violent activity of the preceding session had aroused too much anxiety in the participants.[9]

Intrigued by Batcheldor's results, Colin Brookes-Smith, a retired electrical engineer, began a series of experimental sittings following Batcheldor's prescription. Despite one difference—they conducted their sittings in normal light—Brookes-Smith and his colleague, D. W. Hunt, experienced a variety of dramatic effects, including the repeated activation of a light switch at a distance. In later work Brookes-Smith constructed a specially instrumented séance table that monitored pressure on it from all directions. He was able to elicit strong PK phenomena, and the recording from the instrumented table confirmed that normal forces were not being used.

Brookes-Smith introduced a novel mechanism to generate confidence and expectancy, as well as reduce witness inhibition—the designated cheater. Before an experimental sitting, the sitters would secretly draw lots, and one person would be chosen to "assist" the initial phenomena. The designated cheater would discreetly use normal means to "get the ball rolling," but would stop when paranormal movements became apparent. Of course afterward the cheater would own up and identify what had been done normally. The recordings from the instrumented table easily distinguished the normal from the not-so-normal movements.[10]

The designated cheater, though useful for Brookes-Smith, was not one of the techniques adopted by the Toronto group. In fact they were not even aware of Batcheldor's work when they started, and they spent nearly a year in a fruitless attempt to conjure up an apparition using a meditational technique. On learning of Batcheldor's work, however, they immediately realized that their ongoing experiment provided an ideal setting for duplicating Batcheldor's findings. They adjusted their approach to be more like the traditional sitter group and paid special attention to Batcheldor's advice concerning the right attitude. "Philip" relieved the problem of ownership resistance. Even though they all knew that "Philip" was fictitious, by letting him "take responsibility" for the dramatic physical effects, no single member of the group had to worry that it was his or her own PK. This was just a more imaginative approach to the problem than that taken by Batcheldor's group.

Obviously the importance of these several group-PK projects lies not in the evidentiality of the phenomena. Even though all of the groups, especially the Philip group, demonstrated phenomena to visitors, we must ultimately rely on their own affidavits of good faith as fellow investigators. Films exist of both the Philip group and Batcheldor's group,* but these ultimately depend on the good faith of the filmmaker. We must recognize, however, that evidentiality was not the goal of these groups. They wanted to learn something of the psychology behind the séance and how this might lead to the production of physical phenomena. In this respect they have gained some important insights.

If we are prepared to accept the good-faith efforts of these researchers, then the most dramatic realization to come out of the group-PK research is that quite ordinary folks can produce some amazing phenomena *if the psychology is right*. Believing that the phenomena are possible, expecting that something might happen *right now*, and not worrying about who is "causing" it all, seem to be part of the recipe. This recipe does not tell us anything about *what* is happening, but it certainly suggests that directly observable PK effects may not be so inaccessible for scientists daring enough to look for them.

---

*Not long before Batcheldor's untimely death in 1988 he was visited by a colleague of mine, who reported back that Batcheldor had some "mind-boggling" infrared videotapes of recent sessions. Regrettably at present I am not aware of anyone who plans to carry on Batcheldor's work.

PK Parties

For the most part it looked like any of the thousands of motivational seminars that are given all over the country. The group leader had just spent the last half hour extolling the incredible, unrecognizable powers of the human mind, and now the participants were about to try an exercise in developing their own mental powers. Perhaps three dozen men and women sat in the audience, many with eyes closed—concentrating, concentrating—and each person was gently stroking a teaspoon.

Stroking a teaspoon??? Yes, stroking a teaspoon, or perhaps gently massaging the neck where the bowl joins the handle.

"Bend!" shouts the group leader. "Bend, bend!" responds the group. Eventually sporadic shouts of "bend" emanating from parts of the room give way to shouts of "Hey look, it's going!" and "Wow, look at this!"

I suppose if you were to come upon this scene somewhere in California, you might not think twice about it. But the location for this particular gathering was just outside Washington, D.C. The participants were not a bunch of New Age novices; many were jaded Washington bureaucrats, and there was a generous sprinkling of military personnel with an average rank somewhere around the level of colonel.

What was it? It was a "spoon-bending party," one of dozens led by an aerospace engineer by the name of Jack Houck. Although now such parties are a bit passé, for much of the early eighties Houck took it upon himself to lead similar gatherings around the country for engineers, business people, academics, and even parapsychologists who were interested in his ideas about PK production.

Houck's parties are just demonstrations, not serious research, but with several hundred such gatherings under his belt, he thinks he has learned much about the psychology behind successful PK demonstrations. You may recognize echoes of Batcheldor's approach behind his methods. The party atmosphere helps break down ownership resistance, and Houck's skillful buildup surely prepares most people for a miracle "right now." In place of tilting tables, Houck has substituted bending silverware, a form of PK (if that is what it is) that emerged from one of parapsychology's more frenetic periods of PK research.*

Metal bending started as a psychic fad in the early seventies with the performances of the young Israeli entertainer Uri Geller. A gifted showman whose good looks and engaging personality drew big crowds in Israel, Geller differed from other similar performers in that he claimed that his feats were really psychic. This is something that professional magicians are not supposed to do, so practically from the very start he began to attract critical fire from fellow entertainers, who felt that he was using the same tools of the conjuring trade that they employed. To them Geller was simply a renegade who was not following the magicians' code.

Geller's stage performances are well known. Typically Geller will invite members of the audience to provide a key or similar metal object. Sometimes he will appear to stroke it, and soon the key will be seen to bend. Often Geller will let the owner of the key continue to hold it flat in the palm of his hand while Geller strokes it gently on the top, and then the key appears to bend (usually upward). His stage show often includes demonstrations of apparent ESP as he sketches images that members of the audience are concentrating upon.

Virtually all of what Geller does on the stage can be duplicated almost as convincingly by magicians who do not claim any psychic powers. Of itself that fact does not mean that Geller necessarily uses

---

*At a typical PK party, many folks do start bending spoons and other silverware. The bulk of it involves a degree of ordinary physical pressure, though many who experience this report that the metal becomes soft and the physical pressure used is far less than should be necessary. (At one party I watched a Duke professor crumple a large silverplate serving spoon into a tight ball, much as one would crumple a piece of aluminum foil.)

Toward the end of most parties, Houck can often get a few persons to bend the tines of a fork while holding it at the base (between the thumb and forefinger only). This is done with the whole group watching and is not at all easy to dismiss as mere physical force, since the tines can be observed moving with nothing touching them.

Houck continues to give parties, but his serious research on this phenomenon is done with selected individuals who came to his attention at his parties. Like Batcheldor, Houck does most of his serious research on his own, sharing his findings with fellow scientists and engineers by means of privately circulated reports.

the same tricks, but it does arouse legitimate suspicions. Geller's performances offstage for the various individuals and teams who have sought to test his claimed abilities are, however, considerably more varied and impressive than his stage shows. Although some have claimed that Geller rarely submitted to rigorous examination, the fact is that he has submitted to tests in more than a dozen laboratories in Europe and the United States. On top of that Geller's abilities were examined *up close* on different occasions by at least two experienced and well-respected magicians, who independently declared that they could see no way that trickery could have accomplished what they witnessed.[11]

Geller's most famous laboratory tests took place at Stanford Research Institute. Unfortunately they were famous not for what they demonstrated but for the controversy that surrounded their publication. When Geller was introduced to the SRI researchers (by former astronaut Edgar Mitchell), Russell Targ and Hal Puthoff were involved in remote-viewing experiments, so Geller participated in some similar ESP experiments. Shut in a soundproof, electrically shielded room, Geller attempted to draw a picture of a target that another person was viewing. He was extremely successful at this, and in due course his results were combined with those of Pat Price and other remote viewers for a formal report submitted to the prestigious British science journal *Nature*.*

Although the SRI researchers filmed some of Geller's metal-bending activities, their main interest was in ESP at the time, and it fell to other researchers to do most of the investigations of this phenomenon. Among the first to examine Geller's metal bending

---

*In an unprecedented move thought by many to border on the unethical, the editor of *Nature* preceded the SRI report with an editorial questioning the validity of the experiments and even quoting some of the negative comments made by prepublication reviewers. Furthermore, someone had leaked the report to the popular science journal *New Scientist*, which published a blistering attack on the SRI work even before *Nature*'s report came out. Among other things the *New Scientist* article charged that Geller may have had a miniature radio implanted in a tooth through which a confederate could have given information. (That charge was easily refuted some months later when Geller submitted to a dental examination that revealed no tooth radio and no signs of any prior dental work.) For some time after the publication the letter columns of both *Nature* and *New Scientist* reverberated with charges, defenses, and countercharges.

was Prof. John Taylor of King's College in London. Taylor taped a 20-centimeter brass strip to the platform of a simple letter scale sensitive to one-quarter ounce. Most of the brass strip extended out from the platform parallel to the countertop, and as Taylor closely watched it and the scale, Geller stroked the *top* of the strip with one finger. Although at no time did the scale register a downward force of more than one-half ounce, by the end of the experiment, the brass strip had acquired an *upward* bend of about 10 degrees. Far more disconcerting for Taylor, however, was that as he watched the needle on the scale, the needle itself gradually bent forward (away from the dial) about 70 degrees.

Taylor also investigated whether Geller could influence objects *without* contact. Taylor placed a small crystal of lithium fluoride in a plastic container. Geller held his hands several inches over the container. Within ten seconds the crystal shattered into several pieces. Taylor states that there was no chance for Geller to have touched the crystal, since at all times during the experiment he could see a gap between Geller's hands and the container.[12]

Another team of scientists investigated Geller at the laboratory of Prof. John B. Hasted, professor of experimental physics and head of the physics department at Birkbeck College, University of London. Along with Hasted were Prof. David Bohm, a distinguished theoretical physicist; Edward W. Bastin, a physicist and mathematician from Cambridge University; and several other observers. Geller visited the lab on four occasions in 1974. Hasted's team reported that they were able to observe the often-reported "plasticization" of a metal spoon being handled by Geller. This spoon had already been bent about 30 degrees by one of the metal-bending children that Hasted was also investigating at the time (see page 164). Geller had just arrived at Hasted's office when Hasted began telling him of his experiences with the child who had bent the spoon. He handed the spoon to Geller, who took it by the handle only, not touching the bent part. As Hasted described it, "Within a few seconds, and under our close scrutiny, the bend in the spoon became plastic. It quickly softened so much that the spoon could be held with one end in either hand and gently moved to and fro." Hasted took the specimen in his hands and described the bent part as "soft as chewing gum, and yet its appearance was normal." Hasted set the spoon down in one piece, hoping to preserve it, but later an attempt to move it caused it to fall apart at the bend. Subsequent analysis showed no evidence of corrosive chemicals (one of the "tricks" Geller is alleged to use), and the four scientists present had observed none of the repeated manual bending (nor any evidence of it later) that can be employed to weaken a spoon to the point of breaking.

Later during that same visit Hasted laid out three pill capsules (the clear, cellulose type that pharmacies use), each containing a thin vanadium carbide crystal foil of a type used in electron microscope examinations. Each piece of foil had been prepared and examined at a Cambridge University lab and could be identified if necessary. Before Geller came near the specimens, Hasted placed one hand several inches over them. Geller passed his right hand slowly over Hasted's. Hasted felt a warming sensation in his knuckles, and seconds later one of the capsules gave a little jump (observed by Bastin, since Hasted could not see it). Closer examination revealed that one capsule had indeed moved, *and half of the foil was missing.* Bastin immediately picked up the capsule—Geller never touched it. Later analysis revealed that the severed foil piece was indeed one of the original ones (eliminating a substitution trick as an explanation) and that it exhibited a fracture typical of a mechanical failure of a brittle crystal. The other half of the crystal was never located.[13]

The research on Geller's alleged PK abilities has received severe criticism, primarily from James Randi and others with conjuring and sleight-of-hand experience. In fact Randi has made something of a career as Geller's debunker, having risen from relative obscurity to national prominence through books and television appearances in which he claims to expose Geller's tricks.* Randi and other critics claim that all the scientists who observed Geller's demonstrations were simply duped by conjuring tricks. They maintain—not unrea-

---

*Recently, when scientists complained about Randi's inclusion in a team that the journal *Nature* sent to investigate some controversial French medical experiments, editor John Maddox defended his choice by describing Randi as the debunker of "Uri Geller, the parascientist who claimed he bent spoons by sheer mentation." Of course, Maddox knew very well that Geller never claimed to be a scientist—para or otherwise—but the disingenuous description made *Nature*'s somewhat dubious position look better. ("A Too-Polite Silence About Shoddy Science" *New York Times*, Sept. 26, 1988.)

sonably, I might add—that scientists are particularly easy to fool since they are more or less trained to look for the expected, whereas conjurers are trained in accomplishing their feats through unexpected means. The scientists, goes the standard criticism, simply failed to notice the clever way in which Geller accomplished the feat by normal means.

This criticism makes two important assumptions. First it assumes that the scientists (who may ordinarily be easy to fool with tricks) did not exercise heightened vigilance when dealing with an individual who, at the time, was clearly earning money with his stage performances. Secondly the criticism requires that *what the scientist described was not what actually happened.* So, according to this criticism, Taylor could not have had Geller's fingers under observation for every moment of the scale test: perhaps he was distracted for a second, during which Geller slipped a thumb under the brass strip and levered it upward, or perhaps it was not perfectly straight at the start of the experiment. With the crystal experiment, the criticism goes, Taylor could not have had his gaze fixed on the gap between Geller's hands and the container for the ten seconds or so that it took, or perhaps the crystal was not intact at the start, but Taylor had not noticed. Similarly this view would hold that at Hasted's laboratory the several observers must have been mistaken that the capsule contained a whole vanadium crystal at the start of the session, or that Geller did not distract them for the time that it would take to open the capsule, break the crystal, and reclose it. And so it would go for each lab and every scientist who studied Geller.

The argument that Geller's laboratory phenomena were brought about by conjuring tricks that the scientists failed to notice is, by definition, virtually impossible to refute. If the conjuring was really good, then the scientists would simply never have noticed it, so all their testimony as to what precautions were taken and what observations were made could be absolutely truthful and accurate from their perspective, but irrelevant. Even if the scientists had brought in accomplished conjurors as observers, this would not resolve the problem, since it could always be argued that Geller was "too good" and fooled even them. (Remember that at least two such accomplished conjurers testified that what they had witnessed could not have been done by any conjuring techniques that they knew of.)

It is at this point that we touch the Achilles' heel of this sort of PK research: All of these investigations, no matter how thorough, ultimately boil down to anecdotes—stories about what happened once upon a time. We end up having to choose between the testimony of witnesses who were present and counterexplanations of persons who were not. On the one hand the witnesses may have been mistaken about what they observed, but on the other the counterexplanations may be based on conditions that were not actually present at the time. Of course the weakness of eyewitness testimony cuts both ways. Geller's detractors base much of their case on accounts from witnesses who believe they saw Geller *simulate* psychic effects (key bending or ESP) by normal means. While this "battle of the anecdotes" certainly keeps parapsychology in the popular press, it does little for it as a science.*

I trust the reader will forgive me if I decline to take a stand on whether or not Geller's abilities are genuinely paranormal. Never having had the opportunity to work with the gentleman, my opinion would have to be based upon the testimony of my colleagues, against which I would need to balance the alternative explanations that have been offered by Geller's critics. I *will* say that I do not believe that many of Geller's laboratory demonstrations have been as easily "explained away" as critics would like us to believe, but in the end, they are just anecdotes, and anecdotes do not a science make. Whether or not I believe Geller has psi ability is of little consequence, because all of his demonstrations—even assuming they are genuine—have done little to advance scientific understanding of PK phenomena. That will only come about as a result of a sustained

---

*The Geller saga is a long and complex one. It includes not only much more testimony and charges than what has been mentioned so far, but also rumor, innuendo, alleged "confessions" by members of his entourage and countercharges that the confessions were "bought" or motivated by revenge. The best source for the reports of the research done with Geller is *The Geller Papers*, edited by Charles Panati, a physicist and science writer. (He was *Newsweek*'s science editor at the time.) The most thorough case against Geller is made by James Randi in *The Magic of Uri Geller* (later republished as *The Truth About Uri Geller*). Anyone interested in pursuing the Geller issue further should read both books in order to appreciate fully the quality of the scientific research and the criticism that has been leveled against it.

program of research with Geller or other persons claiming similar abilities.

Rise of the Geller Clones

"We're rolling," I said as I verified that all was in order with the Edinburgh University Psychology Department's latest dual-camera, split-screen, time-stamped video-recording equipment. John Beloff, senior lecturer in the department, asked Fiona, a local lass of about twelve, to show us how she had caused a spoon to bend. Sitting in the center of the room, with a spoon in her hand, Fiona explained that she had seen Uri Geller on the telly and thought that she would try the same thing. As she mimicked Geller's demonstration, she suddenly noticed that the spoon seemed to get soft "right here," she said, pointing to the neck. And then it just flopped over and got stiff again. "Do you think you could do that for us now?" asked Beloff. "Och, aye. I can do it for you," was her reply.

This was 1976. Fiona had come to our attention as the result of an article in the local newspaper, and Beloff had invited her and her mother to the laboratory so that we could examine her ability. Beloff interviewed several witnesses who vouched that they had observed bending that far exceeded anything that she could have done normally. Fiona seemed to be able to do what Geller did, but certainly she could not be accused of being an accomplished conjurer.

I wish I were able to report that I witnessed a miracle, but in parapsychology, failures and near misses are far more common than dramatic successes. As it happened, for over ninety minutes the young lady stroked different pieces of silverware and entertained us with nonstop chatter, but nothing happened. She was even sent to a room to work by herself. The girl seemed extremely puzzled at her lack of results, and her mother gently scolded her to pay more attention to what she was doing, but still nothing happened. Eventually we called it a day and began putting away the equipment. The girl and her mother had gone into the studio control room, where they sat between an American couple who were students there. Fiona had a spoon in each hand, which she continued to rub between the thumb and forefinger and sat dejectedly while her mother chided her for talking too much and not getting on with what she was supposed to do. "These folks came all the way from America to see you," the mother said (quite incorrectly); several seconds later one of the spoons—in the words of one observer— "just went limp and bent over at the neck." Three persons were watching her closely at the time, including one behind a one-way glass window. None saw anything even remotely suspicious in her behavior. No miracles—just another anecdote for the books is all we got for our efforts.

Fiona was not an isolated case. In fact Britain and a few continental countries experienced something of an epidemic of "mini Gellers." These were mostly children who apparently could perform the same metal-bending feats, including the famous plastic deformations, as their Israeli prototype. Hundreds of spoon-bending children would turn up in different countries following one of Geller's television appearances. For a while parapsychologists had a hard time keeping up with all the reports, but researchers did conduct extended research programs with some of these young subjects. Hasted examined several of these children, studying both the sort of contact bending that Geller does as well as noncontact bending in which the subjects are some distance from the metal specimens. Much of Hasted's work uses strain gauges—small instruments attached to the metal specimens that emit electrical signals according to the amount of strain or distortion being produced. In these experiments the strain-gauge signals were continuously recorded, so any unexpected handling, in addition to possible PK effects, would easily be detected. Yet Hasted was able to observe the bending of numerous metal specimens (and associated signals) without the subject touching them—sometimes from several locations in the lab simultaneously.[14]

The young mini Gellers were an interesting phenomenon. For the great majority of them it was easy to ascertain that they were not experienced conjurors. Although it was common for investigators to find that some children "helped" the PK with brute force when they were left unattended, under scrutiny it is unlikely that all of the better subjects could have fooled researchers with sleight-of-hand. Hasted was able to document children bending a special alloy bar that is normally impossible to bend without a constant force over an extended period of time. In other cases he identified unusual structural changes in the bent specimens. The considerable work with metal benders other than Geller himself certainly suggests that at least in some cases a real PK effect is involved. Beyond that, however, Hasted and everyone else who has studied metal bending have been able to offer only the vaguest of speculations about what sort of psychic mechanism might be involved.

And Geller himself? The scientific world may have decidedly mixed opinions on his abilities, but that does not seem to matter to the business world. Geller and his family live quietly on a palatial estate outside London while he reportedly earns a more than handsome living as a psychic consultant to mining, petroleum, and financial firms.

PK Research Chinese-Style

At a congested intersection in Beijing a traffic policeman looked on impatiently as a tradesman finished cleaning up a spilled handcart. As the policeman was about to motion the traffic on, a shrill honking pierced the air, and a foreign luxury car raced up on the wrong side of the road. Ignoring the policeman, the car tore through the intersection, narrowly missing the terrified tradesman.

The policeman shook his head; there was nothing he could do. He knew that car, as did most policemen in the city. The permits on the windshield from the National Defense Committee and the National Security Department gave the driver top-priority clearance. It was Z's car.

Later that evening the driver of that car could be found entertaining guests in Beijing's only five-star hotel—entertaining them not only with a sumptuous meal but also with a display of silverware-bending that left his guests gasping and the waiters wringing their hands. As the evening drew to a close, Z further astounded his guests by summoning taxis for them using his cellular telephone— the first they had seen.

Who is "Z," and why does he merit such privileges? Z, as he was known in scientific papers and early press reports, is Zhang Baosheng, resident psychic at Beijing's Institute of Space-Medico Engineering (ISME). Zhang, quite literally, resides at ISME, along with his wife and young son. According to Zhang's friends, Zhang and his family enjoy a luxurious twelve-room suite, complete with chef, nurse, and servants—all provided by the state, on condition that he never leave the country.

Zhang, now in his mid thirties, has been called "China's Uri Geller." Born in Bengxi City, in the northern coastal province of Liaoning, Zhang began demonstrating apparently paranormal abilities as early as 1976. A group of local researchers brought Zhang to the attention of Beijing scientists in 1982, during a period when Chinese parapsychology, known as Exceptional Functions of the Human Body (EFHB) research, was suffering intense criticism from several quarters.

In the late seventies China had experienced an unusual resurgence of interest in EFHB research among its scientists, and this was followed by a predictable backlash, both from conservative scientists and from Communist party ideologues, who viewed the research as contrary to Marxist doctrine. The ensuing debate came to a head when the Party's National Committee of Science arranged for supporters and critics to conduct joint experiments with a number of leading psychics in April 1982. Most of the psychics failed to produce satisfactory results. The exception was Z, who not only produced impressive results but did so with no evidence of cheating or sleight-of-hand.[15]

For a while after these experiments, Zhang cooperated with researchers at several laboratories in the capital. However, by 1984 Zhang was no longer available to scientists outside the military-controlled ISME, also known as the 507 Institute of the Spaceflight Department. Most of what we know of Zhang's work comes from papers published before 1984, primarily the work of Prof. Lin Shu-huang, of the Physics Department of Beijing Teachers' College. Besides being involved in the April 1982 experiments, Lin headed a team of nineteen researchers who investigated Zhang in a series of experiments that ran from December 1982 through May 1983.

Many Chinese PK researchers deliberately avoid using sophisticated equipment, reasoning that it would be difficult to determine where in a complex system the PK effect is taking place. Instead they prefer simple target systems that must conform to three specific conditions: (a) targets must be unique, or at least extremely difficult to duplicate; (b) targets must be "irreversibly sealed" in whatever container is being used (such that any attempt to open the container would destroy the seal or leave evidence of the opening); and (c) there must be continuous, multiangle observation by the experimenters or video cameras.

Lin's experiments involved Zhang's "specialty"—moving small objects and even live insects in and out of sealed containers. In one experiment specially marked pieces of paper were chemically treated and placed in a glass test tube. The tube was melted to constrict it roughly at the midpoint. Into the top part was placed cotton wads that had been treated with a different chemical that would react if it came into contact with the chemical on the target papers. The top of the test tube was then irreversibly sealed with special paper. With four experimenters watching from different angles, the tube was placed in front of Zhang. Five minutes later the target papers were lying beside the empty tube. The seal on the tube was undamaged and later inspection revealed traces of chemical reaction on the cotton, suggesting that the papers had passed *through* the cotton.

In another experiment of that series a live insect was marked and placed inside a tube. The tube was sealed so that any attempt to open it would break a fine hair glued inside. With two experimenters watching, the tube was placed on a table in front of Zhang. Several minutes later the insect, still alive, was outside the tube.

As far as I am aware, most of Zhang's recent work at ISME has been kept quiet by the authorities. However, in 1987 the Chinese scientific community received a shock when the Spaceflight Department awarded its Scientific Research Achievement Prize (second class) to the ISME team for a film of one of Zhang's experiments. Articles in the press and a Chinese science magazine reported that the ISME scientists filmed the movement of a medicine pill through an irreversibly sealed glass vial.[17] The film was made in color using a high-speed (400 frames per second) Japanese camera. The reports say that three frames of the film clearly show the pill passing through the glass (entering the glass, halfway through, and exiting).*

Although no scientists outside of China seem to have seen the film, in late 1990 researchers both in and outside of China were surprised by the arrival of a new Chinese journal, the *Chinese Jour-*

---

*If only three frames of a 400-frame-per-second film show the object exiting, that might explain why observers never seem to see the objects exiting. To them it seems that one moment the object is in the container, the next moment it is out.

nal of Somatic Science. In it was a report of new experiments with Zhang by the ISME team. Accompanying the report was a series of photos, reportedly from a 400-frame-per-second camera, showing a pill exiting from the bottom of a bottle held by Zhang. The report does not indicate whether the photos are from the prize-winning film, nor does it give much in the way of details about that event, which appears to be more of a demonstration than a controlled experiment. For the present, Western parapsychologists have only sketchy reports to go on, but this latest ISME paper suggests that Chinese researchers are becoming more willing to open up their research to outside scrutiny.

The "New" Psychokinesis

Bob had been a subject in several experiments at the Institute for Parapsychology. He had been polite about the card-guessing tests, but they had been pretty boring, and the dice-tumbling machine was not much better. On this summer's day in 1970, however, he was looking forward to a brand-new experiment, designed by a physicist who had recently joined the staff of the Institute.

The physicist, Helmut Schmidt, met Bob downstairs. "This will be an experiment in psychokinesis, but it is not like the other ones you have seen," explained Schmidt. "I want you to try to use psychokinesis to change the way atomic particles behave in a special machine," he continued. "Atomic particles!" exclaimed Bob. "How am I supposed to see them?" "Don't worry about that," replied Schmidt. "We have an interesting display for that."

Schmidt led Bob to a small room on the second floor. It was not much bigger than a closet, and there were no windows. "So there are no distractions," explained Schmidt. Bob sat down in front of a low table on which sat an aluminum box about a foot square and several inches deep. Nine lamps were arranged in a circle on top of the box, and a cable led from it to the next room. "Now, you do not have to worry about the atomic particles," continued Schmidt. "I have a Geiger counter hooked up so that the atomic particles that hit it will cause these lights to come on in sequence. Some particles will cause the light to move to the next position clockwise, and other particles will cause it to move counterclockwise." With that he turned the machine on and, like a theater marquee border gone awry, the light began a "random walk" around the circle, moving in either direction once each second. "What I want you to do is to use your PK ability to keep the light moving in one direction, either clockwise or counterclockwise."

Bob nodded in understanding as Schmidt turned off the demonstration run. "Which direction do you want to try for?" asked Schmidt. Bob hesitated for a moment. He had not expected to have a choice. "Clockwise, I suppose," he replied. "I'll turn off the room light so that you can concentrate on the lamps," Schmidt said.

Bob set the light box on his lap and waited in the dark for a few moments. The first lamp lit. Then the illumination jumped to the next one, then back, back again, then forward. The display had a hypnotic quality, and soon Bob found his torso tracing small clockwise circles as he tried to push the light along in the right direction. In just over two minutes the run was over, and Schmidt poked his head in the door. "How did that go?" he asked. "That's pretty neat. Sure beats that noisy dice machine," was Bob's reply.

Neither Bob nor any of the other subjects who sat in that dark room realized that the experiment in which they were participating would later be regarded as the biggest revolution in parapsychology since J. B. Rhine began work with ESP cards. This was not simply because Schmidt had made atomic events the target of PK efforts. British and French researchers had earlier attempted to get subjects to influence the rate of atomic decay (as measured by a Geiger counter) using PK. The British were unsuccessful, whereas the French enjoyed modest success. Schmidt, however, parlayed his success in this first experiment into a research program that has opened new horizons in psi research and may ultimately shake the foundations of physics.

In the previous chapter we saw how Schmidt started his parapsychological investigations with several very clever ESP experiments. In those experiments subjects were asked to predict which lamp was going to come on next; in effect they were predicting when the next electron was going to strike the Geiger counter. As we discussed in the previous chapter, Schmidt realized early on that although he called the experiment one of precognition, subjects could have been using another form of psi ability—PK. In other words, instead of predicting which lamp was about to light they could be *causing* their choice to light.

From the point of view of physics, it is just as impossible that a human could influence the timing of an electron emission as it is that a human could predict when an electron would be emitted. Schmidt soon turned his attention from experiments designed for precognition to experiments that would test PK, now dubbed micro-PK for obvious reasons.

To understand Schmidt's PK research, first let us recall the basic construction of a Schmidt-type random number generator (RNG). In his ESP experiments this consisted of a fast ring counter (that simply counted 1, 2, 3, 4, 1, 2, 3, 4, . . .) and a source of true randomness—the emission of electrons (beta particles) as radioactive strontium-90 decays. When the subject indicates his guess by pressing a button corresponding to one of four lamps, a circuit enables the next electron that strikes the Geiger counter to stop the counter at one position. The exact moment that this would happen is impossible to predict, so it is, in principle, impossible to predict which lamp will light (in the absence of psi of course).

Designing a similar machine to test PK was even simpler. There was no need for response buttons and the associated circuitry to lock out multiple responses. The display, however, would have to be reasonably engaging and should let the subject know whether his PK attempts were successful. Schmidt's RNG for PK testing was a binary one, that is, the counter went 1, 2, 1, 2. . . . Electronically this was simply an oscillator that flipped back and forth between two positions. Just as with the ESP machine, the arrival of an electron stopped the oscillator in one of the two possible positions. The display that Bob faced was a ring of nine lights, lit one at a time by the RNG. If the oscillator stopped in one position, the light moved one step clockwise. If it stopped in the other, the light moved counterclockwise. When only chance was operating, the lights did a random walk around the ring, with roughly equal numbers of clockwise and counterclockwise steps.

The subjects were not expected to try to figure out what was going on inside Schmidt's RNG. They were simply asked to "will" the lights to move in a specific direction. Like Bob, many subjects became quite involved, moving their bodies or sweeping their hands over the display, hoping to "pull" the lights along with them. A run in this experiment consisted of 128 binary counts and lasted about two minutes. Four runs comprised a session, usually with breaks between runs.

Schmidt's pilot experiment produced unexpected results. Eighteen subjects contributed a total of 216 runs, but the light seemed disinclined to follow the subjects' wills: the results were almost significantly *below* what chance would predict. Perhaps the display was not engendering the right attitude in the subjects? In any event Schmidt decided to predict negative scoring for the main experiment. This study consisted of 256 runs spread among fifteen subjects—most of them "negative" scorers from the first experiment. The subjects produced a scoring rate of 49 percent (where 50 percent is expected)—not a terribly strong effect but statistically significant, with odds against chance of over 1,000-to-1.[19]

Schmidt's next experiment was a particularly ingenious one in which he attempted to see if there would be any difference in results between a psi test structured for precognition and one structured for PK. For this experiment Schmidt used his four-button machine (see page 126). In the precognition part of the experiment the machine operated as usual: The subject pressed one of four buttons, and a split second later the internal RNG caused one of the lamps to light up. The subject's task was to predict which lamp was going to come on. In the PK test (which Schmidt activated simply by flipping a switch) everything *looked* the same to the subject, but now the machine used the output of the RNG (1, 2, 3, or 4) to count over that many lamp positions from the button that had been pressed. In other words, if the subject pressed button 2, and the RNG came up with 1, then lamp 3 would light. If the RNG produced a 2, then lamp 4 would light. *The only way the subject could get a "hit" was by making the RNG produce a 4.* That of course would cause the machine to step over all four steps and end up back on the lamp associated with the pressed button.

With this experiment Schmidt was able to compare precognition and PK performance under exactly equivalent psychological conditions. In fact the subjects could not tell the difference between the tasks and were simply asked to get as many hits as possible. Schmidt conducted two experiments, one with small groups of subjects and the other with one selected subject. The group experiment produced scoring rates of 30 percent for precognition and 31 percent for PK (where 25 percent is expected by chance). Both of these results were statistically significant. The selected subject (Schmidt's coexperimenter) produced scoring rates of 33 percent for precognition and 30 percent for PK. These results were highly significant. Schmidt concluded that there was no difference between the two conditions: Subjects were able to accomplish either task with about the same degree of success.[20]

Although our intuitive notions of PK and precognition suggest that they are very different abilities, Schmidt's experiments reveal that when we are dealing with micro-PK, we may not be able to distinguish them operationally. After Schmidt's first few experiments researchers adopted the convention of calling the experiment one of PK if the subjects were being asked to affect the RNG, and one of precognition if subjects were asked to predict the behavior of the RNG. In other words the way the test was presented to the subject largely determined how the experimenter decided to label the psi ability that was being tested.

In the following years Schmidt reported a number of successful experiments aimed at unlocking the secrets of PK. One experiment revealed that the speed at which the RNG operates can affect the subjects' scoring rates, with higher RNG speeds producing lower scoring rates. Another experiment used two RNGs with different internal designs—one simple and the other complex. Without the subject knowing it, Schmidt switched between the two machines during the experiment, but the subjects produced equally significant scores with both machines. PK ability was beginning to look like a *goal-oriented* process. In other words the subject's PK appeared to be directed at accomplishing the goal—lighting the designated lamp—and the technological complexity of the RNG seemed to be of little consequence. Thus Schmidt and other researchers began to conclude that as long as the RNG incorporated true random processes, the actual physical properties of the system were unimportant or at least they would not produce detectable differences in PK performance. The important job, they felt, was to make the task simple and appealing for the subject. If the right psychological conditions are present, they believed, PK will be demonstrated no matter what the test device.

PK Through the Time Barrier

Back in his apartment Sean Lalsingh Harribance remembered that he was to do an experiment for Helmut Schmidt. This was as good a time as any, so he sat down on the living room floor, closed his eyes, and meditated a bit to get relaxed. Then he reached for the audiocassette tape that Schmidt had given him and popped it into the player. For the last several nights—when he remembered—Sean had been spending fifteen or twenty minutes with the latest of Schmidt's PK experiments. Sean had already tried his hand (or mind, as the case may be) with the light-ring experiment that Schmidt had started using the year before, and he had been pretty successful with it. Now Schmidt had designed a "take home" PK test; Sean was the first to try it.

What Sean heard on the tape were clicks—strong, loud ones and weak, faint ones—coming at the rate of twenty per second. At that rate he could barely distinguish the individual clicks. His task was to concentrate on the weak clicks and make more of them come out of the player. "Ignore the strong clicks, push for more weak clicks," Schmidt had explained. "C'mon, weak clicks!" Sean thought to himself.

The routine was ten seconds of clicks, followed by twenty seconds of quiet. Sean listened to this for about ten minutes, then paused the recorder to get himself a drink. Comfortable again, he resumed listening to the tape. After another five minutes or so Sean found his concentration wandering. "Time to quit," he thought to himself. That was one thing that Schmidt had emphasized: Don't let yourself get tired or bored. So Sean stopped the machine and carefully removed the cassette so that he could take up where he left off when next the mood hit him.

If you are wondering what sort of PK test this is, you can bet that Sean was wondering too. He knew the researchers over at the Institute for Parapsychology had some pretty crazy notions, but he was willing to humor them and apply his abilities where asked. This experiment was stranger than usual, though.

Strange it may well have seemed to the subjects. To Schmidt's fellow parapsychologists it was nothing short of mind boggling. Schmidt was attempting to demonstrate that PK *effects could go backward in time.* In other words a subject's conscious intention *today* could influence the operation of an RNG *yesterday.* Whether or not he realized it, Sean was actually trying to influence an RNG that had been run the week before. This seems even too wild for science-fiction novels, but is it impossible? Surprisingly not at all. In fact Schmidt has been so successful with this type of PK that it forms the basis of his principal research programs today.

To understand this important line of research, let us examine typical features of a time-displaced PK experiment, based primarily on the experiment in which Sean had participated. Schmidt decided to do an experiment of 20,100 binary RNG trials (0s and 1s) grouped in runs of 201 trials.* In this experiment the 0s and 1s are presented to the subject in the form of "clicks" delivered to either the left ear or the right ear (depending on whether the RNG produces a 0 or a 1) via stereo headphones. (Since Sean did not have a stereo at the time, his clicks were converted into weak and strong clicks on a monophonic player.) Up to this point the experiment is simply a variation on Schmidt's ring experiment. The only difference is that the RNG is connected to an audio device to produce clicks instead of light circuitry.

The next step is where the experiment takes a decidedly different turn. Schmidt runs the RNG in the planned manner, but the runs of 201 clicks are recorded on an audiocassette *without anyone listening to the clicks or otherwise knowing the RNG output.* (The significance of the last requirement will be made clear later.) Later, again without anyone listening to it, a copy of the tape is made to use with the subject. The master copy is locked away. Of course, while preparing the cassette Schmidt also intersperses control tests to ensure that the RNG is producing equal quantities of 0s and 1s. When the subject comes in—which could be any time from a couple of days to several weeks later—he is asked to listen to the clicks and make more of them come in the right ear. To veterans of Schmidt's experiments this seems like a straightforward PK task. In fact often subjects are unaware that they are not listening to the output of an RNG directly but rather to a prerecorded cassette tape of RNG output.

---

*The odd number facilitates later classifying the run as a "hit" run (more than half the trials are hits) or a "miss" run.

Sean of course knew that the RNG had been recorded because he had taken the tape home. Letting the subject do the tests at home does not violate experimental security in this design, since the evaluation of results is based on the master tapes, held securely at the lab.

"What is the subject expected to do?" you might ask. "Change the sounds on the cassette tape?" No! That is not what Schmidt expects to happen, and that is another reason why he keeps a duplicate tape hidden away, to be able to compare the two and make sure that nothing was changed on the experimental copy. *If* subjects are able to affect the clicks, somehow they have been able to use PK *backward in time* to affect the RNG when it was generating the clicks.

So much for the example. Was Schmidt able to get subjects to succeed in actual experiments? He certainly did. In his first few experiments of this type, reported in 1976,* quite a number of subjects were able to demonstrate PK via prerecorded targets. Sean had been the subject in the first of several pilot studies. Schmidt prepared six pairs of cassette tapes as described above; Sean listened to three of the tapes at home. In order to provide a different kind of feedback, the remaining three tapes were fed through an instrument that translated the signals into the movement of a needle on a dial (either left or right) rather than loud or weak clicks. Schmidt evaluated the experiment in terms of the number of runs (blocks, in Schmidt's terminology) that contained more 1s than 0s. Of the 832 runs, 54.6 percent showed more 1s, yielding significant odds against chance of 100-to-one.[21]

Schmidt conducted two additional pilot studies using a four-state RNG (1, 2, 3, or 4) that recorded trials on punched paper tape. The subject's task, when he came in later, was to make one particular lamp of four on a display panel light up each time he pressed the button. In this study the button simply activated a paper tape reader, which read the next hole in the tape to determine which lamp to light. Both experiments employed special subjects, and both were successful. Since the paper tapes contained many more trials

---

*Schmidt actually started pilot experiments with what he termed time-displaced PK as early as 1971, but he did not report them until he had several separate confirmations of the effect.

than were actually used, Schmidt also examined all of the unused trials: They averaged around the expected 25 percent. Only the trials that had been presented to the subjects had the desired deviation from chance.

Schmidt's formal experiments to confirm these time-displaced PK effects involved a complicated RNG arrangement that we will not bother to describe here, but the task amounted to listening to clicks in such a way that a PK effect would shorten the waiting time between them. A pilot experiment confirmed that subjects could do the task in real time (that is, trials coming directly from the RNG), and subsequent experiments not only confirmed the real-time PK effect but also demonstrated an effect of almost equal magnitude for trials that were prerecorded. Each of the three formal experiments yielded results with odds against chance of better than 1,000-to-one. For the prerecorded trials Schmidt actually generated the trials in paired sets (A and B); whether the A set or the B set was presented to the subject depended on a complex mathematical calculation performed just before the test session. Thus Schmidt himself did not know which trials would be the test trials until moments before the subject "worked" on them and could not even inadvertently bias the results by selecting the "better" set of trials. The unused control trials, as before, gave results very close to those expected by chance.

As if that were not enough, Schmidt's 1976 report included another time-displaced PK experiment. This one used a binary RNG that displayed an averaged output on an instrument needle. The subject's task was to keep the needle deflected left as long as possible. Real-time trials were alternated with prerecorded trials, and the subject could not tell them apart. In this experiment, however, the prerecorded trials were presented to the subject four times. Without realizing it, the subjects made one attempt to exert their PK power on the real-time targets and four attempts on the prerecorded targets. The thirty subjects who participated averaged 50.82 percent for the real-time targets and 52.95 percent for the "four times presented" targets. Both results were statistically significant, and although the repeated targets did not quite achieve a fourfold increase, the result certainly suggested that it might be possible to magnify PK effects with repeated presentations.

But Is It Still PK?

By now you may be asking yourself if Schmidt is experimenting with PK as we commonly understand it. His time-displaced PK experiments seem a long way from table levitations and even spoon bending. Are we really dealing with the same phenomenon? Quite frankly parapsychologists are not sure. On the surface micro-PK looks like traditional PK, only with a smaller target. A subject is asked to cause a change in a physical system using only mental effort, and subsequently a change is observed. By all appearances the micro-PK subject has been able to cause an action at a distance, which is one of the traditional definitions of PK.

The difference in targets, however, is more than just one of size. In traditional PK the objects that are apparently being moved are large objects ordinarily governed by the deterministic rules of Newtonian physics. The target objects to which Kulagina directs her PK efforts are stable, normally unmoving objects. Without external force (or PK) they would remain just where they are for a long time. In micro-PK, on the other hand, the atomic particles at the heart of the RNG are governed by the *probabilistic* laws of quantum theory. The target of micro-PK thus becomes nature's purest chance processes.

What we are seeing in the results of micro-PK research is not object movement but *the changing of probabilities of events* in systems based on pure chance processes. In other words the micro-PK subjects are not so much shifting things around as they are *shifting the odds* of an event occurring. Typically in Schmidt's binary PK experiments groups of individuals can shift probabilities from 50 percent to between 51 and 52 percent. Certain individuals have managed over 54 percent. This may not seem like very much, but that it is happening at all raises some very fundamental issues for quantum theory.

Many readers will already be familiar with the profound changes in our thinking about subatomic processes that quantum theory has wrought.* The most basic dictum of quantum mechanics is that *one*

---

*Several recent books have made issues that quantum theory raises more accessible to the lay reader. Among them are *The Tao of Physics* by Fritjof Capra

*cannot observe a subatomic event without changing it in the pro-
cess.* Since we generally associate observing a system—taking measurements on it—with the conscious attention of the human being
who is doing the measuring, some physicists have claimed that consciousness itself must be part of the quantum process. The role that
consciousness plays in quantum physics is one of the burning issues
in physics today, and Schmidt's time-displaced PK experiments bring
parapsychology face to face with that issue.

According to quantum theory the atomic events that are governed
by quantum mechanics do not exist as single, discrete events until
they are measured. Whether a photon will appear as a particle or
part of a wave—two mutually exclusive alternatives—is not determined until it is actually measured. It is not the case that prior to
measurement the electron "really is" a wave or a particle (but we do
not know which) the way a gift "really is" a particular object but
remains unknown until we open it. It is not even as if reality were
rapidly alternating between possibilities—neither the particle nor the
wave exists as such. The electron, prior to measurement, is considered the sum of the probabilities of all possible outcomes. This sum
of probabilities is known as the state vector, and upon measurement
the state vector that describes all possible states "collapses" to a
single state—the one that is observed—while all the other possibilities immediately assume a probability of zero. This strange way of
looking at the world of atomic particles cannot be blamed on parapsychology. It is fundamental to contemporary physics and, though
counterintuitive to the nonphysicist, it is a very successful scientific
picture of the subatomic world.

Obviously we do not live in a world where objects are sums of
probabilities—a chair is a chair, and we can sit in it without fearing
it will mutate into something else when we are not observing it.
How does the transition between the odd world of quantum events,
which lies at the heart of all matter, and the everyday world of
Newtonian physics take place? The act of measurement is a critical
issue for this question, and it is precisely here that we find a number
of diverging interpretations. The interpretations become especially

---

(2nd edition, Boulder, CO: Shambala, 1983) and *The Dancing Wu Li Masters*
(New York: Morrow, 1979) by Gary Zukav.

controversial when they try to explain how atomic events interact with macroscopic systems. The "standard" interpretation of quantum mechanics does not distinguish between a measuring device that makes a macroscopic record of the event (such as a tape recorder) and the observation of a human being—either should collapse the state vector and "fix" reality. However, quite a few leading physicists venture so far as to say that mere measurement by a machine is not enough—conscious observation must be there to bring about state-vector collapse. This interpretation of quantum theory would say that Schmidt's prerecorded but yet unobserved tapes do not have a succession of right and left clicks on them. Until they are observed (by a conscious person listening to them), each click-event exists as a sum or "superposition" of the probability of a right click plus the probability of a left click. Until observation the clicks simply do not exist as discrete events. Remember that this can only be possible because the source of the clicks is a pure-chance process governed by quantum mechanics.

Schmidt and other physicists who study parapsychology believe that it is in the process of observation that the subject exerts a PK effect by producing a slight change in the conventional (without PK) probabilities for the events. The observer is, quite literally, helping specify the reality that he or she will see. This, of course, goes beyond the usual interpretations of quantum theory; standard interpretations permit the observing subject to collapse the state vector to a unique event, but not to help specify what event that will be. Yet, as the evidence from micro-PK experiments mounts, conventional physics may yet have to come to terms with this possibility.[22]

According to the state-vector-collapse interpretation of micro-PK findings, the subject is not actually going back in time, as it were, to affect a past event. The event simply does not exist as a specific outcome until it is observed. It follows from this view that the psychological conditions (motivation, expectancy, and so on) for the subject *at the time of observation* will be salient. They will affect the strength of the PK effect; whatever the subjects or the experimenter may be feeling when the RNG is generating the targets is probably unimportant, according to this view. It also follows that if another person observes the results *before* the PK subject has an opportunity to "work" on them, then a PK effect may be diminished or even eliminated. In fact Schmidt recently reported an experiment to test exactly that. He had two subjects, one with a history of success in PK experiments and one with no apparent PK ability, make consecutive attempts to influence the same prerecorded events. The runs that the PK subject was the first to see produced a highly significant above-chance score, whereas those runs that the PK subject saw only after the control subject had seen them produced only nonsignificant below-chance scores.[23]

It is too soon to propose a precise mechanism by which micro-PK effects might be introduced into the state-vector collapse, but the interpretation so far suggests that it may be an informational process—sort of a reverse ESP. The way one would help select a single event among various alternatives is to add some information into the system. If you have two alternatives, it would require just one item or "bit" of information to specify a single event—the bit that says "*that* one." If you have four possibilities, as in the four-button experiment mentioned earlier, it would take two bits to pick a single event—one to say "greater than 2" and another bit to decide between 3 and 4. Thus instead of being a force that pushes or pulls atomic particles around, micro-PK may prove to be a type of information flow directly from the consciousness of the observer to the collapsing state vector.*

What about macro-PK, the directly observable movements? Can one levitate tables with information? Well, the speculations described above have not extended beyond micro-PK, but they do imply that we might be dealing with two separate phenomena if macro-PK phenomena are genuine. The largely anecdotal status of macro-PK has given the micro-PK theorists reason to ignore it for the time being. One may of course note that even a table is ultimately composed of atoms, but in order to shift all those atoms one foot up, say, one would require an infinite improbability generator, and that has not been found outside of *The Hitchhiker's Guide to the Galaxy.*** More sober appraisals do concede that it would be

---

*This view stems largely from the work of Evan Harris Walker, a theoretical physicist with the U. S. Army Ballistics Testing Laboratories in Aberdeen, Maryland. His theories have been instrumental in suggesting a framework for understanding psi phenomena, and we shall return to them in part III.

**This delightfully funny British radio program (later a TV show and book) by Douglas Adams contains many comical extrapolations of parapsychological issues.

difficult to extend a state-vector-collapse interpretation of PK to macro-PK effects. Tumbling-dice experiments and other PK experiments that involve moving systems can be incorporated into the micro-PK model because the act of tumbling may introduce sufficient quantum-mechanical uncertainty into the system to permit it to be considered a truly random process.

As we discussed earlier, in much of the micro-PK research it is difficult to determine whether the subject is demonstrating PK or precognition. Does the subject influence the random process, or does he somehow "see" into the future so as to know when to press the button (or start a sequence of trials) to get the best result? In real-time PK we simply cannot tell, but when we consider the time-displaced PK experiments, the precognition interpretation begins to look a little less plausible. For some of those experiments a precognition interpretation requires that the experimenter (who would have to be the true subject) precognize the entire course of the experiment and thus know the best time to start recording the RNG sequence to match the rest of the operations in such a way as to produce good results. Schmidt's most recent work with multiple observers further weakens—though does not rule out—precognition as an explanation. As this and similar micro-PK research continues, the precognition interpretation becomes less tenable, though the final verdict may be some time off yet.

PK to Confound the Critics

"Aieeee!" shouted the man as he waved his arm menacingly at the diminutive television. After a few seconds he relaxed and took a few deep breaths. Abruptly he tensed and leapt into an Aikido stance, directing his intense gaze at the hapless TV. Uttering a breathy, "Hunhhh!" he resumed slicing the air with his forearm.

Another viewer fed up with network television? Not this time. The person in question, a master of several schools of Oriental martial arts and instructor of martial arts for the U.S. military, is participating in another of Schmidt's PK experiments—a 1988 version.

The television had done nothing to provoke such hostility. It just happened that this subject felt that the intense concentration he brought to bear in his martial arts work could actually produce PK effects.* All that was on the small (six-inch) television screen was a simple display of a block that shuttled from side to side like a pendulum. The task for the subject was either to increase the amplitude of the block's swings (make it swing more widely) or decrease the amplitude (make it hover closely to the midpoint). Though the display is new, the PK test behind it is familiar: A binary RNG controls the swings, with 0s decreasing the swing and 1s increasing it. The RNG does not control the display directly, though. This is another one of Schmidt's time-displaced PK experiments. In fact this particular experiment is one of several in a three-year project currently under way to deal with a problem that has fascinated Schmidt since Sean first took his click tape home almost two decades ago: Can parapsychologists deliver impeccable PK evidence directly to its critics?

In part, Schmidt's interest in this problem stems from his curious position with respect to parapsychology's critics. We have already seen that Schmidt's ESP research made fraud by the subject extremely unlikely. His regular PK research is designed in much the same way. His general experimental methods have been so careful that parapsychology's regular critics have found little to criticize.** The use of prerecorded targets completely eliminates subject fraud, since the RNG operates before the subjects are even in the building. Furthermore statistical evaluation is based on the master copies of the data, to which the subject never has access. That leaves of course only one possibility: Could Schmidt himself be cheating? None of the many researchers who have worked with Schmidt has ever entertained this thought, but it has not been beyond certain critics to suggest it. The British critic C.E.M. Hansel broadly implied it on a television program some years ago. Ordinarily a researcher has only

---

*Schmidt has recently begun drawing his subjects from groups engaging in "high performance" activities in the hope that the mental state that these persons achieve may be conducive to PK. Among the subjects in a recent experiment have been members of a well-known football team from his current state of residence, Texas.

**One critic suggested that perhaps subjects in one of Schmidt's early experiments had cut into one of the cables and surreptitiously advanced the counters. Schmidt countered this both on technical grounds and by the fact that he was in the room with the subjects most of the time.

his reputation to protect him against such insinuations, but Schmidt has actually done better than that: He has adapted his prerecorded PK methodology to a project aimed at "channeling PK evidence to the desk of the critics," to use his own expression. In this type of experiment the critic (or any outside observer) can actually take part in the experiment in a way that eliminates any possibility of experimenter fraud.

The methodology for Schmidt's "outside observer" experiments is very simple if you are already used to the idea of time-displaced PK. First Schmidt prepares pairs of random binary target tapes (or computer disks, programmable memory chips, or some other recording medium). The random targets are grouped into runs. One tape—sealed and unobserved—is given to the outside observer for safe-keeping. With a copy of the entire experiment already in hand, the outside observer then determines the subjects' goals, that is, which runs should have more 1s and which runs should have more 0s. The observer has complete control over this phase of the experiment and can designate the runs in any manner he or she chooses. The observer gives the goal assignments to Schmidt, who, in turn, instructs the subject as to the goal (0s or 1s) for each run. The targets can then be displayed to the subject in any appropriate and interesting manner. Lately Schmidt has favored the simple pendulum display that our martial arts master was grunting at.

Schmidt has completed only one experiment like this so far, a prototype to see if the method would actually work. It did. The observers—Robert Morris and Luther Rudolph of Syracuse University—were not really critics. Morris is now Koestler Professor of Parapsychology, and Rudolph is a professor of communication engineering at Syracuse. Both, however, were rather skeptical about time-displaced PK and certainly qualified as capable outside observers. The experiment consisted of ten sections, with the observers specifying the target direction for each section. Schmidt served as his own subject. When the observers examined their tapes, they found that nine of the ten sessions reflected the target direction (where five is expected by chance) and the overall results indicated a statistically significant effect with odds against chance of better than 100-to-one.[24]

As this book goes to press, Schmidt is continuing with his large-scale project to channel significant PK evidence to skeptical outside observers. He is choosing his subjects carefully to maximize the PK effect, and he is choosing his observers for maximum impact among critical scientists. If successful, this project could be one of the most important milestones on the way to scientific acceptance of psi research.

PK: An Engineering Perspective

"What a racket!" I exclaimed to Roger Nelson, senior research associate with the Princeton Engineering Anomalies Research (PEAR) program. As a visitor to their basement laboratory in the School of Engineering of Princeton University, however, I was not commenting on their well-funded research program nor on the comfortable (if a bit crowded) laboratory to which I was welcomed. Instead I was referring to the PK test that Nelson had just demonstrated for me. For twelve minutes, nine thousand polystyrene balls clattered their way through an array of nylon pegs mounted in a 6-by-10 foot frame on the wall. Starting from a single point in the center, the balls ricocheted through the array of 330 pegs, finally falling into nineteen collecting bins with digital counters below them to register the number of balls in each bin. The final distribution of the balls is the moundlike arrangement known in statistics as a normal, or Gaussian ("bell-shaped"), distribution. Called the random mechanical cascade (RMC), this device is simply a larger and much more finely engineered version of a Galton board, a common teaching aid for introductory statistics classes.

Probably the most micro-PK research in the world is being done at the PEAR lab of Princeton University. Begun as a pet project of the former dean of the School of Engineering and Applied Science, Robert Jahn, the PEAR lab has grown to include several substantial psi research programs, the largest of which is PK research. The PEAR lab has a distinctive approach to research, the most obvious characteristic being their belief that really large data bases are necessary to draw meaningful conclusions. In keeping with this philosophy, the PEAR team has spent years accumulating large numbers of trials on only a few PK tasks conducted according to unvarying protocols. Not surprisingly engineering concerns are paramount in the PEAR work, and considerable attention has been paid to the

1. Dr. Louisa E. Rhine, in a 1959 photograph, consults some of the letters in her large collection of spontaneous ESP cases. These form the basis of her studies discussed in chapter 1. *(Photo: Foundation for Research on the Nature of Man.)*

1.

2. The Fox sisters (left to right, Margaretta, Kate, and Leah) played a major role in launching Spiritualism as a popular religious movement in the nineteenth century. See pages 58–60. *(Photo: The History of Spiritualism, Vol. 1.)*

2.

3. An artist's conception of one of D. D. Home's more spectacular demonstrations—levitation in good light before witnesses. Several of Home's other feats are described on pages 60–63. *(Photo: Mary Evans Picture Library.)*

3.

4.

4. J. B. Rhine tests a subject while an assistant observes. Rhine is using the "screened touch matching" method of testing, one of several methods used in the early days of the Duke University Parapsychology Laboratory. See pages 66–73. *(Photo: Foundation for Research on the Nature of Man.)*

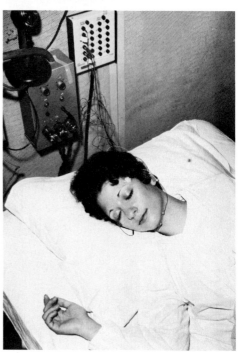

5. A subject sleeps in the Maimonides Dream Laboratory. Wires from her scalp and eye muscles carry signals that will tell investigators when she is dreaming. During dream periods another member of the research team will attempt to "send" her the contents of an art print or similar target. See pages 89–99. *(Photo: Harold Friedman, courtesy of Charles Honorton.)*

5.

Opposite: 6A. A subject relaxes in a ganzfeld experiment at the Psychophysical Research Laboratories (PRL) in Princeton, N.J. The halved Ping-Pong balls covering her eyes, white noise in the earphones, and comfortable chair all help to reduce outside distractions and encourage the subject to focus on inner thoughts and images. During this experiment, an agent in another room will view a film clip several times and try to communicate its contents to the relaxed subject. 6B. PRL researcher George Hansen takes notes while he monitors the equipment that controls the automated ganzfeld ESP tests and records the subjects responses. See pages 105–12. *(Photos: Mort Engel.)*

7. A subject tries her hand with Helmut Schmidt's early ESP test device known as the four-button machine. See pages 123–29. *(Photo: Ansen Seal.)*

6A.

6B.

7.

8. Nina Kulagina, wired for EEG monitoring, attempts a PK demonstration while being filmed by Soviet scientists. See pages 141–47. *(Photo: Copyright Leif Geiges, courtesy of Verena Geiges.)*

8.

9. Members of the Toronto Society for Psychical Research hold one of their regular sittings to conjure up "Philip," an imaginary ghost that seemed to facilitate large-scale PK demonstrations. See pages 151–55. *(Photo: John Cutten, courtesy of Donald Cutten.)*

9.

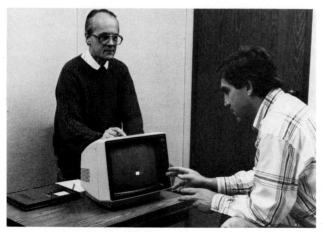

10. While Helmut Schmidt looks on, a subject tries to influence the amplitude of a pendulum-like display on a small TV monitor. The display is governed by one of Schmidt's specially designed random number generators used for PK research. See pages 181–84. *(Photo: Ansen Seal.)*

10.

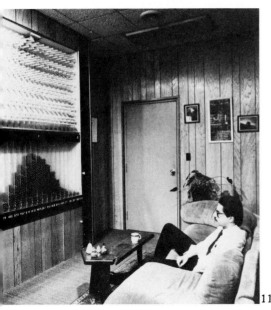

11.
12.

Left: 11. At the Princeton Engineering Anomalies Research (PEAR) Laboratory at Princeton University an operator attempts to influence the distribution of balls in the random mechanical cascade device. See pages 184–87. *(Photo: Margins of Reality, courtesy of the PEAR Laboratory.)*

Right: 12. The author introduces a Duke University student to his "Competitive Game of Chance," a PK experiment that simulates a competition with a student from a rival university. This experiment is part of the author's applied luck project at the Institute for Parapsychology. See pages 187–93. *(Photo: Mort Engel.)*

13. The Cheltenham, England, house in which the Despard family was repeatedly visited by a ghostly widow. Rosina Despard's detailed investigation of the case made it one of the classic ghost stories of early psychical research. See pages 201–8. *(Photo: Harry Price Collection, Mary Evans Picture Library.)*

13.

14. Annamarie, the apparent focus of poltergeist activity in a lawyer's office in Rosenheim, Germany, stands in the entrance hall under a lamp that was often observed to start swinging violently when she was in the office. See pages 216–19. *(Photo: Institut für Grenzgebiete der Psychologie und Psychohygiene.)*

14.

15. Julio, in the warehouse of a Miami novelty distributor where he was the apparent focus of poltergeist activity. See pages 223–27. *(Photo: William G. Roll.)*

15.

16. Joasia Gajewski looks through a badly damaged door in her parents' apartment in Sosnowiec, Poland, that testifies to the havoc wreaked in a 1983 poltergeist episode that centered upon her. See pages 233–40. *(Photo: Nieuchwytna Sila [The elusive force], courtesy of Anna Ostrzycka and Marek Rymuszko.)*

16.

17. Robert Morris records a kitten's activity during OBE detection experiments at the Psychical Research Foundation in Durham, NC. See pages 249–51. *(Photo: Psi SEARCH.)*

17.

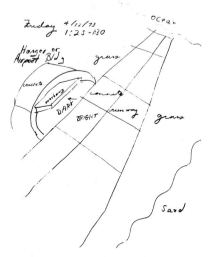

18B.

18A and B. An airport in San Andres, Colombia, visited by researcher Hal Puthoff as a target in one of SRI's remote viewing trials. At right is the sketch produced by the subject. Trials like this suggest potential applications for remote viewing that have interested government funding sources. See pages 319–22. *(Photo: Harold E. Puthoff. Drawing: Russell Targ.)*

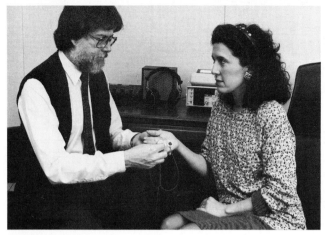

19A.

19A, B, C. Three steps in William Braud's distant mental influence research at the Mind Science Foundation in San Antonio, Texas. At top, Dr. Braud affixes electrodes that will detect changes in the subject's skin resistance that indicate levels of relaxation. While the subject sits "doing nothing" (center), Dr. Braud, in another room, monitors the polygraph that records the subject's skin resistance levels (below). During pre-set intervals Dr. Braud will attempt to calm the subject by his mental influence alone in this experiment designed to investigate the possibility of true psychic healing. See pages 327–30. *(Photo: Ansen Seal.)*

19B.

19C.

physical parameters of the systems targeted for PK effort. This is in contrast to Schmidt's belief that PK is goal-oriented and that the physical nature of the target system is not particularly important. Such differing views are healthy, for at this early stage of understanding, parapsychology can best be served by a diversity of approaches.

The PEAR team has concentrated its PK work on two devices. One is a true (that is, quantum mechanical) random-event generator that produces a random chain of positive and negative pulses. Although more elaborate (and far more expensive), it is functionally equivalent to a Schmidt-type binary RNG. The other device is the random mechanical cascade that had just assaulted my eardrums.

Virtually all of the PK experiments with these two devices conform to a rigid "tripolar" protocol. Each subject tries for a PK effect in one direction (for example, high numbers on the display) on some runs, and the opposite direction (for example, low numbers) on others, as well as doing "baseline" runs where he or she rests and tries to have no effect at all. This three-part protocol is to guard against any possible bias in the physical system that might give the appearance of a genuine PK effect. Both experiments are set up so that *all* the data from formal testing are automatically stored in computer files; thus the PEAR researchers have a virtually unbroken performance record of every subject that ever took part in either experiment.

In the REG experiments a trial consists of 200 binary events. The subject watches a counter that accumulates the binary events, but since the events are generated at the rate of 1,000 per second, the run goes so fast (one-fifth of a second) that the subject simply sees the final number. Chance would predict that these final numbers should average around 100. Subjects do an equal number of runs trying for scores above 100 ("PK+"), scores below 100 ("PK-"), and baseline (BL) efforts. (The aim of course must be declared before the trial.) The actual experimental protocols control a variety of other parameters, but we need not get into those now.

A similar arrangement is used with the cascade device, except here subjects try mentally to "push" more of the balls to land in the right-hand bins on some trials, in the left-hand bins on others, and for baseline trials to let the balls fall naturally. Electric eyes connected to microprocessors count the balls as they enter the bins, and the

counts are displayed below the bins. A run takes about twelve minutes as all the balls clatter through the display.

Data collection on these two projects is an ongoing process, so
publications from the PEAR researchers tend to be in the nature of
progress reports, but the progress is very interesting. In one recent
(1987) report of the REG experiments they had accumulated data
from thirty-three subjects (or "operators" as the PEAR folks like to
call them), who had contributed varying numbers of trials, ranging
from a low of around 2,500 trials in each of the three directions to
a high of more than 55,000 trials in each direction. Overall the
PEAR lab reported over a quarter of a million trials in each direction. The PK$^+$ trials averaged a run score of 100.037 and the PK$^-$
trials averaged 99.966. These averages may look pretty close to
chance, but the odds against chance producing those directional
deviations are more than 5,000-to-one. By way of comparison the
baseline average was 100.004.[25]

A 1988 report of ongoing work with the random cascade presents
a similar picture. With a total of twenty-five subjects and 3,393 runs
(1,131 in each direction), the results indicate that the balls are indeed shifted in the direction intended by the subject, with odds
against chance to the tune of 10,000-to-one. Curiously, the subjects in
the RMC experiment seem to "lean" a bit to one side. RMC operators
are most successful in mentally pushing the balls to the *left*. When they
try to push balls to the right the results are close to chance. The PEAR
researchers are confident that this striking imbalance in performance is
not due to equipment defects, and they suspect it may be a psychological
or neurological effect. Whatever the case, PEAR researchers are continuing to scour the accumulating data for clues that might help them
understand the PK process.[26]

Although the PEAR PK data bases are probably the largest in
existence, the Princeton scientists are not in business just to pile up
numbers. One of their big goals at present is to see if they can
identify operators' individual "signatures"—for example success at
PK$^-$ but not at PK$^+$—in the PK data. In other words, does each
operator have a characteristic way of producing a PK effect across
different types of tasks that could then be predicted when he or she
confronts a new task? Such psychic signatures may not be easy to
find. So far PEAR researchers have reported "encouraging" results

with a few of the operators who seem to exhibit consistent patterns across different experiments. How successful the PEAR group will be in this endeavor remains to be seen.

Another characteristic of the PEAR approach is that they make no effort to preselect subjects on the basis of prior psi ability. This is in direct contrast to the preselection strategy used by Schmidt, who feels that unselected subjects who may have no PK ability will just dilute the efforts of those subjects who do. This issue is more than just one of strategy, however, as it relates to the fundamental question that we examined earlier: Does everyone have psi ability or just a special few? The PEAR researchers feel strongly that their data reveal no evidence of "special" subjects, but merely the wide distribution of abilities characteristic of any human endeavor. Although interpretations may vary for the present, the PEAR data base remains one of the few opportunities for attacking that basic question empirically.[27]

Luck: PK in Daily Life?

"Richard, you had better come and check this out," said Jim Perlstrom, my research assistant, with a puzzled look on his face. I left my office and went with him to the hall outside the room in which one of our subjects was participating in my latest PK test. At first we heard only the electronic beeps and buzzes that the computer game/PK test normally makes. "Yeeehaaaa!" Suddenly a full-blown Southern rebel yell came from the room, and then, "Say your prayers, buddy. I'm gonna blow you away!" Perlstrom and I exchanged glances. I had designed this gamelike PK test to be engaging, but this was the first time anyone had become *that* engaged.

Before we could say anything, a burly Duke University student burst out of the room. "Another Tar Heel bites the dust! I really whipped that turkey!" he shouted with glee. "Hey, terrific," I said, trying to show enthusiasm. "Good going." And then I left him with Perlstrom to wrap up the last few details of the experiment. Fortunately for Perlstrom, the experimental protocol specified that we would not debrief the subjects immediately. We did not want it to get out on the campus that our little "contest" with the rival Tar

Heels of the University of North Carolina was phony. For now we could let our subject savor his victory.

Our Duke University subject had been "playing" the latest in a line of PK tests that I had constructed in the form of games. I have always regarded subject motivation as one of, if not *the*, chief problems facing parapsychologists looking for psi abilities among the general population. Even if one is willing to assume that everyone has some degree of PK ability (and many parapsychologists do not share this assumption), subjects still need some reason to use that ability in your experiment. This is further complicated by the fact that the most obvious characteristic of psi ability is that it is *unconscious* in its operation: in most cases people cannot turn it on and off at will.*

An analogy might give a better picture of what the parapsychologist is facing when trying to obtain evidence of PK. Our local newspaper publishes a crossword puzzle every day. As I have little interest in crossword puzzles, I routinely ignore it and expend none of my language ability upon it. However if someone were to offer me twenty dollars for each completed crossword puzzle, I would probably expend some effort on them; if I were offered fifty dollars for each correctly completed puzzle, I might spend even more effort. Obviously in this case my motivation is purely external to the task. My wife, on the other hand, enjoys the challenge of trying to figure out those obscure word clues, so when she has the time, she will deploy her ability with vigor, simply for the personal satisfaction of mastering the challenge. In her case the motivation is intrinsic and not due to external factors. If what we call psi ability is at all like other human abilities and activities, then we can be reasonably sure that it will respond similarly to human motivation.

Trying to guess what sort of motivation will work in the artificial circumstances of a psi experiment is a tricky business. In general, extrinsic motivators such as money and prizes have not been successful in producing psi results. The best results seem to come when subjects have *intrinsic* motivation to succeed in the test. This motivation can come from several sources. For some successful subjects

---

*It may well be that psi ability has more in common with emotional responses, such as blushing when embarrassed or sweating when anxious, than with more consciously controlled motor and cognitive acts.

psi phenomena may support a personal belief system, so success in a psi task becomes very important to them for confirming their worldview. Some experimenters are very good at creating a climate in which the subject develops a strong desire to succeed, either to please the experimenter, to feel he is contributing to an important scientific endeavor, or for some other reason. Or the task itself may be sufficiently challenging that subjects may try to succeed simply for the satisfaction of personal accomplishment.

This last form of motivation—the one that arises from the challenge of the task—is the logical choice to achieve stable experimental results that can be repeated in different labs. Until recently, however, scant attention has been paid to this feature of psi testing. Through the years J. B. Rhine had placed the burden of inspiring subjects for success on the experimenters; the test was just the test. This approach was still the standard in the mid-seventies, when I entered parapsychology. As a newcomer to parapsychology I found it very frustrating that most of the standard tests I could offer subjects ranged from boring to mind-numbingly dull. When the Psychology Department of the University of Edinburgh, where I was at the time, purchased a new minicomputer with a graphics display, things changed rapidly for me. Within a few months I had my first computer-game PK test in operation.

My first PK game was loosely based on trading in futures on the commodities market. Subjects had "accounts" that accumulated their results (in the guise of play money). The heart of the test was a binary RNG, which translated into the moment-by-moment "market price" of an imaginary commodity. Subjects could select a direction ("Buy" or "Sell" contracts) and a run length based on the number of days the "contract" would run. When the subject was ready, he would "execute" the contract at the current price, and for the next thirty, sixty, or ninety seconds he had to will the price either up or down, according to the type of contract purchased.

Although the initial PK results were very encouraging, I did not stay at the department long enough to report any definitive findings. What I did discover, however, convinced me of the great potential of the game approach. Students (and staff) practically clamored to play the game. (Remember, this was before the days of Apple computers—at the time the only arcade games consisted of bouncing a ball from side to side.) I had to turn away some players lest the parapsychology laboratory wear out its welcome on the department's new computer. Suddenly PK testing had become fun, and the motivation problem, at least for those who liked this sort of game, was largely solved.

That first computerized PK game required a very expensive laboratory computer, but several years later the microcomputer revolution made it possible for any parapsychology laboratory to turn PK experiments into a game. Several researchers did just that, and much of the micro-PK research that has been reported in the last few years has employed games or at least gamelike tests.

Despite my own role in getting PK-gaming started, I must admit that even though this approach may seem to have a lot of advantages for generating subject enthusiasm and motivation, there is no real evidence that it necessarily produces stronger evidence of PK. The gaming approach should be viewed as one method of PK testing that suits some researchers and some research programs. In fact the most productive researchers—Schmidt and the PEAR lab—both prefer simple, straightforward tests for PK. Researchers seem to choose their "style" of micro-PK testing partly on strategic considerations (which style is likely to work in a particular situation) and partly as a matter of taste. Schmidt, a quiet, contemplative person, has told me that he finds PK games too distracting.

PK games may find their greatest utility in studying how motivational factors and the subject's personality affect PK in something approaching a "real life" situation. Parapsychologists have long recognized that they often ask a subject to "use" an ability that he or she has no idea *how* to use consciously. The gaming approach helps to create the circumstances in which a person might *naturally* be inclined to use PK ability without having to think about it. While parapsychologists are not yet ready to set up shop in Las Vegas or Monte Carlo, we can capture a bit of the challenge of "beating the odds" in our laboratories. That is how we hooked our Duke student who thought he'd whipped a Tar Heel.

Our subject was playing a computerized dice game, a highly modified version of a commercially available product. It is not craps, but it does have its own rules. The object is to accumulate a high score (that is, high numbers on the faces of two computer-display dice) and to avoid doubles (which reduce the score). The numbers on the die faces come from a Schmidt-type RNG, so they are potentially influenceable by PK.

We are using this game in several different experiments, but the Duke–Tar Heel match will illustrate how this simple game can help elucidate some of the personality characteristics that may govern how one deploys psi ability in real life. Competition is one of those factors that may play a role in evoking PK abilities, so we decided to present our dice game to subjects as a "competitive game of chance." We told them that our computer was linked to another computer at neighboring University of North Carolina (UNC) at Chapel Hill (home of the Tar Heels). Since most of our subjects were students from nearby Duke University, merely telling them that they would be competing against someone from their sports archrival usually provoked an ample display of competitive spirit. In reality subjects were playing against the computer.

Our subjects played two games during their visit. One was presented as a practice or warm-up game and the other, with a certain amount of fanfare, was presented as the real competition game. In fact both games were played against the computer, but in the competition game the subjects *thought* they were playing against an opponent from UNC. Immediately prior to each game we asked the subject to complete a quick checklist, which gave us a measure of their anxiety level. (The anxiety measure that we used is one commonly employed in sports-psychology research.) People react very differently to competitive sports and games, even when they volunteer to participate, and we wanted to see how anxiety affected their performance.

The only "performance" that would enable subjects to win consistently in the dice game was PK performance. I must confess that our original, naive expectation was that simply by adding the competitive element we would entice PK out of our subjects. Our first experiment proved that expectation wrong. Although the scores in the competitive condition were higher than chance, they were not significantly so, nor were they significantly different from the noncompetitive "practice" scores. The factor that seemed to make a difference, however, was the player's anxiety just before the game. In the noncompetitive game there was no relationship between the game scores and the subject's anxiety. For the competitive game, however, there was a significant *negative* relationship. This meant that subjects who were more relaxed and at ease with the competition game got higher scores and were more likely to win the game. The subjects who were more anxious got lower scores and were more likely to lose the game.

We immediately set about trying to confirm this finding with a second experiment almost identical to the first. Sure enough, precisely the same pattern emerged in the new set of data. In the noncompetitive game there was no relationship between anxiety level and scores, but in the competitive game the less anxious subjects did well, whereas the more anxious ones did poorly. Again, this relationship was statistically significant.[28]

Given parapsychology's history of odd findings that don't seem to fit anywhere, it is very reassuring to find a psi effect that actually makes sense in a broader psychological context. That seems to be the case with our competitive game of chance. Those who were less anxious about the competition, who felt relaxed and perhaps even enjoyed it, did well. Those who were more anxious, perhaps somewhat uncomfortable about the competition, did poorly. It was almost as if they "threw" the game and let the opponent win.

A number of parapsychologists, including myself, have been arguing that if psi is an ability at all, it probably exists to serve human needs. Perhaps the competitive game produced different needs in different subjects. The ones who were relaxed and enjoyed it may have used their psi ability to win. Those who did not care for the competition may have used their psi ability to let their unseen competitor win the game and get it over with.

There are other ways of looking at the relationship between anxiety and PK. Maybe the subject's attitude is the result of PK rather than the other way around. Could it be that some of those subjects know that they are "just lucky" in games, so they naturally felt relaxed in our game? We really cannot say yet, but it does raise another interesting question. Just what is luck? Most people regard it only as fortuitous coincidences augmented by selective memories: we tend to remember the good coincidences and forget the bad or meaningless ones. Yet what has all the micro-PK research been showing? Some people can get random situations—RNGs—to conform to their intentions. If we were to apply that to a casino table, what would we call it? Luck.* Beyond gaming luck, though, keep in mind that life is full of random situations. The brain, for one thing, has numerous random atomic processes. Forgetting, remembering, timing, and so forth, all certainly have their random elements. And then there are the things that are seemingly beyond our control—unexpected equipment failures, other people's random behavior. Suppose one's PK ability extended to those situations. Such a person would not have to exert a really overt PK effect, just what we see in the micro-PK research—shifting the probabilities a little. Would that not look like luck?

Here we must rein in our speculations, at least until the experimental data catch up. For us at the Institute for Parapsychology it is an exciting start to a project that we expect to be working at for a long time. I have nicknamed it the Applied-Luck Project, but clearly we are looking at more than a simpleminded notion of luck. We are seeking to understand what sort of people are able to get random systems to conform to their intentions and under what circumstances. Eventually we may even be able to produce a profile of a "typical" lucky person.

At the Mind-Matter Interface

At the close of the twentieth century, psychokinesis finds itself with a decidedly split personality, and the two sides are not even talking to each other.

Traditional macro-PK research continues, much as it had a century earlier. It has become far more technologically sophisticated, but its status as a collection of astounding anecdotes has not changed markedly. Yet these anecdotes remain much too frequent, and often too well attested, for parapsychology to ignore. With the work of Batcheldor and Brookes-Smith, the "Philip" group, and Houck's PK parties, we can point to modest progress in understanding the psy-

---

*Some gamblers take this interpretation of luck very seriously. In 1966 a well-known gambling research organization, Rouge et Noir, published a book entitled *Winning at Casino Gambling*, which, among other things, advised readers to use their psi ability.

chological conditions that seem to foster directly observable PK, but even that rests on the largely informal reports of a few individuals.

The biggest obstacle to greater progress with traditional PK is that so few parapsychologists are willing to work with it. Traditional PK is saddled with an unsavory reputation. In many instances this reputation is deserved but, if we are to credit only a few of the many reports we have, not in all cases. The encouraging hints offered by the work of those such as Batcheldor, Owen, or Houck languish for lack of takers among the next generation of researchers. I cannot share a common lament of many of my colleagues that the "big phenomena" are no longer to be found. I think we have had the way to these phenomena shown to us, but as a group, we lack the courage to follow the path. For this reason I am not optimistic that we shall see much progress in understanding the fundamentals of large-scale PK, even if it is not all trickery.

In its other guise, however, PK has made enormous strides. Twenty years ago micro-PK research did not exist. Today it is considered the most robust line of research in all of parapsychology. Along the way it has fundamentally changed the way we view PK, from a "mysterious force" to a capability of the human mind to change the probabilities of events. In effect, PK has become the ability of the mind to impose order on chaos—and not just any order, but the order of human needs and intentions.

Apart from the connection with the human mind, there are few similarities between traditional PK and micro-PK. Are they the same phenomenon? Do they originate from the same human ability? We have no answers for these questions, and whether the two sides of this split personality are ultimately reunited or forever sundered remains for the future to reveal.

Today micro-PK is the vanguard of parapsychology for two reasons. The first is that the rapidly accumulating data base continues to reveal a consistent pattern of evidence derived from experiments that meet the most stringent demands of critics. Schmidt, who is largely responsible for starting this line of research, may yet shepherd it into "the breakthrough" for parapsychology with his current program to confront skeptical scientists with incontrovertible PK evidence.

The second reason may be even more important in the long run. The evidence from micro-PK is threatening to make sense in the seemingly crazy world of quantum physics. For decades the cutting edge of physics has been wrestling with conflicting interpretations of the role of human consciousness in determining reality at the subatomic level. This is not parapsychology's problem as such, but it may be an instance—perhaps *the* instance that will make a difference—where the data from parapsychology can contribute to a resolution of the problem. It has been said that the hallmark of a mature science is when its knowledge can be applied to solve problems in other areas of science. Micro-PK research is leading parapsychology into maturity.

CHAPTER 7

Real Ghostbusting

"Spengler, I'm with Venkman. He got slimed!"
"That's great, Ray. Save some for me."[1]

For years after the 1984 film *Ghostbusters* the one question I could always count on being asked when I gave talks in local grade schools was, "Did you ever get slimed?" Much to my young questioners' disappointment, I suspect, my answer invariably was no. Parapsychologists get slimed only in movies. No parapsychologist I know ever got slimed in the line of duty. It comes as a real surprise to kids when I go further and tell them the shocking truth: "Besides, hardly any parapsychologists go hunting ghosts these days."

Adult audiences find this almost as surprising, but it is true. The very word *parapsychology*, which J. B. Rhine promoted in the thirties, was intended to separate laboratory study of the unusual mental abilities of ESP and PK from the traditional investigations of ghosts, hauntings, and poltergeists. These latter phenomena were to remain in the domain of psychical research.

Although the passing decades have permitted these earlier preoccupations to slip back under the umbrella of parapsychology, they remain a very minor part of its contemporary scene. Although part of the reason for this may be fashion—ghosts and poltergeists are scientifically unfashionable, and one rarely meets them at respectable conventions—the chief reason for the decline in this area has to do with scientific efficiency. Even among those who allow that these phenomena are worth investigating, few today are willing to invest the often large amounts of time and trouble that they require. Ghost and haunting investigations are particularly vulnerable to inefficiency, since they can often last for months or years; in the end, all the investigator has is a good story if he is lucky. Even in a meticulously documented story with numerous reliable witnesses and with audio or film recordings, critics will challenge the credibility of the testimony and the authenticity of the recordings. In a few years the event will be just another story, and neither science nor our understanding of these phenomena has been advanced much for all the trouble. This is not to deny the possibility that these phenomena exist, only to explain why few parapsychologists bother with them now.

Yet there remain some parapsychologists who see in the many carefully investigated cases of earlier years the very real possibility that science is ignoring a rare but genuine form of human experience. For them there is a need to continue investigating and documenting these cases, if for no other reason than to keep before parapsychology the awareness that its emerging picture of psychic phenomena may fall short in some areas.

The Candidate's Ghost

The thermometer in the room read 49 degrees Fahrenheit, and the breath of the two young men condensed into little clouds, eerily illuminated by dim shafts of light from their flashlights. They had just lugged two mattresses into place and were preparing to bed down on the floor of an upstairs storeroom in Hannath Hall, a dilapidated Tudor house in the hamlet of Tydd St. Mary, Cambridgeshire, England. The men were Anthony Cornell, a Cambridge County official, and Alan Gauld, a research fellow in psychology at Cambridge University. Both were members of the Society for Psychical Research (SPR) with considerable prior experience in ghost hunting.* They were about to lose a night's sleep in the interest of science, one of many they would lose in their careers.

---

*Cornell is now a Cambridge County councillor, and Gauld is a senior lecturer in psychology at the University of Nottingham.

At the time the house was occupied by Mr. Derek Page, then the Labour party candidate for Parliament (later elected, and now Lord Whaddon), his wife and two children, ages three and five, and his wife's mother. They had moved into the house in August 1957 and shortly thereafter found themselves disturbed by strange noises—thumps on doors, raps, footsteps, and groans. Once a bed was violently jolted. A local journalist learned of the happenings and contacted the SPR, which put him in touch with Gauld and Cornell.

Gauld, Cornell, and two members of the Cambridge University SPR, D. J. Murray and J. M. Brotherton, along with the journalist and two of his friends, visited the house one evening in November 1957. They arrived around 10:30 P.M. and interviewed the adult members of the family. Then they carefully examined the two-story house inside and out, noting the layout of the various bedrooms on the second floor, where most of the phenomena had taken place. One bedroom had been dubbed by the family "the haunted room" because of a story that a previous owner in the nineteenth century had left the body of his deceased wife there for several weeks while he continued to have meals sent up to her. But the phenomena did not seem to focus in that or any particular room.

The stakeout began around 11:45 P.M. Cornell organized a ouija-board séance with the adults in the living room downstairs (primarily to ensure that everyone but the children, who were sleeping, was in view) while Gauld stationed himself in the second-floor gallery from which the bedrooms led off. Twice during the next forty-five minutes Gauld heard noises but concluded that they probably had normal explanations. As is typical in old British houses, this one lacked central heating. By 12:32 A.M. the cold drove Gauld downstairs to join the others.

At 1:25 A.M., with the séance still in progress downstairs, Gauld and Cornell retired to the haunted room and prepared to settle down for the night. The room was primarily used for the storage of unused furniture and had no electricity. With their flashlights they inspected the room again. Their sleeping accommodations consisted of two mattresses laid end to end on the floor.

Only a few minutes after they had turned off their flashlights, gentle taps were heard on the floor about three feet from the mattresses. Flicking on the flashlights, the men saw only bare floorboards where the sounds had been heard. In whispered voices, they called out specific numbers, and the raps—growing louder and moving toward the wall—responded with the correct counts. Using a code, they began to question the rapper, who claimed to be a woman who had been murdered in the house in 1906. (Gauld and Cornell were unable to substantiate this in later record searches.) Later the researchers heard a sequence of six or seven loud knocks, growing in intensity. When Gauld flashed his light in their direction, they stopped; only bare floor was seen.

Eventually the séance downstairs broke up, and the journalist and his two friends left. Murray and Brotherton went upstairs and heard the rappings from outside the haunted room. While Murray waited outside the door, Brotherton ran down to check on the Page family and found them all sitting around the table in the living room. The raps continued throughout. Murray and Brotherton then searched the room below the haunted room, finding nothing.

Gauld and Cornell left the haunted room to ask the others to keep quiet, returning about ten minutes later. Murray and Mrs. Page stationed themselves in the room below; Brotherton and Mr. Page stood in the gallery outside the room. Mrs. Page's mother was alone in the living room. Soon loud raps—loud enough to be heard in the room below—began again, this time on the other side of the mattresses. With further questioning the rapper repeated the earlier information. They asked the month of the rapper's death. Eleven raps were heard. Then someone asked what day of the month. At this a series of raps commenced that moved along the floor toward Cornell's head. The sixteenth rap seemed to come from the air just behind his head. Cornell switched on his light, but the raps stopped, and nothing was seen. When asked to continue counting from ten, the raps resumed, much more faintly, and continued to eighteen. An attempt to learn the rapper's age at death was unsuccessful. After a short while the raps faded away entirely. Gauld and Cornell returned downstairs about 2:45 A.M.

Not long after, the journalist and his friends returned to the house because their car had broken down. Mr. Page drove them to town in his own car and returned to the house around 2:50 A.M. Gauld and Cornell returned to the haunted room at 3:34 A.M., and apart from one strange incident in which a fireplace toasting fork seemed to bolt the door closed when Cornell slammed it shut, nothing else unusual happened that night.

The following week Gauld and Cornell spent another night in the room and heard more rappings, but this time they were faint and distant-sounding. In all they returned twenty times to conduct further inspections of the house. They cleared out the room and inspected the entire floor with a magnifying glass to see if any floorboards had been taken up to conceal machinery. It was tongue-and-groove flooring, and there was no sign that it had ever been removed. They lifted the board below the spot where the first sounds were heard, but again they found nothing. Likewise the ceiling of the room below, also tongue-and-groove boards, was carefully inspected. The rooms were carefully measured and compared with the external dimensions of the house to check for concealed spaces. None were found. At one point they brought in an amateur medium to hold a séance in the haunted room. A woman calling herself Eliza Cullen or Culler "came through," claiming to be the rapper. Gauld and Cornell were unable to trace anyone by that name.

What conclusions can we draw from this investigation? It is not without its shortcomings, of which Gauld and Cornell are well aware. Their biggest regret was that their tape recorder was out of order and they had not brought another one. They also felt that they should have had a minute-by-minute log of everyone's comings and goings. As it was, they only had good estimates for the sequence of events.

How successful had the investigators been at eliminating possible normal explanations for their experiences? Faulty or embellished recollections are always a possibility, but the investigators had taken notes as they went along, always within minutes of the event, and the notes of the various parties agreed. (Copies of these documents were deposited with the SPR in London.) What about auditory illusions that could have made normal sounds seem paranormal? In an ordinary room (as opposed to an anechoic chamber) it would not be difficult for two attentive adults to distinguish sounds in the center of the room from sounds on the window or walls. The rapping "conversation" (heard by all four investigators) rules out random noises, not simply because of the responses but because of the "behavior" of the rapper, appropriately waiting for questions to be completed and pausing when finished. On later visits Gauld and Cornell conducted tests to see if there was any chance of confusing raps from anywhere outside the bedroom with rappings made inside the room. They had no problem in distinguishing between the two.

That leaves the possibility of fraud. Their searches uncovered no signs of rapping machinery secreted between the floor and the ceiling or in any of the adjoining rooms. One of their admitted oversights was not being able to account for the movements of the journalist and his friends throughout the evening, but the rapping had continued while Mr. Page was driving them into town. What about the family itself? There was never any sign of suspicious behavior, and all of the adults signed affidavits stating that they had no part in the production of the phenomena. The children were too young to have been involved, but nonetheless the investigators had checked them regularly throughout the night and had always found them sleeping. Could Gauld and Cornell have been hoaxing everyone else? Apart from the fact that twenty visits to the house and all the tedious searching for alternative explanations seems a rather excessive effort for a hoax, the investigators have only their reputations and avowals of honesty to defend them. For those who know Alan Gauld and Tony Cornell this will be enough; for those who do not know them it may not be sufficient.[2]

This haunting was sufficiently interesting to report, but it was not a very dramatic case. I suspect Gauld and Cornell would dearly have liked to find themselves involved in something a little more exciting, but alas, such cases are rare indeed. To get the flavor of a "classic" haunting investigation we shall have to depart from contemporary parapsychology and go back over one hundred years to Cheltenham, England.

Miss Morton's Ghost

I had gone up to my room, but was not yet in bed, when I heard someone at the door, and went to it, thinking it might be my mother. On opening the door, I saw no one; but on going a few steps along the passage, I saw the figure of a tall lady, dressed in black, standing at the head of the stairs. After a few moments she descended the stairs, and I followed for a short distance, feeling curious what it could be. I had only a small piece of candle, and it suddenly burnt itself out; and being unable to see more, I went back to my room.

The figure was that of a tall lady, dressed in black of a soft woolen material, judging from the slight sound in moving. The face was hidden in a handkerchief held in the right hand. This is all I noticed then; but on further occasions, when I was able to observe her more closely, I saw the upper part of the left side of the forehead, and a little more of the hair above. Her left hand was nearly hidden by her sleeve and a fold of her dress. As she held it down a portion of a widow's cuff was visible on both wrists, so that the whole impression was that of a lady in widow's weeds. There was no cap on the head, but a general effect of blackness suggests a bonnet, with a long veil or a hood.

Thus begins one of the longest and most famous haunting investigations in the annals of psychical research. That narrative was contained in an 1882 letter written by Miss Rosina C. Despard, a nineteen-year-old medical student specializing in forensic medicine.* She lived in a large stone house in Cheltenham, England, and was writing to a close friend in another part of the country.

Six more times over the next two years, Rosina observed the figure, but she told no one, save her friend, of these encounters. Three other people also noticed the figure during this time, but did not take it to be an apparition. One evening Rosina's sister, Mrs. Kinloch, joined the family at dinner. "Who was that Sister of Mercy whom I have just seen going into the drawing room?" she asked. A servant was sent to check but found no one, even though Mrs. Kinloch was quite certain that she had seen the Sister. Later a housemaid saw the same figure and feared someone had broken into the house. In December 1883 Rosina's brother and another boy were playing outside when they thought they saw a woman crying bitterly in the drawing room window. When they ran in to see who it was, they found no one.

Rosina's own experiences with the apparition began to assume a regular pattern. She would encounter the figure upstairs, often after hearing pushing noises at her bedroom door, and follow her down the stairs to the drawing room. The figure would usually assume a position on the right side of a bow window and remain there for a variable length of time. Then she would depart along a passage to the garden door, where she would simply disappear from sight. Be-

---

*She eventually qualified and went on to practice. This was no small achievement for a woman in 1882.

sides the noises at the bedroom door the only sound Rosina would hear would be very light but distinct footsteps, which accompanied the apparition's movement (sounds that, by the way, had different characteristics depending on whether the apparition was moving over carpet or linoleum).

Once Rosina attempted to speak to the apparition. The ghost gave a "slight gasp" and started to depart. "Just by the door," Rosina's narrative continues, "I spoke to her again, but she seemed as if she were quite unable to speak. She walked into the hall, then by the side door she seemed to disappear as before."

In July and August of 1884 the apparition began to be seen more frequently and by more people. One of the early encounters of this period was particularly strange in that Rosina was the only one of several people in the room who noticed the apparition.

One evening, around nine o'clock, Rosina joined her father and sisters who were reading in the drawing room. Rosina sat on a couch near the bow window. Her narrative continues:

> A few minutes after, as I sat reading, I saw the figure come in at the open door, cross the room and take up a position close behind the couch where I was. I was astonished that no one else in the room saw her, as she was so very distinct to me. My youngest brother, who had seen her before, was not in the room. She stood behind the couch for about half an hour, and then as usual walked to the door. I went after, on the excuse of getting a book, and saw her pass along the hall, until she came to the garden door. I spoke to her as she passed the foot of the stairs, but she did not answer, although as before she stopped and seemed as though *about* to speak.

While this encounter might suggest that the widow in black was something only certain persons were permitted to see, a few weeks later several other persons saw the figure jointly or in rapid succession. On this particular evening Rosina's sister, Edith, had been singing in the drawing room when suddenly she stopped and called Rosina from the hall. Rosina reports:

> She said she had seen the figure in the drawing-room, close behind her as she sat at the piano. I went back into the room with her, and saw the figure in the bow window in her usual place. I spoke to her several times, but had no answer. She stood there for about 10 minutes or a quarter of an hour; then went across the room to the door,

and along the passage, disappearing in the same place by the garden door.

My sister M[abel] then came in from the garden, saying that she had seen her coming up the kitchen steps outside. We all three then went out into the garden, when Mrs. K[inloch] called out from a window in the first storey that she had just seen her pass across the lawn in front, and along the carriage drive towards the orchard. This evening, then, altogether 4 people saw her. My father was then away, and my youngest brother out.

It was not until August 5, 1884, more than two years after the first sighting, that Rosina told her father what she and the others had experienced. Her father asked the landlord if he knew of any strange happenings that had occurred before their tenancy, but the landlord did not, having himself only lived in the house a few months. During that August the apparition was seen on several occasions by members of the family as well as by the servants and the gardener. The haunting became noisier, with much more walking on the second-floor landing as well as louder bumps on the bedroom doors and more frequent door-handle rattlings. For a period of time a second set of footsteps was heard—heavy and irregular, very unlike the apparition's—which would continue for most of the night, often three or four times a week.

Sightings continued through the following years with what appeared to be an increase in frequency each July and August. In all, as many as twenty people saw or heard the apparition. Some of these people knew nothing of the apparition prior to their own encounter. Apparently even the household pets sensed the apparition: A Skye terrier that slept on Rosina's bed undoubtedly reacted as if it heard the apparition's footsteps on many occasions. Twice during the daytime Rosina observed the dog run to the mat at the foot of the stairs, acting as if it was about to be affectionately petted, only to slink away suddenly with its tail between its legs and hide under a sofa.

From 1885 on, Rosina was in regular contact with F.W.H. Myers of the SPR, who offered various suggestions on the investigation. Rosina kept a camera ready, but poor lighting thwarted her attempts to capture the apparition on film. She tried to touch the figure, but it would simply disappear if cornered. Attempts to communicate with the figure using signs or gestures also proved futile.

Several times Rosina lightly fastened strings across the stairway at various heights, only to watch the apparition pass right through them.

As the years went on, the apparition came less frequently and curiously appeared fainter when seen. From 1887 to 1889 the figure was rarely seen and the louder noises gradually ceased. Rosina noted that up to about 1886 the apparition seemed "so solid and lifelike that it was often mistaken for a real person," but later it gradually became less distinct. After 1889 the Despards never saw the figure again. There are reports that later residents of the house and neighbors had observed the apparition, but these claims have been too sketchy to permit careful evaluation.[3]

One interesting confirmation of sorts surfaced in 1944. A successful solicitor by the name of George Gooding wrote to the SPR indicating that he was one of the young boys who had seen the tall figure in black while playing with Rosina's brother. He confirmed the description of the apparition and added that while the people did not seem overly concerned about it, the dogs disliked and apparently feared it. He recalled clearly two occasions on which he saw the tall woman in black: one was in bright sunlight in the yard and the other was in the drawing room. In the latter instance the boys joined hands to make a ring around the figure, but she simply passed between them and disappeared.[4]

The Despard family's own investigations suggested that the lady in black might have been a Mrs. Swinhoe, the second wife of the house's first occupant, Henry Swinhoe, who had bought the house in 1860. The description of the apparition was easily recognized by those who knew Mrs. Swinhoe, and Rosina herself identified a picture of Mrs. Swinhoe's sister (who reportedly resembled her strongly) as being most like the apparition. In his letter to the SPR, Mr. Gooding recalled that his godmother, with whom he was living at the time, seemed to know who the apparition was but would never speak of her. Unfortunately there is no romantic story linking Mrs. Swinhoe to the house. Reportedly both Mr. and Mrs. Swinhoe were heavy drinkers and frequently quarreled. Mrs. Swinhoe actually left her husband a few months before he died in July 1876. She went to live in Bristol and apparently never returned to the house. She died in September 1878.

When the SPR heard about the case several years after it began, they were not about to accept Rosina's account solely on faith. Myers, who had been following the case since 1884, interviewed all the principal witnesses and found the testimony satisfactory. He also interviewed a number of people who testified to the good character of the Despard family. Myers's extensive investigations revealed, in his words, "In this case it is observable that the phenomena as seen or heard by all the witnesses were very uniform in character—even in the numerous instances where there had been no previous communication between the percipients." Myers went on to note that with only one trivial exception—a single incident that an elderly man could not recall six years later—he "found no discrepancy in the independent testimonies."[5]

The SPR's first concern was whether it might all be an elaborate hoax, but the arguments against that are substantial. There were simply too many independent witnesses over too long a period. Myers found absolutely no evidence to suggest that Rosina Despard was reporting the events inaccurately. Nor is it possible to conceive of a motive for such an elaborate hoax, since it brought nothing to the family and potentially could have ruined Rosina Despard's hard-earned medical career. Rosina's father, Capt. F. W. Despard, feared for the value of the house, which belonged to a friend, and consented to the publication of the report only if it were written under a pseudonym. (It was published under the name of R. C. Morton, and is often called the Morton Case.)

Another possibility suggested by Mrs. Sidgwick, one of the SPR's most tough-minded and skeptical investigators, was that the figure was an actual living person secretly residing in the house with the connivance of Captain Despard. (His wife had been an invalid for many years.) Mrs. Sidgwick's suggestion, made in 1885, probably accounts for Rosina's experiments with the string and her attempts to touch the figure. That the figure passed through string traps and could not be touched certainly counts against this theory. Furthermore, the figure did not behave as if it were supposed to be hiding, since it often showed up in broad daylight and passed through obviously occupied rooms or even outside. Since this case was included in the SPR's 1892 *Proceedings*, we can be sure that the critical SPR researchers were satisfied that all alternative explanations had been ruled out.

Has the passing of the decades provided investigators with any further clues as to how this incredible story might be attributed to natural causes? In 1958 G. W. Lambert advanced an ingenious theory to account for the noises reported during the haunting. First of all Lambert dismissed the apparition as a secondary effect—perhaps due to suggestion and anxiety about the noises—and concentrated on the sounds: footsteps, twisting door handles, and the like. From his examination of an old survey map Lambert had determined that a stream could have passed near or under the Despards' house. The stream would have received its water from the river Chelt when it flooded, a regular occurrence in those years, at least until upstream reservoirs were created around 1886. Lambert felt that it was a "reasonable inference" that the noises were due to a disturbance caused by the water as it passed underground near or under the house. Lambert admits that his case is based on circumstantial evidence and is not conclusive.[6]

Although clever, Lambert's theory fails to answer a number of questions. If the noises were due to underground water, why should they be concentrated on the uppermost floor of the house? At times the noises were very loud, sufficient to frighten servants into seeking employment elsewhere—hardly the type that rushing water might produce unless there were impacts of some sort. Furthermore, wouldn't someone have been able to feel the vibrations being transmitted through the structure? And why were none of the adjacent houses similarly troubled? Despard's house was not an unstable structure; it was a substantial stone residence that still stands today. Lambert's approach, that of seeking natural explanations first, is fundamental to investigations of hauntings, but in this instance his conjectures are not convincing.

Lambert's assumption that the apparitions were individual *natural* hallucinations brought on, perhaps, by fright combined with suggestion has been the basis of other attempts to explain the case. Once Rosina had described her experiences, the idea goes, the power of suggestion operated on all the others. This hallucination theory, however, fails to account for the several early instances when other household members saw the apparition but were unaware of Rosina's experiences. Also, in the later years several people reported the apparition before learning of the family's experiences. Furthermore, according to Mr. Gooding and others who knew the family, nobody was particularly frightened by the noises. Apart from a period in 1885 when the loud noises commenced, which frightened some of the help and did make the family nervous, none of the family, least of all Rosina, seemed particularly overwrought by the experience. Myers noted that the members of the Despard family "were unusually free from superstitious fears." There were also many times when the apparition appeared without any preceding noises to people in relaxed and congenial circumstances. This natural explanation leaves too many loose ends to be considered satisfactory.

"They don't make 'em the way they used to" could well be the contemporary parapsychologist's lament about ghosts. If only cases like the Morton Ghost would turn up now, when we could use modern video and computer technology to record the phenomena. As it happens, there have been a few occasions, albeit with somewhat less "robust" ghosts, when investigators went in with all sorts of paraphernalia—recording equipment, temperature and motion sensors, you name it—but they have all come away with very little for their troubles. Hollywood is capable of producing far more convincing ghosts than parapsychologists can, and therein lies an almost insurmountable problem. Who would believe the films and recordings today? As a result one of the more interesting techniques for ghostbusting used lately is decidedly low-tech.

Contemporary Low-Tech

"That's a funny sound," thought Phyllis as she moved into the hallway. She stood dead still, listening. "There it is again. Sort of like a long, full skirt brushing against something." Phyllis looked around her own feet, and up and down the hall for something that might have made the sound. She saw nothing. "Better mark that," she thought as she steadied the clipboard that held the house's floor plan.

Phyllis was participating in a novel haunting investigation pioneered by Dr. Gertrude Schmeidler, a professor of psychology at City College in New York City, and her then-graduate student, Michaeleen Maher. In late 1973 friends of Maher reported haunting-type phenomena in their home. Schmeidler and Maher visited the house and interviewed the people involved, but they did not then begin the long and time-consuming "stakeout" in the hope of seeing something for themselves. Instead they took the information that they had gathered and used it to create an *experimental* approach to the investigation. Based on their interviews of the occupants, they compiled a checklist of thirty-seven descriptions, eight that correctly described what the occupants of the house had seen and twenty-nine that did not, the latter group having been selected as controls. They also prepared a map that indicated the sites in the house where the ghost had been seen as well as places where it had not. Next Schmeidler and Maher recruited four people who, for one reason or another, they believed might be psychic. These persons were taken to the house and asked to walk through it and, using their psychic sensitivity, to identify areas of the house where they had "unusual perceptions." After the tour these psychics were asked to indicate which of the checklist items they thought pertained to the reported ghost. To serve as a control group, Schmeidler and Maher had four additional people who were skeptical about this sort of thing also tour the house and complete the same tasks. Presumably this latter group would pick the parts of the house that might appear "spooky" because of lighting or other normal factors. The investigators reasoned that if anything paranormal was happening, the psychics might perceive what the occupants had, but the control participants should not.

On the whole the psychics were able to identify the correct items on the checklist significantly more often than the skeptics. In fact two of the psychics were very accurate. Unfortunately the amount of data collected was rather small, so any conclusions must be considered very tentative, but the method seems promising.[7]

Some might think this method is not as much fun as staking out a haunted room, but it does offer a different perspective on a claimed haunting. The use of the control group provides a handy yardstick against which one can examine the effects of suggestion and other psychological factors. This approach may well become a useful adjunct to more traditional methods, possibly providing an independent corroboration of eyewitness testimony. A big drawback, however, is that there is no way of telling whether the information the psychics picked up comes from the minds of those who knew the correct information—the experimenters and the occupants—or from some "presence" in the house itself.

Common Sense and Nonsense

Perhaps the lowest-tech approach to a haunting investigation is good old-fashioned common sense. Any parapsychologist who has spent even a little time investigating hauntings probably has a much longer list of duds than of truly interesting cases. Often it does not take a great deal of experience to smell a rat. For example what would you think if you were interviewing a family who claimed their house was haunted and in the course of your investigation you came upon a signed contract concerning the proceeds of book and film rights to the story? That actually happened to some colleagues of mine.

Early in January 1976 Jerry Solfvin and Keith Harary of the Psychical Research Foundation, then in Durham, North Carolina (not to be confused with Rhine's Institute for Parapsychology), took a phone call from a Mr. George Lutz in Long Island, New York. Lutz described a most bizarre array of phenomena, which he felt were due to a demonic entity. A brutal mass murder had taken place in the house some years earlier; the caller felt that this event must have some connection. Solfvin and Harary conferred by phone with Lutz several times over the next few weeks, but they didn't believe the case merited a special trip. The phenomena seemed a little too bizarre—not at all like typical cases—and anyway the events were over. The family had moved out of the house and the phenomena had stopped. All they had to offer investigators were their stories.

In March Solfvin happened to be in the New York area, so he stopped in to visit the Lutz family. Quite by chance that same afternoon Dr. Karlis Osis, of the American Society for Psychical Research (ASPR), and Alex Tanous, a psychic who had participated in ASPR research for many years, were visiting as well. At some point the talk turned to the subject of the mass murderer, who was now in prison. The Lutzes produced a sample of the murderer's handwriting for Tanous to examine. The specimen was most interesting, but not what Tanous had expected: The sample was the murderer's signature—on the bottom of a contract for the distribution of the profits from book and film rights to the haunting story!

Osis and Tanous went over to the allegedly haunted house but didn't find much of interest. Later that afternoon Solfvin also visited the house, but by the time he got there, a television crew was already filming and newspaper reporters were prowling about. Since the parapsychologists had nothing more than the family's claims, and given the strong indications of a profit motive behind the whole thing, they concluded there was nothing there to interest them. Sometime later, on a New York radio program, the lawyer for the murderer's family claimed that the whole thing was a hoax—something that he had dreamed up along with the Lutzes—and now he was suing the Lutzes because they tried to cut him out of the profits. The Lutzes were of course countersuing. None of this stopped some folks from making a large bundle of money on the story that became known as *The Amityville Horror*.[8]

Sorting Out the Spooks

If parapsychologists and psychical researchers have had any impact on the spookier side of their investigations, it has been to introduce a measure of order in an otherwise chaotic situation. Ghosts, poltergeists, and hauntings are *not* the same phenomena, although they are frequently confused in the minds of the public, not to mention film and television producers. The patient, careful accumulation and documentation of cases over the years has made it clear to parapsychologists that we are dealing with at least two, and possibly three, distinct classes of phenomena.

In chapter 1 we encountered examples of apparitions—the visual appearance of a person who is not really present. These were *crisis apparitions*—occurring in connection with a crisis for the person who is seen as an apparition—and are almost always one-time events. In contrast to this is the *recurrent localized apparition*—or ghost, to use the colloquial term—that is seen in more or less the same form by different people at different times in roughly the same vicinity. A *collective apparition* is seen by several people simultaneously.

These distinctions in terms do not explain what an apparition is, of course. The preferred explanation by parapsychologists is that the crisis apparition is actually a hallucination brought about by some sort of telepathic contact with the person in crisis. This theory is believed to account for the majority of one-time apparitions. But what about collective apparitions? Assuming there was some telepathic "seed," why should different people generate exactly the same hallucination? And what about the recurrent localized apparition that is seen by many different people (who are ignorant of one another's experiences) on separate occasions, sometimes spread over decades? The notion of a telepathically generated hallucination hardly explains these phenomena.

To account for those instances in which the same apparition is seen by several people or over time, some parapsychologists have advanced the notion of *super-ESP*—psychic ability of a magnitude far greater than that typically found in reported cases in the laboratory. (Super-ESP is also used to explain how mediums get information telepathically from the living, or by clairvoyance.) In applying super-ESP to apparitions, these parapsychologists argue that possibly some terrible event "impregnated" a location with information that later visitors were somehow able to pick up psychically. Others have suggested that the original sighting was simply a hallucination but that the shock and fear felt by the first percipient somehow "reverberates" through the years and is picked up by others later. An important consequence of super-ESP interpretations is that only living individuals are responsible for the psychic manifestations, since it is a living individual who psychically acquires the information necessary to create the hallucination. No input from "the other side" is necessary to explain the experience.

Other parapsychologists theorize that the apparition is in some way caused by a surviving aspect (soul, spirit, consciousness) of a dead individual. This is known as the *discarnate-entity* theory. Although, strictly speaking, the discarnate-entity theory can include such hypothetical beings as angels, devils, and so on, the prevailing interpretation is that some aspect of a human being continues after bodily death. This aspect later serves as a catalyst for the phenomena perceived by the living.

Each of these explanations is purely conjectural, and both arise not out of any hard evidence but from interpretations of admittedly large amounts of testimonial evidence. For the present they serve simply as frameworks around which more comprehensive theories may develop. Unfortunately I cannot even offer the comfort of a statement like "Most parapsychologists believe . . ." since there is little consensus regarding how the evidence should be interpreted. The current focus of parapsychology on the mental abilities of living individuals makes the super-ESP view more fashionable, but, in the end, fashion will have little to do with deciding which of the two views, if either, is correct.

Recurrent apparitions have a number of characteristics besides the one implied in the name. Typically, but not necessarily, a recurrent apparition will appear to engage in the same specific behavior each time it is observed. For instance an apparition may consist simply of a woman pacing up and down a hallway. Another characteristic of recurrent apparitions is that the image rarely interacts with the observers or even acknowledges their presence. The apparition seems to go about its business oblivious of whoever may be watching. Rosina Despard's apparition fits this mold fairly closely except that the widow in black moved over a wider locale (upstairs, downstairs, and sometimes outside) than most. Often an apparition is never seen outside a certain room or hall.

In direct contrast to the relatively unobtrusive character of the recurrent apparition or ghost is the extremely obtrusive nature of the *poltergeist* ("noisy spirit" in German).* Parapsychologists today prefer to avoid the implications of spirit causation carried by the word *poltergeist* and instead use expressions such as "poltergeist phenomena" or "poltergeist outbreak" to describe the phenomena that can occur. In recent years parapsychologists have been using the term *recurrent spontaneous psychokinesis*, or RSPK, in conjunction with a particular theoretical viewpoint that I shall explain below.

The most common types of phenomena associated with poltergeists are noises (generally percussive sounds such as bangs,

---

*The German word means literally a noisy or rattling (*poltern*) spirit (*geist*— obviously related to the English word "ghost"). *Poltergeist* is now a standard English word to refer to this disruptive type of psychic phenomena, but it is not the one that the Germans prefer. To the Germans "poltergeist" connotes a playful silliness that is inappropriate to serious investigation. They use a more serious word, *spuk*, which is clearly related to the English word *spook*, a word English-speaking investigators avoid because of *its* playful connotations.

thuds, rappings, crashes) and object movements (the hurling of crockery and small furnishings, lifting or upsetting of chairs and larger furniture, and so on). Only rarely do apparitions find their way into poltergeist reports, and then they are usually very varied, lacking the apparent consistency of the recurrent-apparition cases.

Perhaps the most striking contrast between poltergeist activity and recurrent apparitions is the matter of duration. Poltergeist outbreaks seldom last more than a few months. In half of the hundreds of poltergeist cases on record, the phenomena ceased within two months. Many occurrences last only a few weeks. By contrast reports of apparitions can continue for years or even decades.

The early, or what we might call the "naive," interpretation of poltergeist phenomena was that some more or less malicious spirit or demon was plaguing the household. Often the local clergyman was called in to exorcise the demon. It is this interpretation that has caused the poltergeist to be lumped together with ghosts, since the poltergeist appeared to be simply a delinquent ghost. Parapsychologists have been able to determine otherwise, however, and this is probably one of the more important advances in understanding these phenomena.

Far from being the activities of a spirit, what we call a poltergeist outbreak seems to be the product of a living individual. Early investigators of poltergeist cases often found that the phenomena typically centered around a living person rather than a particular place. Modern investigations have confirmed this observation and added to the picture. Typically (though not exclusively by any means), poltergeist phenomena are connected with a young person, frequently an adolescent who is under a certain amount of psychological stress.

Parapsychologists now believe that the individual around whom the events center, often called the *poltergeist focus* (or *poltergeist agent*), is producing the phenomena through psychokinesis, hence the term RSPK. Once again, this is not much of an explanation, since we have no idea what psychokinesis really is, but it is more helpful than saying that poltergeist activity is all due to an invading spirit. If the events are caused by psychokinesis, then clearly they are on a scale far greater than has ever been observed in the laboratory, more on the order of D. D. Home's feats. Indeed Home and several of the other physical mediums are often thought of as "tame" poltergeist agents.

It would be nice if parapsychologists could keep all their ghosts in one compartment and their poltergeists in another—and perhaps ultimately they will—but for now there remains a type of case that seems to fall somewhere in between. This is the *haunting*, which bears similarities to both recurrent apparitions and poltergeists.

Hauntings, like recurrent apparitions, are usually centered around a place, often a residence. Haunting phenomena typically consist of poorly defined sounds (thumps, bumps, and rappings) as well as well-defined sounds (footsteps, sounds of doors opening or latches clicking, crockery breaking, and human voices or groaning), all without any apparent normal cause. Objects commonly move. Clothes or bedding are tugged at, lights travel about the room, and doors open or close without any movement of the knob. A haunting might include a ghost or recurrent apparition that appears along with the other phenomena, but many cases consist only of noises and movements. These physical phenomena, particularly those that leave traces, cannot easily be considered hallucinations, which sets hauntings apart from recurrent apparitions. They can resemble poltergeist activities, but are characteristically more subdued and not as concentrated in time.

It is often possible to establish "communication" with whatever or whomever is doing the haunting. Using a simple code of rapping sounds, dozens of careful investigators have conducted question-and-answer sessions in the same manner that Gauld and Cornell did. (Communicating through raps has also been reported in a few poltergeist cases, that is, those with an identifiable poltergeist agent about whom the phenomena center. It is possible that this is simply a classification problem, since most of these reports come from the period when it was believed that poltergeist activity was caused by spirits.) In itself the presence of raps neither confirms nor denies the discarnate-entity interpretation. There is nothing to stop a living agent from paranormally producing raps.

Like recurrent apparitions, hauntings can go on for decades and be observed by many people independently of one another and at widely spaced intervals. Gauld and Cornell's case described at the beginning of this chapter had the characteristics of a haunting without a recurrent apparition.

Whether parapsychologists are dealing with three distinct types of phenomena or just two remains to be seen. Until more progress is made toward understanding the causes behind the phenomena, we can expect this matter to remain unresolved. Fortunately some headway is being made in one of the three areas: poltergeists.

Der Rosenheimer Spuk

On a cold November morning in 1967 most of the employees of lawyer Sigmund Adam were already at work in his chancery in the Bavarian town of Rosenheim. One of the last to come in was Annemarie Schneider, an eighteen-year-old secretary and relatively new employee. She walked down the entrance hall, taking off her coat as she went. As she passed under the hanging lamp, it began swinging, but she did not notice it. As she continued toward the cloakroom, the lamp began to swing more animatedly. Suddenly the lamp in the cloakroom began swinging too. An employee who had eyed her suspiciously when she first walked in suddenly shouted *"Achtung! Die Lampe!"* Annemarie ducked and held up her coat for protection. Seconds later a bulb in the hall lamp, now swinging wildly, exploded, showering glass slivers in Annemarie's direction. The swinging subsided, and with a few words of thanks to the employee who had warned her, Annemarie got a broom and swept up the glass. The rest of the office got back to work. They were getting used to this sort of happening by now.

The lawyer, however, was at his wits' end. His office was rapidly self-destructing and his business grinding to a halt. The fluorescent lights on the ceiling went out time and time again. Once there was a loud bang, and all the lights went out simultaneously. When the electrician climbed up to check them, he found that each tube had been twisted 90 degrees in its socket, breaking the connection. Shortly after he had returned them all to working order, there was another loud bang, and out they went again. Even when they were not on, incandescent light bulbs exploded in their sockets, often leaving the delicate filaments intact. Electrical fuses would blow with no apparent cause, and sometimes the cartridge fuses ejected themselves from the sockets. Telephone disruption was particularly severe; all four telephones would ring simultaneously with no one on the line. Calls were frequently interrupted for short periods or cut off entirely. Telephone bills suddenly soared to unusual levels: Large numbers of calls that had not been made were being billed. The developing fluid in the photostatic copiers would often spill out without any disturbance to the machines.

At first Adam and his staff suspected the electrical supply. Engineers from the municipal power station and the post office (which operates the telephone system) were called in. Monitoring equipment was installed on the power lines to detect any unusual fluctuations or surges. These monitors registered large deflections, which often coincided with observed disturbances. But then the offices were disconnected from the mains and an emergency power unit was brought in to supply "undisturbed" power; the deflections, and the phenomena, continued unabated.

Recording equipment was also installed on the telephone lines to keep track of each call originating from the offices. It started registering calls almost immediately, even though no one in the office was using the phones. The post office equipment registered innumerable calls to the time-announcement number (which is not a free call in Germany), often dialed as rapidly as six times a minute. On October 20, forty-six calls were made to the talking clock in a fifteen-minute period.

Early in November the press got wind of the happenings, and two German television companies produced short documentaries. They showed the destruction in the lawyer's office and the installation of the monitoring equipment. On camera the technicians admitted they had no explanations. A post office official insisted that all the strange calls must have been made in the office, but the employees all denied it. The lawyer himself pleaded for an end to it all. By this time he had filed formal charges making the mischief maker liable for criminal prosecution. At that point the Rosenheim Police CID (Criminal Investigation Division) took charge of the investigation.

Prof. Hans Bender of the University of Freiburg, an experienced poltergeist investigator, arrived with some colleagues on December 1. They were joined one week later by two physicists from the Max Planck Institute for Plasma Physics, F. Karger and G. Zicha, who began to look for physical disturbances in the power and telephone equipment. Bender's team quickly realized that the unusual phenomena and power disturbances occurred only during office hours. It also became clear that the activities centered around Annemarie. Often the first deflection of the power-monitoring equipment registered the very moment that Annemarie crossed the threshold in the morning. Bender's hunch was that they were dealing with RSPK and that Annemarie was the focus.

When Karger and Zicha arrived, they immediately set about examining the power supply. On December 8 they attached additional equipment to the monitors already in place. Between 4:30 and 5:48 that afternoon the recorder registered fifteen strong deflections at irregular intervals. At about the same time they heard loud bangs similar to those produced by especially large sparks, but not every deflection was accompanied by the noise. The noises were recorded on a tape recorder. More equipment was brought in to monitor the electric potential and the magnetic field near the recorder as well as the sound amplitude in the office. On the basis of their investigations the physicists felt they could rule out such causes as variations in the supply current, demodulated high-frequency voltages, electrostatic charges, external static magnetic fields, ultrasonic or infrasonic effects (including vibrations), loose contacts or faulty recording equipment and, finally, manual intervention.

Once Bender had shared his conviction that the disturbances were due to PK, the poltergeist activity began to intensify. Bender's team, as well as power-company engineers and CID officers, watched decorative plates jump off the wall and paintings begin to swing and even turn over on their hooks. Bender captured on videotape the swinging lamps and the banging sounds but was unable to record a picture rotation. Another investigator, using their equipment, was able to record a picture rotating 320 degrees. The Freiburg team witnessed drawers open by themselves and documents move about. Some drawers ejected themselves completely from the cabinet. Twice a filing cabinet weighing nearly 400 pounds moved about a foot from the wall. While this was happening, the investigators noticed that Annemarie was getting more and more nervous. Eventually she developed hysterical contractions of her arms and legs. When Annemarie was sent away on leave, the disturbances immediately ceased. Shortly afterward she found employment elsewhere, and the lawyer had no further problems. At her new office there were some similar disturbances, but they were less obvious and eventually died off.

Bender's budget did not permit him to post observers at the lawyer's office all the time, but he did receive frequent phone reports from eyewitnesses describing events as they were happening. Even this was not easy: one such telephone call was interrupted four times; each time four fuses had to be replaced to resume the call. All in all, the Rosenheim case involved about forty firsthand witnesses, who were thoroughly interviewed. Witnesses included the technicians from the power company and the post office, police investigators, physicians, journalists, and clients of the lawyer. Of the more than thirty-five cases that Professor Bender has investigated, he has always considered the Rosenheim case the most impressive.[9]

Poltergeists Through the Centuries

How typical of poltergeist outbreaks is the Rosenheim case? It is in fact very typical. Except for the involvement of electrical equipment, much of what happened can be found in cases hundreds of years old. Years after their cold night in Hannath Hall, Alan Gauld and Tony Cornell collaborated on a book entitled *Poltergeists*,* which is widely regarded as the most scholarly treatment of the phenomena to date. For this book they examined no fewer than five hundred cases, but only those reported *in detail*, either in diaries, published investigations, or in the records of court cases or commissions of inquiry. Their earliest case dates from 1525–26. It concerned an outbreak of poltergeist activity in a French convent and was the subject of a small pamphlet published in 1528 by the case's investigator, Adrian de Montalembert, almoner and preacher to Francis I of France.

To be sure, not all of Gauld and Cornell's cases were what we would consider clear-cut poltergeist outbreaks—perhaps as many as a third were more like haunting cases—but their chief aim was to compare the different types of cases. Their task was similar to L. E.

*(London and Boston: Routledge & Kegan Paul, 1979.)

Rhine's study of spontaneous cases (see chapter 1), but poltergeist cases involve even stranger happenings, usually consist of reports from several persons who have shared the experience, and continue over an extended period.

Studies of the many poltergeist reports over the centuries and from all parts of the globe have revealed some very curious commonalities. It seems likely that in many cases these distinctive features were observed independently and were not "contaminated" by shared expectations of what "should" happen in a poltergeist outbreak.

As discussed, the most common characteristic of poltergeist cases is object movements. In haunting cases one often gets reports of object *displacements*—something is found in a different place from where it was last seen—but in poltergeist cases objects are frequently *observed* flying around the room. The following incident, witnessed by William Roll, an experienced poltergeist investigator, during an investigation he conducted in Kentucky in 1968, provides an example:

> One time he [a 12-year-old] went out to the kitchen while I followed a few feet behind. When he came to the area between the sink and the kitchen table he turned around facing me. At that moment the table jumped into the air, rotated about 45 degrees, and came down on the backs of the four chairs that stood around it, its four legs off the floor. No one else was in the area.[10]

While some poltergeist movements seem playful, like this one, others can be downright calamitous, as described in the famous Poona (India) case of 1927 that seemed to focus on a nine-year-old boy:

> On April 28, things reached a climax. The little boy's food and toys were repeatedly snatched from his hand, and his drink from his mouth, though he made frantic attempts to retain his hold of these things. His toys came literally in showers from his cupboard when no one was in the room who could have done this. As the child moved through the rooms, he was surrounded . . . by broken glass, scattered liquids (including bottles of citronella oil, liniment, brilliantine, eyedrops, and saccharin, all of which were hurled from their accustomed places), and the noise of crashing objects. The child was exceedingly brave, but hysterical.[11]

Most of the movements reported in poltergeist cases are unusual only in their initiation, that is, once in the air an item behaves like any thrown or dropped object. However a substantial percentage of the reports, perhaps as many as a quarter to a third, describe movements that are in themselves very strange: Objects follow trajectories that would be impossible if thrown normally; they turn in midflight, or strike with unusually weak impacts. For example in an 1818 Austrian case a Mr. H. J. Aschauer, a teacher of mathematical physics, visited his son-in-law's house, where some strange happenings had been reported. Aschauer watched a "big iron spoon," weighing about a pound, suddenly leave a shelf and fly "with great velocity" at a neighbor's head. But instead of seriously bruising the neighbor, the spoon inflicted "only a light touch" and then fell perpendicularly to the floor. Another example comes from a 1709 case that took place on the farm of a Dutchman, Jan Smagge, on the small island of Canvey near the mouth of the Thames River in England. At one point in this very active case the maid and another woman:

> saw a piece of Tile come in of the said Door, about two Foot from the Ground, but very leasurely; and yet so strait, as though it had moved on a Line; and then, in a languid manner, after creeping thus five or six yards in her sight, touching against the Gown of one of them, fell down near her Feet; the other, who was the Maid, ran to catch it up; but let it fall, crying, It burnt her; and a little Blister, in touching it, was raised on her Fore-finger.[12]*

Another curious feature is often noted by observers. To paraphrase the well-known adage about pots, a watched object never moves. Many witnesses report that it is impossible to see an object *start* moving, although often they notice it just after it starts.** It is this

---

*I should mention that, while not being a major characteristic, such heat effects as found in this case are reported in eighteen of Gauld and Cornell's five hundred cases.

**This observation may in part be a result of the physiology of the human eye and brain. Our peripheral vision is well suited to detecting motion but not to identifying objects. Identification of objects takes place in a very small range at the center of the visual field reserved for focal vision. Thus, although motion may be detected at the time it starts, the fraction of a second it takes the observer to bring the moving object into focus may contribute to the impression that the actual start of the motion had been missed. Of course this is a separate issue from some of the cases, in which it almost seems like objects "refuse" to move as long as someone is looking at them.

sort of observation that leads some to conclude that the investigators are being fooled by simple tricks or sleight-of-hand, but
often that is hard to square with the details of the cases. One
example comes from a case that F.W.H. Myers personally investigated in 1891. The outbreak occurred at a carpenter's workshop,
and it principally involved chunks of wood flying about in all directions. Myers complained that he and other witnesses could stare
at an object for many minutes and it would not move, but the
moment they let their attention relax, "that very bit of wood would
come flying at us from some distant point." (In this case, too,
pieces of wood would often follow bizarre trajectories, undulating
in flight or making corkscrewlike spirals.) As Myers described it,
one of the chief witnesses tried hard to outwait the poltergeist, but
to no avail:

> Mr. Crowther, who was a man of leisure and moderate independent
> means, used sometimes to sit in the shed for two or three hours at a
> time, watching to see a piece of wood start on its course. He never
> saw one start; though like the rest of us, he saw many which seemed
> to have just started.[13]

Strange outbreaks of fires have also been reported, erupting on walls
and other unusual places, though they rarely become truly destructive.
Other cases feature water, sometimes appearing in copious quantities
in parts of a house where there is no plumbing. In 1973 Bender investigated such a case in the German village of Scherfede. First small pud-
dles, then large pools of water started appearing in a small row house.
Municipal engineers and plumbers could find no leaks or other source
of water (though tests revealed it to be from the town's springs). Large
pools of water appeared even when the water was turned off at the
main and the village's firemen were posted throughout the house as
guards. At one point large quantities of water came cascading down
the stairs of two adjacent houses. The whole outbreak lasted several
weeks, and Bender concluded that a thirteen-year-old girl was the poltergeist focus.[14]

Showers of stones, raining out of the sky or even inside a house
in full view of witnesses, have been reported, as has the unexplained appearance of large amounts of human excrement. Witnesses' clothes are often torn (while being worn), and very
commonly bedding is disturbed. Surprisingly common (but not as

common as modern filmmakers would have us believe) are assaults on people, though these tend to be on the order of pinches,
scratches, and bites.

This last aspect of poltergeist activity no doubt touches upon a
common concern: Can people get hurt in a poltergeist outbreak?
The answer is generally no. Poltergeist cases often include threatening gestures that do not actually cause harm, such as the flying
spoon described earlier. Cases of serious bodily harm (more than a
pinch or a bite) are uncommon, though not unknown.

In recent decades poltergeist cases have been investigated both
more frequently and more successfully than hauntings. They are less
susceptible to the efficiency problem that hampers ghost and haunting cases, largely because they usually only last a few weeks and the
frequency of events is far higher. The fact that the poltergeist outbreak seems to center on a living person also makes it possible to
isolate the individual and learn more about him or her. Another
1967 case (a good year for poltergeists) illustrates this.

A Poltergeist Among My Souvenirs

"I'm tellin' ya, Sarge, you better get down here and see this for
yourself. If I hand you the report on this without you being here
and seeing it, you'll have me up at the institute or something."

Patrolman William Killin hung up the phone and turned to Alvin
Laubheim, manager and part-owner of Tropication Arts, a whole-
saler of Florida souvenirs and novelty items. "The Sarge is coming
over, but he's not happy. He thinks I've gone nuts." Less than an
hour earlier, it was Killin who thought his dispatcher had gone nuts.
When he received the call to go to the Tropication Arts warehouse
to investigate a report of a ghost smashing the stock, he double-
checked with the complaint clerk; he was not about to be the butt
of someone's joke.

Ten minutes later on that Saturday morning, January 14, 1967,
Killin arrived at the warehouse and found two people there, Laubheim and Julio Vasquez, a nineteen-year-old Cuban refugee who
worked as a shipping clerk. The warehouse had a long row of storage shelves along most of the east wall; three tiers of shelves ran in
the same direction in the center of the building. At the far end were

several tables for packing and shipping. The three men walked to
the back, and while Laubheim and Julio waited there, Officer Killin
proceeded to inspect the aisles. As he rejoined the others, he turned
around, just in time to see a glass from the shelf he had just passed
shatter on the floor. Killin started patrolling the aisles again, and
several more items fell and broke.

It was then that Killin decided to call his sergeant. The sergeant,
not taking any chances, arrived with two additional patrolmen
shortly after noon. Two more people had arrived as well, Howard
Brooks, who was Laubheim's friend as well as a professional magician working at a nearby ice show, and a companion of Mr.
Brooks. With all of these people keeping their eyes on the shelves
and on one another, two more incidents happened. In one, a box
of address books fell into the aisle. Two of the police officers had
noticed that particular box earlier—it had been sitting six to eight
inches from the edge of the shelf—and they were sure nobody was
near it when it fell. The officers shook all of the tiers to see if that
would cause anything to fall. Nothing did.

The events had started about a month earlier. Laubheim had become aware of an unusual amount of breakage but had chalked it
up to the employees' clumsiness. He spoke to them about it, but
items continued to end up on the floor. By January 12 Laubheim
had instructed Julio to lay the mugs (a particularly vulnerable item)
flat on the shelf with the handles facing out to prevent them from
rolling. No sooner did they leave the mugs in that position and walk
away than one of them ended up on the floor. Recalling events later,
Mr. Laubheim lamented:

> From then on, everything started to happen—boxes came down—a
> box of about a hundred back scratchers turned over and fell with a
> terrific clatter over on the other side of the room and then we realized
> that there was something definitely wrong around here.
>
> And for three days we picked things up off the floor as fast as they
> would fall down. It was going on all day—quite violently—but not
> hurting anything, but things would fall to the floor. We tried to keep
> it quiet because we knew it would hurt our business, because we are
> right in the middle of a season—the beginning of a season—and it
> would draw a bunch of curiosity-seekers and the like, so we tried to
> keep it quiet for about four days. Then finally, delivery men saw those

things happen and people coming in and out would see it happen and word got out and there were more and more people coming in. And somebody suggested that with the glasses being thrown around and with the girls crying in the front from fright, we had better notify the police; so I did.

As it happened, Suzy Smith, a writer of popular books about parapsychology, was being interviewed on a radio program on the evening of January 12. One of the employees of Tropication Arts called in on the station's question line and related some of the events that had been going on at the warehouse. Miss Smith visited the warehouse the next day, and several more mysterious falls occurred. She in turn contacted William Roll of the Psychical Research Foundation, probably America's most experienced poltergeist investigator.

Roll arrived on January 19, but there was a marked diminution of incidents in his presence, so much so that he quickly began to wonder if he was somehow inhibiting them. His first instinct was to suspect trickery, but he felt that if trickery had been involved, then the magician, Mr. Brooks, and the two police officers still working on the case would have noticed it by now. Roll interviewed the witnesses, cataloging the numerous happenings. He was particularly interested in Brooks's comments because of his conjuring expertise. At first Brooks had discounted the whole thing as a practical joke and had even surreptitiously tossed an item to show how easily it could be faked. After a week he was not so sure that it was all tricks. Then, after watching two cartons drop to the floor with no one around, he changed his tune. "I can't buy this spook theory at this point," he told Roll, "but something did move those, and I couldn't figure it out." Later Brooks saw other items fall off shelves when he was the closest person nearby. He immediately searched the area but could find no mechanisms that might have triggered the fall.

Eventually, more or less by making himself inconspicuous, Roll was able to be present when several more falls and breakage took place. On his instructions everyone would freeze in position whenever something fell so that Roll could note positions and be the first to examine the fallen item. At this point Roll had to go back to

North Carolina for a meeting, but several days later he returned, this time accompanied by another parapsychologist, J. Gaither Pratt, who had worked alongside Rhine for many decades.

Pratt, who had been introduced only as "a friend," seemed to have less of an inhibitory effect than had Roll, and events happened relatively freely in his presence. Roll and Pratt developed a strategy of prowling around the aisles for a while, then Roll would go outside for a time. At one point Roll asked Julio to place a tray in a particular location from which another tray had apparently fallen earlier. Roll and Pratt inspected the tray several times on their tours; then Roll left the building. Pratt noted what happened next:

> During the period preceding this event I was observing the activity in the room and recording a running description of the situation on tape from my position in the southwest corner of the room. This record continued right up to the instant when the tray fell and broke. The point on the shelf where it was standing was not visible from my observation point. I could, however, see Julio. He was working in the south part of Aisle 3 and was separated from the disturbance by the tier of double shelves. I could see both his hands. In one hand he held a clipboard, and the other was by his side. At the time of the incident he was walking toward my position. No one was in Aisle 2 where the tray fell and broke, and Julio was the nearest person. I was not able to conceive of any way in which the falling of the tray could have been caused to happen in a normal manner.

Moments later, while Roll was still out, two more ashtrays fell and broke.

This apparent encore performance led to more "experiments" of that type. Roll and Pratt began designating certain "target items," which were placed carefully on the shelves and closely monitored throughout the day. Several of these target items later crashed to the floor when the investigators were sure no one was in the vicinity. One time Roll placed a glass on the shelf and then put several small items in front of it. A short while later the glass fell to the floor without disturbing the objects in front of it. Since there was a tendency for objects that had been disturbed once to be disturbed again, Roll took a damaged beer mug from a box of mugs that had just fallen and replaced it on the shelf. When nothing happened to the mug for quite a while, Julio jokingly suggested that the "ghost" might not like the damaged mug and that perhaps he should put a good one there. Roll agreed. Picking up an undamaged mug, Roll thoroughly inspected it and found nothing suspicious. He handed it to Julio, who exchanged it for the damaged one. Roll described what happened:

> At 2:09 P.M., only a little more than half an hour after it had been put out, the new mug crashed to the floor in Aisle 4. . . . This beer mug had been placed behind two small cartons and between a Fanta bottle and a cowbell. Like the glass it too must have moved up into the air to have cleared the obstacles. At the time of this event, I was by the front desk, looking up Aisle 3, where Julio was walking toward me with a broom in his hand. Suzy and a visiting psychologist were next to me near the front desk. No one else was present. The mug moved in a northwesterly direction, its place of origin being about four feet from Julio and the direction of movement away from him. Again I was unable to explain the event normally.

Roll wound up his investigation shortly after this incident.

Julio was later brought to Durham for a psychological evaluation, which revealed him to be an unhappy young man with feelings of unworthiness and guilt. He longed for his mother and his grandfather, who had remained in Cuba. Roll learned that early in December (shortly before events began at the warehouse) Julio's stepmother had told him she wanted him to move out of the house. He had begun having nightmares in October, which became fairly frequent over the next three months. These dreams revealed feelings of need for punishment and even suicidal tendencies.

Not long after his return to Miami, Julio was arrested for shoplifting and spent six months in prison. Not surprisingly, the police had suspected he was the cause (in a conventional way) of all the disturbances at the warehouse, but in the several weeks that they were on the case, they never caught him doing anything wrong. Nor had anyone else. Two years later Julio was working in a gas station and refused to hand over money to two armed robbers. In the scuffle Julio was shot twice and very nearly lost his life. Roll reports that after this incident apparently Julio's "psychical and physical life settled down."[15]

Ruling Out the Normal

When one is faced with a poltergeist case, the first order of business is to look for normal explanations. Despite what critics may think, parapsychologists are no more eager to waste time or be made fools of than anyone else. There have, of course, always been a number of stock explanations for what people witness in some poltergeist cases. Many initial reports of poltergeist activity *do* turn out to have quite ordinary causes, and the families are grateful to the investigators for enlightening them. But not all cases are so easily resolved.

The most obvious conventional explanation for a poltergeist outbreak is fraud. This sits well with the observation that many poltergeist cases center around individuals, especially adolescents. Every parapsychologist who has investigated a poltergeist case has encountered fraud at one point or another. In most of the cases it is fairly simple to detect, though sometimes skillfully executed. Gauld and Cornell's survey showed that in about 8 percent of the cases at least one observer claimed to have seen trickery, though that does not mean that the entire case was deemed fraudulent.

Since we have all seen skillful conjurors in operation but few of us have seen poltergeists, there is a natural tendency to ascribe all of the phenomena to adept conjuring. But this begs the question. Who is the skillful conjuror in poltergeist cases? The skills of a stage magician do not come easily; they take years of study and practice. Small children or teenagers do not become skilled sleight-of-hand artists overnight or train for hours without anyone noticing. Gauld and Cornell noted that of all the cases they have studied, in only one did the apparent poltergeist agent reportedly show a prior interest in conjuring. They are aware of no cases in which a poltergeist agent later went on to become a stage conjurer.

Furthermore, many of the poltergeist cases include phenomena that would seem beyond the capabilities of even the best conjurers of the day. The unusual trajectories and the slow or undulating flights of objects are but a few examples. Were the witnesses mistaken?

Several arguments favor this position. Memory is notoriously unreliable, but in many poltergeist cases the details were written down within minutes or hours of the occurrence. Recent poltergeist investigations also include video records or running commentaries on tape recorders. Many of the cases in Gauld and Cornell's collection consist of reports from not just one or two witnesses, whose memories might have lapsed, but from dozens of witnesses, all supplying corroborating testimony, often before courts of law or investigative commissions.

Perhaps, then, the original observations were erroneous. Again, there is a good deal of research that demonstrates that people can misperceive events for a variety of reasons. Everything from poor visibility to preconceived expectations can influence the accuracy of eyewitness reports. Studies in which an incident was staged have demonstrated that eyewitnesses often misperceive sequences of events or are mistaken about the positions of different parties. But these studies "spring" the event on the subjects unexpectedly, whereas many of the poltergeist phenomena are witnessed by persons who are alert and expecting something to happen that they will want to remember accurately. This experimental literature cannot be used to explain the many instances in which several people collectively witness an event such as an object slowly undulating through the air untouched by anyone. The objective recordings obtained in recent cases, many of which contain the same sorts of phenomena that are found in older ones, also help counter the misperception argument, since these can corroborate the verbal reports.

There have also been attempts to explain poltergeist phenomena by external forces. G. W. Lambert, who attempted to explain the Cheltenham haunting (Rosina's ghost) as underground water movements, has also argued that many poltergeist outbreaks may be due to environmental factors. Underground water channels—streams, old sewers, and so forth—may run under or near the foundations of a house. When pressures build up after flooding, downpours, or abnormally high tides, the house might be subjected to sudden jolts or upward thrusts.[16] Other writers have suggested that mild seismic disturbances could affect the house. The theory is that either the water or the seismic activity might shake the house, causing objects to move or fall off shelves. Certainly this theory might account for *some* of the phenomena reported in poltergeist cases, but only a very small fraction. As residents of California and other earthquake-prone areas can testify, one can feel seismic jolts at magnitudes much weaker than that needed to disturb objects. Frankly it is hard to conceive of any sort of jolt to a house foundation that would knock objects off shelves but not be noticed by the occupants, yet house tremors are virtually never reported, except in the few cases where house shaking seems to be part of the poltergeist outbreak.* Furthermore this theory completely fails to account for the many observations of object movements that go against the force of gravity. Most importantly, it fails to explain why events stop when the focal person leaves the premises.

The Poltergeist Agent

As with haunting cases, if none of the conventional explanations, either singly or collectively, seem to provide a satisfactory explanation for the experiences detailed in the hundreds of poltergeist cases on record, then we are entitled to consider what parapsychology may have to offer. Most parapsychologists have adopted the explanation that poltergeist phenomena are caused by the psychokinetic ability of a living individual. Many of the historical cases and virtually all of the recent ones involve one individual (in rare cases, two) around whom all the commotion seems to focus. When that person is present, things happen; when the person is absent, they cease. There are numerous cases in which the phenomena followed the apparent poltergeist agent to a new location. Typically these have been cases involving fairly young children who are temporarily taken to the house of a friend or relative for closer observation.

---

*Cornell and Gauld actually tested this hypothesis on a house that was slated for demolition. Cornell constructed a motor-driven vibrator (out-of-balance weights on a drive shaft) and cemented it into the wall of the house. Inside the house various objects were placed on mantelpieces and on shelves along the wall with the vibrator. Different vibration frequencies were tested. All were discernible by touch, and the higher frequencies were plainly perceptible through the feet. None of the test objects showed any signs of movement. An impact test (consisting of a 60 pound weight striking the wall) generated very perceptible shocks, but still no movement of the test objects. Eventually Cornell and Gauld sought the help of a vibration specialist from a university engineering department. With his modifications the vibrator produced a thrust on the wall of 1600 pounds and provided the investigators with "quite our most terrifying experience in pursuit of the poltergeist." Even with this force, only four objects moved insignificantly.

Why do these individuals suddenly become able to generate such dramatic feats of PK? Parapsychologists are still groping for answers to this question. The explanation preferred by some investigators, such as Roll and Bender, is that the poltergeist agent is under severe psychological stress. Poltergeist phenomena, they believe, are external manifestations of repressed anger and hostility triggered by stress. In Roll's words, "What we call poltergeist effects may be 'extrasomatic' [exterior to the body] expressions of psychological stress in the same way as an ulcer is a psychosomatic expression of such stress." Fortunately poltergeist outbreaks are much rarer than ulcers.[17]

Even before the age of psychoanalysis, observers had noted that many poltergeist activities, such as assaults by stones, crockery, and so on, seemed to reveal latent hostility toward an individual. In other cases the phenomena clearly seem to be "persecuting" the apparent agent. Psychological testing of poltergeist agents in recent cases reveals precisely the mild psychopathology or stress conditions that investigators would expect. In yet other cases psychologically trained investigators, analyzing the family situations of poltergeist agents, have identified stress factors and underlying psychological problems in the household without formal testing. What has emerged is a picture of the poltergeist agent as someone who is under a certain amount of psychological stress and for whom the phenomena somehow serve as a release for repressed hostilities or anger. Indeed in several recent cases the phenomena quickly abated when the apparent stress-inducing conditions were removed.

We must be careful, however, not to "overpsychologize" our poltergeist agents. As many critics of psychoanalysis have complained, it is easy to find psychopathology and stress conditions anywhere one looks for them. Now that parapsychologists expect to find psychopathology, it is not surprising that they do find it in these cases. If poltergeist outbreaks are simply due to young people with repressed hostility who are under psychological stress, we should expect to see whole school buildings come crashing down by the dozens each year around exam time. At any given time there are probably hundreds of thousands of young people who have more severe psychological disturbances or who are enduring far greater stress than any of the poltergeist agents who have been studied. The real question is, What is the trigger that sets off so very few individuals,

turning them into poltergeist agents? What is it in their psychological (or physical) makeup that can cause such gross violations of the
laws of physics?

Recent advances in neurophysiology and brain research may provide clues to the uniqueness of the poltergeist agent. In a survey of
ninety-two cases Roll found nearly a quarter of the apparent agents
had displayed some sort of dissociative state (such as a trance) or
mild seizure. In several instances the agents were diagnosed epilep-
tics. Roll and his colleagues have recently proposed that there may
be some link between RSPK and epileptic-like disturbances in the
brain. Intriguing though it may be, this remains a highly speculative
theory, and it is likely to be a long time before sufficient hard data
can be gathered to decide its merits. (Julio's brain-wave analysis, for
example, did not show signs of epileptic tendencies.)[18]

There are a few parapsychologists, Gauld and Cornell among
them, who do not find explanations involving living agents, whether
disturbed or not, entirely convincing. They are willing to admit that
this explanation appears to account for many cases, but there remain a large number of cases that seemed to have poltergeist phenomena *without* an identifiable living agent. These cases, and even
some of the ones with apparent agents, often contain sightings of
apparitions and extended "communications" with entities by means
of rappings. These communications seemed to reveal personalities
entirely unknown to the apparent agent. Dr. Ian Stevenson of the
University of Virginia at Charlottesville has argued that there may
be two types of poltergeist cases: those attributable to the psychokinetic abilities of living agents and those that must be ascribed to
discarnate entities—spirits, souls, or the surviving consciousness of
a deceased person.[19]

It is not clear how the differing views—living agent versus discarnate entity—will be resolved, if they ever are. Perhaps it will prove
to be a classification problem: The cases that appear to be
discarnate-entity poltergeist cases may eventually be found to fit best
with haunting phenomena, thus eliminating this particular controversy. It is true that most of the cases that lean toward the
discarnate-entity interpretation are among the older ones; modern
investigations have uncovered very little to support this theory. On
the other hand hardly any of the modern investigators are looking
for evidence that would support the discarnate-entity position, so

perhaps they fail to perform the sorts of tests (for example, trying to communicate with a purported entity) that would lend such support.

Although there is something of a consensus building, parapsychology is still far from having a comprehensive theory of poltergeist phenomena. One can only counsel a "wait and see" attitude, although, for my money, the RSPK interpretation has a clear edge in making sense of most of the cases with which I am familiar.

Reports of poltergeist outbreaks still arise, often several per year, but only rarely does one prove worthy of investigation. Nonetheless every few years one or another intrepid investigator will report yet another amazing case. Precisely that has happened as I write this book.

Yet Another Amazing Case

On the morning of January 28, 1985, Head Nurse Krystyna Kolak was on her way to check on one of the newest residents at the Jasinski Academic Rehabilitation Center in Zakopane, a small Polish town high in the Tatra Mountains close to the Czechoslovakian border. The young lady she was on her way to see, Joasia Gajewski, was not really a patient, but had been admitted to the center two days earlier at the request of the new director, Dr. Eustachiusz Gadula, a respected surgeon and vocational rehabilitation specialist.

There was no secret about Joasia's visit to the center. The unusual "happenings" that centered around the girl had been in and out of the press since 1983. Objects moved in her presence, and reportedly she could bend metal objects merely by stroking them. Dr. Gadula was also known to have an interest in such matters, having often participated in scientific symposia on psychotronics, the East European version of parapsychology.

Nurse Kolak had little time for this nonsense, however; it was of no interest to her. What was of interest was that this was a beautiful winter morning and she wanted to find out if Joasia planned to go skiing that day. As she approached Joasia's room, 309, Kolak met the ward attendant, Maria Wojtas-Opiela, who was cleaning the lavatory directly opposite. Kolak reminded her to wash the mirror in the lavatory, and for a few minutes both women stood chatting at the open lavatory door, directly opposite the closed doors of Room 309.

Suddenly from inside Joasia's room there came a crash of breaking glass—a lot of it. Kolak rushed into the room just in time to see a swirl of glass fragments form into a line and fly at her as if pulled by an invisible magnet. The nurse was showered in glass fragments. Joasia, sitting in a chair, shouted, "Better not come in now."

Recognizing that the shattered glass on the floor used to be a mirror, Kolak instinctively looked at the medicine cabinet over the sink, but that mirror was still there. At almost the same moment the ward attendant in the lavatory turned to wash the dirty mirror that had been called to her attention. *It was not there!* The mirror and the thick fiberboard sheet to which it was attached had simply vanished in the few moments that she had stood in the doorway. Amid the broken glass on the floor of Room 309 lay a thick fiberboard sheet.

Unless we are prepared to dismiss entirely the testimony of these two women—both trusted and longtime employees of the center who had never shown any interest in psychic phenomena—then the inescapable conclusion must be that somehow the mirror went from the wall in the lavatory (where its fiberboard backing was suspended from hooks) into Room 309 without the door being opened or the women noticing. Impossible? Not in the world of the poltergeist. The apparent passage of objects through closed doors and walls is often reported in poltergeist cases, and the behavior of the glass fragments is very reminiscent of the way glass fragments seemed to pursue Annemarie in the Rosenheim poltergeist case. Nor was this incident particularly unusual for Joasia. Things like this had been happening to her ever since the night of April 4, 1983, when all hell broke loose in her parents' small apartment.

Joasia and her parents lived in an efficiency apartment in Sosnowiec, an industrial and mining town in the southern Polish province of Katowice. Her mother worked as a telephone operator in a local office, and at the time her father was a plumber at the local steelworks. Joasia was then thirteen and a sixth-grade student in Primary School 1. Apart from the fact that her grandmother, to whom Joasia was particularly attached, had died some months earlier, leaving the teenager profoundly shaken, life in the Gajewski household was completely unremarkable. Joasia was just entering puberty around then. She was prone to catching colds, but otherwise in good health. Curiously, in the weeks prior to the April outbreak Joasia's family and friends observed that she had seemed unusually charged with static electricity, far more than what one comes to expect in the cold climate of the region. Joasia was described as "crackling" with sounds similar to finger snapping.

On the evening of April 4, 1983, Joasia, her mother, and her visiting grandfather stayed up watching TV. Her father was working the night shift at the steelworks. When it became late, her grandfather decided to stay the night. Her mother bedded down on a cot in the kitchen while Joasia and her grandfather shared the sofa bed in the parlor.

Around 3:00 A.M. a straw mat that hung over the sofa fell on the grandfather. As he tried to fasten it back, it seemed to tear itself out of his hands and dance around. In the dark he first thought it was Joasia playing a trick, but when he checked, she was asleep. Moments later objects started flying about from all directions. Plates and glassware flew everywhere, smashing with great speed into the walls and buffet. Windows rattled and furniture shook. Matches began to flutter around the parlor while Joasia's grandfather chased after and stomped on them lest they start a fire. Most terrifying of all was that fragments of the shattered glassware seemed to fly at the girl, still in bed, and she was cut several times.

Eventually all three abandoned the apartment and ran to upstairs neighbors (who had already been awakened by the din). The neighbors, Jan and Gertrude Jach, at first suspected a joke, but when they went to the apartment and observed the devastation for themselves, they realized that it was no joke. They stood around for a while, but nothing happened, so all five returned to the Jachs' apartment. Later, on hearing noise from below, Jan Jach, Joasia, and her mother ran downstairs. Jach later described the scene to a Japanese television interviewer:

> When the racket downstairs started up again, I returned there and saw glasses, plates, pots and a lot of other objects smash into the wall. The noise was unbelievable.
>
> (Interviewer) You saw objects flying?
>
> Not flying, only when they hit the wall. Nobody was in the room; Mrs. Gajewski and her daughter were standing with me in the door-

way. Those dishes must have been flying incredibly fast because you couldn't see them until they fell.*

Jach admitted to being scared when he saw what was happening, and all three ran back up to his apartment. Later, while they were having some tea, Jach noticed a few things move around his apartment, too, but nothing destructive happened. Eventually Joasia, complaining of a headache and fever that had started the previous day, went to sleep in Jach's apartment, and things quieted down.

Joasia's father fetched the family when he got home from work. Her mother had telephoned him at work, but he could not get off (and, as he later admitted, he thought she was imagining things). Only when he reached the threshold of his apartment was he convinced of the magnitude of the destruction. No sooner had he opened the door than a stoneware pot flew from the kitchen to the parlor, smashing the glass front of the buffet and falling in pieces to the floor.

Over the next few days the destruction actually intensified. The Gajewskis sought help from the authorities but met disbelief and suspicion. A doctor brought in to examine the still-feverish Joasia simply demanded to know which member of the family was mentally ill (to have caused such destruction) and left without even treating the girl. Neighbors, already annoyed at the sheer noise of the disturbances, began to exhibit superstitious fears. The city engineer dismissed it all as subsidence in the building structure. Eventually Joasia's father persuaded several police officers to stay in the apartment. On the first day nothing happened, but on the second, as Joasia returned from a visit to the doctor, Sgt. Tadeusz Slowik, the district constable, saw more than he wanted to. Suddenly glasses,

---

*These quotes, and most of the details of this case, are from *Nieuchwytna Sila* (*The Elusive Force*) by Marek Rymuszko and Anna Ostrzycka, two journalists who had followed the case almost from its inception (and continue to follow it). In addition to spending many hours with the Gajewskis, the authors interviewed numerous witnesses and most of the scientists and medical personnel involved in the case. They were also present at various tests and demonstrations for scientists and the media. The book is not yet available in English, and I am indebted to Mr. Joel Stern for his translation of it. Mr. Stern, an American, is a Polish interpreter who became interested in the case and traveled to Sosnowiec to meet the Gajewskis and learn of recent developments from Rymuszko and Ostrzycka. Virtually nothing has appeared in the Western parapsychological literature, though a few parapsychologists with Polish contacts have been following reports there.

screws, and other objects were flying about. As Slowik looked on, objects flew out of the kitchen, executed a sharp turn in mid-flight, and proceeded into the parlor or slammed into the opposite wall.

The police report convinced the authorities to take the matter seriously. Shortly after, the city engineer came out to inspect the apartment building. No construction defects or evidence of subsidence was found. When the engineer and several other city officials went up to the apartment, they became even more convinced that subsidence was not the problem. All of them witnessed a mustard jar fly out of the kitchen and smash into the wall and several objects move about the room. They also watched as fragments of previously broken glass flew *toward* the girl's hands.

The deputy mayor of Sosnowiec, Jozef Stankiewicz, authorized the municipal authorities to find new housing for the Gajewski family. He had to call a press conference because by now the case was the talk of the town. The move, however, did not stop the destructive phenomena, which continued unabated in the new apartment.

By May of that year Joasia had come to the attention of several Polish scientists, including the physician Dr. Gadula, head of the paraplegic ward at the Miners Medical and Vocational Rehabilitation Center No. 1 in Tarnowski Góry. Gadula organized a team of researchers, including a psychologist, a biophysicist, and a metallurgist. The last member was included because Joasia was apparently able to bend metal after the fashion of Uri Geller. An extensive battery of medical tests revealed there was nothing unusual about the girl apart from several curious features: Thermographic studies revealed that Joasia seemed to have unusual "thermal spots" (warm areas) around her fingers, toes, head, and just above her solar plexus. She also displayed unusually wide and rapid changes in her overall body temperature. Also, Joasia seemed capable of developing exceptionally high static electricity charges on her body that would not dissipate when she was grounded.

During the medical and psychological exams, which took place over several visits to Gadula's facility, all the researchers witnessed unusual phenomena under conditions that they maintain absolutely precluded the possibility of fraud. On one occasion they watched an armchair start moving about *while Joasia was sitting cross-legged in it*. They told her to get out of the chair, which she did, but the chair continued to move. At one point it executed a sharp turn in the air and rotated rapidly. Three men tried to hold the chair down, without success. On another occasion the research team watched a blanket that had been rolled up on a nearby couch glide across the room and cover Dr. Gadula.

The metal-bending studies, however, fell short of the team's hopes. Apparently the researchers knew something of the controversy that surrounded the investigations of Uri Geller* and hoped to be able to obtain high-quality film evidence of Joasia's metal bending. Although she bent countless pieces of cutlery under the scrutiny of observers, she was never able to do so when the camera was on. In the end the team drew no conclusions about her metal bending.

Several attempts to film objects moving have also met with scant success. In most cases nothing moved in the range of the camera. On December 13, 1983, a Japanese film crew set up video recorders to provide a continuous record of parts of the Gajewskis' apartment. That evening, while Dr. Gadula was visiting, a fish-scaling knife hurled itself from the hall to the kitchen and back out again. The video camera caught a portion of the trajectory that was within its range. However, when the videotape was examined, the only unusual occurrence that coincided with the time that the knife moved was a few brief flashes of light that could only be seen under close examination. (Subsequent analysis in Japan confirmed that this was not due to a defect in the tape.)

After a few months the destructive phenomena became more sporadic. However they began to follow Joasia outside the apartment, as the mirror incident indicates. Two days after that event—January 30, 1985—patients and staff reported hearing a loud "detonation" in Room 309. The sound lasted only a few seconds; doctors and nurses were in the room in a flash. What greeted them was beyond belief. The heavy sink lay smashed to pieces on the floor, its waste pipe severed at the elbow. One of the heavy metal stanchions that supported it was ripped from the wall and the other was buckled. The faucet was broken and twisted as if it had been pounded by a sledgehammer.[20]

In recent years furniture movement has become very common and continues to be observed by people outside the family. On the morn-

---

*However they were not so aware as to include a professional conjuror for this part of the research, at least as far as I know.

ing of October 18, 1987, Joasia was alone in the apartment. She reported that she watched her heavy wardrobe "march" out from the wall and return to its place, with the doors against the wall. Joasia phoned her mother at work to tell her that she could not get her school clothes. As she spoke, other furniture began to move and then objects began to fly about. Joasia became scared and ran out to the landing, where she met Adam Imielski, a schoolboy who lived in the same building. In an interview several days later the boy described how he went to help Joasia. He watched the wardrobe march out from the wall again, and then the doors on a three-part wall unit began opening and slamming shut.

> When I saw what was happening, I tried to save the tumblers. I didn't want them to break. Meanwhile, Joasia was standing with her back to the wall unit, picking up glass from the floor. Just then I saw the narrow middle unit lean forward and hit her on the back of the head. I was scared stiff, 'cause I thought it was about to crush her, but it straightened up and returned to its place. I can't imagine how that could have happened. Normally if a piece of furniture tipped over so far it would fall.[21]

Joasia is now twenty. She recently completed her studies at a medical lyceum and is looking toward graduate studies and a career in the health professions, perhaps as a nurse. She has turned down several lucrative offers to go "on tour," preferring instead to continue her studies and work with Dr. Gadula and the other scientists.

As with most poltergeist cases, this one rests almost entirely on human testimony, but there is a great deal of that. Much of it has been published in the popular press of Poland and several other countries. The Gajewskis, Dr. Gadula and his colleagues, and numerous other witnesses have testified on camera, and much of the phenomena has been documented in official reports. Yet the case has only recently come to the attention of Western parapsychologists, and virtually none of the scientific reports has been published outside Poland. At best all I can say now is that this case remains under investigation, though at the moment there is no active research going on. The Polish team ran out of money in 1985, and no other researchers have picked up where they left off.

I need not review all the similarities between this case and what we have seen in other poltergeist cases. In many ways it is a very typical case, save only for its duration, which would place it among the longest on record.

It is possible that this case could be one of the most interesting in decades, but before that can be decided, much work remains. The Polish work already done needs to be scrutinized by others more experienced in such investigations, and further work by parapsychologists and other specialists is needed. Fortunately Joasia and her family have shown every willingness to cooperate with such investigations, and the phenomena continue. Unfortunately few parapsychologists have the financial resources to mount the sort of investigation that is required. The next few years may determine whether this case becomes one of those rare opportunities substantially to augment our understanding of human potential or simply ends up as just another anecdote.

A Final Question

The title song from the film *Ghostbusters* asks, "Who ya gonna call?" In evaluating real-life (so to speak) ghosts and poltergeists, the question is more likely to be, "Who ya gonna believe?" The documentary evidence, including the more recent harder evidence from recording devices, for apparitions, hauntings, and poltergeists is substantial. But just what does this all mean? Does it document the operation of spirits or paranormal forces that we have yet to understand? Or does it document the continuing fallibility and gullibility of human beings when faced with superficially incongruous observations?

Scientific data do not arrive with little "true" and "false" labels attached to them. On the controversial frontiers of science, be they in medicine, physics, or parapsychology, each scientist has to make decisions regarding whether to accept or reject certain data as representative of reality. It is at this point that science ceases to be objective, because in making those decisions each scientist brings with him or her the full weight of past experiences as well as preconceptions and simple blind prejudices.

Controversial data, such as those which we have been discussing in this chapter, tend to lay bare that decision process. They reveal, if you will, a scientist's "boggle threshold," beyond which he or she will accept no more. For many scientists the thought that there might be yet unknown forces operating in the universe is simply too much to accept. They feel that *any* normal explanation for allegedly paranormal events is preferable, regardless of how strong or weak the evidence to support it. For other scientists the possibility of unknown, "paranormal" forces presents no problem, but *discarnate entities? Spirits?* That is asking too much. These scientists feel that ESP or PK will have to explain all that is not amenable to normal explanations.

For the present any person who wishes to form an opinion regarding the reality of these phenomena, or even just select a direction from which an explanation might come, will have to decide whether to trust the analyses of those who feel each case can be explained by some combination of ordinary, conventional mechanisms—fraud, misperception, faulty memory, seismic effects, and so on—or whether to trust the testimony of the witnesses who were there and the evidence. I can assure you that many very capable individuals, scientists, and laypeople alike have lined up behind each of those positions. I, for one, find in the overwhelming amount of testimony reason to believe that the normal explanations have come up far short and that there remain some very unusual phenomena to be understood.

CHAPTER 8

Life After Death?

It was a quiet afternoon, with only a few people going about their errands at the shops along the road. A short way up the road a motorbike approached. Suddenly the screech of tires shattered the quiet as a car abruptly pulled out of an alley directly into the path of the motorbike.

Too late to stop! The bike hit the car almost at full speed. Horrified shoppers looked up to see the motorbike's passenger sailing over the car as if thrown from a catapult. She hit the pavement practically headfirst and lay in a motionless heap. People ran up to her; she looked dead.

In fact she was not dead. Though her body was inert, her consciousness was very much alive, but in a strange sort of way. The young woman survived and she later described what she had experienced:

> I got up from the ground where I lay, surprised that I felt no pain or bruising, and moved away. I saw people running and looked around to see why.
>
> Then I saw that my body was still laying in the road and they were running toward that, some of them passed me as I stood there. I could hear shouts and a woman's voice crying "She's dead."
>
> And then a feeling (I can still feel the awful shock of this whenever

I recall the incident) of terrible fear came to me. I knew I HAD to return to my body before it was touched. There was a dreadful sense of urgency, or it would be too late. It is this sensation of dread that remains so indelible.

I went back and lay down on top of myself. And as I did so I felt the hardness of the road beneath me and all the terrible pains of bruising, lacerations and concussion that I was subsequently found to be suffering from. . . .

I was moving about thinking I was my normal body. . . . Everything looked normal. . . . my "floating self" behaved exactly as my physical.[1]

This woman's experience is commonly known as an out-of-body experience, or OBE. Surveys have revealed that roughly one-quarter of the population reports having had one or more OBEs, though, fortunately, not all of them are the result of such distressing circumstances. The essence of an OBE is the feeling that one's consciousness is temporarily outside one's body. Very commonly, as in the case above, this involves "seeing" a scene or an event—or even one's body—from a perspective that is different from the body's usual perspective. OBEs can last from a few seconds to several minutes (and even longer in rare cases).

Many OBEs do arise from circumstances in which the body has suffered some trauma. Often they happen in hospitals, and the person later reports "watching" an operation from near the ceiling or viewing the resuscitation of his own body from somewhere above the crowd of doctors and nurses. Typically the OBEer can accurately report conversations or details of the actions that took place while he was supposedly unconscious.

The OBE is usually described as an extremely distinctive experience, not easily confused with dreaming, intoxication, or some other altered state of consciousness. Yet, of itself, that does not mean it is a paranormal experience. For example it would not be difficult to explain "local" OBEs (when the altered perspective is not far from the body) simply as mental reconstructions of events based upon sensory information that is getting through to the brain and what is available from memory despite the apparent lack of consciousness. In other words they are a special kind of hallucination.

Although many OBEs are local, and thus could be hallucinations based on partial sensory information, some OBEers report travels farther afield. Sometimes the OBEer returns from the experience with information that could not have been obtained or inferred from what was happening in the immediate vicinity.

Consider this experience of a British woman who was hospitalized and operated on for peritonitis. She subsequently became very ill with pneumonia and was confined to bed. The ward was L-shaped, and from her bed she could not see around the corner.

> One morning I felt myself floating upwards and found I was looking down on the rest of the patients. I could see myself: propped up against pillows, very white and ill. I saw the sister and nurse rush to my bed with oxygen. Then everything went blank. The next I remember was opening my eyes to see the sister bending over me. I told her what had happened; but at first she thought I was rambling. Then I said, "There is a big woman sitting up in bed with her head wrapped in bandages; and she is knitting something with blue wool. She has a very red face." This certainly shook her; as apparently the lady concerned had a mastoid operation and was just as I described.
>
> She was not allowed out of bed; and of course I hadn't been up at all. After several other details, such as the time by the clock on the wall (which had broken down) I convinced her that at least something strange had happened to me.[2]

Collections of OBE cases reveal numerous instances in which the OBEer was able to describe accurately details of situations or events that were far too distant to be accounted for by sensory leakage. Sometimes the OBEer described specific events that took place while his or her body was incapacitated, which were not likely to have been inferred or anticipated. For example one man not only left his body on the operating table but, after watching the operation for a while, left the room and observed a particular interaction between a nurse and a doctor elsewhere in the hospital (which was later confirmed). When this happens, the experience has distinctly paranormal characteristics, but has the person's consciousness really left the body?

The OBE and Parapsychology

The OBE has a long tradition in parapsychology. As with most other types of psychic experiences, cases go back as far as recorded history. Most people who report cases have had only one or two in their lives, and these came on spontaneously, usually triggered by circumstances such as trauma or extreme fatigue. Other experiences seem to be stress-induced, as in the case of a young woman who reported that she took her entire driver's-license examination while viewing it from the roof of her car. However, many cases seem to have no particular triggering circumstances at all. Less common than the spontaneous cases are the examples of individuals who can induce OBEs more or less at will. In former years this activity was known as astral traveling, and the exteriorized consciousness was called the astral body.

The OBE caught the interest of early psychical researchers because of what it might reveal about the independent existence of the soul or consciousness. The OBE seemed a prima facie case of consciousness operating without the body. The experience itself often leaves the OBEer with the profound conviction that his soul or some nonphysical element of consciousness did actually leave his physical body. That these experiences are more than mere dreams or hallucinations is suggested by the many cases in which people not only claim to have "traveled" to a distant location but can also accurately describe objects or events that took place, that they could not have known about. Finally, in a few cases people who were in a location "visited" by the OBEer reported seeing an apparition of the experient or feeling some sort of identifiable "presence" at the precise time of the OBE.

The question that motivated much of early psychical research was, of course, whether or not the soul or consciousness survived the death of the body. The principal effort to answer that question was through the investigation of mediums and the messages that they carried from "the other side." For many investigators, however, studying mediums was not an entirely satisfactory approach. It was terribly inefficient: Too many mediums provided no useful information, and even with the best mediums it was difficult to eliminate explanations based on telepathy or clairvoyance. Researchers began to turn to "astral travel" cases.

From the start, however, astral-travel researchers recognized that their approach had its limitations too. Even if one did demonstrate the existence of the soul in the form of an astral body, this did not prove survival after death, since the body remained alive during the experience. One still had to infer that the astral body would somehow outlast the physical one. Even in its heyday, astral-travel research was a minority approach to the survival question, but curiously it is the approach that has itself survived. Research with mediums is virtually nonexistent today, whereas at least a few parapsychologists conduct OBE research.

The OBE Experience

OBEs vary widely in character, as with most psychic experiences, but there are some common features in the majority of the cases. Typically the experience is described as especially vivid and realistic and distinctly different from a dream. The experient's vision seems brighter and clearer than normal; even when the place "visited" should be in the dark, scenes appear to be lit by a mysterious light. The OBE experient often reports being able to see through walls and other obstacles, and even to pass through them. Experients move by floating or flying, often accompanied with pleasant feelings of lightness and ease. In fact many of the experiences are described as pleasant, enjoyable, and even spiritual, though those experiencing their first OBE often feel uneasy at being separated from their body. Attempts to interact with the physical world, such as moving something or turning on a light, usually fail, as do attempts to make one's disembodied presence noticed by other people.

Parapsychologists generally classify OBEs in two ways. One way is according to the circumstances under which the OBE took place. Although different researchers have focused on different aspects of the triggering event, the basic classification revolves around whether or not the experience was caused by specific events (such as the trauma of an accident, medical emergency, or emotional shock). Cases in which the OBE is brought on by a specific event or condition are usually called enforced or induced OBEs. Another large class of OBEs happen without any apparent reason, however—while relaxing in bed, sleeping, or even just sitting in a classroom. For lack of a better term, these are often called natural OBEs. Most natural OBEs happen spontaneously, but there are a few individuals who apparently can bring on an OBE more or less at will.

The second classification scheme for OBEs is based upon whether or not the person feels he or she is inhabiting a secondary body, as with the motorbike-accident case. In that instance, the secondary body behaved as the normal one might—getting up, walking away, and returning to the scene. More common, however, are reports in which the secondary body "floats" and sails through the air.* In contrast to this is the OBE experience in which consciousness (including a visual perspective) leaves the body, but the experient quite clearly feels that there is no body connected with it, only a "point" of consciousness floating about.

The content of spontaneous OBEs is fairly predictable. In the majority of cases, especially the enforced ones, the experient sees his or her body (or the local scene around the body) from a different perspective, usually from above. In natural spontaneous OBEs this exteriorized consciousness is sometimes more adventurous, taking brief sojourns away from the vicinity of the physical body.

With the OBE adept—one who can have an OBE at will—anything is possible. From the "frequent flyers" of the astral plane one is likely to get reports of travels to all sorts of cities in foreign locations. The actual traveling is typically very swift and foreshortened, but in some cases the OBEer will describe scenes along the way. Almost as common are travels to fantastical locales—heavenly realms on the astral plane or distant planets.**

---

*Traveling about in a secondary or astral body begs an interesting question: What are astral clothes like? Investigators have looked into this issue, and in cases where one's astral clothes were noticed, they seem simply to reflect what the astral traveler would expect to be wearing. F.W.H. Myers reported the case of a young man who became aware that his astral body was naked. When the man's astral self suddenly found itself among two women, it was instantly astrally clothed.

**One famous nineteenth-century OBEer, Hélèn Smith (pseudonym), studied by Theodore Flournoy, routinely astral-traveled to Mars. She provided detailed descriptions of the surface of the planet (as well as of the customs and language of the inhabitants). Needless to say, the American Viking 1 and 2 missions to Mars failed to confirm her observations.

Although for the experient, at least, the OBE is a distinctive and often compelling experience, there is very little in it that is *necessarily* parapsychological. In most cases the experience itself can be regarded as a kind of hallucination or dreamlike experience. Yet it is a curiously stable sort of hallucination, and one of the most characteristic features of an OBE is the sense of realism and authenticity conveyed to the experient. British parapsychologist Susan Blackmore has tried to explain this inconsistency between the OBE and typical hallucinations by relating the OBE to a disruption of the normal cognitive processes that are responsible for maintaining our body image—that mental picture each of us has of our body and how it is positioned within the immediate environment. We do not think about this body image very much, but it is there and ensures that we can safely move about and perform actions within our environment. The body image is constantly being adjusted based on continuous sensory input. If for some reason—bodily trauma for example—there is a sudden disruption of the sensory inputs, then the mind will have difficulty maintaining the body image. Blackmore suggests that the OBE results from the brain trying to put together a "best guess" at what the body image should be when sensory information is disrupted. The components that go into this reconstruction are likely to be either those most recently in the senses (and presumably in recent memory) or those that are familiar and easily remembered (to explain OBEs that occur in familiar surroundings).[3]

This model may account for many of the enforced OBEs, but it doesn't adequately describe how certain individuals can have an OBE at will. One would have to hypothesize that these individuals have an unusual ability to shut down sensory input voluntarily in order to "force" a body-image reconstruction and an OBE. The process may be something similar to biofeedback training or deep meditational states. Most OBE adepts usually enter a state of deep relaxation in order to bring on the OBE, but there is little external evidence for a complete sensory shutdown of the kind associated with trauma-induced OBEs.

But even this theory doesn't account for two types of OBE cases: those in which the OBE resulted in the person having information that could not have come through the senses, memory, or inference, and those in which persons at a "visited" location sensed the presence of the OBEer or reported seeing an image of the OBEer at the time the OBE was taking place. If these reports are accurate, then there is more to an OBE than what a purely psychological model can explain.

Experiments Out of the Body

"Okay, little fella, it's time to do your stuff," said Robert Morris to a small kitten named Spirit. He gently scooped up the little ball of fluff and put him into a long, narrow box. The floor of the box was marked out in a grid of twenty-four numbered squares. The kitten looked up at Morris, but he turned away to pick up a clipboard.

At the same time on this summer evening in 1973, Duke University undergraduate Keith Harary (then known by his nickname "Blue") was stretched out on a bed in the psychophysiology laboratory of the Duke University Medical Center, about a quarter of a mile down the road. Wires from his head, face, and chest led to a rack of monitoring equipment. Harary was here because he was an exceptionally proficient OBEer.

Harary had been having OBEs all his life and very much wanted to understand what was happening. He had chosen to go to Duke University (majoring in psychology) because of its proximity to two parapsychology laboratories. Now he was well into his sixth month of a busy research program at the laboratories of the Psychical Research Foundation (PRF).

Harary chatted idly about great restaurants he had known with his experimenter, John Hartwell, a psychophysiologist and electronics engineer. They were approaching a baseline period, but that meant that Harary was just to behave normally. Hartwell picked up the phone and dialed a number. "Okay, we're ready here. Synchronize clocks . . . three, two, one, now."

Back in the PRF lab the kitten wandered leisurely about the box, occasionally turning to Morris and his assistant and meowing. The experimenters did not acknowledge the kitten's cry or even allow themselves to make eye contact; they just sat still in their raised chairs. In a few moments a buzzer sounded, and Morris began counting the squares as the cat entered them, and counting the meows.

"Thirty seconds," said the assistant, and Morris marked the time on his record sheet.

In the psychophysiology lab Hartwell looked at the clock. "Let's see if it's time for a trip, Blue," said Hartwell, reaching for a coin. Hartwell put the coin in a cup, shook it, and dumped it on the desk. "Heads it is. Go visit your kitten."

Harary closed his eyes and pictured the little kitten. For some months now his routine had been to pay an OBE "visit" to the PRF lab and describe targets composed of objects in various arrangements. Now the researchers were trying something new: Could they somehow detect Harary's disembodied "presence" at the PRF site? Morris, who had done his Ph.D. research in animal behavior, thought it might be possible to use animals as detectors, by comparing their behavior during OBE visits and control periods without an OBE visit. Several attempts to detect Harary's "presence" using small rodents had been unsuccessful,* but Spirit the kitten was different. He was a real pet. When Harary had gone to select two kittens for the project, Spirit had marched right to him, almost as if he had picked *him* to be "his human."

After about three and a half minutes the buzzer sounded again. Morris flipped to the next record sheet. The kitten continued moving about for a few seconds but then wandered to the far end and sat down, looking away from the experimenters. "Hmmm," thought Morris to himself, "that's interesting." The kitten, which had just been so active, hardly moved for the next two minutes. After the final buzzer Morris put down the clipboard, saying, "Well, I'll be real surprised if that wasn't an OBE session."

It was an OBE session, and the kitten seemed to sense it. In this particular experiment there were eight OBE "visits" like this one, as well as eight control sessions in which Harary simply continued to chat with his experimenter. Morris was monitoring the kitten's activity, as measured by the number of boxes he entered and number of meows he uttered during 100-second periods. The kitten's activ-

---

*The rodents had been placed on a special platform that signaled their activity to a polygraph. The experimenters reported simply that there was no difference between the OBE visit periods and the control periods. Having had considerable experience with small rodents myself, I have often wondered if this arrangement would have even distinguished the "presence" of a real person, let alone an astral one. No mention was made of any preliminary testing to address this question.

ity was markedly reduced (to a statistically significant degree) in the periods during which Harary "visited" him, as compared with the control periods. For example during the eight control periods, the kitten meowed thirty-seven times; during the OBE sessions the cat did not vocalize at all.

Over a period of nearly two years Harary participated in about a dozen projects examining his OBE abilities. Many were very exploratory, and others, like the kitten study, were quite formal. Few produced as dramatic results as the study with Spirit, but all contributed to understanding what at least one person's OBE experiences may be like.

The physiological studies revealed that Harary's OBE state is different from normal relaxation, with slightly faster heart and respiration rates during OBE. Also, his OBE state was very unlike his dreaming state. The detection studies showed that at least one animal and several humans seemed capable of detecting Harary's OBE presence, but none of the physical equipment—including detectors for electromagnetic-field changes; visible, infrared, and ultraviolet light; and temperature—was able to detect him. On several occasions research personnel at the visit site spontaneously reported sensing Harary's "presence" at exactly the right time and in the correct place, even though they had no advance knowledge of when and where the OBE was to take place. Hartwell, for example, during a session when he was not with Harary but operating television equipment at the "visit" site, had very strong impressions of Harary's OBE "presence" on four separate occasions, all of which were correct. On one, Hartwell noted on the record sheet that he saw an image of Harary on the television screen. It was later confirmed that at exactly the same time Harary was attempting a "visit" to the part of the room in which Hartwell had observed the image.[4]

The Kidd Legacy

The PRF work with Harary was part of a flurry of OBE research conducted in the early and mid-seventies. Most of this research was a result of a curious bequest from a recluse Arizona miner. In 1949 James Kidd disappeared, leaving an estate valued at over a quarter million dollars. His will stipulated that this money should be given for "research or some scientific proof of a human soul in the human body which leaves at death."

When Kidd was declared dead and the will probated, an Arizona court invited applications from those who thought they could fulfill the miner's wishes. One hundred thirty applications were filed. After weeding out the mediums—including those who claimed to be in touch with Mr. Kidd himself—and the philosophers—who do no research—the court was left with a short list comprising an Arizona neurological institute, the American Society for Psychical Research, and the Psychical Research Foundation. Initially the court awarded the money to the neurological institute for conventional research, but after an appeal the money went to the ASPR. The ASPR, in turn, gave one-third of it to the PRF. Both the ASPR and the PRF chose to put much of the legacy into OBE research as the best bet of meeting Kidd's wishes.[5]

The ASPR's efforts took a slightly different direction from those of the PRF. ASPR Research Director Karlis Osis initially elected to use the OBE "information gathering" approach. The OBEer was expected to visit Osis's office in the ASPR building, stand with his back to the fireplace, and describe what he saw directly ahead. Osis would randomly assemble collections of objects on a table divided by a screen. If the OBEer actually viewed the scene from the indicated spot, some objects would be visible and others would not. This was intended as a nominal control for clairvoyance (which presumably would reveal the entire scene); however other OBE researchers, Morris among them, doubted the effectiveness of this control.

Instead of concentrating on one individual as the PRF did,* Osis cast his net widely. After some pilot studies with Ingo Swann,**

---

*PRF researchers did not work solely with Harary, but most of the OBE research was done with him.

**By now the familiar sound of some of these names may have brought home to the reader just how small a field parapsychology is. This is indeed the same Ingo Swann who later went on to help start SRI's remote viewing (see page 116). Robert Morris, mentioned earlier in connection with the PRF work, is the same person referred to in Malcolm Bessent's precognitive dream at the Maimonides Dream Laboratory (see page 97), and who is now the Koestler Professor of Parapsychology at the University of Edinburgh. As a member of Delphi Associates, Keith Harary later participated in a unique applied psi venture in the silver futures market (see page 338).

which provided encouraging results, Osis put out a nationwide call for OBEers. Over one hundred of the respondents participated in "fly-in" experiments, in which, at the appointed hour, they were to make an OBE visit to Osis's office and describe what they saw. Then subjects reported their experiences on a long questionnaire and sent it to Osis. Promising subjects from the fly-in experiments were later brought to the lab for additional experiments.

The aggregate results from all the fly-in participants were not very impressive. Apparently only some of the volunteers had experiences in which they could "see" things sufficiently clearly to identify the target. Yet Osis was able to discern some general trends. Good sessions with clear vision were usually characterized by the following: The OBEer was not conscious throughout his "exit" from the body; arrival at the destination was sudden; and vision for this OBE was as good as for the person's other OBEs. Sessions in which the subject reported difficulty in leaving the body, consciousness during the exit, a long "flight" to the destination, or difficulty in finding the destination were generally unsuccessful. Osis concluded that success in identifying targets seemed to depend on the quality of the OBE experience itself.

Later research at the ASPR focused on a small number of OBE adepts who worked regularly with Osis and his staff. In an attempt to see if the OBE was more than ESP, Osis created several devices with small viewing windows to restrict ordinary vision to a particular image created within the device. When viewed from a certain perspective, as OBEers claim to do, a composite image would be seen. The presumption underlying the design was that component parts could be perceived by ESP, but not the image available only through the viewing window. These devices were more sophisticated versions of the table-and-screen approach he had used in the fly-in experiments; reports of the actual objects would suggest ESP was operative, whereas descriptions similar to the image available through the viewport would favor the perspective view associated with the OBE.

The results of several years of work proved inconclusive. The better subjects often provided results consistent with the OBE interpretation, yet at other times they produced results indicating that ESP was being used. One subject, Alex Tanous, was able to learn which characteristics of his OBE signaled a good session, and eventually he could produce consistent results suggesting he was using an OBE perspective.[6]

Osis eventually combined the detector approach with his viewing-window devices. In 1980 Osis and colleague Donna McCormick reported a series of OBE sessions in which Tanous reportedly affected strain gauges located near the viewing window. Osis and McCormick felt that the strain gauges may have somehow responded to the presence of Tanous's "astral" body.[7]

Although I think Mr. Kidd's money was well spent, I do not think the research it supported moved us any closer to answering the question he asked. Both the PRF and the ASPR work indicated that several unusual individuals were capable of psychic feats, but it did not demonstrate in any conclusive way that some nonphysical aspect of the body can actually detach itself and move to other locations. Even with Osis's window experiments, there is no reason to assume that ESP might not provide the perspective view as well as the component view. The little evidence arising from the detector studies might be construed as supporting the OBE position were it not for the fact that the same thing could have been accomplished by PK. The OBE may forever remain one of the few human experiences that can convince the experient that his soul can travel free of the body, but it may never convince the scientific community. That is not to say, however, that future research may not permit us a more definitive conclusion.

Until Death Do Us Part

"Code 100, 322 West. Code 100, 322 West." The emotionless voice over the hospital paging system echoed through the corridors. On the third floor an intern dashed into Room 322. Right behind him a nurse wheeled in the "crash cart." Inside, another nurse was already performing CPR on an elderly man in the bed. The intern grabbed an airway from the cart and began to insert it into the man's mouth while the nurse prepared the defibrillator. A second intern arrived and took the defibrillator paddles from the nurse. As the first intern finished, the second placed the paddles on the man's chest and turned on the electrical current. The man's body heaved; he drew in a gurgling breath. "He's coming around," someone said.

The man took more breaths, then turned his head. His eyes opened and focused on the intern still holding the paddles. "Why'd ya do that? Why did you bring me back?" he said to the startled intern. "It was beautiful. I didn't want to come back."

It was not until several days later that the man confided to the hospital chaplain what had prompted his seemingly callous remarks to the medical team that had just saved his life. He found it hard to describe what he had experienced during the minutes he was "dead." Words seemed so inadequate.

> I remember the pain, like my whole chest just seized up and I thought to myself, "This must be a heart attack." Then the pain just went away, and suddenly I felt so peaceful. Next thing I knew, I could see myself on the bed, as if I was looking down from the ceiling. The nurse came running in—must have been some noise I made—and she checked me. Then she grabbed the phone and said something like, "Call a code." I felt like I should tell her not to bother, I was just fine, but that seemed like too much effort. I was so peaceful. The nurse started working on my chest, but I sort of turned away. Suddenly I was outside in some beautiful garden, with sunlight and flowers. I walked—or sort of floated—down a path toward an entrance to some-place. Very brightly lit with a yellowish light. Then I saw my wife— she's been dead three years now—up past the entrance thing. When I started to go to her I heard a voice—or I think I heard a voice—telling me that it was not time yet, and that I had to go back. I didn't want to go back, but I couldn't say anything. Then things got gray, and the next thing I remember was that young doctor with the things in his hands.*

The man was describing what has come to be known as a near-death experience or NDE. Once only rarely reported and usually dismissed as a hallucination, the NDE has suddenly become a surprisingly common experience. Thanks to the wonders of modern medicine, more than ever before doctors are able to snatch

---

*Lest this "case" inadvertently end up in someone's research collection I must note that this is actually a composite, for illustration purposes, drawn from several similar cases.

people from the very jaws of death. Thus more and more people are living to describe what many of them regard as a brief visit to heaven.

Although systematic study of NDEs has been under way only since the mid-seventies, the roots of modern NDE research can be found in the work done in 1959–60 by Karlis Osis when he was with the Parapsychology Foundation in New York City. Following the lead of several early psychical researchers, Osis thought that clues to the survival question might be found in the "deathbed visions" or hallucinations by dying patients that are often reported by medical personnel or other persons at the bedside. Usually these are dismissed as by-products of the increasingly dysfunctional brain, but often the utterances of the dying person and the peace that seems to follow these experiences suggests quite the opposite of brain dysfunction. Osis decided that these deathbed experiences were worth studying systematically, and he sent a questionnaire to five thousand doctors and five thousand nurses. Promising replies led to more detailed interviews and eventually a sizable collection of cases.

Osis's research revealed a pattern of experiences by dying patients characterized by dramatic mood elevations, visions of otherworldly messengers (dead relatives, angels, and so on) coming to take them away, and visions of places of indescribable beauty (often conforming to traditional religious notions of heaven). Osis concluded not only that the pattern of experiences cannot be fully explained by medications or the illness itself, but that the experiences actually run counter to what would be expected from the psychotic-like hallucinations of an oxygen-deprived brain.[8]

This pioneering study was confined to what observers of the dying person had reported. The contents of the visions had to be pieced together from utterances made by the dying patient and recollected by the observers. With the rapid advance of medical resuscitation techniques, it was not long before the patients themselves could give firsthand accounts of the experience. The death experience was now the near-death experience.

The publication in 1975 of Raymond Moody's best-selling *Life After Life** brought the NDE to worldwide attention. Drawing upon a large collection of cases, Moody was able to delineate the partic-

*Raymond Moody, *Life After Life* (Covington, Ga.: Mockingbird Books, 1975).

ular set of features that characterize the NDE. No two NDEs were alike, but most shared some of these features. Moody's work was criticized for lacking supporting statistics, but that was quickly rectified. Within a few years psychologist Kenneth Ring had conducted an interview survey of 102 individuals who had had a close brush with death. Nearly half of these individuals had an experience that conformed to the pattern identified by Moody as an NDE.

Starting from Moody's description, Ring was able to derive a five-stage model of the NDE. A striking feature of Ring's data was that these were indeed stages, and the typical NDE unfolded in an orderly fashion. Not all NDEs go through all stages, so the earlier stages are reported far more frequently than the later ones.

The first stage of the NDE is *deep peace and a sense of well-being.* Nearly 60 percent of those who were near death reported a feeling of peace and contentment that was almost beyond words to describe. It was a "total peace" that removed all fear of death, wiped out all sadness. Many described it as a transcendent experience that relieved them of all earthly concerns.

The second stage is the *separation from the body,* which often has all the hallmarks of a typical OBE. About 37 percent of Ring's sample reported a sensation of being disconnected from the dying body. Almost half of these claimed to have seen their own bodies (and usually the surrounding scene as well) from the elevated perspective common to the OBE. Persons very commonly describe their hearing and seeing as unusually acute during this phase, though their mental processes feel somewhat detached.

In the third stage the separated consciousness goes through a transitional stage, which Ring terms *entering the darkness.* In this stage experiencers report a distinct sense of traveling (usually floating or drifting, but sometimes moving rapidly) through a dark space often described as a tunnel. About one-quarter of Ring's sample reported this experience, which Ring regards as a transition between this world and whatever lies beyond.

As the third stage progresses, many become aware that a momentous decision is being made: whether they shall continue on this journey or return to the living. Although this can occur elsewhere in the NDE, it is commonly reported as part of the transitional journey in the dark. This part of the third stage can be signaled by a life review, in which the person sees what may seem like all or at least parts of his or her life in the form of very vivid and practically instantaneous images. The experience is generally positive—not reproachful or condemning—and the review proceeds with a sense of detachment. Ring reports that about one in four experience a life review. Also characteristic of the decision point is an encounter with "a presence," which is never seen but is sensed or inferred. The presence is sometimes heard to speak, though more common is a telepathy-like direct communication, which may relate to the life review or the impending choice to be made. In conjunction with this some experients report seeing and recognizing "spirits" of deceased loved ones. Finally a decision is made: either the experient decides to return (or in a few cases bargains for a return) or is sent back on the basis of someone else's (often the "presence's") decision.

A certain percentage of experients do not face a decision in stage 3 but instead pass on into stage 4, *seeing the light*. Typically at this stage the darkness is replaced by a brilliant golden light, which either envelops the experient or draws the person to it. In some cases the light is associated with the presence, but not often. Many respondents interpret this stage as the end of the dying experience and the start of a new life. About one-third of the NDEs include this stage.

In the fourth stage the light seems to illuminate the experient or serves as a beacon; in the fifth the experient *enters the light*. Some say it is like entering another world of exceptional beauty, with beautiful flowers, gardens, and meadows of exceptional colors. Wonderful music is sometimes heard. Ring's conclusion is that "plainly, and without equivocation, it is experienced as a beautiful world sans pareil." Ring goes on to observe that it is easy to understand why persons who get this far are unwilling to return.

Ring's research substantially corroborated Moody's observation, and in turn Ring's findings have been corroborated by several other independent studies. Although the researchers often conceptualize the NDE in slightly different ways, their research concurs in revealing an orderly progression of stages. In Ring's words, "it seems to be the same journey with different individuals encountering different segments of what appears to be a single, common path."[9]

The One That Got Away

For parapsychologists interested in the survival question, the NDE would seem the quintessential experience to be studied. Oddly enough NDE research is really on the periphery of mainstream parapsychology today. It is an area that "got away" from parapsychology not long after Osis reintroduced it with his survey of deathbed visions. Although parapsychologists continue to make important contributions to NDE research, the principal work is being done by medical personnel and psychologists based in hospitals, where the data are more easily accessible. The distinctiveness of the NDE and the frequency with which it is reported make it less easy to ignore than other psychic experiences, and this has contributed to near-death research emerging as a minor, and controversial, field within medicine. There is even a small organization to promote such research, the International Association for Near-Death Studies (IANDS).*

The "other world" interpretation of the NDE is by no means widely accepted in the medical community. Many medical researchers regard the NDE simply as a hallucination, most likely the result of a toxic psychosis brought on by an oxygen-deprived brain. The specific contents of the NDE can be attributed to cultural conditioning or religious expectations. Thus, under this view, the "other world" experienced in the NDE need not have any external reality.

NDE researchers, however, argue that several features of the NDE militate against a hallucination interpretation. First of all, hallucinations are typically very varied, often bizarre, and extremely idiosyncratic. NDEs, by contrast, are surprisingly uniform from one experient to the next, and virtually all of them display a logical progression through identifiable stages.

Secondly hallucinations usually take place when the subject is awake

*IANDS, P.O. Box 7767, Philadelphia, Pa. 19101.

and conscious. The NDE experience usually takes place when the person is clinically dead. Some researchers have reported cases in which the NDE took place when the patient's electroencephalogram (brain-wave record) was completely flat. Under such circumstances it is difficult to attribute the detailed and accurate observations of activity surrounding the death scene that NDE experients commonly report to a hallucination based on partial sensory input.

Finally hallucinations typically reported in connection with anoxia (lack of oxygen to the brain) or medications usually display confusion, disorientation, and misperception and are accompanied by fear. NDEs are typically clear and vivid and accompanied by pervasive feelings of joy and peace. Those who have experienced *both* hallucinations and an NDE (at different times) report that the experiences are unmistakably different.

Just as explanations based on hallucinations do not seem to explain the NDE adequately, appeals to religious or cultural expectations fail to provide satisfactory explanations for the content of the experience. The general content of the NDE is the same whether the experient has strong traditional religious beliefs, no religious beliefs, or is a committed atheist. They are all equally likely to experience the presence, go through the life review, and possibly see dead loved ones. After the experience those with religious beliefs will generally interpret the "presence" and the features of the "other world" (if they get to that stage) according to their expectations, whereas atheists will often express disquiet with the implications of the NDE. Thus while religious expectations may influence later interpretations of the experience, they appear to have very little influence on the content of the experience as it unfolds.[10]

The astronomer Carl Sagan, speculating somewhat far afield of his area of expertise, offered a novel explanation for the consistency and universality of the NDE. Sagan proposes that the NDE is a remembrance of the one experience all humans share—birth. The birth experience—traveling down the dark tunnel (birth canal), emerging into the light, and apprehending the powerful presence (presumably the doctor or midwife)—is so indelibly imprinted on the human psyche that it reappears at the moment of death. Sagan's theory encounters problems very quickly when it can be shown that even those born by cesarean section report the tunnel and emergence into the light in NDEs. More importantly, psychological and neurological research has shown that newborns are incapable of perceiving or remembering the detail needed to support Sagan's theory. Finally, even if an infant could remember the birth experience, the prevailing opinion is that the memory would be of a traumatic expulsion *from* a place of peace and serenity, quite the opposite of the welcoming peace of the NDE.[11]

For the present the NDE is in that limbo shared by many parapsychological experiences. That the experience happens is not in doubt, but what it means remains contentious. On the surface the NDE clearly seems to point toward the possibility that consciousness survives the death of the body. But it falls short of being evidence for survival, for it remains only the reported private experience of a person who did not actually die. A variety of explanations based upon normal physiological and psychological mechanisms have been proposed for the NDE, and for many researchers these are good enough. Yet an increasing number find these explanations inadequate. The systematic study of NDEs is only in its infancy, and the one thing we can be certain of is that there is a great deal more to be learned about this most unusual human experience.

Although scientists debate whether the NDE is truly a glimpse of the afterlife or merely a hallucinatory strategy for coping with impending destruction, there is no debate about one aspect of the NDE: For those who experience it, the NDE is a life-transforming event. Almost uniformly an NDE will lessen the fear of death and increase the experient's belief in an afterlife. Most experients find their concern for others greatly enhanced, with greater feelings of compassion, tolerance, and altruism. Many encounter a new personal transcendence that invests life with its own deep meaning and leads to a lack of interest in material gain or personal wealth. Paradoxically, even though the NDE reduces the fear of death, persons who experience their NDE as a result of a suicide attempt seem to be less likely to attempt suicide again than those who did not experience an NDE during a suicide attempt.[12]

NDE research may be one area that has lifted itself out of mainstream parapsychology, but work continues—albeit tenuously—at a few hospitals and medical centers around the world. It remains one of the few instances where research related to questions of survival and the independence of consciousness is demanding a place in orthodox medical research.

Ecological Parapsychology:
Spiritual Recycling

On June 6, 1926, Mr. Kekai Nandan Sahay, a well-known and respected lawyer in Bareilly in the Indian state of Uttar Pradesh, returned from a visit to his family home to attend to his wife, who had been taken seriously ill. While he was home, his three-year-old son, Jagdish Chandra, asked him to get an automobile (which was a great rarity in that part of India at the time). When the father replied noncommittally by saying he would get one "soon," his son became impatient and asked him to do it promptly. "Where do you expect me to get an automobile?" Sahay asked. Much to his surprise, the boy replied, "Get my auto, at the house of Babuji in Benares" (a city on the Ganges River, more than three hundred miles from Bareilly). When Sahay asked his son to clarify who Babuji was, the boy replied, "He is my father."

In other cultures such an exchange might be profoundly worrisome for a father, but Hinduism incorporates a strong belief in reincarnation. Sahay realized that reincarnation could explain his son's comments, but he was not content to leave it as just an article of faith. His legal mind inclined him to document carefully his son's comments and verify them later.

Over the next few days Sahay asked his son to tell him more about Babuji, which he did in surprising detail. For starters Jagdish Chandra claimed that his name was Jai Gopal and that Babuji Pandey was his father. The boy appended the honorific *Pandit* to his name, signifying he was of the Brahmin caste (which was not the caste of his present family). He described the house in which he lived in Benares as having a large gate, a sitting room, and an underground room with an iron safe fixed to the wall. He said Babuji had two automobiles, a phaeton (carriage) and two horses. He also gave many personal details about Babuji, including the fact that he would sit in the courtyard with people and drink bhang (an intoxicant made from Indian hemp), had malish (a type of massage), and before washing in the morning would put a powder or paint on his face. He further said that Babuji had two sons and a wife, all of whom had died.

Before proceeding any further, Sahay enlisted seven friends and colleagues at the high court to witness his son's statements and advise him how to proceed in a scientific manner. They decided that he should first write to the chairman of the municipal board in Benares and ask him to make inquiries. The chairman, a lawyer by the name of Munshi Mahadeva Prasad, replied that everything Sahay's son had said was true, as far as he could determine. In fact, Babu Pandey was a longtime client of his, and he recognized him immediately on reading Sahay's letter.

On June 27 Sahay published a letter in the principal English-language newspaper for the area, describing his son's comments and soliciting further information about Babuji Pandey. This yielded additional confirmations of the details. There was no question but that the person Jagdish Chandra was calling Babuji Pandey was one Pandit Mathura Prasad Pandey of Pandey Ghat (pier), of Benares City. Babu Pandey indeed had a son, Jai Gopal, who had died several years earlier. All the details were correct, except that Babu Pandey did not own the two cars; he only rented them from time to time.

As the case began to attract public and press interest, Sahay had a local magistrate interview Jagdish Chandra and record all of his statements. This produced a very full account of life in the Pandey household, with names and details of personal habits of family members, even to the point of naming and describing a prostitute who would come to the house to dance and sing on special occasions. This was all verified through correspondence by a neighbor and relative of Babu Pandey.

About a month later Sahay and his son visited Benares. With a crowd of onlookers three-year-old Jagdish Chandra pointed the way through a labyrinth of lanes to the house of Babu Pandey. The boy recognized Babu and other members of the household. He also recognized local landmarks and he bathed in the swollen, rushing Ganges River with none of the trepidation one might expect from a three-year-old who had never been near a river before.

Was Jagdish Chandra the reincarnation of Jai Gopal? The one person who has investigated more cases like this than anyone cautiously terms it a "case of the reincarnation *type*." Dr. Ian Stevenson, Carlson Professor of Psychiatry and director of the Division of Personality Studies (formerly Division of Parapsychology) at the University of Virginia at Charlottesville, is the world's foremost investigator of reincarnation cases. In 1961 Stevenson began investigating the Jagdish Chandra case, supplementing the already copious documentation provided by Sahay (who had died by this time). Over several visits continuing through 1973, Stevenson interviewed Jagdish Chandra, as well as his brothers and mother, and Babu Pandey's daughters. He also visited the houses of both families to verify the statements made in Sahay's published account.[13]

Sahay's thoroughness left little for Stevenson to add to the case. Stevenson was able to complete the picture of Jagdish Chandra by learning more of how his apparent former life influenced his later childhood. Most characteristic was Jagdish Chandra's tendency to adopt Brahmin habits that were very out of place in Sahay's family. The boy insisted on eating first, even among his own family, a deference customarily expected by Brahmins. Nor would he eat with non-Hindus, or eat food touched by non-Hindus, a typical trait of orthodox Brahmins. His other eating and dressing habits were also distinctly Brahmin, which he would not have learned from the Sahay family. Jagdish Chandra always retained his fondness for automobiles, even to the present day, and he attributes this to the fact that Jai Gopal, a rather pampered child, was often taken for rides.

In the early years the Pandey family was rather cool to Jagdish Chandra. Apparently, along with the early statements that had been publicly verified, Jagdish Chandra had also made some rather incriminating statements about his former father's activities as a panda (a Brahmin who assists pilgrims wishing to bathe in the holy Ganges). Babu Pandey not only employed a squad of *goondas*, who extracted "donations" of gifts from the pilgrims, but Jagdish Chandra apparently claimed that Babu Pandey had also murdered one pilgrim for his money. After Babu Pandey died, however, the remaining family members welcomed Jagdish Chandra, and he continued to visit them regularly over the years.

Because of the very public manner in which Sahay revealed the details of his son's statements before any verification had been attempted, Stevenson concluded that a hoax was out of the question.

Sahay was a prominent lawyer; he would have had nothing to gain by a faked reincarnation, and, given the public and press interest in the case, everything to lose. Those who knew Sahay said he was a man of outstanding character and that it was purely a matter of scientific curiosity that led him to pursue the case.

Nor is it likely that Jagdish Chandra could have accidentally come upon all the information about the Pandey family that he was later to reveal. The young Jagdish Chandra had spent virtually all of his life within a compound that surrounded the family house. If he went out, it was only with adult family members. Of the family, only Sahay himself had been to Benares on brief visits, and he knew very little of the city; they never had any visitors from Benares. Sahay had a cousin in Benares, but he had never come to Bareilly.

Finally, since Sahay took care to record all the principal statements made by his son before the case became public and before the families met, it is unlikely that the later meeting with the family might have contaminated the child's memories.

Stevenson regards this case as one of the best authenticated of all reincarnation cases. He should know, since for over thirty years he has maintained almost single-handedly the only contemporary research program on reincarnation.* During this time he has published numerous scholarly books and articles, and, to date, has on file over two thousand *investigated* cases.

Reincarnation—the belief that a soul or some other aspect of personality is transferred from one person to another born after the death of the first—is an ancient human belief. Westerners usually associate reincarnation with Hinduism and other Eastern religions, but this belief can be found in many societies that have not been influenced by Judeo-Christian religious thinking. It is common among Shiite Moslems and among several major African tribal groups, who, in turn, carried these beliefs to Brazil, where it remains strong among certain religious sects. Native American tribes in the Northwest believe in reincarnation, as do tribes in central Australia.

By definition *reincarnation* means survival in the sense that the psychical researchers were seeking; the soul or personality in ques-

---

*Stevenson has always acknowledged the many colleagues who have assisted him in his investigations around the world, but he has always been the driving force behind the research itself.

tion would have to survive at least one bodily death, and perhaps exist in some intermediate state, before entering a new body.* Yet reports of reincarnation cases were rare among early investigations. Isolated cases turned up in the literature, but they were generally regarded as mere curiosities until the publication in 1960 of a paper by Stevenson entitled "The Evidence for Survival from Claimed Memories of Former Incarnations." In this paper Stevenson surveyed forty-four cases in which the person who was supposedly being reincarnated could actually be traced and identified. Stevenson argued that these cases may be more frequent than most researchers realize and that careful investigation of future cases could yield important information pertaining to the survival question. As it turned out, that paper was the charter for his own research program; the following year Stevenson began the field studies that have occupied much of his time for the past three decades.[14]

In approaching reincarnation research there are several avenues open to the investigator, but Stevenson feels that only one—investigating spontaneous childhood remembrances of past lives—is likely to yield evidence that might help prove the reality of reincarnation. So-called "past-life readings" of the type one obtains from amateur or professional psychics are of little use to investigators, since they are usually vague and confined to well-known historical periods, the details of which are common knowledge or easily available to the psychic. Besides, most people who have attempted to investigate past-life readings have found that different readers often place the client in vastly different situations and locations for the same dates.

Another strategy, hypnotic regression to "past lives," has become popular lately, though not among serious researchers. Some therapists claim that regressing a patient to earlier lives can uncover the source of present-day personality problems, but such claims are controversial at best. Hypnotism has been shown to facilitate the accurate recall of old memories, when such memories exist. However, in the absence of actual memories, a hypnotized person is very likely

---

*Stevenson has on file a small number of cases in which the "new" body was already several years old when the body of the reincarnated personality died. Stevenson is reasonably sure that errors in recording or remembering dates cannot explain these anomalies, which, needless to say, raise some interesting theoretical issues for a reincarnation interpretation.

to create fake "memories" unconsciously that they cannot distinguish from real memories. Considering that a person under hypnosis becomes very compliant to the hypnotist's instructions, a request to "remember back before you were born" is likely to reveal simply the person's best attempt to construct a past from what can be dredged up from long-forgotten history books, novels, movies, and so on. The drama that a hypnotized person may display in "reliving" past memories, while often very impressive, is no clue to its authenticity—hypnotically regressed individuals may become passionately involved with lives that are blatantly inaccurate historically. If reincarnation is a fact, then there is no reason to think that hypnosis might not be able to reveal earlier lives, but hypnosis itself could never be used to demonstrate conclusively that reincarnation is real.

For Stevenson, investigating spontaneous childhood memories of past lives is likely to be the most productive route for studying reincarnation. Children, especially very young ones, are not likely to have the vast reservoirs of learned but forgotten facts that could be used to construct plausible fantasies. Similarly it is easier to determine if young children have been exposed to the specific information they reveal. In most cases it is the child who has volunteered the information suggesting an earlier life, without prompting or suggestions from adults, which makes it less likely that the child is responding to pressure or encouragement from others.

Stevenson's methods follow in the tradition of the early psychical researchers who painstakingly investigated cases of apparitions. His primary method is to interview the subject and all firsthand witnesses whenever possible. Generally he interviews important informants several times, partly to elicit additional information but also to test the consistency of their reports over time. Stevenson also checks hospital records, birth certificates, and any other sources to substantiate details of the witnesses' accounts. Eventually he accumulates a thorough account of relevant facts of the case as well as a good estimate of the credibility of the witnesses.

The next step in the investigation is to see if the child's memories correspond to the life of a particular individual who had died before the child's birth. Often this will have been done by relatives or friends by the time Stevenson hears about the case, so he will repeat the interviews and investigations with relatives of the alleged previous personality.

In some cases Stevenson (or his colleagues) have been the ones actually to make the identification. Such cases can provide particularly strong evidence, since Stevenson can independently verify the details of the previous personality's life before there is any possibility of these being influenced by the child's family. In three recently published (1988) cases that Stevenson and two Sri Lankan colleagues investigated, they not only made written records of a child's past-life memories before attempting to verify them, but they themselves traced and identified the apparent previous personalities.[15]

An additional four Sri Lankan cases of this type have been investigated in the past three years by Stevenson and his colleagues but have not been published. Stevenson is especially enthusiastic about the cases in which he has been the one to discover and verify the previous personality, since, in his words, "One of these rare cases is worth one hundred of those in which the two families have already met before the investigator arrives on the scene."[16]

Of the more than 2,000 cases on file at the University of Virginia, Stevenson has investigated more than 250 of them extensively. He has investigated about another 1,000 less thoroughly, but considers them of sufficient merit to be included in the collection. The remaining 750 have been investigated by Stevenson's associates or other researchers in whom he has confidence.

Over the years Stevenson has been able to identify several typical characteristics that most childhood cases share. Usually the child begins to speak of a previous life between the ages of two and five. This generally comes about spontaneously, although it is often triggered by an incident or observation that is related to these memories. Often the child uses adult expressions or language skills beyond his years. These memories begin to fade by ages five or six and are usually gone by age eight, unless repeating them for curious visitors has made them familiar.

A very important feature of the more convincing cases is that often more than just visual or verbal memories are involved. Frequently the child will *act* in ways that are strange for the child himself but are entirely appropriate to the previous personality. Recall Jagdish Chandra's Brahmin habits, which he most certainly would not have acquired in a non-Brahmin family. In many cases the child has a phobia unexplainable by his or her own life but that corresponds to the manner in which the previous personality died. In a 1983 case a three-year-old girl who claimed to have died when "a mountain came down on her house" became hysterical when her father took her down the road that led to the site of a 1977 landslide that fit her description. The little girl screamed and refused to go farther. She carried on so much that her father was forced to abandon the trip. Several children who claimed to have drowned in the previous life displayed marked phobias of water. In some cases where the claimed former personality was of the opposite sex, the child showed a marked propensity for dressing and behaving in a manner appropriate to the previous sex. In some cases the behavioral characteristics continue long after the past-life memories have faded.[17]

A smaller number of cases, about two hundred in Stevenson's collection, involve birthmarks that are claimed to be related to the previous personality. Some are claimed to be the mark of a fatal wound, but others are more innocuous. Sahay reported that his son had marks on the upper part of his ears corresponding to the uncommon location for earrings reportedly favored by the pandas of Benares.

Has Stevenson's work made a good case for reincarnation? Stevenson himself has always been somewhat reticent to answer that question directly, preferring to say that they *suggest* reincarnation, but then leaving it up to his readers to decide how they wish to interpret the evidence. Of course his method is to provide sufficient evidence that conventional interpretations of the cases seem inadequate. Though he maintains that his cases only suggest reincarnation, he has been vigorous in defending them against dismissive normal explanations.

The most common alternative explanation for these cases is that they are simply childhood fantasies. Some critics point out that reincarnation cases arise at about the same time that children begin developing imaginary playmates. While those cases in which the claims of a former life were fragmentary, vague, and never subsequently verified may well be fantasy, it is difficult to see how childhood fantasy could explain cases in which there are many *specific and detailed* memories that are later verified. Childhood fantasies would not enable a child to lead the way to the house of the former personality, correctly identify former relatives, or, as in one case, identify the location where the former personality had hidden money.

To support the fantasy explanation, critics often note that the majority of cases arise in cultures predisposed to believe in reincarnation. They argue that parents probably encourage (perhaps unconsciously) the symptoms of a reincarnated personality and then help shape it as the fantasy grows. However, Stevenson has recorded numerous cases of reincarnation in families with no belief in reincarnation or who even express hostility toward it. Many cases come from cultures with no systematic belief in reincarnation. Recently he has published several cases from middle-class, suburban America.

A more convincing alternative explanation is that the cases are real—not fantasized—but are the result of normally acquired information. The child could derive this information from parents and other adults, or perhaps just absorb it from the surrounding culture. Since in many cases the two families—the present and "previously incarnated" one—had met before the case was investigated, the child's initially vague statements of the previous life may have been unintentionally strengthened and have become more detailed or accurate than they originally were. Behavioral traits of the previous personality may have been cued by the adults and learned by the child.

Again, it is possible that some cases could be explained by this reasoning, but there are too many cases in which the detailed information that was communicated by the child was simply not available in the house that the child lived. In enough cases substantial distances separated the families, and written records of the child's statements were made before they ever met. (In some cases the families never did meet, and the verification was done by the investigator or some other third party.) We must not lose sight of the fact that many cases arise almost as soon as the child is able to talk. Often children have to resort to acting out concepts (such as occupations) related to the previous personality, since neither the concept nor the word to describe it is used in the present family.

There are some critics willing to grant that conventional explanations do not suffice to deal with the most convincing of the reincarnation cases, yet they are unwilling to accept the possibility of reincarnation itself. They theorize that the child has somehow picked up information about the previous personality from surviving relatives and friends using ESP. However, reincarnation cases would have to be a form of spontaneous ESP unlike any other. Why should one child suddenly acquire a cluster of ESP cognitions about a certain individual—one of thousands who may have died in the recent past—and yet display no evidence of any other ESP experiences? Why should it suddenly happen many years after the relatives would have ceased grieving about, or perhaps even thinking of, the deceased? Many cases imply several sources of this ESP information, since all the child's claimed memories are not always known to a single individual.

Contemporary ESP (that is, occurring around the time of the child's statements) cannot fully account for the many instances during verifications in which the child recognized people and places that were the same as when the previous personality died but failed to recognize those that had changed in the interim. Similarly, often the child's memories display confusions typical of a child's perspective (for example the ownership of Babu Pandey's two automobiles) but not that of an adult's perspective, from which the presumed ESP is thought to occur.[18]

I think Stevenson can fairly claim that his cases do *suggest* reincarnation. The substantial body of evidence that he has collected, taken as a whole, points in that direction. But few if any parapsychologists would claim that reincarnation has been proven. The evidence rests too heavily on human testimony and the efforts, admittedly diligent, of a single individual. Yet, through Stevenson's efforts, reincarnation seems far more of a possibility than it did thirty years ago. Even though proof, if it is ever to come, may yet be far in the future, Stevenson can at least take credit for reinvigorating survival research with a fresh approach that is providing some of the most challenging data on the issue that parapsychology has seen in some time.

Will There Ever Be an Answer?

The belief in an afterlife is common to virtually all religious traditions. We are entitled to wonder from where it derives. The usual scientific assumption is that these beliefs are purely imaginary concepts that arose from the needs of the living to deal with the sense of loss that the death of a loved one brings. Belief in an afterlife that is better than the present life seems a natural source of comfort and solace to the bereaved. In time, such beliefs became formalized in the religious systems that evolved to explain all of nature's mysteries.

There is another way of looking at the roots of survival beliefs: might they not be early mankind's attempts to explain the very same human experiences that parapsychologists are grappling with today? Why should we assume that OBEs, NDEs, and reincarnation cases represent attempts to fit aberrant mental states into preconceived religious or quasi-religious beliefs? Perhaps they are the *source* of such beliefs. We know from historical sources that reports of out-of-body experiences, near-death experiences, and reincarnation, not to mention apparitions, are as old as recorded history. Should we not assume that our early ancestors experienced, reported, and tried to make sense of NDEs, OBEs, and evidence for reincarnation just as we are trying to do today? The explanation that emerged from their efforts was that something of the human personality continues after the body dies. That such an ancient explanation still seems to fit a good deal of the data should not count against it.

As I noted at the beginning of this chapter, research into post-mortem survival is no longer a major component of parapsychology. The investigations of mediumistic communications and apparitional cases largely played themselves out in the early part of this century. This was not because the evidence that emerged was not good; those who take the trouble to examine the best of this work would find it an impressive achievement. The problem was that it was no longer progressing; new approaches had to be devised.

With the study of OBEs, NDEs, and reincarnation experiences we have, within the last several decades, witnessed a revival of interest in the survival question and the development of intriguing new methodologies. Neither controlled OBE research nor collecting NDE or reincarnation cases will provide the "proof" that so many expect, but each of these approaches is generating interesting data that demand consideration. Whether or not survival is the best explanation remains to be seen. Professor Stevenson has noted that many of the leaders of parapsychology and psychical research died without being persuaded that survival was the correct interpretation of the evidence; today even most parapsychologists are similarly uncertain. "Doubt is therefore not censurable," writes Stevenson. "The only improper stances are denial that there is any evidence worth looking at or the assertion that what we have will suffice."[19]

PART III

The Future of Psi

CHAPTER 9

Adding It All Up

Once again I find myself looking across my desk at yet another reporter doing a story on parapsychology. Same old questions, same old answers.

"Dr. Broughton, when do you think parapsychology will finally begin to achieve recognition by other scientists?" the reporter asks.

That boring old chestnut again; let's try a different answer this time. "When we get into *that* book," I reply glibly, gesturing at a thick volume with a colorful spine on the bottom shelf of the bookcase.

"What's that book?"

"That book" was my aged copy of what is known in academic psychology as "Hilgard and Atkinson." For more than three decades the textbook *Introduction to Psychology* by Ernest Hilgard and Richard Atkinson (with additional colleagues for later editions) was the way most college students first learned what the science of psychology encompassed and what it did not. ESP, psychokinesis, and the other phenomena of parapsychology were firmly placed among those topics that were not entitled to serious consideration. *Introduction to Psychology* has been so influential in defining the bounds of orthodoxy for psychology that I often used it, as I did with this reporter, to symbolize the ultimate hurdle that parapsychology would have to surmount en route to scientific acceptance.

Much to my surprise and delight, those days have come to an end. With the 1990 edition of *Introduction to Psychology** there is now a small section entitled "Psi Phenomena" that provides a fair and accurate picture of a portion of current ESP research. The introduction to the book notes this about-face: "We have discussed parapsychology in previous editions but have been very critical of the research and skeptical of the claims made in the field. And although we still have strong reservations about most of the research in parapsychology, we do find the recent work on telepathy using the Ganzfeld procedure worthy of careful consideration."[1]

Telepathy in *Introduction to Psychology*! It is enough to make a parapsychologist believe in miracles, were it not that it was no miracle at all. It was the result of diligent data collection and the determination of one particular parapsychologist—Charles Honorton—to confront the critics head-on. As the introduction indicated, the authors of *Introduction to Psychology* are willing to consider only a small portion of parapsychology research: the ganzfeld procedure pioneered by Honorton.

Of course diligent data collection has been part of parapsychology since its inception. So why has it taken so long for this measure of recognition? The answer lies in the way the data were presented this time. Several years ago Honorton summed up all the ganzfeld experiments using a relatively new way of looking at data known as *meta-analysis*. It was what meta-analysis of the ganzfeld data revealed that convinced the authors of *Introduction to Psychology* that this research is "worthy of careful consideration." The opening that Honorton has managed to pry in the gates of orthodoxy may soon grow far wider as meta-analysis reveals a good deal of parapsychological data to be much stronger than even parapsychologists thought it to be.

Introduction to Psychology, 10th ed. Rita L. Atkinson, Richard C. Atkinson, Edward E. Smith, and Daryl J. Bem (San Diego: Harcourt Brace Jovanovich, 1990). (The original author, Ernest R. Hilgard, is no longer one of the authors, but the text is often still referred to as "Hilgard and Atkinson.")

Meta-analysis—the Controversy Killer

More than one observer has suggested that part of the reason why psychologists and other social scientists are so resistant to parapsychology is that it reminds them too much of weaknesses in their own sciences. Very often scientists have drawn attention to the fact that in many areas of social and psychological research the results are weak and difficult to repeat. Frequently psychological "effects" are discovered, only to be discarded later when researchers are unable to replicate their findings. In some domains, for example the effectiveness of certain psychotherapies, debates about the reality of the effects continue to this day. Thus within orthodox social science there has been a continuing concern (not to mention a certain touchiness) about how scientists are to interpret weak and often inconsistent results.

In the mid-seventies this began to change as certain statistical procedures were coupled with some basic rules for combining studies, resulting in analytical methods that could yield more objective and quantifiable findings. University of Colorado psychologist Gene Glass is credited with first using the term *meta-analysis* to describe his summary of research dealing with the effectiveness of psychotherapy. Robert Rosenthal of Harvard University became a leading proponent of meta-analysis after he used it to great effect in demonstrating the strength or "robustness" of interpersonal expectancy effects,* a particularly controversial research area that he had opened up many years earlier.[2]

How can meta-analysis put an end to research controversies? Actually the methods are not hard to grasp, and it is worth spending a few moments examining them so that the impact meta-analysis is having on the assessment of psi research can be fully appreciated.

The principal question meta-analysis tries to answer is "Does this collection of experiments demonstrate a real effect?" This of course

---

*Interpersonal expectancy effect is a tendency for investigators in psychological experiments (particularly those with one-to-one contact with subjects) unconsciously to bias the subject's responses in a way that supports the results that the experimenter expects to obtain.

gets right to the heart of the matter for parapsychology, as well as for many areas of psychological research.* The problem in parapsychology is that although researchers A, B, and C may conduct ESP experiments and find significant evidence of ESP, researchers X, Y, and Z may try essentially the same experiments and fail to find significant evidence. Even worse, sometimes when A, B, or C repeat their experiments, they do not always get significant results. Does this mean that ESP results are *not replicable*, or were there subtle (or not so subtle) differences in how these studies were carried out that explain the differences? Critics would like to argue that the inability to replicate results means we do not have to take parapsychological experiments seriously, but meta-analysis is making it harder to justify that sort of rejection in many instances.

To understand how meta-analysis applies to parapsychology, we must first consider what comprises the data of any experiment. The results of any experiment will consist of two elements: signal and noise. The "signal" is the effect on the data caused by the experimental factor that you are investigating. In a simple ESP experiment, for example, the signal would be the number of correct guesses that were due to the ESP-supplied information. The "noise" is everything else that shows up in the data but in which you are not interested. In our ESP experiment the biggest component of the noise is likely to be pure chance—all the correct guesses that were just chance happenings and would be there with or without ESP—but it also includes unknown factors that might cause a person's ESP ability to vary or disappear during the experiment.

The experimenter's task is to extract the signal from the noise, and the discipline of statistics provides the tools. Most basic statistical tests tell the experimenter only if there really is a signal—the experimental effect—among all the noise. But these statistical tests do not provide the experimenter with a definitive answer; they only provide an *estimate* of whether there really is something in all the noise. Like all estimates, the more data that go into a statistical

---

*In discussing the problems that meta-analysis addresses I shall use parapsychological examples, but that should not obscure the fact that presently meta-analysis is being used primarily to address precisely the same issues in many areas of orthodox psychological and medical research.

estimate, the better it will be. The more data that the experimenter can collect, the more likely it is that the statistical tests will detect a signal in it (if there is one to detect).

We find ourselves performing similar "signal extraction" tasks all the time—having conversations in crowded rooms or looking for our ride among the hundreds of cars pulling into the airport pickup area—but a better analogy to the experimenter's situation is the case of a shortwave radio fan. Some shortwave listeners—called DXers—take particular delight in tracking down the weakest, most distant stations possible. If a DXer were to tune to a promising frequency but listen to the hissing and crackling for only a few seconds, he might conclude there was no signal there. But if he listened perhaps for several minutes, he might catch snatches of faint, humanlike sounds. A signal perhaps? Listening even longer—collecting more data—he might be able to determine that someone is speaking. A signal, but is it the correct one? Further listening might even confirm which language was being spoken, and perhaps even that it was the sought-after clandestine radio station of the Tierra del Fuego Liberation Army.

When signals are strong, very little data are needed. You need only a second or two to determine that your local rock-'n'-roll station is alive and well. When signals are weak, however, the amount of data collected becomes critical.

The same situation rises in parapsychological tests. Say you have a subject who can reliably use ESP to guess coin-flips 5 percent of the time. In other words if the person guessed twenty coin-flips, out of the roughly ten correct guesses, *one* would be due to ESP—but you cannot tell which one that is—and the rest are due to chance. If you wish to detect this ability in a test but decide to make your test one hundred coin-flips, you would be in the position of the DXer who listens for a signal for only a few seconds. Your experiment would *fail* to detect your subject's ESP ability nearly 95 percent of the time. Your subject could have the most consistent (though weak) ESP ability in the world, but you would never know it. In technical terms your test lacks the *statistical power* to detect the effect.

Suppose you collect more data, like the DXer listening longer. If your experiment includes one thousand trials, over two-thirds of your tests would provide significant evidence of your subject's ESP ability (assuming he or she can maintain the 5 percent rate). With an experiment of ten thousand trials, you would virtually never fail to detect the subject's ESP. (Do not forget, however, that this process has not told you which particular trials are the ESP hits. Your statistical tools have merely indicated that there is a "signal" present that rises above the noise.)

In parapsychology it is pretty clear that we are dealing with weak effects. Binary RNG-PK effects, for example, seem to range from less than 1 percent to 2 or 3 percent above what is expected by chance. Though parapsychologists often pay lip service to this observation, they do not often take it into account when designing experiments.

The relationship between an experiment's ability to detect an effect and the amount of data collected is a standard part of the researcher's basic education. The amazing fact is that, until recently, probably the majority of researchers in psychology and parapsychology routinely set the size of their experiments with little or no consideration of the strength of the effect they were trying to detect. Often the determining factor was "How many subjects can I run in the amount of time (or with the money) I have?"—not, "How many subjects do I need to detect an X percent effect?" The awkward fact is that where effects are weak—in parapsychology or psychology— most experiments as they are typically designed will fail to detect an effect *even when there really is one.*

In fairness to the researchers, we must recognize that it can often be difficult to predict the size of a given psychological effect. It is virtually impossible at the start of a new line of research unless the researcher can infer it from related studies. Besides, few, if any, effects in psychology are constant; the effect itself will vary according to differing conditions. In theory estimating the required size of an experiment is straightforward; in practice it is quite difficult until a certain amount of data have already been collected. Human nature being what it is, when researchers have to guess, they usually come up well short of the mark. When dealing with replications, however, there is less of an excuse for guesswork, yet many replications fail to reach the criterion of statistical significance simply because insufficient data were collected. Rosenthal calls these "pseudo-failures to replicate."

It is precisely here that meta-analysis shows its usefulness, since meta-analysis is essentially a method of combining many short experiments into one long one. The basic methods of meta-analysis are designed to make different experiments that address the same question statistically equivalent, even though they may have involved differing experimental techniques, had different numbers of subjects, and of course produced different results. With the studies made equivalent, they can then be combined and an overall quantitative assessment of the strength of the effect can be made.

The meta-analyst's first step is to locate *every* study addressing the hypothesis of interest, regardless of the outcome. Successful replications, failures to replicate, and even reversals go into the meta-analyst's pot. The more data that can be combined, the stronger can be the conclusions of the meta-analysis. From this mass of differing results, meta-analysis is capable of extracting a simple yea or nay to a given effect.

Critics of meta-analysis have been quick to point out that simply accumulating a large number of studies can be grossly misleading if studies are not equivalent on grounds other than the statistical result. Should poorly designed, badly executed studies be combined with meticulously crafted experiments? Is it safe to ignore certain differences in procedures? In the past decade these and other questions have actually helped refine meta-analytic methods and made the technique able not only to deal with such issues but also to provide even more meaningful overviews of a particular research area.

Meta-analysis has thus evolved two principal activities. The first is simple accumulation of results. The second is to group the studies according to the different factors that might have something to do with the differing results, technically known as "blocking." Blocking effectively turns the differences between studies—what the early critics regarded as weaknesses—into additional strength for the meta-analysis. Studies can be coded according to the quality of the experiment,* the number or type of subjects, the experimenter, the location, even the date—whatever seems relevant. Often the impor-

---

*It may seem that an intangible such as "quality" may be difficult to quantify, but it is quite possible to do so. A meta-analyst could have other researchers independently rate the studies for overall quality and use their ratings. In parapsychological meta-analyses, as we shall see, it is common to quantify quality by the presence or absence of certain features that researchers (and critics) feel are important for parapsychological experiments.

tant blocking variables will have been suggested by past criticism. In parapsychology, for example, it is often claimed that poor-quality studies show evidence for psi but carefully controlled studies do not. Obviously, then, study quality will be an important blocking variable for parapsychological meta-analyses. Blocking variables need not always be "defensive"; they can be selected to help refine our basic understanding of the basic effect being studied.

Recall that I said that the meta-analyst first looks for all studies done on a particular question. What about all those studies that he or she *did not* find? Odds are that one critical factor common to most unknown studies is that they produced nonsignificant results—they failed to find the desired effect. Because of this the researchers decided they were not worth publishing, so they were just filed away. Rosenthal calls this "the file-drawer problem." Before meta-analysis, when a researcher pointed to a collection of significant studies, critics would claim that if all the failed studies buried in file drawers were added in, then the results would be reduced to chance. Meta-analysis permits the researcher to estimate just how large that file drawer would have to be to bring the observed result below the level of significance. In a small field such as parapsychology these file-drawer estimates can be very revealing; there are so few workers conducting studies that one can easily see that many of these hypothetical file drawers could not possibly exist.

A well-done meta-analysis can therefore determine whether or not an effect is likely to be genuine and what variables may influence that effect. In any controversial area of science this is valuable information indeed. Even if it does not immediately end debate, it permits researchers to make specific predictions for future research—the studies that may just finally settle the question.

Parapsychology, perhaps for even a longer time than psychology, has been trying to accumulate its results in the hope of ending the debate about the reality of psi phenomena. The first of these was a summary of all ESP card-guessing experiments that Rhine and his colleagues assembled in the 1940 volume *Extra-Sensory Perception After Sixty Years* (see page 72). Over the years there have been many summaries of subareas of parapsychological research, but none of these had much impact on scientists outside of parapsychology. In 1985, however, meta-analysis came to parapsychology.

The Great Ganzfeld Debate

By 1985 quite a few ganzfeld experiments had been reported, and it was beginning to look like parapsychologists might have come up with the long-sought repeatable experiment (even though it did not always provide significant results). In that year the *Journal of Parapsychology* hosted a debate between Ray Hyman, a psychologist and frequent critic of psi research, and Charles Honorton, the developer of the ganzfeld technique. The weapon of choice in this contest was meta-analysis, as the two scientists attempted to justify opposite conclusions from the same data base.

I am afraid that what you already know about parapsychology's inclusion in *Introduction to Psychology* removes the suspense regarding who won the ganzfeld debate, but it is worth examining the arguments so that you may judge for yourself how strong the evidence is for ESP in the ganzfeld. From the start of ganzfeld research, in the early seventies, to 1981 (when Hyman and Honorton began the exchanges that culminated in the *JP* debate), forty-two ganzfeld studies were published. An amazing 55 percent of the experiments yielded significant results on the primary indicator of ESP; only 5 percent of the studies would be expected to do this if chance alone were operating.

Hyman opened the debate by claiming that 55 percent was a gross overestimate of the success rate in the data base. He argued that if one considered problems in defining what constitutes a proper replication of the ganzfeld technique, the tendency for some investigators to use more than one measure of ESP (multiple analysis), as well as the possibility of a publication bias (the file-drawer problem that we discussed above), then the success rate would probably be closer to 30 percent. Also, because of certain statistical problems and procedural questions (some real, some just "potential" problems), additional successful studies could be discounted, resulting in a success rate pretty close to what chance would predict. Finally, hoping to administer the coup de grace to the ganzfeld, Hyman presented a statistical analysis claiming to show that the ganzfeld experiments with the most flaws, according to his criteria, were the ones that had the best ESP scores.

Honorton replied that allowing for differences in procedure and using accepted statistical techniques for dealing with multiple analyses would reduce the success rate only to 45 percent—still very significant and far above Hyman's rough estimate of 30 percent. Since many of the problems arose because experimenters had employed different scoring methods, Honorton focused his attention on twenty-eight studies that used the direct-hit method of scoring, that is, when the target picture was ranked first. These twenty-eight studies comprised 835 ganzfeld sessions in ten different laboratories. Forty-three percent of these yielded significant results. The odds against that result arising by chance are greater than one-billion-to-one.

Using the blocking technique, Honorton grouped these studies according to experimenter and was able to demonstrate that the results were *not* due to only one or two experimenters. Grouping studies according to where they were published (an indicator of the relative quality of the study) also showed no differences.

Honorton pulled the rug out from under Hyman's vague claims about how many unsuccessful studies might be buried in file drawers by using the meta-analytic technique to estimate just how many studies would have to be in those hypothetical file drawers to reduce the observed results to chance. It turned out that for every *one* of the direct-hit studies there would have to have been *15* unsuccessful studies to cancel the effect. In other words, instead of there being 28 direct-hit ganzfeld studies, there would have to have been 451, only parapsychologists would have never heard about 423 of them. Given that parapsychology is such a small field and the ganzfeld is a very time-consuming experiment, this is an absurdly high figure. Rosenthal suggests that the "fail-safe" number (the file-drawer estimate) should be at least five times the observed number of studies in order to rule out the file drawer as a potential problem. One can say with absolute confidence that the file-drawer problem does not threaten the ganzfeld research on that calculation alone. In addition some years earlier British parapsychologist Sue Blackmore had conducted a survey of parapsychologists specifically to find out if there was any bias (that is, holding back unsuccessful experiments) in reporting ganzfeld data. She concluded that there was none. Also, for most of the time that the ganzfeld work has been in progress, the Parapsychological Association has maintained an official policy discouraging the withholding of nonsignificant data, a policy unique among the sciences.

Finally Honorton enlisted the aid of a statistician, who exposed Hyman's "flaw analysis" as completely meaningless because Hyman had failed to meet certain basic requirements of the test he was using. (Thus Hyman was guilty of precisely the same charge he often leveled at parapsychologists.)[3]

This was not the end of the ganzfeld debate. About eighteen months after it was published, the *Journal of Parapsychology* opened its pages to a round of further commentary by critics and supporters of parapsychology. For the most part, critical commentators remained unconvinced by the debate, but there was one notable exception: The British mathematician and well-known critic Christopher Scott termed Honorton's reasoning, "the most convincing argument for the existence of ESP that I have yet encountered."[4]

Included in this second round was one commentator who could be considered nonpartisan in the ESP debate yet who is also very experienced in assessing controversial data: None other than Robert Rosenthal himself contributed a commentary, which was both a thorough summary and a penetrating analysis of the debate. After weighing the arguments concerning the impact of procedural flaws, multiple analyses, and other potential weaknesses, Rosenthal's own estimate was that the subject in a ganzfeld-ESP experiment was likely to pick the correct picture 33 percent of the time, where chance would predict 25 percent. He noted there was always a temptation to put off a final decision, saying, "Let's wait for more data." For Rosenthal, "That is not a realistic approach. At any point in time some judgment can be made, and though our judgment might be more accurate later on when those more nearly perfect studies become available, the situation for the ganzfeld domain seems reasonably clear. We feel it would be implausible to entertain the null [that is, that the results are due to chance] given the combined p [probability] from these 28 studies."[5] Translated, that means he is convinced something *is* happening in these experiments.

Perhaps the biggest surprise in the second round of the debate was a paper entitled "A Joint Communiqué," coauthored by

Hyman and Honorton. The two antagonists agreed that the overall significant effects found in the ganzfeld data base "cannot reasonably be explained by selective reporting or multiple analyses." Predictably the two authors did not agree on whether the significant effects should be considered a genuine communication anomaly (ESP) or the result of some yet-to-be identified flaws in the experimental design. But the most important part of the communiqué was that the two authors agreed upon a set of methodological standards that should be met by new studies so that the alleged flaws would no longer be a factor in evaluations. These standards would be both the recipe and the yardstick for future ganzfeld research.[6]

The "more nearly perfect" studies that Rosenthal anticipated were not long in coming. In 1989 Honorton and his colleagues presented the results of eleven new ganzfeld studies (358 sessions) that were carried out according to the guidelines agreed to in the joint communiqué. Ten of the eleven new studies yielded positive results, and the overall success rate—identifying the correct target out of four possibilities—was 34 percent, almost precisely what Rosenthal had estimated. The odds against this result being due to chance are better than 20,000-to-one. When these results are combined with the twenty-eight earlier studies that used the "direct-hit" method of analysis, the odds against chance become truly astronomical—better than 10-*trillion*-to-one.[7]

Meta-analysis has shown that these impressive ESP results are consistent across experiments and experimenters. They are not just statistical flukes (or possibly suspicious results) associated with one experimenter or just a few series. While it would be rash to say that anyone can run a successful ganzfeld experiment, there can be no doubt that *in the hands of a competent experimenter* the ganzfeld-ESP *is* a repeatable experiment.

Meta-analysis and Micro-PK

Undoubtedly the largest meta-analysis of parapsychological findings has appeared not in a parapsychological journal, or even a psychological one, but in the December 1989 issue of *Foundations of Physics*, a leading journal examining controversial issues in contemporary physics. Entitled "Evidence for Consciousness-Related Anomalies in Random Physical Systems," this meta-analysis by Dean Radin (then of the Princeton University Psychology Department) and Roger Nelson (of the PEAR lab in the Princeton University Department of Mechanical and Aerospace Engineering) tracked down 152 reports describing 597 experimental studies and 235 control studies involving the influence of consciousness on microelectronic systems. These studies were primarily of the micro-PK that we examined in chapter 6 and came from 68 different investigators.

The issues facing micro-PK research are very much the same as those facing the ganzfeld studies. Critics charge that the results are not repeatable or are confined to only a small few experimenters (often implicitly casting aspersions on their integrity or competence). They frequently make vague allegations that the equipment is technologically unsophisticated and the methods naive and open to subject fraud. The influential *Enhancing Human Performance* report by the National Research Council, which we shall examine in greater detail in the next chapter, used all of these charges to call the micro-PK research into question. The NRC committee limited its examination of micro-PK research to only the work of Helmut Schmidt, of the Mind Science Foundation, and Robert Jahn, of Princeton University, implying that only a few scientists have conducted such studies. They also referred to an unnamed physicist, allegedly with several years of experience in building random-number devices, who told the committee, "It is quite possible, under some circumstances, for the human body to act as an antenna and, as a result, possibly bias the output."* Although this claim was completely undocumented, the NRC committee suggested that it might

---

*Whatever the unnamed physicist's level of expertise in building RNGs, only someone with a profound ignorance of the methodology employed in most micro-PK experiments would believe this to be a problem in RNG-PK research.

explain some micro-PK experiments. Finally the NRC committee alluded to the possibility that subjects might have tampered with the data, although they offered no clues as to how this might have been done.

Radin and Nelson's meta-analysis was a frontal assault on all of these issues. Did the meta-analysis show evidence of the effect of consciousness on micro-systems? It most dramatically did. For convenience we shall have to use scientific notation to express the odds against chance for the effects. (In scientific notation one writes a 1 followed by a 0 with a superscript to indicate how many times the zero should be repeated. For example 1 million becomes 10^6, 1 billion is 10^9.) The odds that the RNG meta-analysis result arose by chance are about one-in-10^{35}.

Without doubt there is something happening in these experiments, but is it micro-PK? What about the possibility of inadequate equipment or poor methodology? Radin and Nelson assessed each study in the four aspects most often the subject of criticism: procedures, statistics, integrity of data, and the RNG device itself. There was no relationship between the quality of a study and its likelihood of producing evidence for psi. Again, the critics' allegation that results disappear when the experiments are done more carefully stands thoroughly refuted.

To see if the overall meta-analysis outcome might be due to just a few experiments that produced extremely successful results, Radin and Nelson "trimmed" off the extreme studies. This statistical procedure, aimed at producing a more homogeneous distribution of experimental effect sizes, required that 17 percent of the studies be excluded.* Dropping the extreme studies made little difference in the overall results, confirming that the meta-analysis was reflecting the accumulation of many small effects, not just a few exceptionally large ones. Similarly Radin and Nelson also demonstrated that the successful results were *not* confined to just a few experimenters but were broadly spread among the entire group.

Since many RNG studies are automated—easy to set up and run

---

*In meta-analyses in the social and physical sciences it is not uncommon for up to 45 percent of the studies to be dropped in order to obtain a homogeneous distribution. The fact that only 17 percent of the RNG studies had to be dropped indicates that the data base was relatively homogeneous to begin with.

once the basic equipment is in place—it is reasonable to suppose that the file drawer might be larger with the RNG studies than with the time-consuming ganzfeld studies. Experimenters might be more inclined to forget about nonsignificant studies or write them off as "just playing around" with the equipment. Nevertheless the file-drawer estimate that Radin and Nelson calculated completely ruled out selective reporting as an explanation for the overall result; some 54,000 unsuccessful and unknown studies would have been needed to reduce the observed findings to nonsignificance. This is about 90 times the number of known studies, comfortably above Rosenthal's recommended five-to-one ratio.[8]

Radin and Nelson's meta-analysis demonstrates that the micro-PK results are *robust* and *repeatable*. Unless critics want to allege wholesale collusion among more than sixty experimenters or suggest a methodological artifact common to nearly six hundred experiments conducted over nearly three decades, there is no escaping the conclusion that micro-PK effects are indeed possible. Yet Radin and Nelson, in common with most parapsychologists, stop short of claiming that all is proven. All they ask is that physicists (and psychologists) start taking these data seriously. Perhaps the eleventh edition of *Introduction to Psychology* will include a section on the influence of consciousness on physical systems.

Meta-analysis and the Historical Record

As we have just seen, when meta-analysis is applied to two relatively recent lines of research, we find the evidence for psi effects strong and reliable—precisely the opposite of what critics claim is the case. But what about the decades of painstaking research with card guessing and the other traditional tools of parapsychological research? The NRC's *Enhancing Human Performance* report chose to emphasize critic Ray Hyman's favorite charge that over 130 years of research have failed to find any evidence of parapsychological phenomena. Is it really the case that our forebears have simply been spinning their wheels, wasting their time?

Recently parapsychologists have started reexamining older lines of research using the tools of meta-analysis, and the results are nothing less than surprising. Whole areas of research are turning out to be stronger and more consistent than most researchers thought possible.

Precognition

In 1989 Honorton and his colleague Diane Ferrari turned their attention to one of parapsychology's more baffling phenomena—precognition. Systematic precognition research using forced-choice methods began in the thirties with the ESP-card experiments of Rhine and the Duke University researchers. In general these experiments were like other card-guessing experiments except that the subjects' guesses were recorded *before* the targets were even prepared. Researchers recognized that precognition testing had a major methodological advantage over standard ESP testing: There was no chance of sensory leakage contaminating the results.

The first surprise to emerge from Honorton and Ferrari's meta-analysis is the sheer amount of forced-choice precognition research that has been done. Limiting themselves to English-language publications, they retrieved 309 studies conducted by 62 investigators. Over 50,000 subjects participated in nearly 2 million trials. This is not a trivial data base, and Honorton and Ferrari leveled four principal questions at it.

The first question to be asked is, "Is there an overall effect?" The answer is an emphatic yes. Thirty percent of the studies were statistically significant (where 5 percent is expected by chance). The odds of this result happening by chance are about one-in-10^{24}.

Honorton and Ferrari then grouped the studies according to investigator. They obtained roughly the same results, indicating that the findings were not due to a small number of investigators.

Honorton and Ferrari then calculated that over fourteen thousand unreported nonsignificant file-drawer studies would be needed to reduce the observed results to chance. This is about forty-six unreported studies for each reported one, well above the recommended five-to-one margin.

The precognition data base turned out to be extremely heterogeneous, with far more extreme scores than expected. Honorton and Ferrari therefore excluded experimental results in the top and bottom 10-percent ranges, a standard procedure to reduce the influence of extreme scores. This more homogeneous sample still yielded odds against chance of about one-billion-to-one.

Honorton and Ferrari next classified studies according to whether or not the length of the study and its method of analysis were pre-planned, how the targets were randomized, and whether or not there were specific control checks of the randomizing procedure, and how the targets and subject responses were recorded and checked. Honorton and Ferrari found no significant relationship between the quality of the study and the results. If anything, there was a tendency for studies with *stronger* methodology to produce *better* results—exactly the opposite of what critics claim is the case.

One finding was something of a mixed blessing: The effect size—a measure of the experiment's success in demonstrating precognition—remained constant over the more than fifty years under consideration. This shows that the results are stable, but it also reveals that parapsychologists have not learned much about how to *improve* precognition performance in all those years. Perhaps the secret is hidden in the data, waiting only for an astute observer to discover it. It is here that the blocking techniques of meta-analysis prove their worth.

Honorton and Ferrari discovered that subjects selected on the basis of prior performance in earlier tests had a clear edge over unselected subjects. Studies in which subjects received individual attention produced significantly better results than those in which subjects were tested in groups. A particularly interesting question that Honorton and Ferrari asked was whether precognition was better when subjects were asked to peer into the near future or into the distant future. The interval between when guesses were made and targets selected ranges from milliseconds (as with Schmidt's machine) to months (and up to a year in one case). This interval of course also determined how soon after guessing the subject was able to learn whether he or she was correct. The data revealed that results declined as that interval became larger; the best results were obtained with very short intervals, and subjects performed best when they learned if they were correct after each guess (trial-by-trial feedback).

From their analyses, Honorton and Ferrari offered a prescription for successful precognition experiments: use selected subjects, test them individually, and give them trial-by-trial feedback. Out of the whole data base there were eight studies that fit this prescription; seven of them produced significant results. Interestingly there were nine studies in which all three characteristics were the opposite of what should produce good results—unselected, group-tested subjects given no feedback. This second group produced insignificantly negative results.[9]

With Honorton and Ferrari's meta-analysis, a half-century of precognition research has suddenly matured. Precognition in forced-choice testing may be a weak effect *but a stable and highly significant one*. It is not due to just a few experimenters, nor is it a result of poor methodology. Most importantly, the data themselves offer a clear signpost for the future direction of this research.

PK With Dice

In late 1933 a young man visited J. B. Rhine at the Duke University Parapsychology Lab. The visitor claimed he could influence which number came up on a die face simply by wishing for it. At that time psychokinesis was not part of Rhine's research program, but the claim intrigued him, so he put it to the test. The statistical procedures recently developed for his ESP research could easily be adapted to the probabilities of dice tossing.

The visitor did produce results that supported his claim, but even more interesting for Rhine was that some of his top ESP subjects were similarly able to influence the fall of dice. Even Rhine himself had some success at it. Thus began the second major thrust of the Duke Lab—psychokinesis on falling dice—that was to form a smaller but parallel research program for the next several decades. In fact in labs around the world, dice tests remained the standard experimental approach to PK research until the advent of Schmidt's RNGs in the early seventies. The technique continues to be used by some PK researchers, who feel that the RNG experiments may be too easily explained as precognition.

For a variety of reasons the dice experiments were the target of several severe attacks over the years, and it was difficult for parapsychologists, let alone outsiders, to form an overall picture of the success of dice-PK experiments. But in 1990, meta-analysis came to dice-PK with a paper entitled "Effects of Consciousness on the Fall of Dice: A Meta-analysis," by Dean Radin and Diane Ferrari.

The researchers embarked on this project rather doubtful that anything would come of it; like many newer parapsychologists they did not feel that dice tossing had been a particularly successful line of research. Once again, however, the parapsychology data had the capacity to astound even the parapsychologists.

Radin and Ferrari combed the English-language research literature and came up with a total of 148 studies in which the subject attempted to "will" a particular die face to come up. (Quite a few PK studies involved trying to cause dice to fall in certain positions on a grid, but these were not included in the meta-analysis.) Over 2,500 subjects attempted to influence more than 2.5 million dice throws. Forty-four percent of the studies were significant (where chance predicts 5 percent). The odds against chance for this result are roughly 10^{70}-to-one. Thirty-one control studies yielded nonsignificant results.

Of course, as we have often noted, an astounding departure from chance only means that chance is an unlikely explanation; whether or not we can attribute the result to PK depends on the quality of the research. Quality has always been a particularly thorny issue with the dice studies. Research with dice throwing is inherently more difficult than ESP card research. Data recording was more difficult because there was only one relatively short time to record the die faces before they were picked up to be tossed again (or tumbled by the machine). In contrast ESP card decks were often kept intact for later checking, or the target cards were carefully transcribed, so the written guesses could be checked and double-checked. ESP cards could be thoroughly randomized before use, whereas the randomness of dice depended on their physical characteristics and the method of tossing. Over time, steps were taken to address all these problems: high-quality dice were used in good tumblers, cameras recorded die faces, or multiple scorers were employed.

Dean and Ferrari applied the usual meta-analytic approach to the quality issue; they coded each study on about a dozen criteria pertaining to methodological quality. Weighting each study by the quality factor reduced the effect size by about one-half, but the results still remained massively significant.*

---

*Radin and Ferrari noted that methodological quality improved substantially over time, indicating that parapsychologists were responding to constructive criticism throughout this period.

Fourteen of the thirty-nine investigators whose studies went into this analysis reported four or more studies. Radin and Ferrari checked to see if this group of prolific experimenters might have overly influenced the results, which was not the case. They also trimmed off the "outlier" studies (as was done in the other meta-analyses above) to examine whether or not the meta-analysis results were due to just a few extremely successful studies. With 36 percent of the studies dropped, the effect size remained extremely significant.

Finally Radin and Ferrari calculated the size of the file drawer that would be needed to reduce the overall findings to chance—17,974 unreported studies, a ratio of 121 nonsignificant, unreported studies for each reported one.[10]

Clearly Radin and Ferrari's analysis reveals that the PK dice studies show a weak but consistent (and exceptionally significant) effect that cannot be explained by poor methodology or selective reporting. Nor can it be attributed to only a few experimenters or isolated studies. Once again, a venerable old line of parapsychological research has proven to be more robust and substantial than even its supporters imagined.

Winning the Numbers Game

So what do all these numbers mean? Two facts stand out clearly from the several meta-analyses that have been reported, and they seem paradoxical. The first is that several lines of parapsychological research are undoubtedly producing consistent, reliable effects that cannot be attributed to chance, poor methodology, or the vagaries of a few experimenters or unusual studies. The second point—and this is what may seem paradoxical—is that the effects are typically very weak. In fact the effects are so weak that they probably would have been missed in any other branch of science that did not force its practitioners to repeat the same experiments over and over again.

A weak effect, however, is not no effect; weak effects can still be useful in their own way, and techniques can be devised to enhance weak effects. Why psi effects appear weak in our experiments remains a source of speculation. Perhaps psi itself is a weak ability, or perhaps the artificial way in which we try to elicit it in our experiments does not permit it to display its full strength. Or maybe there are other explanations. Whatever the reason, psi ability as parapsychologists have to work with it is weak and hard to detect.

I have used the term *effect size* several times in this chapter without giving a thorough explanation of what this is. It would require a certain amount of mathematics to explain effect size properly, but for our purposes in parapsychology we can describe it as a measure of the difference between the observed results and the results that chance would predict. This measure is useful in meta-analysis because it is the common denominator in comparing many studies that use different numbers of subjects, different numbers of trials per subject, and different statistical evaluations. Calculating an *average* effect size for a particular line of research can tell researchers what to expect in future experiments.

In the meta-analyses so far, our effect sizes range from a low of .0003 for the RNG research through .01 for dice and .02 for precognition, to a high of .29 for the ganzfeld work. It is not surprising that the ganzfeld should produce a much larger effect size since it represents a highly standardized technique aimed specifically at enhancing ESP performance. The other three meta-analyses involved large numbers of different studies, done primarily with unselected subjects working under widely varying conditions.

Despite the smallness of most of the effect sizes, they are by no means unimportant. We have already given you the odds against these results being mere chance, but to put them in another context, let us look at a recent medical study that received a good deal of publicity. You may recall the mid-eighties study designed to see if aspirin can prevent heart attacks. This study was discontinued in 1987 with considerable fanfare because the results (45 percent fewer heart attacks in the experimental group) were so dramatic that it was considered unethical to withhold the treatment from the control group. Yet the actual effect of aspirin is very weak. In fact very few people ever realized that this widely acclaimed medical breakthrough had an effect size of just .03[11]* Parapsychology's finely

---

*Again, recalling our discussion at the start of this chapter on detecting weak effects, it is worth noting that the aspirin study employed over 22,000 subjects. Were it to have been done on a smaller scale—say 3,000 subjects—there would have been no medical breakthrough at all.

honed research program—the ganzfeld—far exceeds this effect size, and the "generic" precognition and dice experiments are not far from it. The mean effect size of Honorton and Ferrari's eight "optimal" precognition studies was .055. This suggests that future precognition studies could be "tuned up" to yield effect sizes even higher than the aspirin study.

Indeed the real way in which meta-analysis is helping parapsychology win the numbers game is in how it points the way for future research. For decades the great quest in parapsychology has been to find the repeatable experiment. Our professional literature contains lengthy discussions on how the concept of a repeatable experiment should be interpreted. Critics generally interpret it as "an experiment that I can do any time I want to and be pretty sure of getting evidence for psi." Meta-analysis has dramatically confirmed statistical repeatability. Now it is going to help parapsychologists write recipes for successful experiments.

At the very basic level, by identifying the expected size of certain psi effects, meta-analysis helps parapsychologists to design replication studies powerful enough to detect the effect. This is an enormous advance for parapsychology.

Even more than this, meta-analysis is identifying factors that have systematic effects on the results. Take, for example, the long line of research attempting to learn if there is a relationship between ESP and the personality dimension of extraversion. Historically researchers had the impression that extraverts are likely to do better in ESP tests, yet the typical experimental attempt to find this relationship often failed to achieve statistical significance. Over the decades parapsychologists had tested for the extraversion-ESP relationship using at least six different ways of measuring extraversion, two basic kinds of ESP tests (free response and forced choice), and many different subject populations and test environments. How are we to make sense of the morass of successful and unsuccessful experiments? How do we plan future research?

Parapsychologists could continue making slightly educated guesses—or they could follow Honorton's lead. As I write, Honorton and his colleagues are completing yet another major meta-analysis, this time of ESP-extraversion studies. With 60 studies from 17 investigators, there is an overall effect size of .09, which gives odds against chance of 250,000-to-one. Far more revealing, however, is the analysis of test conditions. Free-response testing had an effect size more than three times that of forced-choice studies. Among the forced-choice experiments, studies using individual testing (usually experimenter and subject, one-on-one) produced a very respectable effect size whereas group testing—the most common way of testing ESP-extraversion—had an effect size of .00. So it turns out that the most common (and the easiest) way of testing for an ESP-extraversion relationship is a recipe for *failure*. If you wish to maximize your chances of detecting an ESP-extraversion relationship, you will want to use free-response ESP testing administered individually.[12]

In chapter 5 we saw how Honorton's analysis of the ganzfeld studies led to a prediction that a certain number of subjects of a certain type (MBTI, psi experiences, and so forth) should produce ESP scores at a certain level—and our laboratory confirmed that prediction. With his extraversion meta-analysis, Honorton was able to predict that 180 or more free-response subjects should produce a statistical correlation between extraversion and ESP around .20. Using fresh data for the PRL's ganzfeld experiments, Honorton confirmed his prediction almost exactly. The 221 new subjects showed a very significant correlation of .18 between their level of extraversion and their ESP scores.

On the Verge of a Breakthrough

If anyone were to ask me what "major advances" have been made in parapsychology over the past decade, I would not hesitate to point to the application of meta-analysis to psi research. Over a half century of hard and often frustrating research can now be tapped productively to point the way to truly repeatable research. For that reason, parapsychology is incomparably stronger today than it was just five or six years ago.

In the early thirties, when Rhine and his co-workers at Duke were feverishly churning out ESP research, the findings that most excited them—the "breakthrough"—were the indications that psi ability seemed to vary systematically with physiological and psychological factors: Fatigue caused scores to fall off; sodium amytal caused ESP scores to fall to chance; doses of caffeine boosted them.

If psi phenomena could be shown to interact with other psychological factors, it would be a major step on the way to normalizing parapsychology and making its phenomena easier to assimilate into orthodox psychology. Indeed in many ways it is psi's seeming disregard for all the other "laws" of psychology that has made it so hard for psychologists to accept as something that belongs in their study.

Despite the early promise of the Duke work, the intervening decades often made it seem that such lawful relationships were likely to remain elusive for a long time to come. The very success of parapsychology seemed to be the cause of this confusion as a plethora of experimental approaches and settings replaced the uniformity of the Duke lab. Results were coming in from all over, but they rarely led to a coherent picture. The more research that was done, the more elusive a systematic understanding of psi phenomena seemed.

That phase of parapsychology is now at an end. We are now—finally—on the verge of a breakthrough. No, meta-analysis is not the breakthrough, but it is the tool that will help us make it. Never before in the history of this controversial science have we had the power and the data base to identify those long-sought lawful relationships as effectively as we can now. Never before have we had the tools that will enable us to specify precisely how we should conduct our research to confirm these laws. We are on the verge of a breakthrough today, and if parapsychology can rise to the challenge of meta-analysis, we may see the real breakthrough tomorrow.

CHAPTER 10

Are We Ready for Applied Psi?

"I have always been terrible about getting to airplanes on time—still am, actually," said my colleague as we sat in the psychology department common room. This well-respected cognitive psychologist continued, "Usually I get there just minutes before they close the doors, but I never missed a plane—except once.

"I was going to a conference, and for some reason little things kept holding me up, things I probably should have ignored, but this time didn't. I just figured my luck with planes would hold up. I got to the airport and dashed down to the gate, but wouldn't you know it, I missed the plane. First time ever for me. It was just taxiing away from the terminal. Later that day I learned that the plane I missed crashed, killing several of my colleagues. I guess my luck with planes did hold up, but not the way I expected."

My friend was convinced that his missing the plane was not just an accident. Even as he dealt with the trivial matters that detained him, he knew he should not be wasting his time, yet at the time he just felt that he "had" to do them. It was as if some sort of intuition or hunch—ESP?—had been working on his unconscious mind to cause him to miss the flight.

There are few people working in parapsychology who have not

heard many stories such as this. What are we to make of them? Are they merely coincidences which, because of the circumstances, are remembered as being more significant than they deserve to be? Perhaps the dramatic tragedy colored the person's memory of the events that delayed him, or perhaps emotion overlaid the memories of normal delays with a sense of purpose that was never there, as a way of assimilating a distressing experience.

Yet, might not these cases illustrate how ESP could work in daily life? Without conscious awareness my friend had a premonition that caused him to make decisions that ultimately resulted in his avoiding a deadly event. Of course such an instance would never be put forward as evidence of ESP, since it has nothing to distinguish it from ordinary coincidences save the experient's belief that something was out of the ordinary.

Coincidence, or psi in daily life? Today we are nowhere near being able to answer that question. I suspect that even if psi were to become an accepted fact, the question may remain largely unanswerable for most cases. Why I feel that way has to do with the way I view psi.

If humans have the ability to acquire information without the normal senses and to alter the probabilities of events—what we presently call psi ability—then this ability is likely to have certain characteristics in common with our other evolved abilities. Its primary purpose is likely to be the preservation and promotion of the health and well-being of the individual. Psi ability will probably blend relatively seamlessly with other human abilities so as not to call attention to itself and its "unconventional" way of operating.

Of course there remains the question "What about the psi ability of the others in the airplane? Why didn't their psi ability help them avoid danger?" Well, like most other abilities—intelligence for example—psi ability varies from person to person. The exceptional individuals who come to light may simply be the psychic equivalent of rare geniuses or prodigies.

If psi is part of normal human functioning, then there may be more instances of it in our lives than we realize. Perhaps we already do recognize it, but call it by different names. Two concepts that we have already touched upon are intuition and luck, both of which have ordinary psychological explanations that are sufficient for most people, but perhaps not complete.

Intuition

Intuition is an interesting concept. We all use the word, and we have a rough idea of what we mean by it—coming to a decision or making a judgment without quite knowing why. It is typically contrasted with reason, which implies coming to a decision or judgment by a series of logical and usually identifiable steps. When we try to define intuition more precisely, however, we find that there is considerable disagreement among psychologists, in whose province this matter falls.

The conservative (and more common) interpretation is that intuition is a judgment based on information we already have—either in memory or present through the senses—that lies below the threshold of conscious awareness. Thus we might intuit that someone is not to be trusted because of our unconscious perception of his personality or manner. Likewise we may intuit that a financial deal is too risky, an assessment that is really based upon material that we may have read some time ago or overheard at lunch but no longer consciously remember. Since intuition happens below conscious awareness, it may seem mysterious. Couple this with the fact that most people will remember the intuitions that prove accurate and promptly forget those that do not, and we have a perfectly normal explanation of intuition.

A slightly more liberal view of intuition grants that the data on which an intuition is based may be available to the individual, but that the essence of the intuition is the creative "putting together of the pieces" in a way that defies conventional logical analysis. Intuition, then, assumes a status similar to artistic (or even scientific) creativity—normal, but not well understood.

The most liberal view of intuition suggests that it involves, at least in part, ESP. Carl Jung was among the first to offer this interpretation of intuition, though he did not use the term *ESP*. He saw intuition as the direct, nonsensory perception of a truth, or the direct assessment of possibilities, implications, and so forth in a situation. For Jung intuition was a separate mental function, along with sensation, thinking, and feeling, and not reducible to a combination of the other functions.

While parapsychologists today are unlikely to argue that intuition *is* ESP, most would be willing to say that if ESP exists as a human ability, it is likely to be a component of what we call intuition. Undoubtedly the other factors—memories and other data lying below the level of conscious awareness—play a major role, but it may be ESP that supplies the missing piece to complete the picture or connects logically unrelated facts. Any given intuition may well be a mixture of greater or lesser parts of normally acquired data and ESP-acquired information.

In truth, though, this is just a parapsychologist's guess. Studying the hypothesized ESP component of intuition will be extremely difficult within the traditional approach of parapsychology. Standard parapsychological procedure is to isolate ESP from any possible sensory connection, but then how do you study ESP when it augments and blends with normal cognitive activities? At best we can attempt to correlate the performance of persons in ESP tests with their "intuitive ability" measured perhaps by their performance in real life. If successful ESP subjects do well in business, say, or their ability corresponds with some assessment of intuitive functioning, then we might infer that there is a relationship between the two. Beyond this, however, parapsychologists are limited until we are able to devise methods that tolerate the coexistence of sensory and extrasensory information in the same data.

Can psi ability be applied in the workplace? At the higher echelons of business, one is likely to hear a surprising amount of discussion about intuition. Many company presidents, top executives, and successful entrepreneurs will happily relate stories about how an intuition paid off handsomely or how a hunch averted a disaster. There are numerous books purporting to teach one how to *use* intuition in business, and there are high-priced seminars promoting "intuitive management." Intuition has become big business.

Only one project that I am aware of, the Newark (New Jersey) College of Engineering PSI Communication Project, has made any forays into the study of the relationship between business success and ESP. In the early seventies physicists Douglas Dean and John Mihalasky gave precognition tests to corporate presidents to see if they would prove to be much better than average. In fact certain subsets of the presidents did perform significantly above chance, but the project ended before a coherent picture emerged. It was also hampered by an ESP test—subjects had to guess one hundred digits by punching holes in

IBM cards—that must have seemed trivial in the extreme to executives used to having their intuition earn them millions of dollars. Dean and Mihalasky's pioneering effort should certainly be revived with the improved methods of testing that are available today.[1]

Luck

Luck, like intuition, may have a psi component. In chapter 6 I introduced the speculation that luck may have a PK component. This is simply an extrapolation from the growing body of evidence that some individuals can alter the probabilities of random events. Following the principle that psi in human life probably exists to be useful, we can expect that useful PK, when it appears in abundance, would look like our commonsense notion of luck. Certain individuals may use PK to get the random events of life to fall in their favor more than chance would predict. The luck that we are talking about here, however, is not limited to that found in casinos. This luck is more of a general success factor that goes beyond what is achieved through the individual's normal abilities and hard work.

Life is full of randomness, not unlike that which is found in the RNGs that parapsychologists use. The human brain not only contains substantial amounts of random neural firing, but its normal functioning relies on millions of neurons in delicately balanced electrochemical states. Often it only takes an electron or two to start the propagation of a network of neural firings. Years ago no less a brain expert than Nobel laureate John Eccles speculated that telepathy might involve a PK effect on one or more "critically poised" neurons. This, according to Eccles, may trigger the cascade of neural firings that results in a telepathic cognition. Equally possible, of course, would be that such PK on a brain could trigger actions, or inhibit them. In fact if such PK effects on neural circuitry are possible, then the whole range of human behavior might be susceptible to PK influence. Obviously if this happens at all, it is not likely to be a major influence on human behavior, but perhaps only the slightest influence may be needed to provide the "coincidences" that benefit a lucky person. For example a seemingly trivial decision by person A to wait in one location at the airport instead of another may result in a meeting with lucky person B, who happens to be looking for a new job that A can offer. Just chance, or might B have psychically helped A's decision to wait where he did? For the present the latter is pure speculation, but if there is such a thing as psi ability, that is how I would expect it to work.

Even the mechanical and electronic devices that we deal with every day might be candidates for the PK influence of a lucky person. Usually electrical and mechanical devices are not meant to function randomly, but over time they acquire random elements as components deteriorate and fail to perform as designed.* If luck is a form of PK ability, lucky people might be those who can deploy it to change the truly random probabilities in a given situation to probabilities that favor them.

Controlling Psi

All this speculation about intuition and luck is merely to suggest that we—or at least some of us—may be using and applying psi in daily life quite routinely. We simply do not notice it because it may be in psi's nature to be discreet in its operation. When most people talk about "applied psi," however, they mean the deliberate and controlled use of psi. How much research is going on with this type of applied psi?

Unfortunately the answer to this question is "not very much." Parapsychologists have traditionally shied away from applied research for several reasons. First most parapsychologists feel that not enough is yet known about how psi functions. The psi ability that

---

*Some years ago a sore point arose between me and my wife over a problem she was having with our aging automobile. Quite suddenly she began to encounter difficulties starting the normally reliable engine. Twice she was left stranded, yet every time I tried it, it started right up, even immediately after she had been unsuccessful. When I finally took it to the mechanic, he diagnosed the problem as deterioration of the starting points. (The car had two sets, one for starting and one for full-temperature running.) Apparently they were unable to transmit the necessary voltage to provide the spark—except when I tried it. Just luck? Who knows, but I do have a reputation for getting things to work that far exceeds my knowledge of mechanics or electronics.

we have seen in the laboratory seems very unstable and not easily amenable to conscious control. Many parapsychologists feel it is simply too early to begin trying to use psi in real-life situations, where emotions run high and strong expectations can be raised. Another deterrent is the potential public-relations problem. Parapsychology has enough of a problem with its image—particularly among other scientists—that most parapsychologists avoid research that might give the appearance of exploiting people's needs and fears. Finally many parapsychologists assume that those who might be willing to fund applied psi research are likely to have unrealistic expectations about how successful or productive such research will be. So, not much applied research has been done.

Applied psi as an occupation or avocation has a reputation lying between harmless hucksterism and shameless exploitation. At one end of the spectrum is the "storefront psychic," who makes predictions for a modest fee. As long as the prices are not outrageous, this activity can be regarded as a form of entertainment or perhaps comfort for those who seek it. Whether these folks have any true psychic ability is doubtful; it is hardly worth the effort to find out.

At the other end of the spectrum are "psychic consultants," who garner substantial fees for their advice on business and financial dealings, or, as Uri Geller reportedly does, help locate sources of raw materials and valuable minerals. It is not so easy to dismiss these practitioners, if for no other reason than that whoever is paying the bills must feel that their advice is useful. I am not aware of any formal testing of the quality of advice that psychic consultants give, but one would expect that the business world would judge them on the basis of performance: If their advice makes money, then use it, if not, out they go. How much of their advice is truly psychic is impossible to determine at present, but my suspicion is that it would not take much psychic ability to improve upon the predictions of conventional market analysts and consultants.

Somewhere in the middle are the many individuals who appear to be psychically gifted and offer their services—usually at no charge or for expenses only—to assist in missing-person or criminal cases. This middle ground is beginning to attract the attention of researchers for two reasons. First there is a large and growing data base of cases. Secondly it avoids the problems associated with the far ends of the spectrum—low yield, in the case of the shop-front psychics and proprietary or confidential information in the case of business consultants.

Psychic Detectives

I had just started to set out the food when I saw three people walking down the path to the pond where we were. Robert Rhine, son of J. B. Rhine, accompanied two women, whom I did not recognize. The occasion was a picnic for the dozen students of our institute's special summer program in parapsychology. As customary, we had set up camp beside a pond on the Rhine family property near Hillsborough in adjacent Orange County.

I had no idea why Robert would be bringing visitors to our picnic, but the moment he introduced the older woman, I realized why she was there. The woman was composed, though clearly distressed. She explained what we already knew from the newspapers: Her husband and a young helper, who was almost like a son to them, had been replacing a fence on the edge of their property, some distance from their house. The men had come home for lunch, but never returned that evening. For several days helicopters, tracker dogs, and search parties had combed the wooded areas, ponds, and a large section of the nearby Eno River. The police found no trace of the men. Earlier that day she and her neighbor had stopped by the Rhine house in the hope that she might be put in touch with a psychic who could help locate the missing men.

I explained that our institute does not make referrals for psychics, and I gave her our more or less standard response about how psychic ability was too unreliable to be trusted in such circumstances. But the woman was desperate and was practically a neighbor of the Rhines; perhaps there was some way we could help. I told her that if nothing had developed by Monday, she should have the officer in charge of the case phone me.

Early Monday morning a major in the Orange County sheriff's department telephoned, explaining that he was calling at the missing man's wife's request. He had never worked with psychics, but he had heard of cases elsewhere, he said. I provided him with an extended discussion of the pros and cons of trying to apply psychic ability to real-life situations. "I understand," he replied, "but we've tried just about everything we can think of, so it probably can't hurt to try this." I told him that if he was willing to consider it as a sort of experiment—with no promises—I could put him in touch with a local woman who had had some experience using her psychic ability to work with law enforcement agencies.

Two days later Mary* met with the major and other officers at the command post set up at a motel near the site of the disappearance. The major assigned a detective, Joe, to work with her. Her first request was to visit the place where the men had been working.

"We got to the site, and I walked around, but I got nothing. Absolutely nothing. As we drove back up the dirt road, I thought to myself, 'Some help I am going to be.' Then, all of a sudden I got this image of a guy, and then another man," Mary was later to relate. "I turned to Joe and said, 'Do you know someone that looks kinda like a gypsy, you know, dark skin, really black, shaggy hair, and an unkempt appearance? And another guy that is just the opposite—clean-shaven, short hair, and a very neat dresser?' "

Joe slammed on the brakes and turned to her. "How the heck did you know that? You just described our two prime suspects." Although it had not been mentioned in the press, from the start the police had one chief suspect and another they thought was an accomplice. The principal suspect lived near the site of the disappearance and was known to have argued with the missing husband about the fence. Both suspects were former law officers themselves, but had lost their jobs. They were well acquainted with police methods. Unfortunately the police had no evidence that a crime had been committed and no clue where the men had gone.

Over the next several days Mary and Joe visited the sites that the police thought likely candidates for hidden bodies, all of which they had investigated previously. During this time Mary came up with other "impressions" of information that the police already had but had not yet made public. The sites themselves, however, yielded no clues, psychic or otherwise.

One evening Mary suddenly had an impression of a clearing in a woods. There was a trail leading toward it. Across the center was

---

*This is a pseudonym. Our colleague generally shuns press publicity and, in view of the circumstances of this case, preferred to remain anonymous.

a fallen log; off to one side was a weather-beaten wooden crate. With a strong sense that this was where the bodies were buried—she "knew" the men were dead, and this was the general opinion of the police—Mary immediately made a sketch, placing an X to mark the graves. The graves were shallow, with forest debris heaped on top. (Later Mary felt that the men were wrapped in something green—a tarp or plastic bag—and were buried head to toe in a single grave. She also thought they had been murdered at the burial site.)

The next day Mary announced to Joe that they had to find the clearing in her sketch. Off they drove, with Mary issuing directions as they went. "I had no idea where we were headed. I just kept telling Joe to go left here, go right there—purely on intuition," Mary said. Eventually they came to a county road in a part of Durham County where she had never been before. The road ended in a T-intersection. Mary hesitated, then directed, "Turn left." As Joe turned and proceeded up the road, Mary said, "I think there is a dirt road up here on the left. Turn into it." Sure enough, there was, and it led into a large wooded tract of land. "This is it," Mary announced, "I'm sure the spot is around here somewhere."

All that day they wandered through the woods, but they found nothing that looked like her clearing. They returned the next day and the next. In fact on and off for the rest of the summer and into the fall, Mary and Joe searched those woods, as well as several other sites that officers suggested might fit the description, but her clearing could not be found.

Mary braved snakes, bugs, and North Carolina's notorious ticks for weeks on end searching for her clearing. "My family was about to throw me out," Mary recounted. "I was never home. Even when I was home, my mind was on this case. I would do things like jump out of bed in the middle of the night to make notes or review stuff that we had already done."

After a few months the command center was closed and most of the officers were taken off the case. Mary stayed with it, though. For the next three years she checked in with the police and occasionally went out with detectives searching more woods. Yet always she kept coming back to that same area where she first thought she was close to the site. "I feel I'm so close, but I just can't get it," Mary often lamented to me on the telephone. "But I know some terrific places to hide bodies if you ever need one."

The police continued to watch the suspects over the years. By now the prime suspect was in jail for armed robbery. Investigators continued to pressure the second suspect. Eventually he cracked and revealed the details of the slaying. Early on the day of the crime he and his friend had dug shallow graves. They were waiting as the victims returned from lunch. His friend shot the older man first, and then the boy. The older man was very bloody, so they put a large plastic garbage bag over him and drove both bodies to the grave site. They buried them and spread pine straw, leaves, and branches to cover the fresh digging.*

Almost exactly three years after the disappearance, the second suspect led the police to the bodies. He took them to the same T-intersection on the county road that Mary and Joe had come to, but he told the police to turn *right*. About a mile down the road they turned right onto a dirt road. From there a trail led to a clearing. The bodies were found buried head to toe in a single shallow grave in the center of the clearing.

Several days later police took Mary to the grave. It was just three and a half miles down the road from where she and Joe had spent weeks searching in vain. As she circled the clearing, Mary noticed something the police had not. About fifteen feet from the grave were the decaying remains of an old wooden crate. This was the clearing she had been searching for.

"If I had just turned right instead of left, we would have found the bodies three years ago," Mary later explained to a fresh group of summer students, three years after the picnic that started her adventure. "On a map the grave site is almost exactly a mirror image of where we were."[2]

Close, but not close enough to save the police three years of investigations. Was Mary a psychic detective, or was it just guesswork? Obviously it is not possible to say for sure. Perhaps the information that Mary reported to the police—which surprised them greatly—was something she had picked up unconsciously in overheard conversations or from documents in the command center. Perhaps the similarity between her sketch and her description of the graves was just coincidence or guesswork. Yet, of all the locations to which the killers could have driven in a couple of hours, is it

*Mary's feeling that the men were killed at the grave site was incorrect.

mere coincidence that Mary focused her search within just a few miles of the actual site?

Mary's adventure is not unusual in many respects. Psychics *are* assisting law enforcement agencies in surprising numbers. When asked officially about the use of psychics, most law enforcement agencies routinely deny having anything to do with them. Sometimes they may admit to having had psychics volunteer information, but deny that it was of any use. If you talk to the officers on the beat, however, a different picture emerges, as private investigators Whitney Hibbard and Raymond Worring found out while researching their book *Psychic Criminology.** They visited dozens of law enforcement agencies in the western United States and Canada and found that "the vast majority have informally experimented with the use of psychics as an adjunct to traditional investigative procedures." Often this arose when a local psychic volunteered information or, as in Mary's case, through a request by relatives of the victim. Even more surprising was that Hibbard and Worring met quite a few officers who routinely turn to psychics for assistance when traditional methods fail, or even just to narrow the focus of an investigation.

My own experience confirms this. Our institute gets several phone calls a year from law officers. Typically the call opens with the brisk identification of the caller and the jurisdiction, followed by some hemming and hawing before the caller gets to the point. Often the call is about a specific case and is made at the request of relatives. Increasingly common, however, are calls from officers who have heard about cases that were helped by psychics and are simply seeking more information should the need ever arise in their department.

Regrettably the information that parapsychologists can offer is scanty. It has long been a dream of several of my colleagues to obtain funding for a large-scale evaluation of the effectiveness of psychics in law enforcement, but this has not yet transpired. The closest approximation to this is a project directed by Marcello

---

Psychic Criminology: An Operations Manual for Using Psychics in Criminal Investigations (Springfield, Ill.: Charles C. Thomas, 1982). Although the authors are rather uncritical of much anecdotal and experimental evidence for psi ability, they offer a practical and sensitive guide to dealing with psychics in criminal cases. The publisher is a leading publisher of forensic texts.

Truzzi,* a sociologist at Eastern Michigan University in Ypsilanti. Truzzi's Center for Scientific Anomalies Research (CSAR) specializes in collecting criminal and missing-person cases involving psychics (both successful and unsuccessful). Recently he has summarized the findings of this ongoing project in a book *The Blue Sense: Psychic Detectives and Crime.***

Truzzi is quick to note that the standards by which one must evaluate instances of psychic assistance in these cases are *not* the same as those of a scientist. The chief concern when a scientist evaluates data is to avoid committing what is called a Type I error, that is, concluding that something is happening when really nothing is happening. The social scientist's use of statistics largely revolves around avoiding Type I errors, as evidenced by the expression often encountered in this book "the odds against chance for this result. . . ."

When lives or justice are at stake, however, the chief concern is to leave no stone unturned, no lead uninvestigated. In police investigations it is the scientists' Type II error—concluding that nothing is happening when in fact something is—that could be disastrous. If there is any chance that a psychic's information might be accurate, can the police afford to ignore it?

For the police, of course, following a psychic's leads accrues the same costs in time and manpower entailed in following up any tip, so whether or not to use a psychic's information boils down to the same cost-benefit analysis that law officers make all the time. The reputation of the psychic, the officers' experience with this or other psychics, how well the information corroborates other facts of the case, as well as the hidden costs (such as potential embarrassment to the department), will all be weighed. In Mary's case her early statements convinced the officers that her information might be useful, and by then they had no other leads. Mary's shunning media attention helped too. Very commonly the police will not bring in a psychic until they have exhausted all other conventional methods and are willing to adopt a "Well, what can we lose?" attitude.

---

*This is the same person who cofounded the organization of skeptics, CSICOP (see page 81).

**Arthur Lyons and Marcello Truzzi, *The Blue Sense: Psychic Detectives and Crime* (New York: Mysterious Press, 1991).

Although it is doubtful that a definitive study of psychic assistance in law enforcement is likely to be done soon, projects such as Truzzi's are helping to assemble a reasonable picture of the data and issues involved. Predictably the picture is complex, with no simple "Yes, they work" or "No, they're a waste of time" judgments on the horizon.

There is already a collection of cases in which a psychic *has* definitely helped investigations. Psychics have led police to bodies or have described locations so accurately that police could find them. Psychics have saved precious time in locating lost children and uncovered vital clues in criminal investigations. In a few cases psychics were able to describe a suspect or lead police to him, whereupon traditional methods completed the investigation. For many of these cases sworn law officers have stated that the case *would not have been solved without the psychic's help*.

A tragic 1987 case provides a good example of this level of psychic assistance. On Tuesday, June 9, 1987, Andre Daigle was leaving a New Orleans poolroom and bar with a buddy when a woman he had never seen asked for a lift home. A generous person, Andre agreed, and said good night to his buddy, who had his own car. That was the last time Andre was seen alive.

He was reported missing the next morning, but his large, close-knit family was not content to wait for the police to begin a search. Brothers and sisters fanned out all over the city, systematically checking every street and ally. By Saturday there was still no sign of the missing man or his truck. One sister, who lived in southern California, paid a visit to psychic Rosemarie Kerr. Kerr immediately said she felt pain all around her head and then said Andre would be found near water with a span bridge and railroad tracks nearby. The number 7 was important, she added. Andre's sister produced a map of Louisiana, and almost immediately Kerr put her finger on Slidell, a small town some thirty miles northeast of New Orleans, across Lake Pontchartrain. If they wanted to find Andre, they had to go there quickly. Kerr emphasized the urgency, "Do it quick!"

The sister went home and immediately called her family in New Orleans. By 11:30 that evening the Daigle family had piled into two cars and were headed to Slidell. As the brother, another sister, and Andre's buddy in one car approached Slidell, they were shocked to see Andre's truck pass them on the highway—but Andre was not in it! They followed the truck, which soon pulled off the road, the occupants aware that they were being followed. The Daigles chased the truck with the aid of a police car that happened on the scene. A few minutes later the truck was stopped, and Charles Gervais and Michael Phillips were arrested on suspicion of grand theft-auto.

While in custody, Gervais confessed to the brutal murder of Andre Daigle. The woman had lured Daigle to an apartment, where the two men had bludgeoned him to death by blows to the head "just to see if they had what it took to be criminals." Gervais led police to the body. Andre Daigle was found next to a body of water alongside a span bridge for Interstate 12, some twenty miles west of Slidell. Just to the east was a parallel railroad bridge. Interstate Exit 7 led to this area. Rosemarie Kerr had been surprisingly accurate.[3]

Not all cases are as dramatic as the Daigle case. In a large number of cases the psychic supplied information that helped, or corroborated known information, but did not of itself result in solving the case. Often this occurs because the psychic's information was incomplete or the police did not follow it up, so the accuracy of the psychic's information became apparent only after the case was solved. Often in these cases the police or family members will report that the psychic could not have known the information normally, yet in the end the information made little difference.

Mary's case might fall into this category. Her heroic efforts did not shorten the investigation at all, yet the police who worked with her were sufficiently impressed with what she could offer that they are willing to work with her again should the need arise.

Hibbard and Worring relate a case of their own in which they inadvertently put a twist on a psychic's information that rendered it useless even though it was very accurate. They had asked a psychic to give a reading on a missing girl. The psychic said that the girl would be found in an area where there were two Quonset huts; there was something to do with garbage and a parking area nearby, she added. A log house was within sight of the body, she noted, and there was a large red tank and a large pipe or pipes that might be part of a pumping station. The psychic gave other specific details and went on to say that the body would be found around the middle of the following month. The private investigators relayed this information to the sheriff's office by phone, commenting that it sounded like the psychic was referring to a highway rest area or an oil field pumping station. The sheriff organized search parties and searched every oil field and rest area for miles around, to no avail. In the middle of the following month some children found the girl's scarf, which led to the discovery of her body in a ravine below the city sewage pump house. Nearby was a large red gasoline tank for filling city vehicles, and garbage trucks were parked there. Three Quonset huts were in the vicinity, and the whole site was overlooked by an undersheriff's log cabin on a distant hill. All the other details checked out too. The sheriff's office was convinced that they would have recognized the place immediately had they seen the original notes rather than receiving only a verbal report with the added interpretation.[4]

Finally there is the most common way in which psychics interact with the police: They are no help at all. Even if we ignore the numerous times self-styled psychics offer unsolicited and unhelpful information to the police, we find that often even psychics with impressive track records simply miss the mark on cases. Sometimes they simply "get nothing" on a case, but more often than not they are likely to come up with information that proves to have no relation to the case. At worst this can result in costly mistakes, as in a 1960 case cited by Hibbard and Worring in which the New York Police Department bulldozed a four-foot-deep ditch for an entire square mile on information from a psychic. They were looking for a missing judge, but he did not turn up in the excavation.

Perhaps the best-known recent case in which psychics were unable to help was that of the Atlanta child murders. For over a year, ending in June 1981, a serial killer stalked Atlanta, Georgia, killing young, usually black children—twenty-seven in all. For many parents the agony was prolonged, since the children were often missing for months before being identified among the dead. As the hunt for the killer dragged on, media attention intensified. Few Americans were unaware of the city's agony as one name after another was added to the list of missing children. In just the last six months of the manhunt no fewer than 146 persons who could be considered psychics volunteered information. Other psychics had visited the city earlier in the case. Among them was Dorothy Allison, a New Jersey psychic with a remarkable track record. Yet none of the psychics was able to offer any significant assistance to the police. In the end it was old-fashioned police work that tracked down Wayne B. Williams and resulted in his conviction.[5]

Psychic ability as an aid to law enforcement remains something of a hit-or-miss proposition. There is much to suggest that the potential exists for a truly productive alliance, but this will require psychics to become more adept at recognizing the really important information. At the same time police departments will have to develop ways of working effectively with psychics, adapting to their sometimes quirky and idiosyncratic ways. Some psychics, such as Dorothy Allison, or Greta Alexander of Delevan, Illinois, have acquired considerable experience (and impressive reputations) in working with law officers around the country.

Although the better-known psychics often charge fees for private clients, they will typically work for expenses alone when contacted by law enforcement agencies. The majority of psychics who help police do so simply out of compassion for the victim or relatives, or out of a sense of civic duty. Most prefer to keep their names out of the press for fear of retribution by the criminals caught with their assistance. With so little to be gained by this activity it is not surprising that there is scant evidence of systematic fraud in these cases.

Unfortunately fraud is not entirely absent, however. Hibbard and Worring offer commonsense advice against getting involved with psychics who are too concerned with their reputations or too eager to get money for their efforts. A recent example is that of the Dutch psychic Gerard Croiset. In the fifties and sixties Croiset was quite famous for his claimed successes in locating missing persons and solving crimes, but most of the cases were reported by or through his promotor, the Dutch psychical researcher W.H.C. Tenhaeff. When Piet Hein Hoebens, an investigative reporter for the Dutch paper *De Telegraff*, tracked down the principals in several of the cases, he found the facts to be rather different from the way Tenhaeff had presented them. In fact Hoebens turned up enough evidence to charge that Tenhaeff systematically misrepresented Croiset's successes in order to promote his own position as a leading parapsychologist. Although Croiset's reputation is not based solely on Tenhaeff's reportage of events, it appears that Croiset was willing to go along with Tenhaeff's misrepresentations for his own career purposes.[6]

When psychics do provide useful information to the police, is it really psychic? Again, it is impossible to say. In many of the cases it seems reasonable to say that it is unlikely the psychic could have obtained the information normally, but in the uncontrolled and often hectic circumstances surrounding police investigations, who can be sure? The fact is that the police and the relatives do not really care. If it works, use it.

In at least one recent case the question of whether or not the information was obtained psychically was of more than academic interest. While at work on December 17, 1980, Etta Louise Smith, a young mother of three, heard a news report about the house-to-house search for a missing nurse. As she listened, she "knew" the nurse was not in a house. She had an image of a canyon area where she thought the nurse might be. At first she was afraid to go to the authorities with nothing more than her impressions, but as she drove home that day, her sense of duty prevailed and she went to a police station. She described her vision to a detective and even located an area on the search map where she thought the body was to be found. That area had not been searched yet, but the detective said they would check it out.

When she got home, she described her experience to her children. The vision kept bothering her, so she and her children decided to drive out to the nearby canyon to see for themselves. As they drove along, one of the children spotted something. They got out to investigate. As they got close to the object, Smith suddenly noticed white shoes—nurses' shoes. They all ran back to the car and drove to the nearest phone booth to call the police. After leading police to the site, Smith and her children returned home.

Unfortunately that was not the end of Smith's involvement in the case. Later that evening she was taken to the police station and questioned for ten hours, then arrested and charged with the murder. Smith was held in jail for nearly four days, until a man confessed to the murder and implicated two other men. The men had no connection with Smith.

Six years later Smith sued for wrongful arrest. Although the city attorney argued that the police acted reasonably when confronted with a tale of a psychic vision, the judge thought otherwise and ruled in her favor. In March 1987 she was awarded $26,184 in damages. The police continue to maintain that she had learned of the body through neighborhood gossip or other natural means.[7]

If psychics are using ESP when they assist in these cases, it is not surprising to see that it works very much like the spontaneous cases of noncriminal ESP that we encounter—sporadic, sometimes frustratingly vague, other times shockingly accurate. Undoubtedly we are some way from being able to use this sort of ESP information reliably, but it is no longer an issue that can be dismissed out of hand. Equally certain is that more than just your local police are interested in that question.

Of Spies and Psychics

"Cue ball. Four ball. Eight ball. Rackup. Side pocket."

"Are we going to get laughed at, or what?" thought Hal Puthoff as he read the pool-game terms in the letter in his hands. The Monday-morning mail had brought a fat envelope from a Mr. Patrick H. Price, and at the moment Puthoff was beginning to question the wisdom of an impulsive decision he had made late on the previous Friday afternoon.

Pat Price was eventually to become one of the top subjects in a series of experiments conducted at Stanford Research Institute (SRI), in Menlo Park, but as Puthoff read the letter, Price was very much an unknown quantity. Puthoff had met him briefly several years earlier, and on Friday had had a long telephone conversation with the former Burbank, California, police commissioner. Throughout his police career, Price felt he had unusually good intuition or luck in tracking down suspects. Once he had such a clear picture of a certain event (which proved to be correct) that he began to wonder if he had some psychic gift. He explained all this to Puthoff by way of volunteering to participate in the SRI experiments.

"On an impulse," as he was later to describe it, Puthoff gave Price a set of map coordinates for the target in a very special remote-viewing experiment that was under way. The coordinates described an area roughly 135 miles southwest of Washington, D.C. A little bit of geographical research could have yielded a pretty good description of the general locale. What Price gave Puthoff, however, .

was far more than the researcher expected—a five-page running commentary of a tour that began 1,500 feet above the site and went through a complex of buildings and underground storage areas. The letter described communication and computer equipment manned by Army Signal Corps personnel and even the names on desks in the buildings. The pool terms came from the labels on file folders in a locked file cabinet in one of the rooms.

Puthoff sent the detailed description to what the SRI team termed their "East Coast challenger," but not without some trepidation. This was no ordinary remote-viewing experiment. It was a high-stakes challenge, and the outcome could determine the future of SRI parapsychology research. The project was called SCANATE for "SCANning by coordinATE," and their challenger was a CIA case officer.* The targets were prepared by CIA headquarters personnel, who selected them randomly from potential targets around the world (including sites in the Soviet Union and China that could only be verified later by satellite surveillance). The coordinates were passed to the National Security Agency, which encrypted them and transmitted them to their people assigned to monitor projects at SRI. No one outside CIA headquarters, not even the "challenger" himself, knew what the targets were.

Much to Puthoff's surprise, not only did the CIA not laugh at Price's report, they confirmed that it was essentially correct.**

---

*These are not the sort of details that come out at parapsychology conferences or in reports, and even among impecunious parapsychologists it is still considered bad form to toss off questions like "Gee, Hal, where is all that research money coming from?" The details of this government connection with parapsychological research were brought out by investigative journalists. John Wilhelm of the *Washington Post* first broke the story in an article entitled "Psychic Spying" in the Sunday magazine (August 7, 1977). Ron McRae expanded the topic in his book *Mind Wars* (New York: St. Martin's, 1984). McRae interviewed the "East Coast challenger" to confirm SCANATE details.

**This story is not without its ambiguities. McRae reports that the CIA officer confirmed that the pool terms were secret codes and that the description was accurate. Wilhelm, however, reported that he had seen the SCANATE report and visited the site described by the coordinates that Price had been given. What he found was a sparse hillside with sheep grazing. The place was called Bullpasture Mountain, and there was no military installation anywhere nearby. When Wilhelm confronted James Foote, the Navy project manager for SCANATE, with this in-

They were also sure that there was no way that Price could have obtained his information by normal means. Price had made the team.

Project SCANATE ran from 1973 to 1975. Many of the gifted subjects who participated in the better-known Bay Area series of experiments were at the same time remote viewing for the CIA. Apparently hundreds of trials were done with targets as diverse as the location of Soviet submarines or meetings inside CIA headquarters. Ingo Swann's descriptions of Kergeulen Island (see page 117) and of an apparent missile site were part of this project.

How successful was SCANATE? The CIA was satisfied with the results. When they contracted an independent intelligence expert to evaluate the project, he concluded that SCANATE demonstrated ESP sufficiently well to justify considering practical applications. He cautioned, however, that ESP was not sufficiently reliable to replace traditional methods of intelligence gathering, although it could supplement and guide them. More than this is difficult to say, since the official report on the project remains under a top-secret classification.[8]

As we noted in chapter 5, parapsychologists are continuing to do remote-viewing experiments, but these are mostly in the nature of pure science, devoid of any immediate utility. Yet, almost by definition, remote viewing implies practical applications just as soon as the method is sufficiently reliable. Perhaps the parties who are interested in practical applications of remote viewing are simply waiting for parapsychologists to refine the technique, or maybe they have already determined that it is useful but too important to leave in the hands of scientists outside of their agencies.

After SCANATE, remote viewing for both the Navy and the CIA continued for some years at SRI, until the researchers left for other positions.* Parapsychology continues at SRI under the supervision

---

formation, Foote thought something must be wrong. After consulting with his contacts "across the river," however, Foote confirmed that from what he had seen, the (presumably CIA) investigators were satisfied that it had been a valid test. McRae suggests that Price's report might describe an area at the NSA's Fort Meade, Maryland, headquarters.

*Russell Targ left first to become a senior staff scientist at Lockheed Palo Alto Research Laboratories. Later Hal Puthoff took a post at the Institute for Advanced Studies, Austin (Texas).

of physicist Edwin May, and its scope has broadened beyond remote viewing to include "electronic perturbation techniques" (PK to the rest of us) and intuitive decision making (precognition). Its funding continues to come from unspecified government sources, at times as much as a couple of million dollars a year. Like many controversial topics, however, parapsychology is not always in favor in Washington.

Parapsychology in the Military

"Perhaps our strongest conclusions are in the area of parapsychology," continued the speaker, reading the prepared statement. The room was quiet as the speaker paused for a slight dramatic effect and then went on. "The committee finds no scientific justification from research conducted over a period of one hundred thirty years for the existence of parapsychological phenomena."[9]

The speaker, John A. Swets, was addressing a roomful of journalists attending a December 1987 press conference announcing the findings of a committee charged by the National Research Council (NRC) to review human-performance technologies—certain techniques that seem to enhance human abilities beyond normal levels—in which the Army was interested. Swets had chaired that committee, and the report that he was announcing, *Enhancing Human Performance: Issues, Theories and Techniques,** was the fruit of this two-year, nearly half-million-dollar project.

The project had its start about four years earlier when the Army Science Board's panel on Emerging Human Technologies recommended to the Secretary of the Army that the service look into enhancing human performance with such techniques as neurolinguistic programming, biofeedback, sleep learning, and other nonconventional learning techniques, guided imagery, meditation, and parapsychology. The U.S. Army Research Institute for the Behavioral and Social Sciences (ARI) was given the job, which they elected to subcontract to the NRC, an arm of the National Academy of Sciences charged with advising the federal government on matters of

*National Academy Press, 2101 Constitution Avenue, N.W., Washington, D.C. 20418.

science. This move was entirely appropriate; if the Army did want to employ some of these technologies, it would help to have NRC backing should questions arise.

Although the Army (and ultimately the taxpayer) had a real need for an impartial evaluation of these behavioral technologies, from the start it did not look like they were going to get it. ARI normally appoints an unbiased observer to monitor outside research contracts—the Contracting Officers Technical Representative. To supervise the NRC contract, ARI appointed Dr. George Lawrence, a civilian Army psychologist and former deputy director of human resources at the Pentagon's Advanced Research and Projects Agency (ARPA). Lawrence already had a record of being firmly opposed to some of the technologies under study. Among other things, in 1972 he and University of Oregon psychologist Ray Hyman were instrumental in getting one of SRI's ARPA-funded parapsychological projects canceled.[10]

When the NRC began to form the subcommittees to look into the different areas, several parapsychologists—myself among them—contacted the NRC to offer assistance in selecting experts for the parapsychology subcommittee. The NRC declined any assistance from parapsychologists and instead appointed Hyman to head the parapsychology subcommittee. No one with parapsychology research experience sat on the committee. In addition to his earlier association with Lawrence, Hyman is a founding member of the Committee for Scientific Investigation of Claims of the Paranormal (CSICOP), the advocacy group widely known for its crusade against parapsychology.

The NRC committee commissioned several reports from outside experts. For parapsychology, no recognized expert was consulted, but instead they commissioned psychologist James Alcock of York University to prepare a report. Alcock is also a charter member of CSICOP and is widely known for his books and articles attacking parapsychological research.

Psychologist Robert Rosenthal of Harvard University was commissioned to prepare an evaluation of all the areas of interest to the NRC committee. Rosenthal is widely regarded as one of the world's experts in evaluating controversial research claims in the social sciences and has spent much of his career developing techniques to provide objective assessments of conflicting experimental data. Neither Rosenthal nor his coauthor, Monica Harris, had taken any public position on parapsychology and were probably among the most objective of any participants in the NRC study.

The report prepared by Harris and Rosenthal determined that the "research quality" of the parapsychology research was the best of all the areas under scrutiny. The ganzfeld research (see page 99) was given an overall quality rating of 19 (out of a possible 25), while ratings for the nonparapsychological areas ranged from 3 to 13. Incredibly, in a move thought by many to border on scientific dishonesty, committee chairman Swets asked Rosenthal to withdraw the parapsychology section of his report. Rosenthal refused. In the final document the Harris and Rosenthal report is cited only in the several sections dealing with nonparapsychological topics; there is no mention of it in the parapsychology section.*

Did the Army get what it paid for—an objective and unbiased assessment? Certainly not where parapsychology was concerned. The Parapsychological Association (PA), of which I was president at the time, responded immediately by creating a committee to reply to the NRC report. Authored by John Palmer, Charles Honorton, and Jessica Utts, the PA's reply concluded:

> We have documented numerous instances where, in lieu of plausible alternatives, the Committee's attempts to portray parapsychology as "bad science" have been based upon erroneous or incomplete descriptions of the research in question, rhetorical enumeration of alleged "flaws" that by its own admission frequently have no demonstrable empirical consequences, selective reporting of evidence favorable to its case, and the selective omission of evidence not favorable to its case. Moreover, with respect to the Committee's central mission for the U.S. Army, we have shown that the Committee's prejudice against parapsychology has led it to ignore research, the further development of which could have important implications for our national security.
>
> The scientific and defense communities are entitled to a rigorous and unbiased assessment of this research area. A strong prima facie

---

*According to Col. John Alexander, U.S. Army, Ret., Swets even tried to have the report dropped from the supporting documentation normally available with the NRC report. Apparently he was not successful, since the Harris and Rosenthal report, *Interpersonal Expectancy Effects and Human Performance Research*, is available from the National Academy Press under their "documents on demand" program.

case has been made for the existence of psi anomalies, and meaningful relationships between such events and psychological variables have been reported in the literature. Further efforts and resources should be expended toward the identification of underlying mechanisms and the development of theoretical models, either conventional or "paranormal," that can provide adequate understanding.[11]

As battles between parapsychology and the powers of scientific orthodoxy go, the encounter with the NRC was one of the more interesting, if for no other reason than for what it revealed about the inner workings of one of our premier scientific institutions. Parapsychologists, however, have been fighting these battles for decades, and there was really nothing new in the NRC's sweeping rejection of the entire field. What *was* new was the context: parapsychology as a "technology" for possible application in the military. In the end, *did* the NRC committee tell the Army effectively to "forget about parapsychology?" Surprisingly, given their general dismissal of the past 130 years, they did not. Their recommendation was that the Army should *monitor* the work being done in the Soviet Union and the best of the work in the United States. Included in the latter category is the work of the PEAR lab and SRI, Honorton's ganzfeld work, and Schmidt's RNG work. Further, the committee recommended that the monitoring include future cooperative research between parapsychologists and skeptics, paying particular attention to the practical application of any effects discovered.

The NRC report's mention of parapsychology in the Soviet Union was indeed curious. There is no evidence that the committee was even familiar with, let alone had studied, parapsychology research in the Soviet Union. Yet they were willing to put it on a par with the "best" U.S. research. The fear that the Soviet Union might beat us at something, which in the past has probably caused more military money to be spent on parapsychology than any other factor, dies hard, even in the era of glasnost.

Over the decades several branches of the military have looked into parapsychology, many of these investigations inspired by the fear of being left behind by other countries. In the seventies alone, several assessments of Soviet and East European psi research were commissioned, and while none was conclusive, they all contained the ominous warning that the communist governments were spending large amounts of money on military-oriented psi research.[12]

It is difficult to guess how much U.S. military psi research has been carried out in secret. It does not take any fancy technology or even special expertise to conduct basic parapsychological research, so it is entirely possible that military psi research programs could go on completely unnoticed by others working in the field. Certainly even before the SRI work began, rumors abounded about secret experiments in submarine detection, psychics on government payrolls, and the like. Judging from such evidence as the NRC report, as well as material available through the Freedom of Information Act, however, it seems safe to say that the military has not made any secret breakthroughs in this area. C. B. Scott Jones, a retired naval commander and former intelligence officer now serving as a special adviser to Sen. Claiborne Pell on human-potential research, summarized his impression as follows: "My personal speculation is that most of the classified government activity has been a series of attempts to apply what is understood from the open research already accomplished. I suspect that a chart of these application attempts would show sharp peaks and valleys reflecting the coming and going of individuals in various departments and agencies who were able to try an application attempt based on strong personal interest in the field and whatever opportunity their particular assignment provided."[13]

As far as more open military interest goes, the Army began funding some of Rhine's work at Duke University as early as 1952. The Air Force began its own ESP experiments in the early sixties using an early automated test device called VERITAC (see page 125). Throughout the seventies some of the SRI remote-viewing work was funded by the Navy, and it is widely believed that the military still funds at least part of the research there.

The military continues to keep track of parapsychological research, even while it may wish to keep its own hands out of it. The NRC report is but one example of this. Several years before that report was produced, ARI commissioned parapsychologist John Palmer to do a separate (and extensive) evaluation of parapsychology research. All of this of course is entirely appropriate for the military. Military authorities face a similar situation regarding the

use of psychic abilities that law enforcement officials face in dealing
with psychics, only with greater potential consequences. If psychic
ability *might* impinge on matters of national security, Type II errors—ignoring an effect that is real—could have devastating consequences. If there is a possibility that psi ability is real and can be applied,
then the government would be seriously negligent to ignore it.

Despite what one might think is a strong mandate to be involved
in psi research, the biggest deterrent to greater governmental involvement seems to be the threat of public ridicule or charges of
wasting money. Prior to the commissioning of the NRC study, there
had been revelations of Army involvement in several schemes that
some government officials may have identified with parapsychology,
but actually made orthodox parapsychology look conservative. Some
military supporters of psi research speculate that the NRC brief grew
out of a backlash to these revelations. It was an attempt to show
that the Army had a responsible and sober attitude toward such
matters.

Many of my colleagues, however, do not welcome military involvement in psi research, no matter how bad the nonmilitary funding situation gets. Besides being unwilling to subscribe to the
inevitable demands for secrecy, most of these researchers feel that
psi ability, should it be understood and perhaps harnessed, must be
reserved for helping and healing functions—not allied with weapons
of destruction.

Healing Psi

"Okay, Janet. Now, during this session I want you just to sit comfortably, watch the colored display, and listen to the sounds in
the earphones. As I explained, I shall be trying to calm you psychically, but you should not think about that. Just make a wish that
you will become calm at the appropriate times and that such effects
will occur effortlessly and automatically."

These were the instructions that William Braud was giving to the
young woman seated in the armchair. He answered a couple of her
questions and said he would explain anything else when the session
was over. While Janet commented nervously about the light display,

Braud double-checked the electrodes on her fingers and prepared to leave. "All set, then?" he asked as he stood by the door.

"I guess so," Janet replied, though she still felt nervous about what she was expected to do. When she'd volunteered for the experiment, she feared that she might not get her instructions right and make a mess of the experiment. Now that her instructions were just to sit here and do nothing, she was wondering if she would be able to "do nothing" properly. Braud dimmed the light a little more, then he strode down the hall to the experimenter's room.

In the experimenter's room the polygraph was slowly tracing a line that represented Janet's skin-resistance response as measured by the electrodes on her fingers. Now Braud's job was to be the "influencer": He would try to calm Janet in the other room simply by mental effort alone. At the appointed time he would relax himself and imagine Janet relaxing, calming down. Sometimes he would watch the polygraph tracing, picturing the small and infrequent deflections of the pen that indicated the subject was in a calm state. That Janet seemed unusually nervous in the experiment was no accident. She was among a number of subjects chosen because they exhibited a greater need for calming than most people, because of either stress-related complaints, excessive anxiety, tension headaches, or any of several other symptoms.

Braud verified that the polygraph was operating correctly and then started the computer that digitized and recorded the data and timed the influence sessions. Then he retrieved from the desk an envelope left there by an assistant, tore it open, and took out a stack of cards. In a few moments he heard a tone, and Braud turned up the first card.

"Control," read the card. That was Braud's signal to do nothing. He tried to think of something else, daydream, think about anything but the experiment. He glanced at the watch. Thirty seconds passed slowly, but then the period was over and he rested briefly. Another thirty seconds passed less self-consciously, then came the tone again. "Influence," said the card. Now Braud began to relax himself and simultaneously pictured Janet in her chair relaxing, calming herself. "Relax, Janet, relax," he repeated in his mind. He looked at the polygraph pen. It seemed to be moving a bit less, but rather than get distracted by that, he closed his eyes again to picture a relaxed Janet.

So it went for a total of twenty such periods. Janet was one of thirty-two subjects who participated in this study. Half, like Janet, were in the group who especially needed calming, and the other half were relaxed to start with and were in the low-need group.

What was going on in this experiment? The expression Braud prefers to describe this work is "distant mental influence," but it could also be called PK with human targets. From yet another perspective, it can be viewed as an experimental version of what is known as psychic healing, in which one person attempts to affect the physiology of another paranormally.

During the past decade Braud and his colleagues at the Mind Science Foundation in San Antonio, Texas, have conducted a total of thirteen experiments along the same basic lines as the one in which Janet found herself. There have been 323 sessions with 271 different subjects. Four experimenters have served as influencers, along with nearly sixty other volunteers (including a few practicing healers). Not all of the studies involved calming efforts. For some the influence was to be an activating one; other experiments mixed calming and arousing influence periods. Six of the experiments yielded independently significant results, and in all but one of the experiments the results were in the expected direction. In Janet's experiment the subjects who needed calming showed a very significant calming reaction to the experimenter's psychic influence, while those subjects without that need showed virtually no effect. A combined assessment of all thirteen experiments gives odds against chance of better than 43,000-to-one.[14]

In parallel with the distant-influence experiments on humans, Braud has also been conducting experiments to see if biochemical processes can be influenced outside of the body. A particularly successful design employs human red blood cells as the target system. Since the blood cells come from the subject who will serve as influencer, this design amounts to trying PK on one's own body (at a distance of course). The blood is drawn by a nurse and placed in test tubes containing a saline solution. This induces hemolysis, or slow destruction, of the blood cells. The subject's task is to try to slow down the rate of hemolysis, effectively retarding red-cell destruction. The rate of hemolysis is automatically monitored via a spectrophotometer connected to a computer, and the statistical evaluation compares the rates for the influence periods with those of the

interspersed control periods. As of a 1990 report Braud has completed sixty-four formal test sessions and, as with the human distant-
influence studies, the subjects are very successful. The rate of
hemolysis in the influence tubes is significantly retarded when compared with that of the controls, with odds against chance of nearly
200,000-to-one.[15]

Braud's impressive results represent a bridge between the atomic-
level PK effects being demonstrated on RNGs and the biochemical
processes of human physiology. His work also represents an even
more important bridge between psi demonstrations in the laboratory and the eventual use of psi to alleviate suffering.

Psychic healing has always been a tempting but troublesome area
for parapsychologists. Perhaps more than other areas of human endeavor in which psi might possibly be involved, psychic healing has
the greatest potential for good, yet it is also fraught with methodological difficulties and ethical conflicts that scare off most researchers.

To start with, there is great confusion about what is meant by
psychic healing. One hears of mental healing, spiritual or prayer
healing, shamanic healing, or similar terms, yet all of these carry
different connotations. The practice of unorthodox healing comes
in more forms than can be imagined. They range from the diagnoses
and prescriptions that the shamanic healer may make in consulta-
tion with dead ancestors to the "healing services" that Americans
can watch almost daily on television. Some healers require the patient to be present so that there can be contact or a "laying on of
hands," whereas other healers have no difficulty practicing without
ever seeing their patients.

Unorthodox (by Western standards) healing can be found in all
corners of the globe. In parts of Africa, Asia, and South America it
is often the only healing easily available. In many other places, such
as Brazil and parts of Africa, it is the *preferred* method for many
people even when Western-style medical care is available. Even in
some Western countries, for example the Netherlands, unorthodox
healers are legally operating in parallel, and often cooperatively,
with the orthodox medical establishment. Dutch researchers found
that where both orthodox and unorthodox treatments were available, people tended to make their choices based on results, not preconceptions. The practical-minded Dutch chose their treatments not

because of some prior belief system or religious conviction, but because the treatment seemed to work. Often Dutch patients turned to unorthodox treatments only when they were dissatisfied with orthodox treatments.[16]

Just because healing is unorthodox does not mean it is psychic. In fact most of what comes within the rubric of unorthodox healing probably has nothing to do with parapsychology. Medical research over the years has revealed that the body has amazing self-healing powers. Perhaps the best-known example of this is the placebo effect, wherein simply the belief that a pill (in this case an inert substance called a placebo) will work results in a measurable physiological improvement. In a similar way, belief in the effectiveness of a certain preacher could trigger such a self-healing process, as could simply the extra attention and encouraging words brought by a lay healer. At present a great deal of medical research is being devoted to understanding the body's self-healing powers and to harnessing them where possible. Visualization techniques (for example visualizing one's cancerous tumor growing smaller) have been shown to have dramatic effects for some individuals. Other techniques of coping with illness, such as psychotherapy, have been associated with improvements of physiological conditions. Some researchers argue that just getting patients to "take charge" of their own health can liberate amazing self-repair abilities.

All of this, however, is not what the parapsychologist is primarily concerned with. What the parapsychologist means by psychic healing is that some healing or amelioration of symptoms occurs in the *absence* of normal factors such as the placebo effect. Typically this requires that there not only is no contact between the healer and the patient, but that the patient does not even know that such a treatment is being attempted. The obvious implication is that the process that we call psychokinesis when applied to inanimate systems also underlies psychic healing.

If there is a psi component to unorthodox healing, I suspect that we will find a situation similar to what I suggested is the case for intuition and luck. The psi component will be merged discreetly with all other operative factors. This, in turn, means that trying to extricate the psi component from the rest experimentally will be a frustrating, if not futile, endeavor.

For the present the best approach for parapsychology seems to be what Braud is doing, developing experimental parallels to the healing process in which all of the normal factors can be excluded or controlled. This means using the traditional methods of parapsychology within creative, new experimental contexts. In fact Braud's work follows a long line of parapsychological research showing psychic-healing-type effects. Often these experiments are labeled "PK on living systems" or "bio-PK," but it is the desire to understand psychic healing that is usually at their root.

In the mid-sixties Bernard Grad of McGill University in Montreal worked with a healer, Oskar Estabany, in a series of experiments examining Estabany's effect on mice with experimentally induced medical problems. In one of the biggest experiments, three hundred female mice had a small oval portion of skin removed. Wounds were measured, and matched sets of three mice were randomly assigned to three conditions. In the first condition Estabany placed his hands around cages containing ten mice each and practiced his healing for fifteen minutes twice daily. The cage was inside a paper bag, and the treatment was done either by placing hands inside the bag (for half the cages) or by simply holding the bagged cage between his hands. In the second condition medical students performed the same actions as Estabany. In the third condition the cage containing the mice was simply placed on a table for the fifteen minutes. At the end of sixteen days the wounds were measured. Estabany's mice showed significantly smaller wounds than those of either of the other conditions. The wounds of the mice held by the medical students healed no differently from those of the mice that were not held at all.[17]

Grad and other experimenters have examined PK or healing effects on "sick" plants grown under adverse conditions. In a series of experiments reported in 1965, Grad's healer, Estabany, "treated" saline solutions by holding the bottles between his hands. In a fully blind experimental design, both treated and untreated saline solutions were used for the first watering of barley seeds. Subsequent measurement of seedling growth revealed that the seeds watered with the treated water grew significantly taller than those watered with the untreated saline. After successful pilot studies three of four confirmatory experiments demonstrated a significant growth advantage for the seeds watered with healer-treated saline. Grad's conclusion was that Estabany's treatment could reduce the adverse effects of the saline.[18]

In another line of research Graham and Anita Watkins, working at our institute, found that persons serving as healers could reduce the time it took a mouse to revive from anesthesia. Watching through a one-way glass, the healer was able to "wake up" one randomly chosen mouse of a matched, anesthetized pair faster than the control mouse.[19]

The past decade has seen a veritable explosion of healing research in China, where more than two hundred universities, medical centers, and independent laboratories are using twentieth-century science to help understand the ancient system of Chinese healing known as qigong. Actually qigong is a program of deep-breathing exercises that are meant to promote one's health and well-being. In Chinese philosophy *qi* is a type of fundamental vital energy, and qigong exercise helps the individual master the flow of this energy within the human body. Extended qigong practice eventually may enable a person to "externalize" his *qi* and direct it toward others for healing purposes. Persons with this ability are known as qigong masters and frequently serve as healers, either informally or in "traditional medicine" clinics. Recently some Western-style hospitals have opened traditional medicine departments in which qigong masters work alongside conventionally trained physicians.

Of particular interest to Western parapsychologists is research into *qigong waiqi*, or qigong external emission (QGEE), which in many cases resembles Western-style PK research on biological systems. For several years Lu Zuyin of Qinghua University's Department of Chemistry and Biological Science,* one of China's leading QGEE researchers, has been investigating the paranormal abilities of Yan Xin, a renowned qigong master and healer. Lu and his colleagues first reported their work in the March 1987 issue of *Acta Biophysica Sinica* and continue regular publications in the wider-circulation *Ziran Zazhi (Nature Journal)*, often with Yan, himself a doctor of traditional Chinese medicine, as senior author.[20]

Lu's research consists of a series of experiments examining the QGEE effects on different biological and chemical preparations. In

*In 1990, Lu moved his research to the Institute of High-Energy Physics in Beijing.

most of the experiments qigong master Yan exerts his efforts at a distance of seven to ten kilometers, though successful results have been reported with Yan as far away as two thousand kilometers. In a typical experiment researchers prepare the specimens and allow a sufficient waiting period for the preparation and the measuring equipment to stabilize. Researchers begin taking measurements, and at some point during this stage Yan is instructed to direct his *qi* toward the preparation. The treatment usually lasts only ten to fifteen minutes. Depending on the type of preparation, researchers may continue to take measurements for hours and even days after the treatment.

Using a U.S.-made Laser Raman Spectrometer, Lu's team observed dramatic shifts in the spectral characteristics of ordinary tap water. A huge peak in the spectrograph appeared at 1970 cm^{-1} wavelength immediately after treatment and gradually declined to normal over several hours. Physiological saline (0.9%) normally shows a characteristic peak at 246 cm^{-1}, but shortly after treatment this peak disappeared or was shifted to 237 cm^{-1}. Again this effect decayed over time. Yan's treatment of a 50% glucose solution produced an elimination of one normally occurring peak and the intensification of others. All the experiments have been repeated several times. The researchers interpret these findings as signs that the molecular structure of the solutions is being temporarily altered by QGEE.[21]

Using similar methods, Lu's team have reported that Yan's QGEE can produce certain chemical reactions under conditions in which they should not occur, as well as alter the ultraviolet-absorption characteristics of DNA and RNA preparations.

Western parapsychologists are understandably cautious about Lu's work, since no one outside of China has had the opportunity to confirm his findings. Nevertheless even though the Chinese researchers seem unaware of this fact, at least some of their findings are supported by earlier work of Western parapsychologists. Grad found that saline solutions similar to those used in his barley-seed experiments produced different infrared-absorption spectra depending on whether or not they had been "treated" by a healer. In 1983 Douglas Dean, working at Kings College, London, reported similar effects when samples of distilled water were held by two different healers. Samples held by another person who was not a healer showed no effects. Thus, far from being isolated findings, Lu's results actually take their place in a modest tradition of related findings.[22]

For the present all these reports are but tantalizing hints to suggest that it may be possible eventually to understand the operation of psychic healing at the physiological level. If human consciousness, through psi, can affect physical systems, then why not biophysical systems too? Braud's work certainly indicates that psi *can* be a component of unorthodox healing; whether or not it *is* a common component remains to be learned.

As research on unorthodox healing increases in this country and abroad, the possibility grows that parapsychologists may eventually find themselves working with medical researchers to help harness the healing powers of the mind. Learning the answers to parapsychological questions is not likely to be any easier in the medical field than it is elsewhere, and it may even be more complex. As with other areas of applied psi, parapsychologists will need to tread a narrow line between raising false expectations and doing what they can to help others who are in desperate need of help.

The Continuing Search for Practicality

"So, if the mood report indicated that the subject was a hitter, we took the binary responses as they were given. If the mood report indicated a misser, then we reversed the guesses, + became 0, 0 became +. Then we summed over all subjects, and this is what we got," said the speaker, pointing to the column of +s and 0s on the board.

The speaker was Dr. James Carpenter and he was presenting the results of a very unusual ESP experiment to fellow researchers at the Institute for Parapsychology. In his experiment Carpenter had been trying to see if coded messages could be communicated via ESP by individuals who did not even know that they were communicating a message. Before the experiment started, Carpenter had someone choose a word and encode it in the traditional Morse-code dots (*dit*) and dashes (*dah*). Then he had dozens of students from his classes at the University of North Carolina take a simple ESP test consisting of guessing several runs of twenty-four binary targets (0 or +). Unknown to the subjects, twelve of those targets encoded the "message" word, while the remaining targets were part of another aspect of the study. During the ESP testing, each subject also completed a mood adjective checklist to describe his or her state of mind at the time.

Carpenter's method is complex—and still evolving—but there are two important features at the heart of his procedure. The main feature is the *majority-vote* technique, in which the guesses are *summed* across subjects for a single, composite set of guesses. In other words, for this experiment the twelve message targets were the same for all subjects, so for each target the number of 0s and +s were tallied over all subjects, and the symbol with the highest count became the composite guess for that target. This permits weak but consistent correct guessing (if it is there) to be "distilled" into a strong representation of the target sequence. It is equivalent to averaging a noisy signal to cancel the noise and leave only the signal. It is not a new technique, and parapsychologists have used it successfully before, but Carpenter added a new twist. Among the UNC students, there were likely to be some who will consistently score below chance (called psi-missing). Their guesses would cancel those of the hitters, obviating the benefit of the majority vote. Their guesses *could* be used, however, if there was some way *independent of the message trials* to predict who was going to be a misser and then *reverse* their guesses on the message targets before combining them with the hitters' guesses. This is where the mood reports come in. Carpenter's earlier research had shown that subjects who checked certain adjectives to describe their mood during testing were more likely to produce hitting on their ESP results. Another cluster of adjectives seemed to predict missing, or below-chance scores. In this experiment, if the mood reports predicted more hits than chance, then the guesses for the message were used as they were written. If the mood reports predicted fewer hits than chance, then the run was considered a missing run, and the guesses at the message targets were *reversed*.

"The majority votes on the twelve targets were," Carpenter continued, tracing down the column, "0, +, +, 0, 0, 0, +, +, +, 0, +, 0, 0. Translating the first four into Morse code, we get ditdahdahdit, or 'P'. Next, a single dit for 'E', ditdah for 'A', dahditdahdit for 'C', and finally dit for 'E'. Ladies and gentlemen, the target word was 'PEACE'. The group's guesses decoded it with one hundred percent accuracy."[23]

Not all of Carpenter's majority-vote experiments since that time have been so successful, but they have achieved impressive results in terms of the percentage of correct guesses. There is more than a hint here of practical application. Eventually a method such as Carpenter's could be used to extract psychic information from persons who are not particularly psychically gifted. This work is in its infancy, and now Carpenter is examining personality and mood variables in the hope of identifying subjects and situations that might yield more stable scoring.

Carpenter did his research by hand, and it took a long time—too long for practical use. Computerization will speed up the process, and many people can work simultaneously with almost immediate analysis. Messages need not be long, either, perhaps only a single word or digit sequence that is an encryption key to decode a longer, conventionally transmitted message.

Carpenter's work is still very exploratory, and it will be a long time—if ever—before we can think about making practical use of it. Yet this work is representative of several applied psi projects that even parapsychologists regard as somewhat avant-garde. Stephen Schwartz of the Mobius Society in Los Angeles has been using a majority-vote technique involving converging remote-viewing information from experienced viewers to locate archaeological sites. Schwartz's group typically enlists several successful remote viewers— some veterans of the SRI research—who work more or less independently to provide information that is then collated to provide the best guess at potential sites to be searched. The psychics are told what the goal of the search is and are asked to use their psychic sense to help locate it. Working first with maps, the psychics identify areas that they feel may contain the goal. Schwartz's team collates the responses and then focuses on areas on which there is some consensus among the psychics. The researchers repeat the process with progressively more detailed maps, until they feel they have a manageable area to search. Eventually a few of the psychics will go into the field with Schwartz's team and continue their psychic assistance on site. Schwartz claims that this technique was successful in locating previously unknown sites in Alexandria, Egypt, and, in 1987, a sunken ship off the Bahamas.[24]

"Psychic archaeology" is not new, and Schwartz is but one of several researchers who, in the seventies, began using psychics to help locate sites or identify artifacts. It remains difficult to separate truly psychic information from inspired or informed guesswork, so evaluation is problematic. As in any avant-garde program, the work is controversial. Critics of Schwartz's work note that in an ancient city such as Alexandria, digging anywhere will probably turn up something. Also, the ship his team found on the Bahama Banks was an undistinguished American brig carrying molasses, not the Spanish treasure galleon that reportedly was their goal. Schwartz, for his part, points to unique features of the site and close correspondences with the allegedly psychic information that argue against simple chance as the explanation.[25] In the end, however, practical applications of psi are not going to be judged by academic scientists but by the marketplace. If the technique is cost-effective, or if the backers of such research are satisfied with the return, the research will continue—and perhaps all of science will be the better for it. If not, then the research will quickly fade away.

Psychic Riches

Perhaps the ultimate test for practical application of psi in capitalist countries is "Can it make money?" Though anecdotes abound in the business world and some psychics seem to be making comfortable livings as business consultants, there is very little published research that directly addresses this question. Perhaps the closest attempt in recent years to "make a bundle" with psi ability came from a unique team of researchers and investors.

In 1982 Keith Harary, Russell Targ, and Anthony White formed a partnership called Delphi Associates. Harary, a veteran of much parapsychological research as both subject and experimenter, and Targ, fresh from the successful SRI remote viewing trials, described Delphi Associates' purpose as "to apply psychic abilities to the modern market place."[26] Targ, for one, had long been convinced that the way to win acceptance for parapsychology would be to do something that the *Wall Street Journal* would publish, so applying psi to the marketplace seemed a logical first step.

The Delphi strategy was based on two observations that the SRI researchers had made during their remote-viewing work. The first was that remote viewers could successfully view locations that would not even be selected until some future time. In fact precognitive remote viewing seemed even more successful than real-time remote viewing. The second observation was that remote-viewing impressions tend to be pictorial and visual instead of analytical and abstract. Some years earlier, in a project with Stephen Schwartz of the Mobius Society, the SRI researchers had developed a technique that they called "associative remote viewing," in which easily visualized objects were individually associated or linked with more abstract concepts. Rather than asking the subject to obtain the abstract concept by ESP, the researchers asked the remote viewer to view the associated object.

Delphi Associates combined these two concepts to create an informal study of associative remote viewing into the future. Concrete objects (and locations in later work) would be associated with future events. The events? The price of silver in December 1982 as traded on the COMEX in New York. On Thursday Harary, the viewer, would try to describe the object which he would be shown the following Monday. That object would be determined by whether the price of silver went up or down. If Harary's description corresponded to the "up" object, then the team bought silver. On Monday they would show Harary the object that corresponded with the market's actual movement (whether or not he was correct).

With the backing of a person whom Targ describes as an "enthusiastic investor," Delphi Associates made nine weekly forecasts for the price of silver in December. All nine forecasts were correct, and Delphi Associates shared in the $120,000 profit. And, yes, the story did appear in the *Wall Street Journal*, October 22, 1984, under the headline "Did Psychic Powers Give Firm a Killing in the Silver Market?"

Did Delphi Associates go on to corner the market? Well, not exactly. The following year they started a second series of informal trials aimed at March silver but met with disappointing results that sent the team back to basic research before tackling the market again.

Hal Puthoff, then still at SRI, got into the act later that same year.

Puthoff, however, set up a series of associative remote-viewing trials to benefit a philanthropic cause. With seven viewers making thirty forecasts and the results combined by majority vote, Puthoff managed twenty-one correct forecasts. That netted his charity $25,000 in a relatively flat market.

Targ continues to experiment with the associative remote-viewing approach, now computerized and employing the majority-vote technique. His latest version yielded eight hits out of nine trials, but he did this experiment without any money at risk, just to be safe.[27]

The various tentative attempts to apply psychic ability to real-world problems that we have seen in this chapter show that Russ Targ's notion about doing things that the *Wall Street Journal* might notice is not entirely frivolous. Many parapsychologists share this same feeling that demonstrating practical, reliable applications for psychic abilities will make debates about the reality of psi take a back seat. Yet, research toward that goal faces an essential dilemma that is cast into sharp relief by projects like the silver futures venture. The risks are high—be they of reputation or of purse—but the potential rewards are enormous. For the time being, applied psi research will remain the province of only the most intrepid of scientists and boldest of speculators. The future will judge these persons as either fools or visionaries.

CHAPTER 11

Glimpsing the Future

"All telemetry channels are locked in, sir," snapped the young electronics engineer with his customary military precision. "Thank you, Jim," responded his lab chief, Dr. Jones, "Now please go get our subject."

Mary, a middle-aged "gifted" subject, was slightly apprehensive about this experiment. Sure, Mary had worked in parapsychology labs before; the testing did not bother her. It was something about Dr. Jones—the way his foreign accent seemed mismatched to his common name; the temporary nature of this parapsychology lab set up in the bedroom of a rental house near the California coast. Still, Jones and his team were very nice, and they were paying her handsomely for her time—something no other parapsychology lab had ever done.

"Sorry to keep you waiting, Mary," said Jones, "but I think we are ready to start now. Do you remember what to do?" Mary nodded and sat down in front of the green computer screen. Along the bottom were lots of what looked like little bar graphs jumping up and down, not unlike the indicator lights on late-model stereo systems. Her task was to get the bars on the far right side to move up higher than the rest. It was different from other PK tasks she had participated in, but not that different. Evidently her performance had been good, because Jones seemed very pleased with the work last week.

"Now, Mary, today I want you to wait until I tell you to start. We are testing, er, well, let's just call it 'time locking'," said Jones. Mary looked around as she waited. Jones's assistant, Jim, was on the phone with someone, just listening. Abruptly he nodded to Jones, who turned to Mary and said, "Okay, Mary, let's see your best effort now." Immediately Mary began the slow, rhythmic deep breathing that she felt helped her effort. Then she focused her eyes on the right part of the screen. "Up, up, little fellows, up." Gradually the half-dozen bars on the right began to make increasingly larger leaps upward. The previously flat profile started to resemble a slope. After about thirty seconds the little bars suddenly collapsed to a flat green line. Before Mary could ask Dr. Jones what happened, he said, "Oh dear, we seem to have a problem. I think we had better call it quits for now."

Jones ushered Mary to the living room. To Mary he appeared in remarkably good spirits for someone whose experiment had just gone awry. "You can see yourself out, then?" he asked. "Should I come back tomorrow?" Mary asked. "Ah, no. Not tomorrow. We'll call you, okay?" replied Jones.

Later that evening Mary was watching the news. The television showed a familiar picture of a missile streaking out over the ocean. "There was another failure in the test program of the new X-40 missile today," the announcer intoned. "About thirty seconds after launching, this missile went out of control and had to be destroyed by range officers." The missile on the screen veered sharply and then burst into an orange ball of flame. "Officials are investigating the cause of the failure, but a spokesperson said there appeared to be a fault in the command-telemetry system," continued the announcer. Mary just shook her head. "I wonder how many millions of dollars went up in smoke that time," she thought to herself.

STOP! Before you read any further, read this carefully: *The preceding scenario did not take place.* At least I am not aware that it or anything like it has taken place. "Dr. Jones's" experiment is purely fictional—for the present.

Could this be the future of parapsychology? It is entirely possible. As we have seen in the preceding chapters, there is a large body of data—hundreds of experiments from dozens of laboratories—showing that humans can influence certain probabilistic com-

ponents of electronic systems. The scientists who conduct this research feel that it demonstrates that human consciousness can shift
the probability of an event from its "natural" or purely random
probability to one that favors the intention or desires of the human
operator.

But, one might argue, parapsychologists' experiments use special
equipment *designed* to have a purely random element in it. This
fictional experiment suggests that Mary interfered with a sophisticated missile-guidance system, something that should not have such
random elements. What evidence is there that humans can influence
the functioning of ordinary electronic equipment?

At the moment we have very little evidence that humans can influence properly functioning computers.* Yet, there are a few factors that you might want to consider before you relegate "Dr.
Jones's" experiment to the world of pure fantasy.

Consider: I said "properly functioning" computer. What if something is not quite right? Suppose the power supply is failing and not
putting out the proper voltage? The memory chips will begin to produce errors—"forget bits," if you will—more or less randomly, and
instructions or data will become corrupted. Suppose a central process-
ing unit develops an intermittent flaw? The consequences of this in
your home computer are not serious: The program simply goes wacky
or fails to work at all. But our lives are being given over more and
more to microprocessor control. From our automobiles and household
appliances to the airplanes we travel in and the complex weapons we
create to defend ourselves, microprocessors, memory chips, and other
delicate electronic devices are being entrusted with an enormous number of small decisions that can directly affect our well-being. Many of
these devices have to function in fairly hostile environments that push
the devices past the manufacturer's specifications.** Could such cir-

---

*There are numerous accounts of equipment malfunctioning or otherwise going
"haywire" during parapsychologists' investigations of certain psychics or macro-
PK subjects. Likewise, reports of recent poltergeist cases (for example the
Rosenheim case, page 216) suggest that PK disruptions of various kinds of equipment are indeed possible. However, all of these instances seem completely sporadic
and not subject to the conscious intention that seems to guide the effects of the
micro-PK findings.

**Of course in circumstances where lives are at risk, such as in aircraft and in

cumstances—where electronic components are stressed beyond their normal tolerances—introduce just enough randomness that someone's PK ability might make a difference?

Consider: In the quest to make computer components smaller and faster, scientists are already exploring ways to build microcircuits based on quantum-mechanical effects—the same statistical properties that are exploited in the parapsychologist's RNG. While practical use of "nanoelectronics" (smaller than microelectronics) employing quantum transistors may still be years off, the large research effort in this area completely ignores parapsychology's evidence that human intention can alter the statistical properties of quantum-mechanical systems. It would be ironic if the computers of the future turned out to be as temperamental as their operators because their circuits were actually responding to the operators' moods.

Consider: There is an increasingly important need for true randomness in certain electronic engineering situations. Recently AT&T introduced an integrated circuit—the T7001—that is a true RNG on a chip. This is a commercial product designed for digital noise simulation and—notably—for data encryption. Might it be possible for human intention to interfere with the normal working of this commercial RNG the way parapsychology subjects interfere with experimental RNGs?

We already have a tentative answer to this question. No sooner was the AT&T chip on the market than Dean Radin, a scientist with the large communication technology company Contel, attempted to answer precisely that question. In a 1990 paper provocatively titled "Testing the Plausibility of Psi-Mediated Computer System Failures" Radin reported the results of two experiments in which he, as the subject, attempted to influence the output of the T7001 chip. Both of these experiments showed statistically significant deviations in the runs that Radin attempted to influence. These results, combined with other PK research, support the possibility that, in Radin's words, "*in principle*, some computer failures may be psi-mediated." Before you think you have the answer to your

---

military uses, a great deal of effort is expended to make computers fault tolerant. As the complexity of these systems grows, though, there is a corresponding increase in the opportunity for failure.

problems with computers, however, you should note that Radin feels that the "some" in his statement is probably in the range of tenths of a percent.[1]

Radin's work is continuing. Recently he has speculated about the possibility of creating "psibots," robots that can respond to the mental intentions of human operators. Such devices—say, to assist severely handicapped individuals—could be a combination of conventional robot technology (already well under way), physiological monitoring equipment (also well advanced), and banks of RNGs tuned to respond to human intention. These components would be linked by sophisticated computer software employing artificial-intelligence technology to integrate and interpret the inputs and control the robotics. Pure fantasy or possible future reality?[2]

Although devices such as Radin's psibot may not be the sort of thing we see in the near future, it *is* likely that one of the principal "growth" areas for psi research will be the interface between the human mind and emerging technology.

Judging from present work, it is likely that the interaction between psi and technology will proceed along two lines. One will follow the lead of the micro-PK research and investigate intentional psi effects on electronic equipment. This is the route that may lead to psibots and other "psi-responsive" technology that could have immense benefits for humankind. Whether or not it leads to experiments such as that of "Dr. Jones" along the way will probably depend more on the prevailing global political climate than anything inherent in psi research.

The second line of research will investigate unintended psi effects on technology. As electronic systems grow more complex and pervasive, the need to understand why components sometimes fail becomes increasingly urgent. Great efforts are being made to identify, anticipate, and prevent failures in computers and other control systems. Yet, for all these efforts, there inevitably remains a residue of mysterious failures, unexplained by our best understanding. Could psi have a role in these failures?

That may seem a silly and unnecessary question. We certainly do not need to invoke psi power every time something breaks down but we do not know why. Left unchecked, that attitude would quickly return us to a world of superstition well left behind. Nevertheless the question is not entirely frivolous. If individuals can influence physical systems by mind alone, and if this ability is subject to the unconscious desires, hopes, and fears that influence so much else of human behavior, what might occur when a human encounters a piece of equipment that has become unstable? As we have already noted, a proportion of modern technology might be operating at a suboptimum state—waiting to break down, if you will. Taking this speculation one step further, suppose the operator really hates working with that piece of equipment, or perhaps hates the job connected with it. For the present I think we need not fear that the photocopier service technician is going to start probing our inner feelings about his brand of machine, but it is something to think about.

The lab lore of high-tech research facilities around the world is rich with anecdotes about people who were walking technological Typhoid Marys. Physicist and writer George Gamow relates that the noted theoretical physicist Wolfgang Pauli was notorious in this respect: "Apparatus would fall, break, shatter or burn when he merely walked into the laboratory."[3] Modern labs, chock-full of computers and sensitive electronics, often have unwritten rules about some professor being forbidden to enter lest his or her very presence upset things. Silly superstitions? Perhaps, but widely shared by scientists, who should know better if there were not a grain of truth behind it.

The possibility of human-machine interactions on the psychic level has not escaped the notice of several parapsychological laboratories. The PEAR lab in Princeton University's School of Engineering has conducted pilot experiments to see if human consciousness could influence ordinary computer memory chips "stressed" by operation under suboptimal conditions. Before he was appointed Koestler Professor of Parapsychology at the University of Edinburgh, Robert Morris was in the Computer Science Department of Syracuse University, where he developed a strong interest in the role of psi in human-machine interactions. Morris has carried this interest with him to Scotland, a country that is experiencing a mild boom in microtechnology development.

Personally I have little doubt that this is going to be a major thrust of parapsychology in future years. I also feel that it will be among one of the first areas of psi research to drop out of the public view, not from sinister military motives but under the cover of corporate "proprietary information" and routine industrial research and development secrecy. At some point in the not-too-distant future (perhaps it has already happened) R&D executives in the multinationals—IBM, AT&T, NEC, Hitachi, and so forth—will decide that the evidence is too strong to ignore, because to ignore it might imperil corporate profits. Then psi research will really take off, but don't expect to read about it in a book like this, at least not until "the product" is out in the market.

A Uniquely Human Ability?

Earth's population had been stabilized, about the middle of the twenty-first century, at eighteen billion. The Fertility Board, a subsection of the United Nations, made and enforced the birth control laws. For more than half a thousand years those laws had remained the same: two children to a couple, subject to the judgment of the Fertility Board. . . .

And so each year the Fertility Board totalled up the year's deaths and emigrations, subtracted the year's births and immigrations, and put the resulting number of Birthrights into the New Year's Day lottery. . . .

For the past two centuries, between ten and thirteen percent of each human generation has been born by right of a winning lottery ticket. What determines who will survive and breed? On Earth, luck.

And Teela Brown is the daughter of six generations of winning gamblers. . . .[4]

In Larry Niven's 1970 science-fiction classic *Ringworld* Teela Brown is a naive young woman sought by an alien who is forming a crew to undertake an extremely hazardous space-exploration mission. Teela was needed on this mission, not for her skills in spaceflight, defense, or exploration—she had none of these—but for her *luck*, a quality that the alien race had determined only humans possessed.

Of course I am not going to tell you the plot. *Ringworld* is still a very good read, and like many science-fiction classics, it may just anticipate a certain amount of science fact. Is luck—a notion as old as history—science fiction threatening to become science fact?

In *Ringworld* the reality of luck is a given. It is a uniquely human ability, and a psychic one at that. In the novel luck is treated like other abilities, and selective breeding can enhance that ability in certain individuals. Although in this future world ESP is "well understood" as a particular type of brain function, luck remains mysterious—an unusual ability of some individuals to get life's "random" events to come out in their favor. It is almost as if they can "influence" the course of the universe to favor them.

In our late twentieth-century world, however, the notion of luck is most often considered nothing more than the operation of selec-. tive memory—remembering fortunate occurrences and forgetting the unfortunate or meaningless ones. Is it possible that that idea will have to be revised in some future age? If all we have to rely on is anecdotes and memory, it probably will not. Yet we do have a robust line of parapsychology research showing that some individuals *can* influence the probability of events—the micro-PK research. Is it possible, as I suggested in the preceding chapter, that what we colloquially call luck has the same basis as this probability-altering PK research?

Whether we call it luck, PK, ESP, or just generic psi ability, I believe the second main thrust of future psi research will be the examination of psi as an unusual but practical human ability. It is true that most of the history of parapsychology has implicitly treated psi as some kind of ability, but all too often this view has been coupled with a degree of mysticism. Psi, even as an ability, was a "gift" without much practical significance except in the rare instances where a psychic experience conveyed useful information.

I suspect the future will see an increasingly pragmatic approach to psi. Scientists will say, "Okay, we accept the reality of psi ability. Now, what is it for? How did humans acquire this ability?" Curiously parapsychologists themselves have only rarely asked these questions.

Several years ago I was president of the Parapsychological Association, an honor that carries with it the obligation to deliver the presidential address at our annual convention. For parapsychologists like myself, who spend most of our time doing experimental research, the presidential address affords an opportunity to indulge in the sort of wild speculation that one cannot get away with in research publications. I decided to speculate on the answers to those questions.[5]

I chose for the title of my speech "If You Want to Know How It

Works, First Find Out What It's For," a borrowed expression* that pretty much typified the direction implicit in my own research. For decades parapsychology had been conducting experiments that treated psi as if it were a human ability—like seeing, hearing, reasoning, and so forth—but it rarely asked, "What is psi ability for; what purpose does it serve?" It seemed to me if we could formulate some answers to this question, parapsychologists might be far better able to design experiments to observe psi "doing its thing," whatever that might be.

The usual answers that come to mind are inadequate when given some thought. If ESP were meant to be a means of communicating information, it is woefully unreliable—whether in spontaneous experiences or in experiments. PK seems a ridiculously inept way of affecting the environment around us, considering all the ways in which we can affect things using our bodies. It seems we have not quite put our finger on the real purpose behind psi ability.

One parapsychologist who has spent some time thinking about this question is Rex Stanford, of St. John's University, New York. In the mid-seventies he introduced his concept of the psi-mediated instrumental response or PMIR. The idea behind PMIR is that a person uses psi to accomplish something (the instrumental response) that fulfills certain needs he or she has. The person may not even be consciously aware of those needs, but psi "knows" what is needed and seeks to fulfill the need. This would translate into real-life experiences much like those that introduced the preceding chapter—seeming coincidences or unusual good luck that proves advantageous.

Stanford's PMIR model of psi function is fairly elaborate and has a certain amount of experimental support. Its biggest impact, however, has been to highlight the need for researchers to consider the "functional significance" of psi abilities. For Stanford the most basic functional significance of psi abilities is to serve human needs. The PMIR model was derived from observations of how psi appears to operate in ordinary life, along with a variety of clever

---

*It came from my friend John Hartwell during a lecture at our institute's Summer Study Program. This is the same John Hartwell who, years earlier, had been one of the experimenters doing OBE research with Keith Harary (see page 249).

experiments that artificially created needs that a subject's psi could help serve.[6]

There is an even more fundamental way of looking at psi as a human ability, however. If psi is a human ability, then its function is probably the same as for all other abilities with which evolution has seen fit to provide human beings. If we ask evolutionary biology "what is psi for?" we are likely to find a very simple answer. Contemporary interpretations of Darwinian theory have a very basic bottom-line explanation for any ability: It serves to help the organism survive and pass on its genes to the next generation. The purpose of psi ability is *survival*.

If psi is a product of human evolution, then its chief function is to ensure the individual's biological survival. Psi would have to be fundamentally need serving, and the needs would relate directly to matters that contribute to the health and well-being of the individual, and probably that of the individual's offspring. Ultimately psi ability would have to be considered as one of the "weapons" in the battle for survival.

I think that it is entirely possible that the sort of psi ability that has traditionally attracted the attention of parapsychologists—that of D. D. Home, or even Kulagina—may be aberrations, completely unlike "normal" psi ability. If psi is a need-serving ability, then its normal form is likely to look much more like what we call intuition and of course luck—just what is required to get the job done, and no more. As I hinted at in the last chapter, both of these concepts would need to be expanded somewhat from their common meanings. Intuition would not be limited to occasional creative flashes but would include the act of acquiring the information to guide the mass of petty decisions that go into being in the right place at the right time, or avoiding the wrong place at the right time. Thus the psi component of intuition would comprise whatever nonsensory information could be gathered to confer a competitive advantage in the game of survival. Similarly luck would not be simply winning lotteries or card games. Luck as we mean it here would be a generalized success factor—getting more than one's share of life's breaks. The psi component of luck would be similar to what is seen in micro-PK experiments—shifting the odds in one's favor—only here the RNGs are the innumerable chance processes one encounters in daily life.

The evolutionary battle for survival takes place over generations. The winners are those who get to pass their genes on to the next generation. For much of the human race survival is not the physical struggle that it was centuries ago. Yet life remains full of evolutionary competition in finding and holding suitable mates, achieving sufficient economic success to ensure the survival of the family, and leaving the offspring well positioned for continued reproductive success. In many ways for *Homo sapiens* physical competition has been replaced by psychological competition. The evolution of consciousness has given our species an enormous—almost insurmountable— advantage over other species. Perhaps psi is just that ability that has evolved to provide a competitive edge to individuals *within* a species that has consciousness.

Viewing psi as an evolved ability might clear up other mysteries. Psi could well be elusive and obscure by its nature. The most effective psi might be imperceptible psi, since if it became too obvious, one could get into trouble. It was only a few centuries ago that witches were being burned. Ostentatious displays of psi ability could severely limit one's chances of reproductive success. It could even be that psi has evolved to be deliberately self-obscuring because it works best when it is unhampered and unnoticed by the individual it is serving.

If *you* have some psi ability, then very likely *I* have some psi ability, too, and there is going to be a lot of other competing psi out there as well. Some of it might be more effective than yours. This is true of all abilities and traits that contribute to evolutionary success. Some years ago the British biologist John Maynard Smith introduced into evolutionary theory the concept of an evolutionary stable strategy (ESS). This is defined as a strategy—that is, a pattern of behavior—that, if adopted by most members of a population, cannot be bettered (in terms of survival and genetic transmission) by an alternative strategy. In a population of many competing individuals the strategy that persists, once evolved, will be the one that cannot be bettered by any deviant individual. The ESS model can go a long way toward explaining, at least theoretically, why populations of animals will develop certain behavioral strategies in competing for food or mates. An ESS grows out of an implicit cost-benefit analysis of the behavior for the individual in a particular population. Given a certain food supply and a certain number of available mates, it might turn out that the most stable pattern of behavior for males encountering males might be for an individual to be aggressive for, say, 60 percent of the encounters and submissive for 40 percent. Of course this can be extrapolated to all forms of behavior, but the important thing to realize is that we are not talking about *conscious* strategies (even in humans). These are patterns of behavior that have, over time, proven to be the most effective in promoting an individual's ability to pass on its genes.[7]

If psi is an evolved ability (and let us not lose sight of the big *if* that that statement involves), then the way this psi ability is deployed in life probably conforms to an ESS. How we "use" psi has undoubtedly evolved, vis-à-vis all the competing psi of the other members of our species, as the strategy that is most likely to benefit us in the long run: gain a little advantage here, give a little ground there. Obviously it is premature to attempt cost-benefit analysis of the evolutionary advantages of psi since we know so little about it, but the odds are that it fits the ESS model.

Several years have passed since I shared these notions with my colleagues, and I am still not sure whether it is wild speculation or just common sense. In any event I am quite sure that parapsychologists in the future will be spending more time looking at psi as a *functional human ability*.

What does this all mean for future psi research? Will we be searching for the Teela Browns of the world? Perhaps not yet, but the questions parapsychologists ask will change. Psi will have to be considered not as a somewhat ephemeral "gift" but as a functioning component of human biological survival. Rather than seeking persons who do or do not have the gift, we shall be looking for those capable of *effective deployment of psi ability* in practical situations. That is not likely to show up in card-guessing tests, so we shall need to rethink many of our testing strategies.

If there is something to psi ability, these developments will all come in time. One does not have to be a science-fiction writer to appreciate that. Suppose in the future scientists are able to identify "psi-effective" (lucky) individuals. Don't you think that the business world, not to mention certain government agencies, might have more than a passing interest?

Playing Dice With the Cosmos

God does not play dice.
—Albert Einstein[8]

Albert Einstein's comment was meant to convey his dissatisfaction with the view of the world that was emerging from quantum mechanics. Along with many others, Einstein found a world in which classical causation was replaced by collections of possible events profoundly unsettling, hence his unwillingness to concede the possibility of a world governed by statistical probabilities. Yet quantum theory has not only persevered but has been immensely successful in describing the realm of atomic events. In a sense God does play dice with the cosmos, and it is beginning to look as if humans can load those dice.

Quantum mechanics grew out of the realization, early in this century, that at the subatomic level, basic physical quantities, such as energy or electrical charge, were found to come in discrete quantities—quanta. An electron orbiting a nucleus will be at one energy level or another, but never in between. The same is true of its charge, or "spin."

In pursuit of the quantum world, physicists soon discovered that the particles of the subatomic realm did not behave in the same way as objects in the familiar world of our senses. In the old view, particles had definite properties. One could specify a precise velocity and an exact position. In the quantum world that was no longer true.

Both the logic of quantum physics and various experiments pointed to a view of the world in which subatomic particles do not have definite properties until the moment they are measured. It is not simply a question of the properties being unknown until measured; the properties do not *exist* until measured. Before the moment of measurement a particle's properties—its spin, or charge, for example—can only be described as a collection of probabilities describing the states in which the particle might be found when measured.

It was this view of the unseen subatomic world as collections of probabilities that disturbed Einstein. He proposed the famous

Einstein-Podolsky-Rosen paradox as a means of illustrating the absurdity of the probabilistic view. Take, for example, one of the measurable properties of an electron, its spin. According to quantum mechanics, when no measurement is taken the electron does not really have any spin. Now, suppose a pair of electrons are split off from an atom. The general laws of physics tell us that the electrons will be spinning in *opposite* directions. We do not know which direction (clockwise or counterclockwise) either electron is spinning, but we do know the directions are opposite one another. Let the electrons travel light-years apart so that they cannot possibly communicate with one another, and then measure one. If it is clockwise, we know instantly that its distant counterpart must be counterclockwise, without ever measuring it. Einstein argued that the nonmeasured electron must have really had counterclockwise spin to start with, thus quantum mechanics must be incorrect on this point.

Although the EPR paradox was troubling, it did not deter the march of quantum physics. In the mid-sixties the Scottish physicist John Bell proposed what amounted to an experimental test of the EPR paradox. Bell's theorem (as it has come to be known) predicted that the particles split off in the atomic reaction would have different characteristics if their atomic properties were really there to begin with (Einstein's view) from those they would have if described by a probabilistic wave function.

For many years Bell's theorem pointed to a hypothetical experiment that few thought would ever be done. Technology has moved on, however, and within the last decade quite a few extremely clever experiments have put Bell's theorem to the test. The verdict: Einstein was wrong. The predictions of quantum mechanics hold; electrons have no spin before measurement; electrons are really nowhere when they are not being observed.

The flurry of recent experiments examining some of the strange properties of quantum mechanics have highlighted even stranger consequences of the quantum view. Experiments similar to the paired-electron experiment have been done in such a way that, after the electrons are split off, one electron is suddenly constrained to spin in a certain direction. The other electron of the pair always turns out to be spinning in the opposite direction. But the direction in which the first electron will be constrained is decided *after* they split, when the electrons are too far apart to communicate even at the speed of light. *How does the second electron know in which direction it must spin?*

Don't expect an answer to that question yet. That is about as far as physics has gotten so far. Several physicists, including Nobel laureate Brian Josephson, regard experiments of this type as the best evidence yet for the existence of something like telepathy. For the present most physicists are ignoring the implications of this recent research, though a few are truly disturbed by these data.

So what has all this quantum mechanics to do with the future of parapsychology? Well, if several of my colleagues are correct, it *is* the future of parapsychology. Parapsychology's links to quantum mechanics may be more fundamental than the suggestions of telepathic-like phenomena emerging from EPR-type experiments.

The act of measuring in quantum mechanics is obviously very important. Prior to measurement, particles, charges, and spin do not literally exist, but the moment they are measured, they are found to be discrete entities or have discrete values. In the language of quantum mechanics the "state vector" that described all possible states before measurement has been "collapsed" to a single state by the act of measurement. Simple enough? No. For physicists this is actually the starting point for the problem of measurement. Since a quantum system is really a rather "fuzzy" set of probable states prior to measurement, what is it that "selects" the particular state that is observed?

This problem becomes particularly apparent when the state vector describes equally probable states. It is often illustrated by a thought experiment known as the Schrödinger's Cat experiment (after the Austrian physicist Erwin Schrödinger, who developed the wave-function equations). Suppose a cat is locked in a room along with a radioactive source that has an exactly fifty-fifty probability of decaying within one hour. A Geiger counter will register that decay, if it occurs, and will cause a hammer to fall and strike a flask containing a poisonous gas. According to the equations of quantum mechanics, after one hour the cat is neither dead nor alive, but in a "linear superposition" (a mixture) of the states of being alive and being dead. When the experimenter opens the door and looks, however, the cat is going to be in only one of those states.

Contemporary physics deals with the measurement problem in several ways, none of them universally accepted. The most widely accepted stance, sometimes called the Copenhagen interpretation, is that the state vector does not represent some physical reality but simply a measure of how much information an observer has about a system. Measurement simply happens, and the sudden increase of the observer's knowledge of the system is accompanied by the sudden collapse of the state vector.

From the early days of quantum mechanics a number of the leading physicists did not feel this was a complete picture. They argued there must be some "hidden variables" in the quantum system required for a complete description of quantum reality. The hidden variables might be what cause the wave function to collapse into a particular state. In 1961 the American Nobel Prize–winning physicist Eugene Wigner suggested that consciousness itself was the hidden variable that decided which state actually occurs in state-vector collapse. For Wigner it is the consciousness of the observer that determines the state in which Schrödinger's cat ends up.

Although this interpretation of state-vector collapse is subscribed to by only a minority of physicists, it is a growing and influential minority. Some, such as Princeton physicist John A. Wheeler, have suggested that the term *observer* fails to convey the new view of the relationship between reality and consciousness. Wheeler offers *participator* as a more accurate replacement. Indeed the inescapable conclusion from this line of reasoning is that consciousness plays a role in determining what reality will be.

Wigner's model of the measurement process is not a radical reworking of quantum theory. It requires only minimal modifications to the standard version and only at the last stage of measurement, when the observer comes into play. Since consciousness enters the system only at the moment of observation, Wigner's model (unlike the Copenhagen interpretation) permits macroscopic states (that is, ones we can see) to exist ambiguously, like Schrödinger's cat, as long as they are not observed by a conscious being. Schmidt has exploited this feature in his time-displaced PK experiments (see page 173), where the PK targets are recorded, but not observed, before the subject is asked to influence them.

It is through this minority view of quantum mechanics that parapsychology comes face to face with modern physics. For decades parapsychologists have been conducting experiments that demonstrate that consciousness can directly affect physical reality. Hundreds of carefully conducted experiments reveal observers to be influencing—selecting, if you will—the observed states in probabilistic systems. For about the same time physicists have been wrestling with the problem of consciousness. Working from the basic principles of quantum mechanics, they have added consciousness as a variable in their equations. It is not just a passive consciousness but a consciousness capable of bringing about the selection of the observed state of physical reality.

It seems that parapsychologists and physicists, traveling down two different roads, have arrived at the same place. Only a few physicists and parapsychologists have begun to realize this, however. Over the years several leading physicists (including Einstein himself) have looked sympathetically upon the struggles of parapsychology, often offering speculations on how psi phenomena might fit into physical theory. In the early seventies physicist Evan Harris Walker began a sustained attempt to incorporate psi phenomena within the framework of quantum mechanics. Walker's theory explicitly links consciousness to the hidden variables of quantum theory, and he endows consciousness with a "will" factor that serves to exchange information with the state vector as it collapses. Helmut Schmidt, the physicist responsible for many of the innovative experiments that have made explicit the connection between psi and quantum mechanics, has also proposed a theory of psi function based on quantum-mechanical principles.[9]*

To the extent that physics will continue to grapple with the role of consciousness in the determination of reality, we can expect that parapsychology will find itself an increasingly useful partner in the search for understanding. Perhaps, if parapsychology's data continue to accumulate and if the climate of tolerance among the established sciences improves, then parapsychology, so long the shunned outsider of the sciences, may become a full participant in the search for answers to some of the most fundamental questions science can ask.

*Both of these theories are too complex and technical to deal with in a book for the general reader. The list of additional reading material will identify the basic expositions of these theories for those who wish to learn more.

Normalizing the Paranormal

In the foregoing I have outlined three general approaches in which I expect much of the interest in parapsychology will concentrate in the future. They are not meant to be independent categories by any means. In fact not only do they overlap, but it could be argued that they are all simply different research perspectives on the same phenomena. Yet they are rather different orientations and will probably be pursued by different scientists with different goals and expectations: the technologists, interested in the use and application of psi; the social scientists, interested in who we are and how we do what we do; and the physical scientists (and perhaps the philosophers), interested in the ultimate workings of the universe.

There is another, more important factor common to these approaches. Each, in its own way, represents the gradual normalization of what we now call paranormal. That is not to suggest that all of what we now call psi ability will suddenly be explained by known physical mechanisms, nor is it to imply in any way a trivialization of psi. It is nothing more than the progress of science—understanding that which was not understood before. Whether or not this understanding will require a major revolution in the basic assumptions of science remains to be seen. Certainly many scientists both in and out of parapsychology feel that this will be necessary. Yet, as we have seen, a small but influential number of physicists think that psi phenomena already have a place in quantum physics. But even if a major upheaval is required to accommodate psi phenomena into our worldview, what is wrong with that? It has happened many times in the course of scientific progress, and it will inevitably happen again.

You have probably noticed that my glimpses of the future have overlooked a few of the areas of parapsychology that attract public interest. This is not because I do not expect any progress in those fields but because I see only continued slow progress or progress that follows in the wake of the areas already outlined.

For psychic healing (as well as for other forms of applied psi), I think our understanding of these will grow only in tandem with a broader understanding of the interaction between consciousness and physical systems. In other words, progress in these areas will be subsumed under progress toward a more general understanding of psi phenomena. In keeping with its newfound maturity, parapsychology will see more of the dialogue—and creative tension—between basic and applied research that is often found in other sciences. Nevertheless it will be some time before applied psi research entirely overcomes its image problem, so progress will be slow. Reliability of results is the key to that image problem, and indeed the key to the very notion of applying psi abilities, and that will require more basic research first.

Ghosts, reincarnation cases, and other evidence suggesting life after death will remain with us, but I would not expect any breakthroughs that give us "the answer" to the question that so motivated the founders of our enterprise over a century ago. Evidence will continue to accumulate, and it will continue to challenge the prevailing assumptions of science and philosophy, but I see little prospect of the topic moving beyond the stage of being an issue about which reasonable men and women can disagree.

Poltergeists, as a form of unruly PK, as well as the more controlled displays of macro-PK that certain individuals seem to display, are something of a "wild card" in the future of parapsychology. For Western scientists poltergeist agents are too problematic and gifted macro-PK subjects too few and far between for either to afford much possibility of progress at the rate we are going today. Yet there remains the possibility that the techniques pioneered by Kenneth Batcheldor to "liberate" macro-PK phenomena may become sufficiently refined to bring macro-PK truly within the orbit of experimental research. Another possibility is that our colleagues in the East may be able to tap the reported abilities of ancient techniques like qigong to produce experimental macro-PK subjects in sufficient quantity to advance our understanding.

The Pitfalls of Prognostication

Parapsychologists may study prognostication, but they are notoriously bad at practicing it. I have identified three approaches or areas of interest in which I would expect to see research activity and advances in scientific understanding. Precisely what might develop, or when, I really cannot say, since that depends far more on external factors than on the state of the science itself.

When I entered parapsychology in the early seventies, the field was riding the crest of a wave of optimism. Parapsychology was still benefiting from popular enthusiasm for exploring consciousness, especially in its somewhat altered forms. When I was doing my graduate studies at the University of Edinburgh, there were nearly a dozen fellow graduate students pursuing parapsychological research at various universities. Only a few years earlier the Parapsychological Association had been accepted as an affiliate of the American Association for the Advancement of Science. New laboratories for psi research were opening in America and in Europe. It seemed to us graduate students that we were getting in at the start of parapsychology's final push for integration within mainstream science.

Today parapsychology is no more integrated into mainstream science than it was twenty years ago. Of my fellow graduate students, I am the only one employed full-time in the field. Hardly any of them lost interest in parapsychology; the opportunities for employment simply did not materialize or soon faded away. The laboratories that opened during those years (three, that I can think of) have since closed due to lack of funds.

What has gone wrong? It may surprise you, but I do not think anything has gone wrong. All we are seeing are the ups and downs of a controversial science that has not quite made the transition to orthodoxy. For the past decade in the United States at least, funding for all branches of science has been relatively slow. With vigorous—some might even say brutal—competition for research funds, it is only to be expected that parapsychology would have trouble attracting research money. Private foundations, traditionally the chief source of parapsychology research money, are finding it necessary to support a larger share of the orthodox scientific and medical research as government support dwindles. Some observers might trace at least a few of parapsychology's present problems to the vigorous public relations campaign of the Committee for the Scientific Investigation of Claims of the Paranormal (CSICOP). For about fifteen years this group has been aggressively marketing its narrow brand of scientific fundamentalism to a ready market of true believers in their cause. But there are signs that this market is saturated, and more and more scientists—whether or not they even care about parapsychology—are becoming uncomfortable with the notion that a small group of zealots can dictate which scientific questions are worth asking and which are not.

Parapsychology is in no danger of fading away. Perhaps, more than anything else, it is this realization that most infuriates parapsychology's ardent critics. By many of the popular criteria of pseudoscience, parapsychology should have long ago passed into oblivion. But it has not. As we have seen with the ganzfeld debate, the harder critics try to explain away parapsychology's data, the stronger these data become.

There is a certain irony in parapsychology's present situation. Leading researchers in parapsychology agree that the funding situation and thus the prospect for serious research is bleaker than it has been in decades. Yet most of these researchers, along with many scientists outside the field, also agree that parapsychology's data are looking more convincing than ever before. In the end, however, it is the data that will determine parapsychology's fate, and I have confidence the field will weather the current crisis and emerge the stronger for the trial. Such optimism does not diminish the sadness I feel at seeing so much exceptional skill and talent languishing for lack of the relatively trivial sums that could sustain productive psi research programs.

If the present difficulties for psi research are but a temporary setback in the long history of this endeavor, they are to a certain extent only a local problem as well. The United States and Europe are not the only places in which scientists are investigating psi. In virtually all corners of the world where science is practiced, there is some interest in psi phenomena. In some countries the research interest is considerable, though little of the work is shared with other countries.

The Soviet Union and several of the former Communist-bloc countries have had long-standing interests in psi research, albeit with a somewhat different orientation owing to their Marxist materialist approach. How the political changes in the Soviet Union will affect psi research in that country remains to be seen; however, a small but steady stream of Russian scientists continue to visit American parapsychologists and their laboratories. American scientists have visited several Soviet research institutes, too, and have reported that our colleagues there are well aware of Western research. They are also perfectly capable of conducting very sophisticated psi research, though little of it is published outside Russia.

The fall of the Communist regimes in the former satellite countries has liberated a tremendous interest in parapsychology. Within only a few months of the momentous events of late 1989 and early 1990, the Institute for Parapsychology began receiving requests from Rumania, Hungary, and Poland for books and scientific papers—anything that could bring them up-to-date about the status of psi research.

India has government-funded parapsychology programs at several universities. A large research institute for the study of yoga and consciousness (including psi phenomena) was recently established at Andhra University in Andhra Pradesh. It is staffed by psychologists, physiologists, and accomplished practitioners and teachers of yoga. The millennia-old yogic tradition provides an intellectual tolerance, even acceptance, of the direct interaction of consciousness and the physical world. With justifiable pride in their ancient traditions, Indian scientists are now seeking a scientific understanding of yogic practice and experiences.

China likewise is seeing a tremendous surge of scientific interest in its ancient wisdom. Just since 1980 many dozens of laboratories and research centers have been established to study qigong, or traditional Chinese medicine. The majority of these are in universities or established science and technology institutes, such as the Institute of Space Medico-Engineering (ISME), which we encountered in chapter 6. In 1981, when one of China's best-known scientists, rocket pioneer Dr. Qian Xuesen, brought psi research (called exceptional-functions-of-the-human-body, or EFHB, research) into ISME, it was just as controversial as psi research is elsewhere. After a heated debate in the nation's science journals, the Communist party's Propaganda Department was prevailed upon to issue guidance. In 1982 the Party issued a diplomatic judgment that "officially" discouraged EFHB research but still permitted limited research as long as it was discreet. Research continued quietly at the universities, but it has flourished at ISME since, as a branch of the military, it is largely exempt from the Party's decision.

Since 1987 the Party's directive seems to have been quietly dropped. A vigorous movement to promote research into qigong has grown up, but this time the emphasis is on the health-giving aspects of qigong, including both the effects on a qigong practitioner's own health and the healing effects of qigong masters (those whose advanced state of practice enables them to channel their *qi* to others). As if to accent this change, in 1987 none other than Qian Xuesen was named chairman of the Chinese Science and Technology Association, a quasi-governmental agency that directs the nation's scientific research. Among his first actions, Qian strongly endorsed qigong research, stating, "Chinese qigong is modern science and technology—high technology—absolutely top technology." Reportedly the work of Lu Zuyin and colleagues with the qigong master Yan Xin (see page 333) was influential. With a certain amount of nationalistic pride, Qian recommended to the editors of the Chinese *Journal of Biophysics* that Lu's work "should be published immediately, to announce this Chinese achievement to the whole world."* It seems that qigong research and related EFHB studies will be flourishing in China for the foreseeable future.[10] Although not much Chinese research is being published in the West, parapsychologists in most U.S. centers can testify to a noticeable increase in Chinese interest and visits. Both qigong master Yan and researcher Lu spent several weeks in the summer of 1990 lecturing at major U.S. universities (as well as raising funds for a traditional-Chinese-medicine institute). Chinese scientists are particularly interested in adapting Western-style statistical and microelectronic approaches to their own research programs.**

There is one more country whose interest in parapsychology bears

---

*In fact much of the very interesting Chinese qigong and EHFB research is published only in "restricted" journals not meant for circulation outside the country. While individual Chinese scientists are generally eager to share information with their Western counterparts, the government still keeps a tight rein on potentially "useful" scientific findings, especially those that might be uniquely Chinese.

**Although many leading EFHB and qigong researchers, Qian among them, have stated explicit preferences for the macro-PK-type research, other scientists see the Western approach as more likely to gain recognition outside of the country.

watching. In this case it comes complete with rumors of strong government support for psi research as well as emphatic denials of government interest. Paradoxically we are aware of only a few small research programs, yet, outside of North America this country has the largest number of subscribers to the *Journal of Parapsychology*, the professional research journal that we publish at the Institute for Parapsychology. The country? It probably will not surprise you to learn that it is Japan.

Is Japan quietly conducting psi research programs for possible commercial applications? At the moment I am not aware of any evidence of this, but that may not mean much. Over the decades Japan has quietly assumed leadership in the exploitation of several technologies. With their advanced programs in robotics and recently accelerated efforts in artificial intelligence, "neural networks," and "fuzzy logic"* computer applications, I would put my money on Japan as the place where we are likely to see Dean Radin's Psibot Mark I show up.

Some years ago it was fashionable to contrast the parapsychology research programs of Western countries and the Soviet Union as a "psychic arms race." In fact this coverage was largely the product of overenthusiastic journalists. Although the Soviets did (and still do) have several very competent research programs in parapsychology, there is no evidence of anything approaching all-out competition with the West. I would not want my listing of other countries' interest in parapsychology to have a similar effect. I think we can fairly say that the United States still leads the world in terms of the quality, quantity, and creativity of parapsychological research. How long this will continue is a legitimate question, however. Remember, it is neither difficult nor expensive for any country to mount a very sophisticated program in psi research; all the basic methods and findings are easily available. The goals of such research programs may not be for military advantage, as some have feared, but for economic advantage.

---

*Neural networks and fuzzy logic are types of computer applications that effectively "learn" and adapt to changing situations as they run. Numerous appliances are already on the market in Japan that use fuzzy logic programs to determine the details of routine tasks (like how long to wash the laundry, or how much soap to use) with very little human intervention.

The Coming of Age for Parapsychology

If there is one word that best characterizes the period of parapsychological research that I have surveyed in this book, it is *maturation*. Even though parapsychology already had a long history, it entered the seventies with a show of youthful exuberance. New methods for ESP and PK research were being developed, and talented young researchers were taking up the challenge of psi research. By 1980, however, a sense of disillusionment set in as the exuberance was replaced by a feeling that the burst of research that had just taken place might not, in the end, bring the field any closer to understanding the phenomena or to acceptance by the scientific community. By the end of that decade, however, the disillusionment was replaced by a renewed confidence that the results of psi research *are* starting to make sense. Meta-analysis is confirming that parapsychology is dealing with real effects, not statistical chimeras or methodological mirages.

This time parapsychology is not experiencing just another bout of wide-eyed optimism. As our science heads into the nineties and the next millennium, parapsychologists have an optimism based upon hard numbers and—perhaps for the first time in its history— a realistic assessment of the size of the effects we are dealing with in our experiments. Armed with this fresh perspective on decades of data, parapsychologists should be able to bring to the field the level of replicability and predictability needed to make it a *useful* science. In scientific terms this is maturity.

I shall avoid the trap of attempting to predict how parapsychology will become useful, or when it will achieve the reliability that will bring it into mainstream science. I used to think this would not happen until someone clever enough came along to design *the* repeatable experiment, or figure out how to use psi with undeniable effectiveness. Now, reflecting parapsychology's growing maturity, I think the answer to how soon it will be before psi is reliable and useful will depend less on the arrival of a talented genius and more on those same factors that the rest of science depends so heavily upon: money and manpower.

Teasing psi's weak effects out of the morass of chance and unknown factors is not easy. It took over fifty years of systematic experimentation before we could even begin to do that with some confidence. Enhancing those psi effects to the point where they might be effectively used is likely to be even more difficult. But if those psi effects are truly there—and I believe the evidence is now quite clear that they are—we can rest assured that the secrets of psi and its application will be available to whomever chooses to commit the necessary resources to unlocking them.

APPENDIX

Sources of Information

If I have been at all successful in presenting this guide to parapsychology in the manner that I set out to, then perhaps it will stimulate some percentage of my readers to inquire further into this controversial science on their own. I earnestly hope that among the readers of this book will be the scientists (now and of the future) who can take parapsychology farther from the margins of science into the mainstream, possibly even to the vanguard.

This appendix provides several sources from which interested readers can obtain additional information on most topics in this book. A selective bibliography is the primary source, followed by a list of organizations and, finally, some comments on educational opportunities in parapsychology.

For Further Reading

Parapsychology in General

In the first section I have listed a selection of books that cover all or most of parapsychology. Except for the books by Eysenck and Sargent, Grattan-Guinness, and Irwin, most are aimed at scientists or academics and are not light reading. In many cases, however, they are standard reference works for the serious student of parapsychology.

Edge, Hoyt L., Robert L. Morris, John Palmer, and Joseph H. Rush. *Foundations of Parapsychology: Exploring the Boundaries of Human Capability.* Boston: Routledge & Kegan Paul, 1986. [A university-level textbook.]

Eysenck, Hans J., and Carl Sargent. *Explaining the Unexplained: Mysteries of the Paranormal.* London: Weidenfeld and Nicolson, 1982.

Grattan-Guinness, Ivor, ed. *Psychical Research: A Guide to Its History, Principles and Practices.* Wellingborough, England: Aquarian Press, 1982.

Irwin, Harvey. *Introduction to Parapsychology.* Jefferson, NC: McFarland, 1989.

Krippner, Stanley, series ed. *Advances in Parapsychological Research.* [This continuing series contains comprehensive treatments of many topics within parapsychology. Most volumes contain very useful annotated bibliographies by Rhea White.]

    Volume 1: Psychokinesis. New York: Plenum, 1977.

    Volume 2: Extrasensory perception. New York: Plenum, 1978.

    Volume 3. New York: Plenum, 1982. [ESP, PK, Life after death]

    Volume 4. Jefferson, N.C.: McFarland, 1984. [PK, Mental healing, Mental imagery and psi, Criticisms, Psi and psychology]

    Volume 5. Jefferson, N.C.: McFarland, 1987. [Recent PK, Ganzfeld, Theories, Criticisms]

    Volume 6. Jefferson, N.C.: McFarland, 1990. [PK, PMIR model, Psi and cerebral cortex, reincarnation]

Wolman, Benjamin B., ed. *Handbook of Parapsychology.* Jefferson, N.C.: McFarland, 1986. [First published in 1977. Thirty-one contributors, glossary, and extensive references.]

Professional Journals

European Journal of Parapsychology. (1975–) Department of Psychology, University of Edinburgh, 7 George Square, Edinburgh EH8 9JZ, Scotland [formerly at the University of Utrecht, Holland].

Journal of the American Society for Psychical Research. (1907–) American Society for Psychical Research, 5 West 73rd Street, New York, N.Y. 10023.

Journal of Parapsychology. (1937–) Parapsychology Press, P. O. Box 6847, Durham, N.C. 27708.

Journal of the Society for Psychical Research. (1882–) Society for
Psychical Research, 1 Adam and Eve Mews, London W8 6UG, England.

Journal of the Society for Scientific Exploration. (1987–) Pergamon Press,
Fairview Park, Elmsford, N.Y. 10523. [Wider scope than just parapsychology, but often includes parapsychological papers.]

Specific Topics

Chapter 1: What Is a Psychic Experience?

Angoff, Allan, and Diana Barth. *Parapsychology and Anthropology.* New
York: Parapsychology Foundation, 1974.

Mintz, Elizabeth. *The Psychic Thread: Paranormal and Transpersonal Aspects of Psychotherapy.* New York: Human Sciences Press, 1983.

Rhine, Louisa E. *Hidden Channels of the Mind.* New York: William Morrow, 1961.

———. *The Invisible Picture: A Study of Psychic Experiences.* Jefferson,
N.C.: McFarland, 1981.

Chapter 3: Origins of the Science

Gauld, Alan. *The Founders of Psychical Research.* London: Routledge &
Kegan Paul, 1968.

Inglis, Brian. *Natural and Supernatural.* London: Hodder & Stoughton,
1977.

———. *Science and Parascience: A History of the Paranormal, 1914–1939.*
London: Hodder & Stoughton, 1984.

Mauskopf, Seymour H., and Michael R. McVaugh. *The Elusive Science:
Origins of Experimental Psychical Research.* Baltimore: Johns Hopkins,
1980.

Rhine, Louisa E. *Something Hidden.* Jefferson, N.C.: McFarland, 1983.
[Biography/autobiography of the Rhines.]

Rogo, D. Scott. *Parapsychology: A Century of Inquiry.* New York: Tap-
linger, 1975.

Chapter 4: Why Does the Controversy Continue?

Braude, Stephen E. *ESP and Psychokinesis: A Philosophical Examination.*
Philadelphia: Temple University Press, 1979.

Collins, Harry M., and Trevor J. Pinch. *Frames of Meaning: The Social*

Construction of Extraordinary Science. London: Routledge & Kegan Paul, 1982.

Kurtz, Paul, ed. *A Skeptic's Handbook of Parapsychology.* Buffalo, N.Y.: Prometheus, 1985.

McClenon, James. *Deviant Science: The Case of Parapsychology.* Philadelphia: University of Pennsylvania Press, 1984.

Chapter 5: Contemporary Extrasensory Perception Research

Jahn, Robert G., and Brenda J. Dunne. *Margins of Reality: The Role of Consciousness in the Physical World.* San Diego: Harcourt, Brace, Jovanovich, 1987.

Sargent, Carl L. *Exploring Psi in the Ganzfeld.* Parapsychological Monographs No. 17. New York: Parapsychology Foundation, 1980.

Targ, Russell, and Harold Puthoff. *Mind-Reach: Scientists Look at Psychic Ability.* New York: Delacorte, 1977.

Ullman, Montague, and Stanley Krippner, with Alan Vaughan. *Dream Telepathy: Experiments in Nocturnal ESP,* Second Edition. Jefferson, N.C.: McFarland, 1989.

(Also, Volume 2 of the *Advances* series and chapters in Volumes 3, 4, and 5. Several chapters in *Handbook of Parapsychology* and *Foundations of Parapsychology* deal with recent ESP research.)

Chapter 6: Contemporary Psychokinesis Research

Hasted, John. *The Metal-benders.* London: Routledge & Kegan Paul, 1981.

Jahn, Robert G., and Brenda J. Dunne. *Margins of Reality (op. cit.)*

Oteri, Laura, ed. *Quantum Physics and Parapsychology.* New York: Parapsychology Foundation, 1975.

Owen, Iris M., and H. M. Sparrow. *Conjuring Up Philip.* New York: Harper & Row, 1976.

Panati, Charles, ed. *The Geller Papers: Scientific Observations on the Paranormal Powers of Uri Geller.* Boston: Houghton Mifflin, 1976.

Randi, James. *The Magic of Uri Geller.* New York: Ballantine, 1975.

Robinson, Diana. *To Stretch a Plank: A Survey of Psychokinesis.* Chicago: Nelson-Hall, 1981.

(Also, volume 1 of the *Advances* series and chapters in Volumes 3, 4, and 5. Several chapters in *Handbook of Parapsychology* and *Foundations of Parapsychology* deal with recent PK research.)

Chapter 7: Real Ghostbusting

Auerbach, Loyd. *ESP, Hauntings and Poltergeists*. New York: Warner, 1986.

Gauld, Alan, and Anthony D. Cornell. *Poltergeists*. London: Routledge & Kegan Paul, 1979.

MacKenzie, Andrew. *Hauntings and Apparitions*. London: Heinemann, 1982.

Roll, William G. *The Poltergeist*. Metuchen, N.J.: Scarecrow Press, 1976. [See also his chapter in the *Handbook*.]

Chapter 8: Life After Death?

Blackmore, Susan. *Beyond the Body: An Investigation of Out-of-the-body Experiences*. London: Heinemann, 1982.

Greyson, Bruce, and Charles P. Flynn. eds. *The Near-Death Experience: Problems, Prospects, Perspectives*. Springfield, Ill.: Charles C. Thomas, 1984.

Irwin, H. J. *Flight of the Mind: A Psychological Study of the Out-of-Body Experience*. Metuchen, N.J.: Scarecrow Press, 1985.

Lundahl, Craig R., ed. *A Collection of Near-Death Research Readings*. Chicago: Nelson-Hall, 1982.

Osis, Karlis, and Erlendur Haraldsson. *At the Hour of Death*. New York: Avon, 1977.

Ring, Kenneth. *Heading Toward Omega: In Search of the Meaning of the Near-Death Experience*. New York: William Morrow, 1984.

Roll, William. "The Changing Perspective on Life After Death." In *Advances 3*. New York: Plenum, 1982.

Stevenson, Ian. *Children Who Remember Previous Lives*. Charlottesville, Va.: University Press of Virginia, 1987.

Chapter 9: Adding It All Up

Honorton, Charles. "Summarizing Research Findings: Meta-analysis Methods and their Use in Parapsychology." In Lysette Coly, ed. *Psi Research Methodology: A Re-examination*. New York: Parapsychology Foundation, 1991.

Rosenthal, Robert. *Meta-analytic Procedures for Social Research*. Newbury Park, Calif.: Sage, 1984.

Chapter 10: Are We Ready for Applied Psi?

Dean, Douglas, John Mihalasky, Sheila Ostrander, and Lynn Schroeder. *Executive ESP.* Englewood Cliffs, N.J.: Prentice-Hall, 1974.

Druckman, Daniel, and John Swets eds. *Enhancing Human Performance: Issues, Theories, and Techniques.* Washington, D.C.: National Academy Press, 1988.

Ebon, Martin. *Psychic Warfare: Threat or Illusion?* New York: McGraw-Hill, 1983.

Hibbard, Whitney S., and Raymond W. Worring. *Psychic Criminology: An Operations Manual for Using Psychics in Criminal Investigation.* Springfield, Ill.: Charles C. Thomas, 1982.

Lyons, Arthur, and Marcello Truzzi. *The Blue Sense: Psychic Detectives and Crime.* New York: Mysterious Press, 1991.

McRae, Ronald M. *Mind Wars: The True Story of Government Research Into the Military Potential of Psychic Weapons.* New York: St. Martin's, 1984.

Palmer, John A., Charles Honorton, and Jessica Utts. *Reply to the National Research Council Study on Parapsychology.* Research Triangle Park, N.C.: Parapsychological Association, 1988.

Solfvin, Jerry. "Mental Healing." In *Advances 4.* Jefferson, N.C.: McFarland, 1984.

Chapter 11: Glimpsing the Future

Oteri, Laura, ed. *Quantum Physics and Parapsychology.* (*op. cit.*)

Stokes, Douglas M. "Theoretical Parapsychology." In *Advances 5.* Jefferson, N.C.: McFarland, 1987.

Organizations and Information Centers

American Society for Psychical Research (ASPR), 5 West 73rd Street, New York, N.Y. 10023. (212) 799-5050. Membership society open to the public. Publishes *Journal of the American Society for Psychical Research*, *ASPR Newsletter*. Reference library, lectures, workshops, educational information, mail-order books.

Foundation for Research on the Nature of Man (FRNM), P.O. Box 6847, College Station, Durham, N.C. 27708. (919) 688-8241. Research laboratory (Institute for Parapsychology). Publishes *Jour-*

nal of Parapsychology, FRNM Bulletin. Reference library, two-month intensive summer study program, advanced training program (for researchers), educational information, mail-order books.

Mind Science Foundation, 8301 Broadway, Suite 100, San Antonio, Tex. 78209. (512) 821-6094. Research laboratory, reference library, seminars, newsletter.

Parapsychological Association, Inc., P.O. Box 12236, Research Triangle Park, N.C. 27709. (919) 688-8241. A professional association of parapsychologists and interested scientists and academics. Holds annual conferences (open to the public). Publishes members' newsletter. News-media referrals.

Parapsychology Foundation, 228 East 71st Street, New York, N.Y. 10021. (212) 628-1550. Sponsors and publishes proceedings of topic-centered professional conferences, monographs (available by mail). Reference library.

Parapsychology Sources of Information (PSI) Center, 2 Plane Tree Lane, Dix Hills, N.Y. 11746. (516) 271-1243. Run by Rhea White, parapsychologist and professional librarian, the PSI Center offers comprehensive bibliographies on parapsychological topics and customized bibliographic searches for scholars and researchers (fees charged).

Society for Psychical Research (SPR), 1 Adam and Eve Mews, Kensington, London W8 6UG, England. 071-937-8984. Membership society open to the public. Publishes *Journal of the Society for Psychical Research, SPR Newsletter.* Reference library, lecture series, study days, conferences.

Spiritual Emergence Network (SEN), Institute of Transpersonal Psychology, 250 Oak Grove Avenue, Menlo Park, Calif. 94025. (415) 327-2776. Provides counseling referrals for people experiencing "psychospiritual crisis" (for example as a possible result of troubling psychic experiences). Public workshops, forums, and conferences. Supported by public and professional memberships, and by donations.

Educational Opportunities

Opportunities for formal education in parapsychology are very limited. As a rule I generally discourage students from becoming overly concerned with studying parapsychology while they are still undergraduates. I recommend instead that any prospective parapsychologist get solid training and a good degree in a related branch of orthodox science. The specialized training for parapsychology can be obtained later, either in one of the few postgraduate programs or in independent-study programs such as the one that our institute conducts.

Despite the scarcity of formal programs, at any time there are numerous instructors offering introductory and even advanced courses in parapsychology at many universities. There are a few university departments and individual faculty members who are willing to work with students in obtaining advanced degrees for thesis work that includes parapsychology. The best source of this frequently changing information is the ASPR (see previous section), which publishes its "Educational Opportunities in Parapsychology" list. This is available for a small fee to cover production. Usually the FRNM and the SPR can provide information as well.

The graduate programs that I am aware of now are as follows:

Andhra University, Department of Psychology and Parapsychology, Visakhapatnam 530 003, India. Three-year Ph.D. program. (It is possible to arrange to conduct thesis research at FRNM.) Direct inquiries to Professor P. V. Krishna Rao.

Saybrook Institute, 1550 Sutter Street, San Francisco, Calif. 94109. Graduate students in the Human Sciences Program may specialize in parapsychology. Contact Dr. Stanley Krippner, director.

University of Edinburgh, Department of Psychology, 7 George Square, Edinburgh EH8 9JZ, Scotland. Prof. Robert Morris supervises a very limited number of Ph.D. students specializing in parapsychology.

West Georgia College, Department of Psychology, Carrollton, Ga. 30118. Students in M.A. program can specialize in parapsychology.

For independent study in parapsychology there is no better opportunity than the Summer Study Program offered by the Institute for Parapsychology in Durham, N.C. (See FRNM in previous section.) This runs for eight weeks in June and July of each year and provides a comprehensive introduction to all aspects of parapsychology. Although primarily aimed at researchers (and would-be researchers), the program is also very useful for educators who wish to incorporate parapsychological topics into their courses. It is often possible to arrange credit for students already enrolled in a university. Contact Dr. John Palmer.

Finally students at accredited institutions can become "student affiliates" of the Parapsychological Association (see previous section). Following the activities of PA scientists and meeting them at conventions is an excellent way to learn about study and other opportunities in the field. Contact the PA for further information.

NOTES

Chapter 1: What is a Psychic Experience?

1. From the author's own collection.

2. George Gallup, *The Gallup Poll, Public Opinion, 1978* (Wilmington, Del.: Scholarly Research, 1979). In December 1989, CBS television conducted a poll in connection with a broadcast of a "48 Hours" program on psychic experiences. The results were given at the end of the show and were reported in greater detail in the *ASPR Newsletter*, Spring 1990.

3. For a discussion of the pros and cons of Rhine's approach see Debra H. Weiner and JoMarie Haight, "Charting Hidden Channels: Louisa E. Rhine's Case Collection Project" in K. Ramakrishna Rao, ed., *Case Studies in Parapsychology* (Jefferson, N.C.: McFarland, 1986).

4. Louisa E. Rhine, "Subjective Forms of Spontaneous Psi Experiences," *Journal of Parapsychology.* 1953, **17**, pp. 77–114.

5. Case reported in Louisa E. Rhine, *Hidden Channels of the Mind* (New York: William Morrow, 1961), p. 32. Reproduced with permission.

6. *Ibid.* p. 47.

7. *Ibid.* p. 49.

8. *Ibid.* p. 65.

9. Louisa E. Rhine, *ESP in Life and Lab: Tracing Hidden Channels* (New York: Macmillan, 1967), p. 148. Reproduced with permission.

10. *Ibid.* p. 152.

11. Louisa E. Rhine, "Precognition and Intervention," *Journal of Parapsychology.* 1955, **19**, pp. 1–34.

12. Quoted directly from the L. E. Rhine Collection of Spontaneous Psi Experiences, Institute for Parapsychology. Reproduced with permission.

13. *Ibid.*

14. Rhine, *Hidden Channels of the Mind. op. cit.*

15. E.F. Torrey, *The Mind Game: Witchdoctors and Psychiatrists* (New York: Bantam, 1973).

16. Adrian K. Boshier, "African Apprenticeship," in Alan Angoff and Diana Barth, eds., *Parapsychology and Anthropology* (New York: Parapsychology Foundation, 1974), pp. 273–284.

17. See, for example, Stanley Krippner and Alberto Villoldo, *The Realms of Healing*, 3rd ed. (Berkeley, Calif.: Celestial Arts), 1988.

18. Joseph K. Long, "Shamanism and Voodoo Death: Stress Theory in Medical Anthropology," in Joseph K. Long, ed., *Extrasensory Ecology: Parapsychology and Anthropology* (Metuchen, N.J.: Scarecrow, 1977), pp. 257–270.

19. Joan Halifax-Grof, "Hex Death," in Alan Angoff and Diana Barth, eds., *Parapsychology and Anthropology* (New York: Parapsychology Foundation), 1974, pp. 59–73.

Chapter 2: Mapping the Territory

1. For a personal account of the effort to win AAAS acceptance from one of the persons principally involved see E. Douglas Dean, "20th Anniversary of the PA and the AAAS, Part I: 1963–1969" *ASPR Newsletter*, Winter 1990, pp. 7–8, and "Part II: December 30, 1969–Present" *ASPR Newsletter*, Spring 1990, pp. 19–20.

2. Edmund Gurney, Frederic W.H. Myers and Frank Podmore, *Phantasms of the Living*, two volumes (London: Trubner, 1886). Laura A. Dale, A Series of Spontaneous Cases in the Tradition of *Phantasms of the Living*," *Journal of the American Society for Psychical Research*, 1951, **45**, pp. 85–101. Gerhard Sannwald, "Statistische Untersuchungen and Spontanphenomenen," *Zeitschrift für Parapsychologie und Grenzgebiete der Psychologie*, 1959, **3**, pp. 59–71.

Chapter 3: Origins of the Science

1. Herodotus. *The Histories of Herodotus*, translated by H. Carter (New York: Heritage, 1958).

2. This quote is taken from a deposition made under oath and quoted from earlier sources in Herbert Thurston, *The Physical Phenomena of Mysticism* (Chicago: Henry Regnery, 1952), p. 12.

3. Witnesses to Joseph of Copertino's levitations also testified under oath for the *Promotor Fidei* (around 1665–66). See Thurston, *op. cit.*

4. Renée Haynes, *Philosopher King—The Humanist Pope Benedict XIV* (London: Weidenfeld and Nicolson, 1970).

5. Richard Deacon, *John Dee: Scientist, Astrologer & Secret Agent to Elizabeth* (London: Muller, 1968).

6. For more on mesmerism and the origins of psychical research see

Frank Podmore, *Modern Spiritualism*, vol. I (London: Methuen, 1902), pp. 51–66.

7. R. Laurence Moore, *In Search of White Crows: Spiritualism, Parapsychology, and American Culture* (New York: Oxford University Press, 1977), pp. 11ff.

8. E. E. Lewis, *A Report of the Mysterious Noises Heard in the House of Mr. John D. Fox, in Hydesville, Arcadia, Wayne County* (Canandaigua, N.Y.: by author, 1848).

9. E. E. Lewis, *op. cit.*

10. Austin Flint, Charles A. Lee, and C.B. Coventry, Letter to the Buffalo *Commercial Advertiser*, 17 February 1851. See S. Brown, *The Heyday of Spiritualism* (New York: Hawthorn, 1970).

11. The confession was reported in the *New York Herald* on 24 September and 10 October and in Reuben Briggs Davenport's *The Death-blow to Spiritualism* (New York: G.W. Dillingham, 1888). See Alan Gauld, *The Founders of Psychical Research* (New York: Schocken Books, 1969) and Herbert G. Jackson, *The Spirit Rappers*, "The Horrible Deception" (Garden City, N.Y.: Doubleday, 1972), pp. 201–215.

12. See George Zorab, review of *The Enigma of Daniel Home: Medium or Fraud* by Trevor Hall. *Journal of Parapsychology*, 1985, **49**, pp. 103–105.

13. Earl of Dunraven (Lord Adare), "Experiences in Spiritualism with D. D. Home," *Proceedings of the Society for Psychical Research*, 1926, **35**, p. 135.

14. William Crookes, *Researches in the Phenomena of Spiritualism* (London: J. Burnes, 1874). (Reprints of his *Quarterly Journal of Science* papers.)

15. "Objects of the Society," *Proceedings of the Society for Psychical Research*, 1882, **1**, pp. 3–6.

16. Helen de G. Salter, "Impressions of Some Early Workers in the S.P.R.," *Journal of Parapsychology*, 1950, **14**, pp. 24–36. Quotation is from Salter's recollection of a conversation with Yeats (p. 31).

17. "Report of the Committee Appointed to Investigate Phenomena Connected with the Theosophical Society," *Proceedings of the Society for Psychical Research*, 1885, **3**, pp. 201–400 (quotation, p. 207).

18. Charles Richet, "La Suggestion Mentale et le Calcul des Probabilités," *Revue Philosophique*, 1884, **18**, pp. 609–674. Charles Richet, "Relation de Diverses Expériences sur la Transmission Mentale, la Lucidité, et Autres Phénomènes non Explicables par les Données Scientifiques Actuelles," *Proceedings of the Society for Psychical Research*, 1889, **5**, pp. 18–168.

19. John Beloff, "Historical Overview," in Benjamin B. Wolman, ed.,

Handbook of Parapsychology (New York: Van Nostrand Reinhold, 1977), pp. 3–24.

20. Letter from Rhine to Joseph De Wyckoff and the ASPR board of trustees, 15 July 1926. Quoted in Seymour Mauskopf, and Michael McVaugh, *The Elusive Science* (Baltimore: Johns Hopkins University Press, 1980), p. 76.

21. J.B. Rhine, *Extra-sensory Perception* (1934; reprint ed., Boston: Bruce Humphries, 1973).

22. J.B. Rhine and J.G. Pratt, "A Review of the Pearce-Pratt Distance Series of ESP Tests," *Journal of Parapsychology*, 1954, **18**, 165–177.

23. J.B. Rhine, *New Frontiers of the Mind* (New York: Farrar and Rinehart, 1937).

24. J.G. Pratt, J.B. Rhine, Burke M. Smith, Charles E. Stuart, and Joseph A. Greenwood, *Extra-Sensory Perception After Sixty Years* (New York: Henry Holt, 1940).

25. The definitive account of the early years of the Duke University lab is Mauskopf and McVaugh, *op. cit.*

Chapter 4: Why Does the Controversy Continue?

1. Margaret Mead speaking to the members of the AAAS Council, December 30, 1969. Quoted in E. Douglas Dean, "20th Anniversary of the PA and the AAAS, Part I: 1963–1969." *ASPR Newsletter*, Winter 1990, pp. 7–8. (Originally privately circulated in 1970 as "The Parapsychological Association Becomes Affiliated with the American Association for the Advancement of Science.")

2. John A. Wheeler, "Drive the Pseudos Out of the Workshop of Science" (Address to the Annual Meeting of the AAAS, January 8, 1979). Reprinted in *New York Review of Books*, May 17, 1979.

3. Robert G. Jahn, "On the Representation of Psychic Research to the Community of Established Science," in Rhea White and Richard S. Broughton, eds., *Research in Parapsychology 1983* (Metuchen, N.J.: Scarecrow, 1984), pp. 127–138.

4. Lucien Warner and C. C. Clark, "A Survey of Psychological Opinion on ESP," *Journal of Parapsychology*, 1938, **2**, pp. 296–301. Christopher Evans, "Parapsychology—What the Questionnaire Revealed," *New Scientist*, 1973, **57**, p. 209. Mahlon W. Wagner and Mary Monet, "Attitudes of College Professors Toward Extra-Sensory Perception," *Zetetic Scholar*, 1979, **5**, pp. 7–16.

5. James McClenon, *Deviant Science: The Case of Parapsychology* (Philadelphia: University of Pennsylvania, 1984).

6. O. Costa de Beauregard, "Quantum Paradoxes and Aristotle's Twofold Information Concept," in Laura Oteri, ed., *Quantum Physics and Parapsychology* (New York: Parapsychology Foundation, 1975), pp. 91–102.

7. Brian Josephson speaking on the BBC World Service radio program "The Unexplained," May 5, 1987.

8. John Palmer, "Progressive Skepticism: A Critical Approach to the Psi Controversy," *Journal of Parapsychology*, 1986, **50**, pp. 29–42. John Palmer, "Conceptualizing the Psi Controversy," *Parapsychology Review*, 1988 (Jan.–Feb.), **19**(1), pp. 1–5.

9. George R. Price, "Science and the Supernatural," *Science*, 1955, **122**, pp. 359–367. George R. Price, "Apology to Rhine and Soal," *Science*, 1972, **175**, p.359. Letter from Price to Rhine, Jan. 22, 1972. (J.B. Rhine papers, Manuscript Department, Perkins Library, Duke University).

10. Paul Kurtz, "Committee to Scientifically Investigate Claims of Paranormal and Other Phenomena," *The Humanist*, 1976 (May/June), p. 28.

11. C.E.M. Hansel, *ESP and Parapsychology: A Critical Re-evaluation* (Buffalo: Prometheus, 1980). For numerous examples of Hansel's misstatements see Charles Honorton, review of *ESP: A Scientific Evaluation* by C.E.M. Hansel, *Journal of Parapsychology*, 1967, **31**, pp. 76–82. Charles Honorton, "Beyond the Reach of Sense: Some Comments on C.E.M. Hansel's *ESP and Parapsychology: A Critical Re-Evaluation*," *Journal of the American Society for Psychical Research*, 1981, **75**, pp. 155–166. Ian Stevenson, "An Antagonist's View of Parapsychology. A Review of Professor Hansel's *ESP: A Scientific Evaluation*," *Journal of the American Society for Psychical Research*, 1967, **61**, pp. 254–267.

12. For example, Ray Hyman, "Further Comments on Schmidt's PK Experiments," *Skeptical Inquirer*, 1981, **5**(3), pp. 34–40.

13. Although much of this affair is public knowledge, an insider's report from one of the McDonnell laboratory researchers details the correspondence and interactions with Randi during this period: Michael A. Thalbourne, "Science vs. Showmanship: The Case of the Randi Hoax" (Privately circulated, February, 1984). See also, Loyd M. Auerbach, "Project Alpha: Showmanship vs. Science," *ASPR Newsletter*, 1983 (April), **9**(2), pp. 1–2.

14. William J. Broad, "Magician's Effort to Foil Scientists Raises Questions," *The New York Times*, February 15, 1983.

Chapter 5: Contemporary Extrasensory
Perception Research

1. This example is adapted from Montague Ullman and Stanley Krippner with Alan Vaughan, *Dream Telepathy: Experiments in Nocturnal ESP*, 2nd ed. (Jefferson, N.C.: McFarland, 1989). Quotations reproduced with permission.

2. Sigmund Freud, "Dreams and Telepathy," in George Devereux, ed., *Psychoanalysis and the Occult* (New York: International Universities Press, 1953), p. 86.

3. For a good summary of the Maimonides studies see Irvin L. Child, "Psychology and Anomalous Observations: The Question of ESP in Dreams," *American Psychologist*, 1985, **40**, pp. 1219–1230.

4. Ullman and Krippner with Vaughan, *op. cit.*, p. 139.

5. Ullman and Krippner with Vaughan, *op. cit.*, pp. 143–144.

6. Ullman and Krippner with Vaughan, *op. cit.*, p. 172n.

7. This ganzfeld report is from the files of the Institute for Parapsychology. I am grateful to experimenter Nancy Zingrone and subject Anne for permission to reproduce it.

8. See Charles Honorton, "Psi and Internal Attention States," in B. B. Wolman, ed., *Handbook of Parapsychology* (Jefferson, N.C.: McFarland, 1986), pp. 453–472 (First published, 1977). Charles Honorton, "Psi and Internal Attention States: Information Retrieval in the Ganzfeld," in Betty Shapin and Lisette Coly, eds., *Psi and States of Awareness* (New York: Parapsychology Foundation, 1978), pp. 79–90.

9. Transcript quotation from Marilyn Jean Schlitz and Charles Honorton, "ESP and Creativity in an Exceptional Population" (Paper presented to the Thirty-third Annual Convention of the Parapsychological Association, Chevy Chase, Md., August 18–20, 1990). My thanks to Marilyn Schlitz and Charles Honorton for permission to reproduce this.

10. The original sheep-goat work is in Gertrude R. Schmeidler and Robert A. McConnell, *ESP and Personality Patterns* (1958; reprint ed., Westport, Conn.: Greenwood Press, 1973). For a recent summary see John Palmer, "Extrasensory Perception: Research Findings," in Stanley Krippner, ed., *Extrasensory Perception,* Advances in Parapsychological Research, Vol. 2 (New York: Plenum, 1978), pp. 59–243.

11. Carl L. Sargent, "Extraversion and Performance in 'Extra-sensory' Perception Tasks," *Personality and Individual Differences*, 1981, **2**, pp. 137–143.

12. Quoted descriptions of MBTI types are from M. Carlyn, "An Assessment of the Myers-Briggs Type Indicator," *Journal of Personality Assessment*, 1977, **41**, pp. 461–473.

13. Charles Honorton and Ephraim Schechter, "Ganzfeld Target Retrieval with an Automated Testing System: A Model for Initial Ganzfeld Success," in Debra H. Weiner and Roger D. Nelson, eds., *Research in Parapsychology 1986* (Metuchen, N.J.: Scarecrow Press, 1987), pp. 36–39.

14. Richard S. Broughton, H. Kanthamani, and Anjum Khilji, "Assessing the PRL Success Model on an Independent Ganzfeld Data Base," in Linda Henkel and John Palmer, eds., *Research in Parapsychology 1989* (Metuchen, N.J.: Scarecrow Press, 1990).

15. Quotations from this and the following SRI experimental transcripts are from Russell Targ and Harold E. Puthoff, *Mind Reach: Scientists Look at Psychic Ability* (New York: Delacorte, 1977). My thanks to the authors for permission to quote.

16. Russell Targ and Harold Puthoff, "Information Transmission under Conditions of Sensory Shielding," *Nature*, 1974, **251**, pp. 602–607.

17. David Marks and Richard Kammann, *The Psychology of the Psychic* (Buffalo, N.Y.: Prometheus, 1980).

18. See David Marks, "Sensory Cues Invalidate Remote Viewing Experiments," *Nature*, 1981, **292**, p. 177. Harold E. Puthoff and Russell Targ, "Rebuttal of Criticisms of Remote Viewing Experiments," *Nature*, 1981, **292**, p. 388. Charles T. Tart, Harold E. Puthoff, and Russell Targ, "Information Transmission in Remote Viewing Experiments," *Nature*, 1980, **284**, p. 191.

19. Harold E. Puthoff and Russell Targ, "A Perceptual Channel for Information Transfer over Kilometer Distances: Historical Perspective and Recent Research," *Proceedings of the IEEE*, 1976, **64**, pp. 329–354.

20. Quotations from Marilyn Schlitz and Elmer Gruber, "Transcontinental Remote Viewing," *Journal of Parapsychology*, 1980, **44**, 305–317. I am grateful to Marilyn Schlitz and the *Journal of Parapsychology* for permission to reproduce them.

21. C.E.M. Hansel, *ESP: A Scientific Evaluation* (New York: Charles Scribner's Sons, 1966), p. 241.

22. Helmut Schmidt, "Quantum Processes Predicted?," *New Scientist*, 1969 (16 Oct.), pp. 114–115. H. Schmidt, "Precognition of a Quantum Process," *Journal of Parapsychology*, 1969, **33**, pp. 99–108.

23. Helmut Schmidt, "Clairvoyance Tests with a Machine," *Journal of Parapsychology*, 1969, **33**, pp. 300–306.

24. Charles Honorton, "Automated Forced-Choice Precognition Tests

with a 'Sensitive,' " *Journal of the American Society for Psychical Research*, 1971, 65, pp. 476–481.

25. Charles Honorton, "Precognition and Real-Time ESP Performance in a Computer Task with an Exceptional Subject," *Journal of Parapsychology*, 1987, 51, pp. 291–320.

26. James C. Carpenter, "Quasi-Therapeutic Group Process and ESP," *Journal of Parapsychology*, 1988, 52, pp. 279–304.

27. Dean I. Radin and Edwin C. May, "Testing the Intuitive Data Sorting Model with Pseudorandom Number Generators: A Proposed Method," in Debra H. Weiner and Roger G. Nelson, eds., *Research in Parapsychology 1986* (Metuchen, N.J.: Scarecrow, 1987), pp. 109–111.

Chapter 6: Contemporary Psychokinesis Research

1. For further details on this encounter see J.G. Pratt and H.H.J. Keil, "Firsthand Observations of Nina S. Kulagina Suggestive of PK upon Static Objects," *Journal of the American Society for Psychical Research*, 1973, 67, pp. 381–390.

2. Benson Herbert, "Reports on the Kulagina Cine Films," *Journal of Paraphysics*, 1969, 3(3 and 4), and 1970, 4(1, 3, and 4).

3. For full details, see Benson Herbert, "Spring in Leningrad: Kulagina Revisited," *Journal of Paraphysics*, 1973, 7, pp. 92–104. See also, H.H.J. Keil, Montague Ullman, Benson Herbert, and J.G. Pratt, "Directly Observable Voluntary PK Effects," *Proceedings of the Society for Psychical Research*, 1976, 56, pp. 197–235.

4. See Larissa Vilenskaya, "Scientists Study Phenomena of Nina Kulagina," *Psi Research*, 1984, 3(3/4), pp. 66–73. Also, V.N. Volchenko, G.N. Dulnev, K.I. Krylov, V.V. Kulagin, and N.V. Pilipenko, "Measurements of Extreme Values of Physical Fields of the Human Operator," in *Tekhnicheskie Aspekty Refleksoterapii i Sistemy Diagnostiki* [Technical aspects of the reflex therapy and diagnostic system] (Kalinin: Kalinin State University, 1984), pp. 53–59 [in Russian]. My thanks to Larissa Vilenskaya of *Psi Research* for providing details of Kulagina's later activities.

5. The offending article was V. Strelkov, "Resurrection of Dracula, or Who Spreads Mysticism," *Chelovek i Zakon* [Man and law], 1986 (Sept.), 9 (189), pp. 28–46 [in Russian]. The court-directed retraction appeared in "The Editorial Office Answers," *Chelovek i Zakon* [Man and law], 1988 (May), 5 (209), p. 70 [in Russian].

6. Charles Honorton, "Apparent Psychokinesis on Static Objects by a 'Gifted' Subject," in W.G. Roll, R.L. Morris and J.D. Morris, eds., *Re-*

search in Parapsychology 1973 (Metuchen, N.J.: Scarecrow Press, 1974), pp. 128–131.

7. Graham K. Watkins and Anita M. Watkins, "Apparent Psychokinesis on Static Objects by a 'Gifted' Subject: A Laboratory Demonstration," in W.G. Roll, R.L. Morris, and J.D. Morris, eds., *Research in Parapsychology 1973* (Metuchen, N.J.: Scarecrow Press, 1974), pp. 132–134.

8. Adapted with permission from Iris M. Owen with Margaret Sparrow, *Conjuring up Philip* (New York: Harper & Row, 1976).

9. K.J. Batcheldor, "Report on a Case of Table Levitation and Associated Phenomena," *Journal of the Society for Psychical Research*, 1966, **43**, pp. 339–356. Kenneth J. Batcheldor, "Contributions to the Theory of PK Induction from Sitter-Group Work," *Journal of the American Society for Psychical Research*, 1984, **78**, pp. 105–122.

10. C. Brookes-Smith and D. W. Hunt, "Some Experiments in Psychokinesis," *Journal of the Society for Psychical Research*, 1970, **45**, pp. 265–281. C. Brookes-Smith, "Data-tape Recorded Experimental PK Phenomena," *Journal of the Society for Psychical Research*, 1973, **47**, pp. 69–89.

11. Artur Zorka (as Chairman of the Occult Investigations Committee), "Official Report: Society of American Magicians, Assembly 30, Atlanta Chapter," in Charles Panati, ed., *The Geller Papers* (Boston: Houghton Mifflin, 1976), pp. 157–167. Leo Leslie, "A Magician Looks at Uri Geller," in Panati, *op. cit.*, pp. 243–246.

12. John G. Taylor, "A Brief Report on a Visit by Uri Geller to King's College, London, June 20, 1974," and "Analyzing the Geller Effect," in Panati, *op. cit.* pp. 213–227.

13. John B. Hasted, "My Geller Notebooks," in Panati, *op. cit.*, pp. 197–212.

14. John B. Hasted, *The Metal-benders* (London: Routledge and Kegan Paul, 1981).

15. Combined Committee for EFHB Tests, "Report on Tests of the Authenticity of EFHB," *Renti Teyigongneng Yanjiu* [EFHB research], 1983, **1**, pp. 9–22 [in Chinese].

16. Lin Shuhuang, Zhang Congqi, *et al.*, "PK Experiments: Objects Moved Into or Out from Sealed Containers," *Renti Teyigongneng Yanjiu* [EFHB research], 1983, **1**, pp. 110–118 [in Chinese].

17. Huo Yaohua, "Qigong Miracles and Research Developments," *Xinhua Wenzhai* [New China digest], 1988, **2**, pp. 172–175 [in Chinese].

18. Song Kongzhi, Lan Rongliang, Li Xianggao, and Zhou Liangzhong (Subject: Zhang Baosheng), "The Research of the Break Through Spatial Obstacle Function," *Chinese Journal of Somatic Science*, 1990 (July), pp. 22–31 [in Chinese].

19. Helmut Schmidt, "A PK Test with Electronic Equipment," *Journal of Parapsychology*, 1970, **34**, pp. 175–181.

20. Helmut Schmidt and Lee Pantas, "PK Tests with Internally Different Machines," *Journal of Parapsychology*, 1972, **36**, pp. 222–232.

21. Helmut Schmidt, "PK Effect on Pre-recorded Targets," *Journal of the American Society for Psychical Research*, 1976, **70**, pp. 267–292.

22. Helmut Schmidt, "Collapse of the State Vector and Psychokinetic Effects," *Foundations of Physics*, 1982, **12**, pp. 565–581.

23. Helmut Schmidt, "Addition Effect for PK on Pre-recorded Targets," *Journal of Parapsychology*, 1985, **49**, pp. 229–244.

24. H. Schmidt, R. Morris, and L. Rudolph, "Channeling Evidence for a PK Effect to Independent Observers," *Journal of Parapsychology*, 1986, **50**, pp. 1–15.

25. R. G. Jahn, B. J. Dunne, and R. D. Nelson, "Engineering Anomalies Research," *Journal of Scientific Exploration*, 1987, **1**, pp. 21–50.

26. R. D. Nelson, B. J. Dunne, and R. G. Jahn, "Operator Related Anomalies in a Random Mechanical Cascade Experiment," (Princeton Engineering Anomalies Research, School of Engineering/Applied Science, Princeton University, Technical Note PEAR 88001, June 1988).

27. B. J. Dunne, R. D. Nelson, Y. H. Dobyns, and R. G. Jahn, "Individual Operator Contributions in Large Data Base Anomalies Experiments," (Princeton Engineering Anomalies Research, School of Engineering/Applied Science, Princeton University, Technical Note PEAR 88002, July 1988).

28. Richard S. Broughton and James R. Perlstrom, "PK Experiments with a Competitive Computer Game," *Journal of Parapsychology*, 1986, **50**, pp. 1–15.

Chapter 7: Real Ghostbusting

1. Columbia Pictures, *Ghostbusters*, Copyright 1984.

2. This case is taken from Alan Gauld and Anthony D. Cornell, *Poltergeists* (London: Routledge & Kegan Paul, 1979), pp. 312–318.

3. R. C. Morton, "Record of a Haunted House," *Proceedings of the Society for Psychical Research*, 1892, **8**, pp. 311–332. For the most recent update on sightings see, Andrew MacKenzie, "Continuation of the 'Record of a Haunted House,'" *Journal of the Society for Psychical Research*, 1988, **55**, pp. 25–32.

4. The Gooding letter is reported in Andrew MacKenzie, *Hauntings and Apparitions* (London: Heinemann, 1982), pp. 50–51.

5. F.W.H. Myers, Prefatory note to R. C. Morton's report, *Proceedings of the Society for Psychical Research*, 1892, **8**, p.311.

6. G.W. Lambert, "The Cheltenham Ghost: A Reinterpretation of the Evidence," *Journal of the Society for Psychical Research*, 1958, **39**, pp. 267–277.

7. Michaleen Maher and Gertrude R. Schmeidler, "Quantitative Investigation of a Recurrent Apparition," *Journal of the American Society for Psychical Research*, 1975, **69**, pp. 341–352.

8. While some of these incidents are generally known among parapsychologists, my colleague Loyd Auerbach collected the details and reported them in his book *ESP, Hauntings, and Poltergeists: A Parapsychologist's Handbook* (New York: Warner Books, 1986), pp. 295–303.

9. Hans Bender, "Modern Poltergeist Research—A Plea for an Unprejudiced Approach," in John Beloff, ed., *New Directions in Parapsychology* (London: Paul Elek, 1974), pp. 122–143. F. Karger and G. Zicha, "Physikalische Untersuchung des spukfalles in Rosenheim 1967" [Physical investigation of the Rosenheim psychokinetic phenomena 1967], *Zeitschrift für Parapsychologie und Grenzgebiete der Psychologie*, 1968, **11**, pp. 113–131. [in German]

10. William G. Roll, "Poltergeists," in B.B. Wolman, ed., *Handbook of Parapsychology* (New York: Van Nostrand Reinhold, 1977), pp. 383–413 (quotation, p. 287).

11. Harry Price and H. Kohn, "An Indian Poltergeist," *Journal of the American Society for Psychical Research*, 1930, **24**, pp. 122–130, 180–186, 221–231 (quotation, pp. 129–130).

12. Cited in Gauld and Cornell, *op. cit.*, pp. 211–219.

13. Frederic W.H. Myers, "On Alleged Movements of Objects, Without Contact, Occurring Not in the Presence of a Paid Medium," *Proceedings of the Society for Psychical Research*, 1891, **7**, pp. 383–394. Quotation (p. 391) is from Myers's notes on his conversation with John Bristow who was an apprentice at the shop during the activity.

14. Bender, "Modern Poltergeist Research . . ." *op. cit.*

15. Adapted from William G. Roll, *The Poltergeist* (Metuchen, N.J.: Scarecrow Press, 1976), pp. 104–147. My thanks to Professor Roll for permission to quote selected passages.

16. Lambert presented his views in a series of papers in the *Journal of the Society for Psychical Research*. See Anthony D. Cornell and Alan Gauld, "The Geophysical Theory of Poltergeists" and Lambert's reply, *Journal of the Society for Psychical Research*, 1961, **41**, pp. 129–147, 148–155.

17. Roll, *The Poltergeist, op. cit.*, p. 173.

18. See William G. Roll, "Towards a General Theory for the Poltergeist," *European Journal of Parapsychology*, 1978, **2**, pp. 167–200.

19. Ian Stevenson, "Are Poltergeists Living or Are They Dead?" *Journal of the American Society for Psychical Research*, 1972, **66**, pp. 233–252.

20. Adapted from Anna Ostrzycka and Marek Rymuszko, *Nieuchwytna Sila* [The Elusive Force] (Warsaw: Rój, 1989) in an as-yet unpublished translation by Joel Stern. I am indebted to Mr. Stern and the authors for permission to quote the selected passages.

21. Activities since the original publication are reported in Joel Stern, Marek Rymuszko and Anna Ostrzycka, "Polish Teen Shows Extraordinary Psychokinetic Powers," *Pathways* (Washington, D.C.), March 1990.

Chapter 8: Life After Death?

1. Charles McCreery, *Psychical Phenomena and the Physical World* (Oxford: Institute of Psychophysical Research, 1973), pp. 35–36. I am grateful to the Institute of Psychophysical Research (Oxford, England) for permission to quote.

2. Celia E. Green, *Out-of-the-Body Experiences* (Oxford: Institute of Psychophysical Research, 1968), p. 121. Reproduced with permission.

3. See Susan J. Blackmore, *Beyond the Body* (London: Heineman, 1982), pp. 225–252.

4. Adapted from Robert L. Morris, Stuart B. Harary, Joseph Janis, John Hartwell, and W.G. Roll, "Studies of Communication During Out of Body Experiences," *Journal of the American Society for Psychical Research*, 1978, **72**, pp. 1–21, and D. Scott Rogo, "An Experiment with Blue Harary," in D. Scott Rogo, ed., *Mind Beyond the Body: The Mystery of ESP Projection* (New York: Penguin, 1988), pp. 170–192. My thanks to John Hartwell for his assistance.

5. For an entertaining account of the Kidd legacy and its settlement see John G. Fuller, *The Great Soul Trial* (New York: Macmillan, 1969).

6. Karlis Osis, "Out of Body Research at the ASPR," *ASPR Newsletter*, 1974 (Summer), pp. 1–3.

7. Karlis Osis and Donna McCormick, "Kinetic Effects at the Ostensible Location of an Out of Body Projection During Perceptual Testing," *Journal of the American Society for Psychical Research*, 1980, **74**, pp. 319–329.

8. Karlis Osis, *Deathbed Observations by Physicians and Nurses*, Parapsychological Monographs no. 3 (New York: Parapsychology Foundation, 1961). See also, Karlis Osis and Erlendur Haraldsson, *At the Hour of Death* (New York: Avon, 1977).

9. Kenneth Ring, *Life at Death: A Scientific Investigation of the Near-*

Death Experience (New York: Coward, McCann, & Geoghegan, 1980). Also, Kenneth Ring, "Frequency and Stages of the Prototypic Near-Death Experience," in Craig R. Lundahl, ed., *A Collection of Near-Death Research Readings* (Chicago: Nelson Hall, 1982), p. 145.

10. These issues are discussed at length in Lundahl, *op. cit.*, and Bruce Greyson and Charles P. Flynn, eds., *The Near Death Experience: Problems, Prospects, Perspectives* (Springfield, Ill.: Charles C. Thomas, 1984).

11. See Carl Sagan, "The Amniotic Universe," and C. B. Becker, "Why Birth Models Cannot Explain the Near Death Phenomena," in Greyson and Flynn, *op. cit.*, pp. 140–162.

12. Kenneth Ring and Stephen Franklyn, "Do Suicide Survivors Report Near-Death Experiences?" in Lundahl, *op. cit.*, pp. 180–201.

13. Adapted from Ian Stevenson, *Ten Cases in India, Cases of the Reincarnation Type*, Vol. I (Charlottesville, Va.: University Press of Virginia, 1975), pp. 144–173.

14. Ian Stevenson, "The Evidence for Survival from Claimed Memories of Former Incarnations," *Journal of the American Society for Psychical Research*, 1960, 54, pp. 51–71 (Part I), pp. 95–117 (Part II).

15. Ian Stevenson and Godwin Samararatne, "Three New Cases of the Reincarnation Type in Sri Lanka with Written Records Made Before Verification," *Journal of Scientific Exploration*, 1988, 2, pp. 217–238.

16. Personal communication from Professor Stevenson, November 1990.

17. See Ian Stevenson, *Children Who Remember Previous Lives* (Charlottesville, Va.: University Press of Virginia, 1987).

18. See James G. Matlock, "Past Life Memory Case Studies," in Stanley Krippner, ed., *Advances in Parapsychological Research 6* (Jefferson, N.C.: McFarland, 1990), pp. 184–267, and Ian Stevenson, "Reincarnation: Field Studies and Theoretical Issues," in B. B. Wolman, ed., *Handbook of Parapsychology* (1977; reprint ed., Jefferson, N.C.: McFarland, 1986).

19. Ian Stevenson, "Survival after Death: Evidence and Issues," in Ivor Grattan-Guinness, ed., *Psychical Research: A Guide to Its History, Principles & Practices* (Wellingborough, England: Aquarian Press, 1982), pp. 109–122 (quotation, p. 120).

Chapter 9: Adding It All Up

1. Rita L. Atkinson, Richard C. Atkinson, Edward E. Smith and Daryl J. Bem, *Introduction to Psychology*, 10th ed. (San Diego: Harcourt Brace Jovanovich, 1990), pp. vi, 234–241.

2. Gene V. Glass, Barry McGaw, and Mary Lee Smith, *Meta-Analysis in Social Research* (Beverly Hills, Calif.: Sage, 1981). Robert Rosenthal, *Meta-Analytic Procedures for Social Research* (Newbury Park, Calif.: Sage, 1984).

3. Ray Hyman, "The Ganzfeld Psi Experiment: A Critical Appraisal," and Charles Honorton, "Meta-Analysis of Psi Ganzfeld Research: A Response to Hyman," *Journal of Parapsychology*, 1985, **49**, pp. 3–49, 51–91.

4. Christopher Scott, "Comment on the Hyman-Honorton Debate," *Journal of Parapsychology*, 1986, **50**, pp. 349–350.

5. Robert Rosenthal, "Meta-Analytic Procedures and the Nature of Replication: The Ganzfeld Debate," *Journal of Parapsychology*, 1986, **50**, pp. 315–336.

6. Ray Hyman and Charles Honorton, "A Joint Communiqué: The Psi Ganzfeld Controversy," *Journal of Parapsychology*, 1986, **50**, pp. 351–364.

7. Charles Honorton, Rick E. Berger, Mario P. Varvoglis, Marta Quant, Patricia Derr, Ephraim Schechter, and Diane C. Ferrari, "Psi Communication in the Ganzfeld: Experiments with an Automated Testing System and a Comparison with a Meta-Analysis of Earlier Studies," *Journal of Parapsychology*, 1990, **54**, pp. 99–140.

8. Dean I. Radin and Roger D. Nelson, "Consciousness-Related Effects in Random Physical Systems," *Foundations of Physics*, 1989, **19**, pp. 1499–1514.

9. Charles Honorton and Diane C. Ferrari, " 'Future Telling': A Meta-Analysis of Forced-Choice Precognition Experiments, 1935–1987," *Journal of Parapsychology*, 1989, **53**, pp. 281–308.

10. Dean I. Radin and Diane C. Ferrari, "Effects of Consciousness on the Fall of Dice: A Meta-Analysis" (Paper presented at the 33rd Annual Convention of the Parapsychological Association, Chevy Chase, Md., August 16–20, 1990).

11. Steering Committee of the Physicians' Health Study Research Group, "Preliminary Report: Findings from the Aspirin Component of the Ongoing Physicians' Health Study," *New England Journal of Medicine*, 1988, **318**, pp. 262–264.

12. Charles Honorton, Diane C. Ferrari, and Daryl J. Bem, "Extraversion and ESP Performance: A Meta-Analysis and New Confirmation. (Paper presented at the 33rd Annual Convention of the Parapsychological Association, Chevy Chase, Md., August 16–20, 1990).

Chapter 10: Are We Ready for Applied Psi?

1. Douglas Dean, John Mihalasky, Sheila Ostrander, and Lynn Schroeder, *Executive ESP* (Englewood Cliffs, N.J.: Prentice-Hall, 1974).

2. I am grateful to "Mary" for permission to reproduce parts of her narrative from a presentation she gave at the Institute for Parapsychology, July, 1988.

3. From the files of the Mobius Society, Los Angeles, Calif. Mobius Society investigators collected interviews and affidavits from judges, prosecutors, and police officials as well as courtroom testimony and police forensic reports.

4. Whitney S. Hibbard and Raymond W. Worring, *Psychic Criminology: An Operations Manual for Using Psychics in Criminal Investigation* (Springfield, Ill.: Charles C. Thomas, 1982), pp. 65–66.

5. William G. Roll and Roger C. Grimson, "A Majority-Vote Study of Impressions Relating to a Criminal Investigation," in Rhea A. White and Richard S. Broughton, eds., *Research in Parapsychology 1983* (Metuchen, N.J.: Scarecrow Press, 1984), pp. 72–74.

6. Piet Hein Hoebens, Gerard Croiset, "Investigation of the Mozart of 'Psychic Sleuths' "—Part I. *Skeptical Inquirer*, 1981, VI, pp. 17–28. Piet Hein Hoebens, Gerard Croiset, and Professor Tenhaeff, "Discrepancies in Claims of Clairvoyance," *Skeptical Inquirer*, Winter 1981–82, VI(2), pp. 32–40.

7. Jan Klunder, " 'Psychic Vision' Woman Wins False Arrest Suit Against LAPD," *Los Angeles Times*, March 27, 1987. (Stories appeared in the *Los Angeles Times* on March 21, 24, 27, and 31, 1987.)

8. Russell Targ and Harold E. Puthoff, *Mind Reach: Scientists Look at Psychic Ability* (New York: Delacorte, 1978). Ronald M. McRae, *Mind Wars: The True Story of Government Research into the Military Potential of Psychic Weapons* (New York: St. Martin's, 1984).

9. Daniel Druckman and John A. Swets, eds., *Enhancing Human Performance: Issues, Theories, and Techniques* (Washington, D.C.: National Academy Press, 1988), p. 22.

10. For an insider's perspective (retired Army colonel) see John A. Alexander, "Enhancing Human Performance: A Challenge to the Report," *New Realities*, 1989, 9(4), pp. 10–15, 52–53.

11. John A. Palmer, Charles Honorton, and Jessica Utts, *Reply to the National Research Council Study on Parapsychology* (Research Triangle Park, N.C.: Parapsychological Association, 1988). Reproduced with permission.

12. For example, Defense Intelligence Agency, *Paraphysics R & D—Warsaw Pact* (Unclassified) (Washington, DC: Defense Intelligence Agency, March 30, 1978 [#DST-1810S-202-78]). J.D. LaMothe, *Controlled Offensive Behavior—USSR*, (Unclassified) (Washington, DC: Defense Intelligence Agency, 1975 [#ST-CS-01-169-72]). L.F. Maire and J.D. LaMothe, *Soviet and Czechoslovakian Parapsychology Research* (Unclassified) (Washington, DC: Defense Intelligence Agency, 1975 [#DST-1810S-387-75]).

13. C.B. Scott Jones, essay review of *Psychic Warfare: Fact or Fiction?*, *Journal of Parapsychology*, 1989, 53, pp. 141–150.

14. William Braud and Marilyn Schlitz, "Psychokinetic Influence on Electrodermal Activity," *Journal of Parapsychology*, 1983, 47, pp. 95–119. William Braud and Marilyn Schlitz, "A Methodology for the Objective Study of Transpersonal Imagery," *Journal of Scientific Exploration*, 1989, 3, pp. 43–63.

15. William Braud, "Distant Mental Influence of Rate of Hemolysis of Human Red Blood Cells," *Journal of the American Society for Psychical Research*, 1990, 84, pp. 1–24.

16. H. Attevelt, "Research into Paranormal Healing" (Ph.D. thesis, Department of Psychology, University of Utrecht, Netherlands, 1988).

17. Bernard Grad, Remi J. Cadoret and G. I. Paul, "The Influence of an Unorthodox Method of Treatment on Wound Healing in Mice," *International Journal of Parapsychology*, 1961, 3(2), pp. 5–24.

18. Bernard Grad, "Some Biological Effects of the 'Laying on of Hands': A Review of Experiments with Animals and Plants," *Journal of the American Society for Psychical Research*, 1965, 59, pp. 95–127.

19. Graham K. Watkins and Anita M. Watkins, "Possible PK Influence on the Resuscitation of Anesthetized Mice," *Journal of Parapsychology*, 1971, 35, pp. 257–272.

20. Lu Zuyin, Zhao Nanming, Li Shengping, Zheng Changxue, and Yan Xin. "Observations on Qi Emission Effects on the Structure and Properties of Some Substances." *Shengwu Wuli Xuebao* [Acta biophysica sinica], 1987, 3, pp. 93–94 [in Chinese].

21. Yan Xin, Li Shengping, Yu Jianyuan, Li Baike, and Lu Zuyin. "The Effect of Qigong on the Raman Spectra of Tap Water, Saline and Glucose Solution," *Ziran Zazhi* [Nature journal], 1988, 11, pp. 567–571 [in Chinese].

22. Douglas Dean, "Infrared Measurements of Healer-Treated Water," in William G. Roll, John Beloff and Rhea A. White, eds., *Research in Parapsychology 1982* (Metuchen, N.J.: Scarecrow Press, 1983), pp. 100–101.

23. James C. Carpenter, "Toward the Effective Utilization of Enhanced

Weak-Signal ESP Effects." (Paper presented at the Meeting of the American Association for the Advancement of Science, New York, N.Y., January 1975). See also, James C. Carpenter, "Prediction of Forced-Choice ESP Performance," Parts I and II, *Journal of Parapsychology*, 1983, **47**, pp. 191–236.

24. Stephan A. Schwartz, *The Alexandria Project* (New York: Delacorte Press/Eleanor Friede, 1984). Stephan A. Schwartz and Rand De Mattei, "The Discovery of an American Brig: Fieldwork Involving Applied Archeological Remote Viewing," in Linda A. Henkel and Rick Berger, eds., *Research in Parapsychology 1988* (Metuchen, N.J.: Scarecrow Press, 1989), pp. 73–78.

25. See Keith Harary, "On 'The Discovery of an American Brig'," and Stephan A. Schwartz and Rand De Mattei, response to Harary, *Journal of the American Society for Psychical Research*, 1990, **84**, pp. 275–281, 283–295.

26. Keith Harary and Russell Targ, "A New Approach to Forecasting Commodity Futures," *Psi Research*, 1985 (September/December), pp. 79–88.

27. Russell Targ, "ESP on Wall Street," *The Explorer*, 1988 (April), **4**, pp. 1, 4.

Chapter 11: Glimpsing the Future

1. Dean I. Radin, "Testing the Plausibility of Psi Mediated Computer System Failures," *Journal of Parapsychology*, 1990, **54**, pp. 1–20.

2. Dean I. Radin, "Putting Psi to Work," *Parapsychology Review*, 1990, **21**(2), pp. 5–9.

3. George Gamow, "The Exclusion Principle," *Scientific American*, 1959, **201**, pp. 74–86.

4. Larry Niven, *Ringworld* (New York: Del Rey, 1970), pp. 27–29. Permission to quote these passages is gratefully acknowledged.

5. Richard S. Broughton, "If You Want to Know How it Works, First Find Out What It's For," in D. H. Weiner and R. L. Morris, eds. *Research in Parapsychology 1987* (Metuchen, N.J.: Scarecrow Press, 1988), pp. 187–202.

6. Rex G. Stanford, "An Experimentally Testable Model for Spontaneous Psi Events: I. Extrasensory Events, II. Psychokinetic Events," *Journal of the American Society for Psychical Research*, 1974, **68**, pp. 34–57, and 321–356. For an updated version, see Rex G. Stanford, "An Experimentally Testable Model of Psi Events," in Stanley Krippner, ed., *Advances in Parapsychological Research 6* (Jefferson, N.C.: McFarland, 1990) pp. 54–167.

7. See Richard Dawkins, *The Selfish Gene* (Oxford: Oxford University Press, 1976).

8. "Gott wurfelt nicht." B. Hoffman, *Albert Einstein, Creator and Rebel* (New York: New American Library, 1973).

9. See Helmut Schmidt, "The Strange Properties of Psychokinesis," *Journal of Scientific Exploration*, 1987, 1, pp. 103–118, and Evan Harris Walker, "Measurement in Quantum Mechanics Revisited: A Response to Phillip's Criticisms of the Quantum Mechanical Theory of Psi," *Journal of the American Society for Psychical Research*, 1987, 81, pp. 333–369.

10. For a full account of recent Chinese psi research activity see Leping Zha and Tron McConnell, "Parapsychology in the People's Republic of China: 1979–1989," *Journal of the American Society for Psychical Research*, 1991, 85, pp. 119–143.

INDEX

Index